The arts of mankind

EDITED BY ANDRÉ MALRAUX
AND ANDRÉ PARROT
MEMBER OF THE *INSTITUT DE FRANCE*

EDITOR-IN-CHARGE
ALBERT BEURET

Europe of the invasions

J. Hubert - J. Porcher - W. F. Volbach

EUROPE
OF THE
INVASIONS

GEORGE BRAZILLER • NEW YORK

Translated by Stuart Gilbert and James Emmons

Library of Congress Catalog Card Number: 75-81858

Printed in France

Published 1969 by arrangement with Editions Gallimard.
All rights reserved. No part of the contents of this book may
be reproduced without the written consent of the publisher,
George Braziller, Inc., One Park Avenue, New York, N.Y. 10016.

Contents

HOMAGE TO JEAN PORCHER

In the course of such an immense enterprise as 'The Arts of Mankind,' *it was but to be expected that one or another of the participants should not live to see it through. But there is an especial poignancy when death leaves a gap in an unfinished task. Hence the shock for all of us when, on April 26, 1966, we learned of the death of Jean Porcher, honorary Chief Curator of the Cabinet des Manuscrits in the Bibliothèque Nationale, and joint author of the two volumes in our series dealing with the Merovingians and the Carolingians.*

Jean Porcher was one of the most likable of men. Small, sprightly, with sparkling eyes and an alert expression, he had a frankly optimistic nature, an infectious cheerfulness. Speaking of him, one of his friends quoted his own words to remind us that he sprang from that Norman race of men, 'inquisitive, aggressive, impetuous yet level-headed, who can affirm and deny in the same breath so as the better to encompass the truth of the matter.' An alumnus of the Ecole des Chartes, exceptionally gifted, speaking several languages (including Russian), he lived contentedly among his books and manuscripts. No one could have been better qualified to deal with an age that he knew by heart, that of the great illuminated manuscripts. He had organized three exhibitions of them (1954, 1955, 1958) which Malraux described as 'a cultural landmark of the present century' since, thanks to them, 'the amazing painting of the centuries without painting at long last entered history.'

After his retirement in 1962, Jean Porcher worked harder than ever. Renowned at home and abroad, his services were in constant demand. For this reason, he was frequently invited to Dumbarton Oaks. None of us suspected that he was already suffering from an incurable disease. Some months later, Jean Porcher was irremediably lost. Pendent opera interrupta. But there could be no question of resigning ourselves to this tragic frustration of our hopes. The work begun by him has been brought to completion. The chapters entirely written by his hand remain a moving memorial to the author, a testimony to a dedicated faith in his calling, and a scholarly enthusiasm that never faltered, even when he knew the end was near.

ANDRÉ PARROT

June 1967

Introduction

Greek, then Roman antiquity had built up through the ages a civilization center-
ing on and ancillary to man and his terrestrial existence, after which he led a
life that was but half alive, as a drifting shade, harmless or malevolent as the case
might be, never at rest, exiled from light and all the joys of living. Like the civilization
itself, its art was dominated by man and his environment; it represented him existing
in space, as he really is—if perceptible appearances are envisaged as the sole
reality and the function of art is to give an illusion of them. Even the gods of antiquity have human forms, they share man's passions and foibles, his virtues and his
vices; even ideas and abstractions were personified by art. In virtue of an underlying
equilibrium, whose laws the artist sought to elicit, the forms of nature reflected the
physical and moral harmony of a universe made to man's measure, and beauty
was a product of these laws.

The passing of the ancient world put a stop to this art, but this ending did not
come abruptly. Between its premonitory signs and the time (towards the fifth century)
when a new Europe came to birth, there was a long interval, marked by cataclysmic
upheavals. The Roman Empire fell to pieces under the onslaughts of the barbarians
who, from the second half of the third century on, had begun to overrun its frontiers
and establish themselves in the West, where they became the seminal centres of our
modern nations. For this break-up of a civilization peerless of its kind, Rome herself
was partly to blame, politically, to begin with, as a result of the autocratic nature
of the central government. In an earlier age the Roman citizen had conquered the
world; he lost it by tamely submitting to the dictatorial rule of upstarts and dema-
gogues less and less qualified to hold for long the reins of power. The imperial
economy was unable to stand up against this regime and to meet the cost of constant
wars beyond the frontiers. None the less, so lasting was the imprint that Greco-
Roman antiquity had made on the mentality of Europe that western man never
could cease looking back to it with a nostalgic yearning; in times of doubt and trouble,

◄ 1 - ECHTERNACH GOSPELS. BIBLIOTHÈQUE NATIONALE, PARIS.

he turned invariably to antiquity, as the source of all the spiritual values that give life a meaning. These periodical returns to the past are usually described as 'renascences.' They took a number of different forms and the pages that follow are devoted to one of them, the Carolingian renascence of the ninth century and the events leading up to it.

But if classical antiquity in its decline left this abiding imprint, the reason was that it appealed even more to the soul than to the mind. Imbued at an early hour with the spirit of the mystical religions of the East, which freed it from a sterile materialism, it had embraced Christianity in the fourth century and in so doing opened to man the portals of eternity. Henceforth Rome was inseparable from Christ, Roman art equaled Christian art.

After the Edict of Milan which, in February 313, set its seal on the union of Church and State, Constantine transferred the capital to Byzantium in the eastern Mediterranean. Before his death he divided the Empire between his sons, Constantine II, Constans, and Constantius, who succeeded him in 337. The early period of this divided Empire was marked by the rivalry between the new rulers. But a much more serious peril than these domestic feuds menaced the safety of the whole Empire. As far back as 276 Franks and Alamanni had crossed the Rhine, invaded Roman Gaul and established themselves in the north-east of the province as far as Autun. Constans and, after him, Valentinian, while striving to contain them in Gaul and Brittany, had to defend the Danube frontier against the Sarmatians (354-375).

In 375, brushing aside the Ostrogoths, the Huns began a new advance. Three years later (August 9, 378) a horde of western Goths (Visigoths), who had swept down across the Danube, utterly defeated the Romans at Adrianople. From the reign of Theodosius (379-395) on, began a gradual infiltration of barbarians into the Roman army, even into the imperial administration, which was ready now to compromise with them, thus postponing its final downfall. The definitive settlement of barbarians in the West took place in the fifth century.

While the Vandals and their allies, the Suevi, crossed the Rhine in December 406, invaded Gaul, then Spain, and finally conquered Roman Africa in 429-439, Alaric's Visigoths, after ravaging the East of the Empire, launched an attack (in 401) on the West. Despite the stout resistance put up by Stilicho, Honorius' 'captain-general', the Goths entered Rome on August 24, 410, and sacked it—though as Christians (if Arians) they spared the churches. Next, by way of Aquitaine, under the command of Athaulf (Alaric's brother-in-law), they invaded Spain. In 455 Rome was pillaged once again, this time by the Vandals, who under the leadership of Genseric had established themselves in Africa. Now the barbarians became the effective rulers of the West: when on August 23, 476, the Herule chief Odoacer, commander of the imperial troops, deposed the child-king Romulus Augustulus, the Empire of the West came to an end.

After defeating Odoacer and capturing Milan (in 493), the Ostrogothic king, Theodoric, made Ravenna his chief place of residence, under the nominal authority of the Emperor of the East. Theodoric died in 526, and thanks to the enterprise of Justinian (527-565), the sixth century was the age of the Byzantine reconquest, an age of alternating peace and war. Justinian's famous general, Belisarius, invaded Africa, wiped 'Vandalia' off the roll of nations in a brief campaign, then turned to Italy, entering Rome in 536. After recapturing part of Italy, the Gothic king Totila was defeated and slain by Narses, Belisarius' successor, in 552. The whole of Italy was reunited under Byzantine rule, and at about the same time Justinian turned his attention to Spain. The Mediterranean was once again a Roman sea. Byzantium had partly restored the cohesion of the old Empire, and here we have perhaps one of the causes of the revival of Byzantine influence and the classical tradition which characterized the seventh century throughout the western world. Justinian had surrendered transalpine Gaul to the Franks. In Great Britain Germanic peoples (Frisians, Angles, Saxons, Jutes), all of them heathens, had, in the middle of the fifth century, invaded and settled in the South and East of the old Roman province. Christianity was introduced into these regions by missionaries dispatched first from Rome, then from Ireland, in the first half of the seventh century. Justinian died in 565 and three years later a new band of invaders, the Lombards, poured into Italy. After taking Milan in 569, they occupied the whole interior of the country, and there installed a string of duchies, most important of which were Spoleto in the north and Benevento to the south of Rome. After a relatively tranquil period lasting over a century, the Lombards under their king Liutprand resumed their victorious advance. When Ravenna fell to them in 751, the East had no longer any foothold in Italy, and the sole representative of the Empire in the peninsula was the Pope. Such was the situation in the West at the beginning of the second half of the eighth century when, hard pressed by the Lombards, Pope Stephen II appealed for aid (in 753) to Pepin, King of the Franks, father of Charlemagne.

The West had been thoroughly transformed by these upheavals and the only refuge for what survived of the ancient Empire was in the eastern provinces, where the towns had kept intact their schools, their administration and their artists' workshops. This explains why the cultural and artistic idiosyncrasies of the eastern regions enjoyed a wide diffusion in the lands of the West, then undergoing a disastrous economic crisis: a diffusion that was further promoted by successive invasions of the Mediterranean and African East, first by the Persians, then by the Arabs (605-678). But this final débacle of Roman power should not make us overlook those glorious centuries when the might of Roman arms had converted the Mediterranean into a Latin sea; the moral unity of the Empire was fated to outlast for many years the political dismemberment of the western world. But now that world was to be shaken by cataclysms—this time of a religious order.

Only a few years after its destiny had become tied up with that of the Roman Empire, the Church embarked (round about 318) on the momentous doctrinal controversy due to the rise of Arianism. Its struggles with the heresy of Arius, complicated by the need to combat the Donatist schism, were followed in the early fifth century by the dispute which led to the condemnation of Nestorius by the council of Ephesus in 431. Next came the heresy of Eutyches, that of the Monothelites and, last and most serious in its impact on art, that of the iconoclasts (image-breakers) which lasted for over a century, from 726 to 843. The germinal centre of these controversies was Constantinople, in the very palace of the monarch on whom the whole life of the State depended. Thus, from its earliest days, the eastern sector of the Empire was deeply involved in the most arduous, most abstract theological disputations. This fact, of capital importance, partly accounts for the progressive transformation of art, in which from now on the Church was to play a dominant role. It was in the first decade of this, the fourth century, that the Greek scholar Porphyry died in Rome; he had been the commentator on the *Enneads* of the Neoplatonist Plotinus, and author of the *Introduction to the Categories of Aristotle*, a passage in which gave rise to the controversy as to the nature of Universals which so greatly preoccupied medieval scholars.

Do ideas exist *ante rem*, independently of the mind, or are they its creations, mere collocations of words? Do we live in the midst of transient appearances, mere reflections of a reality that underlies their diverse aspects? The art of the Church —all art—took sides and opted to be 'realist' in the philosophical sense of the term, as was to be the art of the Early Middle Ages, including that of the Carolingians, despite their efforts to avoid this. Carolingian art, as we shall see, spelt the triumph of abstraction, hints of which were visible early in the century of Constantine and Theodosius. Abstraction steadily gained ground in the next century, and all tokens of earthly life were gradually drained away from the painted and carved images, of which until now that life had been the pretext and mainstay.

The notion of space tends to die out and by the same token that of relief. Forms are flattened, isolated, and are no longer organized in relation to each other on a plane created and demarcated by our horizon-line, nor do they go to compose pictures peopled with figures like those we see in daily life. Devoid of weight and substance, these forms seem to have broken contact with the ground; they float up and hover one above the other, reduced to the condition of signs—rather like writing on a wall or on the pages of a manuscript. Signs of beings and things whose real nature is garbled by the appearances that meet the eye, they can be grasped as they truly are only by the thinking mind. In these signs it is the message alone that matters, 'vain' appearances cease to count, the artist makes no effort to represent depth or any sort of empty space, and he soon becomes incapable of doing so. Each scene, however crowded or intricate, is depicted on the frontal plane exclusively: all that lies behind is shown on top of the main scene or outlined in an independent row, the upper figures signifying a rearward, the lower, a forward, position. In short the third dimension is ignored completely.

Images thus delivered from their material context are particularly suitable for the representation of divine beings. Representations of this kind naturally bulked large in a milieu in which the Church, theological problems and religious ceremonies were the prime concern. But these sacred figures were also differentiated from the others by their immobility; for movement pertains to the world of men, where all is in a state of flux, change and decay, and will so continue till the end of time—a world of generation and corruption. Whereas Heaven and its denizens are eternal and unmoving. No trace of emotion ruffles the faces of God, the Virgin and the saints, and this attitude of superb aloofness also befitted certain sacred personages such as the emperor. To render this demeanour nothing could have been more appropriate than the use of a single plane, suppressing space and the movement it generates. That stalwart adversary of the Monothelite heresy, St. Maximus the Confessor, spiritual leader of Greek orthodoxy, who died in 662, voiced the opinion of the contemporary theologians, an opinion no less operative in the domain of art than in the thought of his contemporaries, and harmonizing with the philosophic and cosmographic views of the age. 'Godhead is motionless at every point and therefore immune from any outside interference, no matter what its source. How, indeed, could anything mundane climb to that high, closed tower from which God contemplates the universe? His peace is unperturbable, His stability unshakable, safeguarded by the serenity of His being.'

There was no novelty in this dictum; for a long while, as a result of contacts with the religious thought of the East, ancient art had taken to assigning to the immortals and to heroes a gaze, a posture, even a stature, in keeping with their supremacy over ordinary mortals and their supramundane functions. But what had been, so far, only a vague tendency, now became the rule; the narrative genre was henceforth confronted, sometimes in one and the same scene, and by the hand of the same artist, with the hieratic genre, which soon imposed its formulas on art at large. Those aspects of the perceptible, concrete world in which the artist saw but a coarse reflection of the sacred were blotted out. There is no question that this evolution was speeded up by the current theological controversies, for art is necessarily bound up with its environment and the spirit of the age; but they did not give rise to it, there had long been premonitory signs of this change. To attribute it to the barbarian invasions would be a mistake, for it much preceded them. Nonetheless, the foreigners who, after taking over the reins of power, became the new patrons, often too the practitioners, of art, did much to develop it, in virtue of their decorative instinct, essentially coloristic and hostile to any effects of relief. In promoting these pictorial methods, the Church authorities adapted to their own ends the Bible imagery which had developed in the holy places of Palestine, its natural and traditional setting, and made it capable of embodying constant allusions to the Christian's hopes of eternal life in the Other World.

The generalization of these methods, which took place in or about the fifth century, is a fact far more significant than the technical degeneration to which it tended (incidentally) to give rise. Severed from its terrestrial links and oriented

XV

towards the divine, the art of the West was henceforth, with alternating periods of regression and advance, to restore slowly and tentatively the broken links and to retrieve a foothold, at the human level, in man's life on earth. This process took full effect only in the fifteenth century, the century of humanism when, after a thousand years, medievalism had run its course and men's eyes were opened to a new vision of the world.

Antiquity did not die out abruptly. Not only did its towns and palaces, their furniture and decorations, silent witnesses of its achievements, survive, but there still lived men cast in its mould and whole families who treasured memories of the splendid unity of the Roman world. As late as 416 one of their poets, Rutilius Namatianus, voiced this nostalgic yearning when, acclaiming Rome, he wrote, *Fecisti patriam diversis gentibus unam:* 'Thou didst make for diverse peoples a single fatherland.' Though the barbarians could not share the regrets of a Gallo-Roman, they could admire the culture of these men amongst whom they now lived and feel a very real respect for the material vestiges bequeathed by that bygone culture. This admiration and respect for the Roman past were never to die out. In the Carolingian age and the age leading up to it, we are on the threshold of a long period of history, that of the making and shaping of modern Europe. We are witnessing a birth, our birth, in which two radically different mentalities participated, two 'families' of thought with whose unequal imprint we are still marked, token of a deep-seated cleavage that many centuries were hard put to it to efface. Art, letters, even ways of thinking were long to oscillate between two heritages, constantly pitted against each other and striving towards an equilibrium, but always losing it again once it had been precariously achieved.

That equilibrium was harder to achieve in this early phase, when the conflict between the two trends had an instancy that time was to abate, than in any other; but also in some ways easier, in view of the fact that classical antiquity was still an abiding presence, close at hand, always ready to assert its high prerogative, a claim insisted on, compulsive, as it was never again to be in afteryears.

PART ONE

Architecture and Decorative Carving

I N the fifth century the civilized world was convulsed by a momentous event: the occupation of a large part of the Roman Empire by the barbarians. Historians of the last century differed widely in their interpretation of this event, according to the view they took of Roman civilization. Opinion was divided between Romanists and Germanists, soon to be opposed by a third group—those whom recent explorations in Asia had convinced of the overriding importance of the ancient civilizations of the East. The scholars of that day indulged freely in hypotheses. Since then, half a century of excavations and methodical research has taught us to think twice before venturing on risky generalizations.

On the eve of the barbarian invasions, art, and in particular Christian art, then in its early stages, exhibited throughout the Empire, both in Europe and in the eastern provinces, an impressive unity of style. Western Europe still held the lead in the creation of forms. This has been strikingly demonstrated by the fourth- and fifth-century monuments discovered or cleared since the last war (San Lorenzo, Milan; Trier Cathedral; St Gereon, Cologne; Saint-Pierre, Metz). These have revealed ground plans and architectural forms which do not appear until slightly later in the churches of the East.[1] So far as our present knowledge goes, the oldest baptisteries with corner niches and a lantern tower are to be found in France, not in the East, as used to be supposed. It is only fair to add, however, that the architects employed at Milan and in Gaul could have been natives of the eastern provinces of the Empire; it was as easy at that time to bring in a team of master-builders from a distant province as it was to transfer a legion. The unity of the Roman Empire explains how offshoots of the trunk retained enough features in common to convince art historians that there must have been, in after times, new and wholesale exchanges of architectural forms. One point, however, is worth emphasizing: after the period of the great invasions the finest, most vigorous offshoots developed in those parts of the former Roman Empire which were never occupied by the barbarians or which they only passed through. Syria, Armenia and part of Asia Minor

1. To facilitate comparison, all the plans are grouped together on pp. 294-307, most of them reproduced on a common scale.

◀ 2 - FRÉJUS, BAPTISTERY. DOME AND DRUM PIERCED WITH WINDOWS.

1

4 - FRÉJUS, BAPTISTERY. EXTERIOR.

shared this privilege with Byzantium. As regards architecture, these parallel developments account for the resemblances—to take one example—between sixth-century Syrian churches and French Romanesque churches. As regards decoration, the successive waves of influence are explained, on the contrary, by the exportation of textiles and luxury objects from the great cities of the East to regions as remote as Gaul and, later, by the exodus of Coptic and Syrian artists fleeing from the Arab invasions.

Architecture and all the arts dependent on it were introduced into Gaul by Roman civilization.

The early cathedrals, some of them built on a colossal scale, as shown by the vestiges found at Trier and Aquileia, were vast halls of rectangular plan designed to hold large crowds of worshippers. More ingenuity was demanded of the architects of the Later Empire when it came to building baptisteries, places of Christian initiation, and funerary basilicas, portals to eternity. The cathedrals of Aquileia and Trier date to the fourth century. The baptisteries of Fréjus and Albenga appear to date to the late fifth century. The Fréjus baptistery is a solid, well-designed construction on a square plan with corner niches and a central dome resting on a drum pierced with many windows. The Albenga baptistery, near the Italian frontier, has

◀ 3 - FRÉJUS, BAPTISTERY. INTERIOR.

3

6 - ALBENGA, BAPTISTERY. VAULT MOSAIC.

a high interior colonnade like that of Fréjus, but its plan is a polygon, from which radiates a series of niches, alternately rectangular and semicircular. The handsome mosaics still adorning some of the vaults show how magnificently these first sanctuaries of triumphant Christianity were decorated; the imagery, still very sober, evokes the vault of Heaven and the symbol of salvation.

There were some very fine mosaics, too, in the basilica erected in Cologne towards the end of the fourth century, on the spot where forty soldiers of the Theban legion had been martyred, and known in the time of Gregory of Tours as 'the church of the golden saints.' In the Middle Ages this church bore the name of St Gereon. Remnants of the original structure were brought to light during World War II: it was an oval-shaped building, with niches, reproducing the plan of certain ancient mausolea.

◀ 5 - ALBENGA, BAPTISTERY. INTERIOR.

7 - MILAN, SAN LORENZO. WEST COLONNADE OF THE ATRIUM.

8 - MILAN, SAN LORENZO. VIEW FROM THE SOUTH-EAST.

The basilica erected in honour of the martyred St Lawrence outside the ancient walls of Milan, to the south, was probably built to house the tombs of members of the imperial family; several bishops of Milan were also interred there. This church with a central dome and a high tribune was surmounted on all four sides by tall square towers. Of all the buildings of this period, throughout Christendom, which have come down to us, this is without any doubt the most skilfully constructed one. It is preceded by an imposing colonnade, which closed off the west side of a vast atrium.

7

10 - MILAN, SAN LORENZO.   INTERIOR FROM THE SOUTH-EAST.

◄ 9 - MILAN, SAN LORENZO.   INTERIOR FROM THE SOUTH-EAST.

9

12 - MARSEILLES, CHURCH OF SAINT-VICTOR, CRYPTS OF NOTRE-DAME-DE-CONFESSION. MOSAIC.

Shortly after the grandiose church of San Lorenzo was built in Milan, a tiny edifice with groin-vaulted aisles was erected in Marseilles, at the back of a quarry where the martyr Victor had been buried. Recent excavations have shown it to be a mausoleum. In front of this commemorative monument stood a colonnade extending round three sides, like the porticoes of an atrium. A fine piece of mosaic, with a vine-pattern on a gold ground, can still be seen on the intrados of an arch, part of which has miraculously escaped destruction. Also, at the entrance of one of the

◀ 11 - MARSEILLES, CHURCH OF SAINT-VICTOR, CRYPTS OF NOTRE-DAME-DE-CONFESSION.

11

13 - MARSEILLES, CHURCH OF SAINT-VICTOR, CRYPTS OF NOTRE-DAME-DE-CONFESSION. VINE-BRANCHES DECORATING AN ARCH.

aisles of the mausoleum a stucco ornament of vineshoots has survived. Both mosaics and painted stuccoes were characteristic elements of the decoration of religious edifices in early Christian times.

In less than two centuries Gaul had been endowed by its Roman conquerors with some sixty magnificent cities, their streets intersecting at right angles and forming a clear-cut chequer-work pattern, so far as the lie of the land permitted. The forum was the centre of public life. Around it stood the temples, the basilica where the law courts sat, the curia, seat of the municipal assemblies, and the theatre. But this sumptuous way of life lasted only for a time. In the year 276 seventy towns and cities of Gaul were annihilated by a gigantic horde of invaders from Germany. Subsequently the barbarians returned to their own lands, but only after having devastated the richest provinces of Gaul from the Rhine to the Pyrenees. To guard against the danger of another such calamity, a measure was taken which, while all to the good for purposes of defence, proved disastrous for the future of urban civilization in Gaul. From the North Sea to the Rhone, all along the Loire Valley and at the strategic approaches to the valley of the Garonne, some fifty cities, hitherto unenclosed by walls, were converted into strongholds. The quarter of the old open city which happened to stand on rising ground or had some natural means of defence was girdled with high walls, quadrangular or curvilinear, which were crenellated and flanked with towers. These fortified towns of the Later Empire proved their strength and lasted for centuries, but they checked the growth of urban life. Air and light were lacking within these grim strongholds, the largest of which covered an area about the size of the garden of the Tuileries. The decay of the towns is all the more significant for the art historian because it was peculiar to Gaul. Nothing of the sort happened in Italy and Spain. In many of our old French towns, the stout walls of the Later Empire, whose facing of small stones was often reinforced with courses of bricks, were demolished only in the nineteenth century. They were found to contain many pieces of sculpture and the debris of monuments which had been utilized to add bulk to the construction material. These remnants, which have done so much to enrich our archaeological museums, came either from buildings wrecked by the barbarians or from others which had to be razed in order to clear a sufficient area for defence, a no man's land, around the stronghold. Beyond this perimeter there remained inhabited districts which had once formed part of the old open city, but excavations have in many cases shown that these suburbs rapidly decayed and made way for vast cemeteries, and that the first signs of an active revival of urban life hardly occur before the second half of the sixth century. The decline of the towns in Gaul, beginning under the Later Empire, led to the development in the open countryside of *villae*, fortified or not, where the aristocracy took the habit of residing.

In the time of Constantine Christian churches had been erected in most of the Roman cities of Gaul. It is known that at first they were built on the periphery of the cities. The oldest of them were so small and so ramshackle (this was the case in Paris) that three centuries later, in the time of Gregory of Tours, no one even knew where they had stood. It was not long before they were given a more honourable and better protected position within the walls of the stronghold. By the beginning of the fifth century all the towns in Gaul had their bishop, and little by little each one became a sort of 'holy city' where the living and the dead had their sanctuaries. In the most favoured cities the bishop's church, styled the *ecclesia*, was composed of three buildings: a place of prayer for the catechumens, those who were to be initiated into the faith through baptism in the baptistery (second of the three buildings) as a preliminary to their admission to the third building, the church, where the religious services were celebrated, and which, much later, became known as the cathedral After the Peace of the Church, the lowering of the minimum age required for baptism made the rites of initiation superfluous, but the force of tradition remained so strong in religious architecture that in the eighteenth century, on the eve of the French Revolution, the city of Auxerre still had its two ancient episcopal churches with a detached baptistery. Outside the city walls the community of the dead, kindred to that of the living, spread out its graves in the shelter of another church, the 'basilica,' which was complemented by chapels for private worship or funerary monuments having the form of vaulted shrines half sunk into the earth.

Little is known of the decoration of the churches erected in Gaul at that period, except that the presbytery and some of the walls were covered with mosaics and paintings. The walls were not adorned with bas-reliefs of figure subjects, but

14 - MARSEILLES, ABBEY OF SAINT-VICTOR. ALTAR SLAB. MUSÉE D'ARCHÉOLOGIE, MARSEILLES.

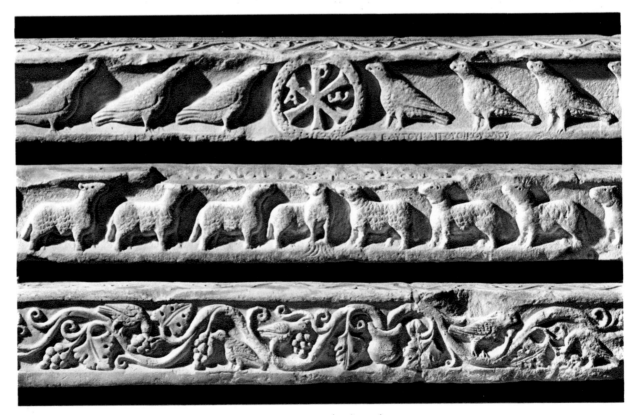

15 - MARSEILLES, ABBEY OF SAINT-VICTOR. ALTAR SLAB, DETAILS. MUSÉE D'ARCHÉOLOGIE, MARSEILLES.

16 - ARLES, CEMETERY OF LES ALISCAMPS. SARCOPHAGUS OF CONCORDIUS. MUSÉE LAPIDAIRE CHRÉTIEN, ARLES.

such reliefs were used to beautify the tombs of the rich, following a practice that went back to pagan times. Mythological scenes carved in marble on the visible sides of the sarcophagus were now replaced by Christian scenes of a historical or symbolical nature. A large number of these fine marble sarcophagi have been preserved at Arles. They closely resemble those of Rome and Italy. There was a time, however, when historians were convinced that in the last days of Roman domination a great school of sculptors flourished at Arles; hence the remarkable abundance of carved sarcophagi preserved there. But this belief was erroneous. As Fernand Benoît has shown, these stone coffins came from Italy ready-carved. Historical circumstances explain why they were imported in such large numbers. About 395, Trier being threatened by the barbarians, the imperial court was transferred to Arles, with a consequent influx of civil servants and high-ranking officials into the new capital. Arles thus became the centre of an active courtly art which influenced even the burial of the dead. Nonetheless, the carvings made in Italian workshops continued to play an important part in the artistic life, first of Gaul, then of France. They were admired, attempts were made to copy them, and, from Carolingian times on, the handsomest sarcophagi were re-employed, either to bury persons of rank or as reliquary shrines.

15

17 - NARBONNE. RELIQUARY OF THE HOLY SEPULCHRE. MUSÉE LAPIDAIRE, NARBONNE. — 18 - PILASTER, DETAIL. MUSÉE LAPIDAIRE CHRÉTIEN, ARLES.

The occupation of Gaul by the barbarians changed the fortunes of this region. The evidence provided by excavations enables us to gauge the scope and consequences of this event in the domain of material culture.

Our early archaeologists, working at a time when knowledge of the period was still rudimentary, were led to believe that the invaders had brought with them a rich, entirely new civilization. Excavations were carried out in barbarian cemeteries chiefly with a view to enriching local museums and private collections with the jewellery found in the graves. The beautiful objects of personal adornment discovered in the tombs were thought to have belonged to the early invaders, the Goths, Burgundians and Franks of the fifth century. More systematic methods of excavation and archaeological research have enabled the finds to be fitted into a precise chronological sequence, and this has brought into prominence a fact of the highest importance. The grave goods of the fifth century, other than those of the royal tombs, tend to be inferior. An abundance of high-quality artifacts made in local workshops is found only in tombs dating from the middle of the sixth century on. Stylistic analysis shows that this production of finer work resulted from a progressive fusion between the descendants of the invaders and the indigenous peoples; and history tells us that it was promoted by an economic revival and an increased volume of

19 - SAINT-MAXIMIN, BASILICA OF SAINTE-MADELEINE. ENGRAVED SLAB: THE VIRGIN AS A YOUNG GIRL. ▶

20 - SAINT-MAXIMIN, BASILICA OF SAINTE-MADELEINE.   ENGRAVED SLAB: THE SACRIFICE OF ISAAC.

21 - SAINT-MAXIMIN, BASILICA OF SAINTE-MADELEINE. ENGRAVED SLAB: DANIEL IN THE LIONS' DEN.

22 - SLAB WITH THE SACRED MONOGRAM. CHURCH OF SAINT-GERMAIN, AUXERRE.

trade, which becomes perceptible in Gaul at just this time. It was now that the new barbarian world began to acquire the refinements of civilization, not only in Gaul but also in Spain and Great Britain. In the lands north of the Loire, despite the upheavals of the eighth century, living conditions steadily improved until the advent of the Carolingians.

The early barbarian invaders cannot be credited with any particular skill as builders or stone carvers. It is common knowledge that the Germanic peoples did not build in stone, and they do not even seem to have had any marked influence on timber construction. Real proficiency in the art of building with wood can never be acquired by semi-nomadic tribes, for that art is bound up with a knowledge of forestry and a settled way of life, just as the art of stone-carving is bound up with quarrying. That this knowledge existed in Gaul several centuries before the invasions is a fact borne out by many discoveries.

Scholars today no longer refer to the early medieval churches of Spain as monuments of 'Visigothic art'; they speak of them as belonging to the Visigothic period. This distinction also applies to the Franks of Gaul and the Lombards of Italy. It may be said to the credit of the new overlords, first, that they took pains to improve their standard of life by adopting the language, religion and some of the basic

23 - READING-DESK ATTRIBUTED TO ST RADEGUND. ABBEY OF SAINTE-CROIX, POITIERS.

institutions of the peoples they had conquered; and, secondly, that they encouraged art by their patronage.

It is a significant fact that the two pieces of sculpture which there are grounds for associating with the name of a barbarian ruler are both works in the Mediterranean tradition: the altar cross set up in the basilica of Saint-Germain at Auxerre by order of Queen Clotilda (died 545) and the wooden lectern of Queen St Radegund (died 587) preserved by the nuns of the abbey of Sainte-Croix at Poitiers.

Contemporary chronicles leave no doubt as to the havoc wrought by the barbarians in the early phase of their occupation of the ancient Roman provinces of northern Gaul and northern Italy. Yet they already had behind them a long familiarity with the amenities of Mediterranean civilization. Under the Empire large numbers of them had already been permitted to settle in Gaul. Land had been given to them to clear and bring under cultivation, and thus whole colonies of Germani settled in the midst of the Gallo-Roman population. The *foederati*, mercenaries recruited

21

24 - CHARENTON-SUR-CHER, ABBEY. SARCOPHAGUS. MUSÉE DU BERRY, BOURGES.

among the barbarians, were authorized to occupy a third of the houses and lands as a reward for their services. In 418 the Visigoths were permitted to establish themselves in south-western Gaul between Toulouse and the Atlantic coast, and about 443 the Burgundians peacefully occupied Savoy. Attila himself, reputed the most savage of the barbarian chiefs, maintained friendly relations with Byzantium and had had stone thermae built beside his wooden palace.

The new masters of Gaul were content for the most part to live in palaces and *villae* dating from the Gallo-Roman period. The so-called 'Burgundian palace' discovered by Louis Blondel in Geneva reveals a makeshift adaptation, in quite a small area, of a complex of ancient buildings grouped round a small courtyard. The new owner did no more than add an oratory to the existing group. About 565 the poet Fortunatus published an enthusiastic description of a fortified estate not far from Koblenz which was owned by Nicetus, bishop of Trier. His long account of the place is worth citing in full, for it is striking evidence of the persistence of Roman culture under the barbarian kings. Nicetus was a native of Auvergne or the Limousin. He had been a monk before being appointed to the important see of Trier by the Austrasian king Theodoric I. Gregory of Tours commends his asceticism. All the same, a bishop at that time was expected to 'live like a lord,' for the

25 - CHARENTON·SUR·CHER, ABBEY. **SA**RCOPHAGUS, DETAIL. MUSÉE DU BERRY, BOURGES.

26 - GÉMIGNY. FRAGMENT OF A DISK. M. HISTORIQUE, ORLÉANS.

new masters found it expedient to make the head of each cathedral church a kind of high provincial functionary. Here is a translation of this interesting text. 'A defensive wall flanked by thirty towers surrounds the mountain on which stands a building occupying the site formerly covered by a forest; prolonged on either side, the wall runs down to the bottom of the valley, all the way to the Moselle, whose waters bound the estate on this side. At the summit of the rock is built a magnificent palace, like a second mountain placed on top of the first. Its walls enclose a vast area, and the house itself forms a kind of fortress. Marble columns sustain the majestic building, from the top of which, on summer days, boats can be seen gliding along the river. It has three storeys and when one has reached the highest, one gets the impression that the edifice covers up all the fields below. The tower that overlooks the ramp leading up to the castle contains a chapel consecrated to the saints, as well as the weapons kept there for the use of the warriors. There is also a double ballista whence projectiles fly forth, spreading death and havoc on their course. Water is brought in by channels following the slopes of the mountain, and the stream serves to turn a mill which grinds the corn that goes to feed the people of the region. On these once barren hills Nicetus has planted vines bursting with sap, and the rock which once was covered with brambles is now carpeted with green vineshoots. Orchards of fruit-bearing trees grow here and there, filling the air with the fragrance of their blossoms.'

In barbarian society it was a point of honour for the king to show an interest in the arts; it was a matter of prestige. The royal treasury was made up not only of the reserves of gold and silver needed for the administration of the realm. It also contained the 'collection' which elevated the monarch in the esteem of cultivated men. Chilperic proudly showed Gregory of Tours the medallions sent him by the emperor Tiberius II, bearing on one side the emperor's effigy and on the other a quadriga with the motto *Gloria Romanorum*. He was even prouder of the pieces which he himself had struck. He would not have it thought that the artists in his service were inferior to those of the Byzantine emperor. Pointing to a large *missorium* (i.e. a gold dish) which had been wrought and enriched with precious stones at his command, he told Gregory: 'I had this made to add lustre and distinction to the nation of the Franks. If God grants me life, I will make many more still.' In the same spirit Queen Brunhilda had commissioned a large golden shield encrusted with gems, which she sent to the king of the Visigoths with two wooden paterae plated with gold and studded with rare stones.

Kings, queens and nobles erected basilicas—the only public monuments of the period—with a zeal in which pride counted for at least as much as piety. Fortunatus wrote a poem in honour of Duke Launebolde who built in Toulouse (c. 570) a basilica dedicated to St Saturninus, praising 'this man of barbarian blood' for having done what no 'Roman' before him had thought of doing. In a rather curious passage, Gregory of Tours relates that Queen Clotilda, in her eagerness to bring about the conversion of Clovis, decorated the church, where their son Ingomer was baptized, with precious veils and hangings, hoping to win him over to the faith by glamour where exhortations had failed.

27 - TOULOUSE, CHURCH OF SAINT-SERNIN. SARCOPHAGUS, DETAIL. MUSÉE DES AUGUSTINS, TOULOUSE.

28 - TOULOUSE. CAPITAL. MUSÉE DES AUGUSTINS, TOULOUSE.   29 - TOULOUSE. COLUMN, DETAIL. LOUVRE, PARIS.

For, like the Romans, the barbarians realized that art could be a potent instrument of propaganda. In the days when Rome was extending her conquests over the known world, the colonial cities were built on a more lavish scale than those of Italy. Similarly, three or four centuries later, in Gaul at least, the Frankish kings seem to have devoted more care and effort to church-building than to improving their own residences. Contemporary accounts extol the churches but say nothing of the palaces.

25

At Auxerre Queen Clotilda had erected a basilica on the tomb of St Germanus. After his conversion, King Clovis had another built in Paris as a shrine for his own tomb; it was dedicated to the Holy Apostles. It also served as the last resting place of St Genevieve, so that something of the royal lustre was reflected on the patron saint of the Parisians. Preceded by an atrium with porticoes on each side of it, this church was probably adorned with mosaics. Like the Byzantine emperors, the Frankish kings were not content to fill their treasury with rare coins, they also 'collected' relics from which they hoped to get protection and prestige. After his return from an expedition against the Visigoths of Spain, Childebert had a basilica erected on the left bank of the Seine to house the relics of the Holy Cross and those of St Vincent, the martyr hallowed at Saragossa. This church became the royal necropolis before taking the name of an illustrious churchman subsequently interred there, Germanus, bishop of Paris; its popular appellation, Saint-Germain-le-Doré, suggests that it was built with a certain magnificence.

In the closing years of the sixth century the basilica of Saint-Martin was erected on the outskirts of Autun by Queen Brunhilda and Bishop Syagrius. Its fine marble columns, timbered ceiling and mosaics were much admired in the Middle Ages. The ground plan is known from a drawing made in the seventeenth century, and descriptions of the same period give us an idea of the general appearance of this church after a partial restoration carried out in the eleventh century.

It was too readily assumed by scholars of an older generation that the basilicas of barbarian Gaul must have been in all respects similar to those still extant at Ravenna and Rome. We still have a sadly imperfect knowledge of Christian architecture in the West under the Later Empire. But in all probability that architecture strongly influenced building practices in Gaul for centuries to come, for in the religious architecture of this region certain features can be distinguished which unquestionably antedate those introduced in the sixth century by the master-builders of the Byzantine provinces.

The basilica of Saint-Martin at Tours was described only briefly by Gregory of Tours. It was not a very large building and measured only some 160 feet in length. Yet it had 120 columns, 8 doors and 52 windows. From this it has been inferred that it must have been an elaborate structure with double aisles and galleries. I do not share this view. The old basilica of Saint-Pierre built at Vienne, in Dauphiné, in the fifth century, has undergone many modifications since then, but it has preserved one feature which must date from its original foundation: two superimposed orders of marble columns lining the side walls. The interior of this timber-roofed basilica thus recalled the stately internal disposition of the great edifices of the Gallo-Roman period. Now the number of columns here is almost the same as in the basilica of Saint-Martin as described by Gregory of Tours. And as the interior of Saint-Laurent of Grenoble and Germigny-des-Prés was later lined with columns in the same manner, rather to adorn the wall than to strengthen it, this feature must be regarded as a widely generalized survival of the architectural methods of the Late Empire.

◀ 30 - VIENNE, CHURCH OF SAINT-PIERRE. INTERIOR.

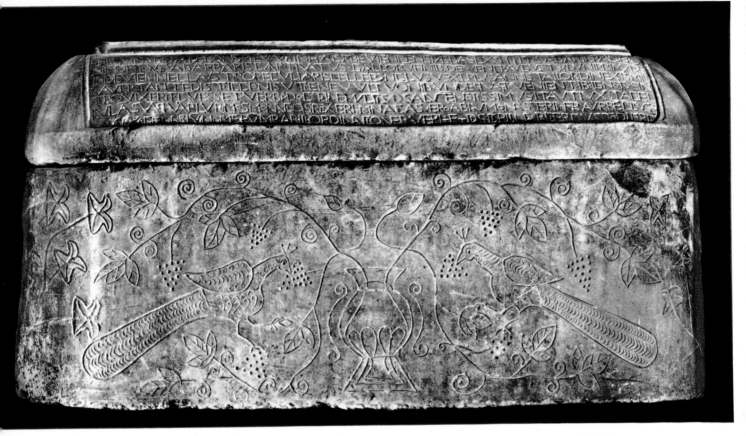

31 - VIENNE, CHURCH OF SAINT-PIERRE. SARCOPHAGUS WITH ENGRAVED DESIGNS AND MEDIEVAL INSCRIPTION.

32 - LANGEAIS. STELE. MUSÉE ARCHÉOLOGIQUE, TOURS.

33 - SELLES-SUR-CHER. EARLIER COLONNETTES AND CAPITALS RE-USED AS FAÇADE DECORATION.

To these examples must be added that of Selles-sur-Cher, which is still more significant. Before 558 a basilica had been erected there by order of King Childebert to glorify the memory of the hermit Eusicius, who had predicted the king's successes on the battlefield.

When this Merovingian basilica was rebuilt in the Romanesque period, care was taken to imitate one of its original features by reinstalling several of its finest marble capitals in a colonnade set flush with the wall at the foot of the façade. Here good use could be made of the columns of marble or hard stone salvaged from ancient monuments falling into ruin. The same use could not be made of capitals of

34-35 - SELLES-SUR-CHER. EARLIER CAPITALS RE-USED.

the classical epoch: the capital was too fragile an element not to be damaged in the course of demolitions, and this was certainly one of the reasons for the activity of the workshops of marble masons in Aquitaine, who carved capitals and exported them to the whole of Gaul in the sixth and seventh centuries. Considering the obscurity that shrouds the material culture of the Merovingian period, a clue of this kind is of exceptional value. It does not tell us what the determining principles of that architecture were, but it vouches for a fidelity to ancient practices which can only be explained by an unbroken continuity of building methods from antiquity onwards.

Further evidence of this is provided by the constant recourse to geometry for

36-37 - SELLES-SUR-CHER. CAPITAL AND SCHEMA OF TRIANGLES ON WHICH ITS DESIGN IS BASED.

the working out of proportions. Pattern-books compiled from Vitruvius and the 'geometers' have been preserved. Small monastery churches of the seventh century found at Saint-Denis, Jouarre, Nivelles and Echternach show the simplest ground plan that can be adopted for a sacred edifice: a plain rectangle, but a rectangle which in fact is exactly equal to two squares. Here is proof that the builders of these churches were deliberately applying geometric principles so as to safeguard the harmony of the proportions. A subtler use of geometry was made by Aquitanian stone-carvers: the ornamentation of marble capitals of the seventh century is often based on a schema of equilateral triangles, and the decoration of tombs on a chequer-work of squares.

31

Some Merovingian basilicas, as we know from contemporary descriptions, had a dome or a bell-tower; it stood over that part of the church which separates the nave from the apse. Such was the case at Saint-Julien of Brioude, built about 476, and at Saint-Antolien of Clermont, which was at least as old a church as Saint-Julien, for it was already in ruins in the time of Gregory of Tours. The same feature may have existed in Saint-Martin of Tours, and certainly did in the cathedral of Nantes, consecrated about 567. In the latter church, according to Fortunatus, the lower storey of the tower was pierced with arcades which let in so much light that reflections from the metal roof mingled their colours with those of the vault mosaics. At Clermont there were also marble arcades, but the dome was decorated only with paintings.

The church of Notre-Dame at Manglieu, in Auvergne, as it was described shortly after 700, was surmounted by a pentagonal tower with a square base. The bell-tower at Brioude was close to the apse and must have stood directly over the altar, like the tower at Clermont.

An examination of the plans of Saint-Pierre of Vienne and the basilica built by Queen Brunhilda near the monastery of Saint-Martin of Autun reveals that these two churches were also crowned with a light tower, for in both the last bay of the nave, just before the apse, is much wider than the others. Since this feature appears only very rarely in the churches of Italy, some archaeologists have seen it as convincing proof of the direct importation into Gaul of the Oriental type of domed basilica. Here the 'Oriental mirage' is easily dispelled, for in fact the domed church appears in the West earlier than in the East and it certainly derived from the martyria of the Later Empire. A few years ago, at Lyons, the earliest form of the church of Saint-Irénée was brought to light: it comprised a dome based on a square structure by means of pseudo-squinches composed of ordinary stone lintels. The upper part of the Fréjus baptistery, with its dome and its drum pierced with windows, probably gives a fairly accurate idea of what the dome-shaped towers of Merovingian churches were like. These towers had something of a sacred character. More effectively than the ciboria of Latin churches, they provided protection for the altar and the saint's tomb by means of a vault forming an integral part of the church roof. They were the symbol of Heaven. Of them it might have been said what a sixth-century poet wrote of the church of St Sophia at Edessa:

'Its lofty dome is comparable with the Heaven of Heavens and it is like a helmet. As the golden stars shine in the firmament, so it glows with golden mosaics. Its arches call to mind both the angles of the world below and the arch of the clouds.'

In the West these towers, destined to have a long line of descendants, were built as yet only on a very modest scale. But they must have given the martyria-churches of Frankish Gaul a quite distinctive aspect. Through the windows in the drum streamed in a flood of light focused on the most sacred place in the church. The church roof, covered with tiles of tin or gilt bronze, could be seen gleaming in the sun from a long way off and seemed to invite men to 'lift up their eyes to Heaven'; these were the words used in one of the inscriptions in the basilica of Saint-Martin at Tours.

38 - SCHOOL OF REIMS. UTRECHT PSALTER, DETAIL. UNIVERSITY LIBRARY, UTRECHT.

Excavations have brought to light another peculiarity of early medieval churches. In classical times there was no large building of any kind but had porticoes either in front of it or all round it. Covered walks, sheltered from sun and bad weather, were so much appreciated in antiquity as an added amenity in large architectural complexes that they came to figure even in modest country *villae*. From quite early times, both in the West and in the East, Christian architects adopted these outer porticoes, and they became standard elements of the sacred edifice. In North Italy, Gaul, Spain and England, the covered walks on three or even all four sides of the church (as in the baptisteries of Fréjus and Riez in the early fifth century) had none of the imposing monumental character they were given in Armenia in the sixth century, particularly at Tokor and Ereruk, but they seem to have been more highly developed than in Syria. The reason is that Western architects took to using these porches flanking the north and south sides of the church as shelters for the privileged dead who were buried in the sacred precinct; excavations have shown this to be the case at Veurey-Voroize, Saint-Romain-d'Albon, Saint-Martin of Angers and Saint-Laurent of Lyons. At Canterbury St Augustine, who in 597 had founded the monastery on the east side of the town, was entombed in the north porch of its main church in 613, while the south porch was reserved for royal tombs. The term 'cloistered church' has been wrongly given to this composite type of edifice whose historical development is perfectly clear. If, on the plan, the side porticoes give the illusion of forming an organic whole, it is only because they adjoin a cruciform church and because they extend from the nave exactly in line with the projecting arms of the transept, of which they appear (on the plan) to be a

33

39 - SOISSONS. SARCOPHAGUS OF ST DRAUSIUS. LOUVRE, PARIS.

prolongation. Moreover, these porches were not originally intended to house altars; these were set up only when the tombs located in them became an object of such veneration as to make them necessary. The history of these side porticoes is an example of the changes that came over religious architecture in the barbarian kingdoms. To the plans, structures and formulas bequeathed by the builders of the Later Empire, nothing essential was added, but ingenious improvements of a utilitarian character were made by the Franks in the designs transmitted to them by tradition. Thus architecture kept pace with the evolution of religious usage.

On the strength of the discoveries made in tombs, maps have been drawn showing the distribution of objects of personal adornment over the territory of Gaul. Two regions are shown to have excelled in the number and quality of their workshops: Aquitaine, from the upper Garonne to the lower Loire, and north-eastern Gaul, from the mouth of the Seine to Switzerland.

Aquitaine had greatly prospered in the Gallo-Roman period, and became prosperous again from the second half of the sixth century on. A surprising number of the court officials, churchmen and missionaries of the period hailed from Aquitaine. The circulation of currency testifies to a marked increase in the volume of trade and to a revival of urban life. At Cahors Bishop Desiderius girdled the town with defensive walls and built aqueducts, but he did not confine himself to utilitarian constructions. He saw to it that his cathedral city was given new houses, a monas-

40 - SOISSONS. SARCOPHAGUS OF ST DRAUSIUS, CENTRAL DETAIL. LOUVRE, PARIS.

tery and several churches. One of the export industries of Aquitaine was that of marble carvings—capitals and sarcophagi—which were made not far from the quarries at the foot of the Pyrenees, in the Toulouse area, and then sent eastward as far as the Rhone Valley and northward to the valley of the Seine.

In this conveyance of heavy objects over long distances we see an extension of the sea, river and land transport which had been so ably organized in Gaul under the Romans. The working of the marble quarries was itself a survival of the old industrial activities of Gaul.

The capitals carved in the sixth and seventh centuries derive from classical models, but their ornamentation, in which a direct study of nature can often be detected, shows a variety, an elegance and an inventive faculty which rival the virtuoso carving of the last workshops of Romanesque sculptors centuries later. The Aquitanian sarcophagi are very different from those of other Christian lands, and their technique is much closer to that of Syro-Egyptian art of the sixth or seventh century than to classical art. This fact is all the more significant since the capitals carved in the sixth century for the basilica of Selles-sur-Cher were still very similar to the antique types. Figures continued to be carved in low relief on the sides of sarcophagi, but it was only in the purely ornamental designs that these artists excelled. In this respect Gaul followed an evolution very similar to that of the workshops in the Eastern Mediterranean.

41 - NANTES, CATHEDRAL. CAPITAL. MUSÉE DOBRÉE, NANTES.

42 - NANTES, CATHEDRAL. CAPITAL. MUSÉE DOBRÉE, NANTES.

43 - VERTOU, ABBEY. CAPITAL. MUSÉE DOBRÉE, NANTES.

44 - VERTOU, ABBEY. CAPITAL. MUSÉE DOBRÉE, NANTES.

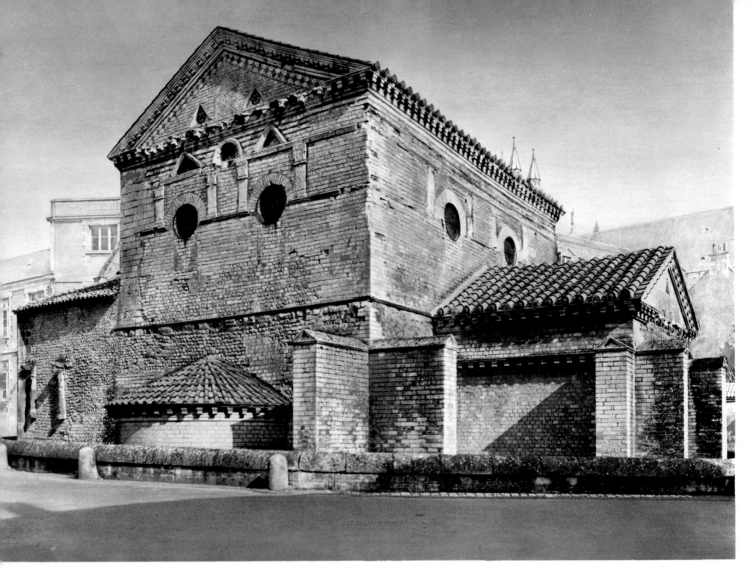

45 - POITIERS, BAPTISTERY OF SAINT-JEAN. VIEW FROM THE SOUTH-EAST.

From the late sixth to the early eighth century, the conditions of life in Poitou were favourable to art. This is clear from the flourishing state of tomb sculpture. The tombs of this period that can be positively dated, either from inscriptions engraved on them or by the level at which they were found in the cemeteries, have high artistic qualities. Some carvings skilfully imitate the embroidered textiles with which the dead were clad. The most characteristic of them have been preserved and can still be seen at Poitiers in the baptistery of Saint-Jean, a famous monument which, like the tombs, dates to the seventh century.

This dating has been contested—on insufficient grounds—by local archaeologists; for them, this fine old building symbolizes the ancient civilization of this part of France, and they would push back its foundation into the remotest past. But apart from the Gallo-Roman vestiges on which it rests and the Romanesque modifications of the entrance and the whole interior, what we have here is a cruciform edifice, with apses originally square, whose ground plan is at once very different from that of the fifth- and sixth-century baptisteries with corner niches, and quite

46 - POITIERS, BAPTISTERY OF SAINT-JEAN. VIEW FROM THE NORTH-EAST.

close to the layout of the Venasque baptistery which dates back only to the early Middle Ages. Above the apse roofs, the outer masonry of the walls has remained unchanged since the seventh century except for the insertion of round windows. The triangular pediments of the façades have been likened to those of pagan temples and of the mausoleum of Galla Placidia at Ravenna. But the Poitiers pediments are supported by tall pilasters embedded in the masonry, and this arrangement has more in common with another piece of architecture typical of the Later Empire: the façade of the Salvatore basilica at Spoleto. The layout of the two buildings is too similar for them not to have a common origin. But at Poitiers the forms have degenerated so much that the triangular pediments of the windows are replaced by flat slabs of stone devoid of any relief, and their ornamentation recalls the simulated embroideries on the stone tombs of this region mentioned on the previous page. In the chronology of forms the Poitiers baptistery comes long after the Spoleto basilica and shortly before the decoration of pilasters and mitre arches which once existed at Saint-Ursanne and can still be seen on the façades of the monumental gate of the atrium

47 - POITIERS, BAPTISTERY OF SAINT-JEAN. NORTH FRONT.

of the abbey of Lorsch. Stress must be laid on this point. For it suggests that Merovingian Gaul practised a religious architecture whose forms continued or imitated,
with varying success, those of the Later Empire. Too often it aimed at trivial 'effects';
there was no logical connection between the ornamentation and the structure.
This art form owes its historical significance to the fact that by the seventh century
it had spread over a large part of Gaul, as is proved by the carved slabs like those of
the baptistery which have been found at Poitiers itself in the ancient church of Saint-
Pierre-le-Puellier and by the slabs which still exist at Saint-Jouin-de-Marnes (one
of the foundations of St Martin, abbot of Vertou, who died early in the seventh
century) and at Mazerolles, an ancient monastery rebuilt by Bishop Ansoald of Poitiers
at the end of the seventh century. We find further links with the vestiges of other
early medieval buildings of this region. The upper register and ponderous cornices
of the Poitiers baptistery contain modillions and large decorations in terracotta.
In Nantes Museum there are similar pieces, some coming from monasteries founded
by St Martin of Vertou, others found in the vicinity of Nantes. To be sure, not all

48 - POITIERS, BAPTISTERY OF SAINT-JEAN. SOUTH FRONT, DETAIL. ▶

40

49 - POITIERS, BAPTISTERY OF SAINT-JEAN. EARLIER CAPITAL RE-USED.

these fragments of figured terracotta went to adorn façades; some of them undoubtedly served as brackets supporting decorated ceilings in the antique manner. Here we have yet another proof of the survival in Gaul, throughout the Merovingian period, of the architecture of the Later Empire.

In France the coffered ceiling disappeared from religious architecture towards the end of the Carolingian period, while, in the Loire Valley and neighbouring regions,

50 - POITIERS, BAPTISTERY OF SAINT-JEAN. EARLIER CAPITALS RE-USED. ▶

51A - ANTIGNY. SARCOPHAGUS. — 51B - POITIERS, CEMETERY OF SAINT-LAZARE. SARCOPHAGUS. BAPTISTERY OF SAINT-JEAN, POITIERS.

, SAINTE-CATHERINE CEMETERY.   SARCOPHAGUS. — 51D - POITIERS, SAINT-LAZARE CEMETERY.   SARCOPHAGUS.   BAPTISTERY OF SAINT-JEAN.

53 - POITIERS, BAPTISTERY OF SAINT-JEAN. CARVED SLAB (CAST).　　　　54 - MAZEROLLES, CHURCH. CARVED SLAB (CAST).

church fronts of the early Romanesque continued to be adorned with alternate courses of brick and stone, and with triangular inserts of masonry decorated with billet mouldings. Here the frieze of figured stonework took the place of terracotta. A century ago two Touraine archaeologists, Abbé Bourrassé and Abbé Chevalier, published a large book in which they sought to demonstrate that these early Romanesque churches were Merovingian. The mistake they made hardly deserves the ridicule some critics have heaped upon them, for these churches with their elaborately adorned façades manifestly represent the last phase of an architecture rich in colour and visual effects whose principles had been formulated in Italy under the Later Empire, and which found enthusiastic exponents in Gaul during the seventh century, as is proved by the handsome façades of the Poitiers baptistery and the traces of ornamentation we have drawn attention to. Nothing of the kind is to be found in the early Middle Ages in Italy, Spain or the British Isles. It may justly be concluded, therefore, that Gaul (and Aquitaine in particular) played an essential role as an intermediary between antique and Romanesque art, between the decorative reliefs

◀ 52 - POITIERS, BAPTISTERY OF SAINT-JEAN. PILASTERS DECORATING THE EXTERIOR (CASTS).

47

55 - TUNISIA. PANEL: ADAM AND EVE TEMPTED BY THE SERPENT. MUSÉE DU BARDO, TUNIS.

of the Later Empire and the architectural sculpture of France in the early twelfth century. A similar observation may be made with respect to the sculptured marble capitals of the sixth and seventh centuries in the Toulouse area. Fine examples of them can be seen in the interior of the Poitiers baptistery, but they were placed there only in the Romanesque period. Not everything in this art is the outcome of a long tradition or a true survival.

The terracotta bas-reliefs from churches or mausolea in the Loire Valley carry vine-patterns and figures which undoubtedly were copied from antique carvings then still extant. Here we may justly speak of a renascence.

On the other hand, the terracotta panels with Christian imagery and the 'Holy Faces' certainly derive from models created under the Later Empire, for there are striking similarities between these works of seventh-century Gaul and those of early sixth-century Africa—similarities which can be accounted for only as stemming from a common 'art language' current throughout a large part of the Christian world before the great invasions of the mid-fifth century.

56 - VERTOU. PANEL: ADAM AND EVE TEMPTED BY THE SERPENT. MUSÉE DOBRÉE, NANTES.

57 - TUNISIA. CHRIST (?). MUSÉE DU BARDO, TUNIS.

58 - PARIS. HEAD WITH A CROSS. PARIS.

59 - NANTES. FIGURED PANEL IN IMITATION OF THE ANTIQUE. MUSÉE DOBRÉE, NANTES.

60 - VERTOU. FRAGMENT OF A PEDIMENT. MUSÉE DOBRÉE, NANTES.

61 – VERTOU. FRAGMENT OF A PEDIMENT. MUSÉE DOBRÉE, NANTES.

62 – NANTES. FRAGMENT OF A CORNICE. MUSÉE DOBRÉE, NANTES.

51

63 - NANTES. PANEL WITH THE SACRED MONOGRAM. MUSÉE DOBRÉE, NANTES.

64 - VERTOU. FRAGMENT OF A PEDIMENT. MUSÉE DOBRÉE, NANTES.

65 - NANTES. ARCH-STONE WITH A FIGURE. MUSÉE DOBRÉE, NANTES.

66 - SAINT-DENIS, BASILICA. PART OF A CLOSURE SLAB. DÉPOT LAPIDAIRE, BASILICA OF SAINT-DENIS.

67 - SAINT-DENIS. CLOSURE PILASTER. DÉPOT LAPIDAIRE, SAINT-DENIS.

As against this art of the Loire Valley which had been so profoundly marked by Mediterranean influences, mention must be made of the very unusual partition slabs, fragments of which were found in the basilica of Saint-Denis during the excavations conducted by Jules Formigé. These carvings probably date to the seventh century. The design on one of them is like an enlargement of the curves and counter-curves which were a favourite motif with the barbarian goldsmiths.

69 - POITIERS, HYPOGEUM: 'HYPOGÉE DES DUNES.' LONGITUDINAL SECTION (AFTER LE PÈRE DE LA CROIX).

Another monument at Poitiers, though less imposing than the baptistery, is equally renowned, for it has contributed a great deal to the understanding of the Gallo-Franks of the seventh century whose beliefs and way of life still remain something of a mystery. In 1878, a funerary oratory was discovered in an ancient cemetery south-east of Poitiers; it came to be known locally as the Hypogée des Dunes. Lying partly underground and roofed at some time in the past with a semi-circular vault, this small hypogeum recalls the stone-built tomb chambers in which wealthy Gallo-Romans had themselves interred. Here is a striking example of the survival of a type of edifice already four centuries old at the very least. The only differences lie in the rough masonry of the walls and the new use made of the building. Inscriptions and the presence of an altar prove that it served both as an oratory and a place of burial. Ten steps led down to the underground chamber. 'Here is the tomb of Abbot Mellebaude, Christ's debtor. Hither men come to worship Christ. Hence go consoled the faithful who came laden with the grievous burden of their sins.' The inscription continues on the door-jambs and ends on a minatory note: 'If there be any man who here refuses to worship Our Lord Jesus Christ or dares to destroy this work, may he be anathema for evermore!' Further precautions were taken against possible violation of the tomb. The three steps nearest the door are

◄ 68 - POITIERS, HYPOGEUM: 'HYPOGÉE DES DUNES.' OVERALL VIEW FROM THE WEST.

70 - POITIERS, HYPOGEUM: 'HYPOGÉE DES DUNES.' THREE STEPS OF THE STAIRWAY.

71 - POITIERS, HYPOGEUM: 'HYPOGÉE DES DUNES.' MAGIC INSCRIPTION AT THE ENTRANCE.

decorated with motifs incised deeply enough in the stone for the foot to trip over them. On one step are three intertwined snakes, on the second some fishes, on the third some ivy tendrils. Fish and ivy were symbols of immortality in early Christian times. Intertwined snakes are a motif of Germanic origin; they occur very often on the bronze buckles discovered in seventh-century tombs. That all three motifs are used here with a magical intent is shown clearly by the cabalistic rune engraved on the step serving as the threshold of the tomb:

GRAMA GRVMO ANA-AY CAX PI/IX.

72 - POITIERS, HYPOGEUM: 'HYPOGÉE DES DUNES.'
CROSS SECTION (AFTER LE PÈRE DE LA CROIX).

73 - POITIERS, HYPOGEUM: 'HYPOGÉE DES DUNES.' LOWER PART OF THE ALTAR.

Inside the hypogeum there is no trace of this primitive sorcery. For the protection of his tomb, Abbot Mellebaude trusted to the sanctity of the altar—a cube of masonry painted on the main side with a cross embellished with glass beads—and to that of relics enclosed in stone shrines. These shrines are roughly carved with figures of apostles, archangels and saints.

74 - POITIERS, HYPOGEUM: 'HYPOGÉE DES DUNES.' NORTH SIDE OF THE SANCTUARY. ▶

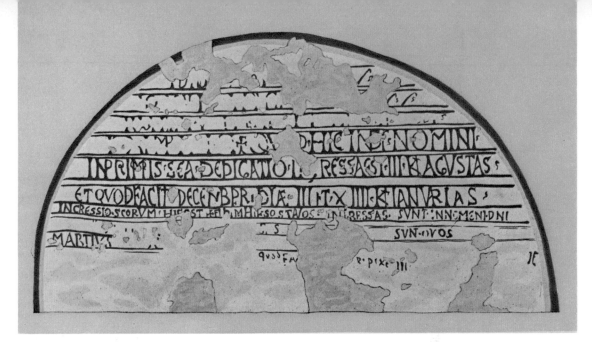

75 - POITIERS, HYPOGEUM: 'HYPOGÉE DES DUNES.' COPY OF AN INSCRIPTION (AFTER LE PÈRE DE LA CROIX).

Carved on a stele are two figures, each bound to a cross, who for a long time were thought to be local martyrs. Victor Elbern has shown, however, that this fragment of sculpture represents the two thieves undergoing punishment at the foot of the Cross. This is an important discovery, for this work, taken in conjunction with the cross of St Eligius formerly at Saint-Denis, proves that monumental crosses existed at that time in churches and cemeteries. This one, so far as its height can be judged from the surviving fragment, was too tall for the small hypogeum. It was a monumental cross made to figure in a large choir or the open air. It may have stood originally in the large basilica which must have existed in the Cimetière des Dunes, as in all the suburban cemeteries of the Merovingian period. The basilica having been burned down or demolished by the Arabs, the fragments of the cross would then have been placed in the hypogeum to safeguard them from desecration. (This of course is purely conjectural.) In any case the stone-carved crucifixion at Poitiers proves that bas-reliefs were used to decorate churches or the approaches to them. It should be noted that in this period the Aquitanian sculptors showed less skill in figure carving than in ornamental work on sarcophagus lids.

In its origin and development, Christian iconography was of a character radically different from that of pagan religious statuary. In the East, the doctrines of Neo-Platonism encouraged the creation and proliferation of a copious imagery which, by its very excesses, gave rise eventually to a violent reaction—iconoclasm. The resulting quarrel over images had little effect on the art of the West. At Poitiers the sculpture is of poor quality, but the painted and engraved inscriptions—and of these there are many—speak for a fairly high standard of culture. The Latin is correct and the lettering elegant. One of these inscriptions, however, expresses a deep-seated pessimism: 'All things go from bad to worse and the end of time is near!' This resigned expectancy of the coming end of the world was not an attitude conducive to progress.

76 - POITIERS, HYPOGEUM: 'HYPOGÉE DES DUNES.' BASE OF A MONUMENTAL CROSS. ▶

From Aquitaine in south-western France, we may turn now to the Marne Valley east of Paris. Here we find a funerary edifice approximately contemporary with the hypogeum of Poitiers: the famous 'crypts' of Jouarre, an abbey founded about 630 near Meaux, in a region then still thickly wooded but fertile, settled and controlled by barbarian nobles. And here we see the rise, in the first flush of its brilliant promise, of that new world despaired of by Abbot Mellebaude of Aquitaine. It is an arresting contrast, one that brings home to us the fact that, by the end of the seventh century, the northern lands had become the true continuators of the Mediterranean civilization.

Jouarre was one of the seven abbeys founded in the Marne Valley by the Irish monk Columban. In Poitou very few monasteries had been built in the opening years of the seventh century, whereas north-eastern Gaul at that time was being almost literally 'conquered' by the monks. The number of monasteries founded there from the late sixth to the early eighth century can be reckoned at something over two hundred. Many of them were housed in the surviving structures of the old Gallo-Roman estates. The churches were plain, rectangular buildings, as we know from excavations and the early plans of those at Nivelles, Moûtier-Grandval, Fleury and Nouaillé, but each abbey had more than one. In the seventh century it was the custom, if not the rule, for both monasteries and cathedrals to be surrounded by several churches, forming an imposing group of buildings often covering a vast area. By the end of the seventh century the abbey of Jumièges had been girdled with a square wall fortified with towers. The finest buildings, described by a contemporary chronicler as 'admirable,' stood at the entrance and were set aside as guest quarters. The edifices reserved for the monks stood between two large churches and three oratories; they were adorned with gushing fountains and porticoes with stone columns. Facing south, the dormitorium measured over 300 feet in length. It was a two-storey building, well lit by large windows. On the ground floor were living quarters, kitchens and other dependencies. Such is the description of Jumièges that has come down to us; it tells us nothing of the nature of the architecture and little enough of its actual appearance. Nevertheless this was a period of fairly intense building activity, for the total surface area covered by the monasteries founded in the seventh century represents twenty or thirty times the area of Paris in the Gallo-Roman period. That this architectural activity extended also to the towns is proved by the number of suburban churches erected at this time whose exact site is known. At Le Mans, in the late sixth and the seventh century, eight monasteries and hospitals were built outside the town walls, on the Roman highways, at distances varying from 200 to 900 yards from the town.

The foundress of Jouarre, Abbess Theodechilde, belonged to one of the families of barbarian nobles in close touch with the court, to whom had fallen the lion's share of the great landed estates as well as the high offices of Church and State. Jouarre in the Middle Ages included two churches near the monastic buildings and a third, dedicated to the hermit Paul, which stood inside a cemetery. Excavations made in 1867 brought to light the original walls of this cemetery church. They

77 - JOUARRE, ABBEY. NORTH CRYPT FROM THE SOUTH-WEST. ▶

78 - JOUARRE, ABBEY. NORTH CRYPT, WITH THE SOUTH CRYPT AT THE FAR RIGHT.

formed a rectangle, and inside it were found three superimposed tiers of tombs. The walls of this church are no longer visible, but the vast burial vault built under the apse in the late seventh and early eighth century has survived, and it testifies to the high civilization of the late Merovingian period.

This burial vault became a crypt, in the modern sense of the word, only after the original layout had been altered. An underground, tunnel-vaulted passage was built beneath the central axis of the church of St Paul, and as a result the floor level was raised. This passage enabled worshippers to enter the burial vault directly, without passing through the church. Originally the east vault was level with the

79 - JOUARRE, ABBEY. WEST WALL OF THE NORTH CRYPT.

church, of which it formed the back part of the apse. Privileged burial places of this kind were frequent in the seventh century, as we learn from the records, and a similar one has been found in the apse of the main church of the monastery of Nivelles. The vault at Jouarre was altered in the Romanesque period, but it has retained its original west wall and the original marble columns, crowned with fine Aquitanian capitals, which supported what was probably a barrel vaulting by means of stone architraves, of which a few fragments survive in an annexe built in the eighth century to house the tomb of Ebregesilus, bishop of Meaux. The masonry of the west wall reproduces the most ingenious device transmitted by Roman architects—*opus reticulatum*. Here, as at Lorsch a little later, the wall surface is divided into three registers filled successively by square, lozenge-shaped and octagonal stones. These dressed stones were not taken over from an earlier building, and it is apparent that the masonry is quite as carefully bonded as in similar stonework of the Gallo-Roman period.

This is neither a creation of 'barbarian art,' nor a slavish copy. Such fine

80 - JOUARRE, ABBEY. CAPITAL IN THE NORTH CRYPT.

masonry called for great skill on the part of both stonecutter and mason. It can only have been executed by highly specialized workers, men who probably roamed far afield, catering for rich and powerful patrons. As in Gallo-Roman times, the aristocratic art of the early Middle Ages was not limited to any special place, nor was it dependent on materials available locally. The same remark applies to the columns and the handsome capitals crowning them.

The columns are 'second-hand'; they were taken over from ancient monuments, and were probably delivered by teams of craftsmen who ransacked existent Roman ruins, in order to procure materials conforming to the same module. The capitals, however, are not Roman work. The quality of the marble and the peculiarities of their ornamentation prove that they were made in the seventh century by Pyrenean stone-carvers.

They must have been shipped to Jouarre by sea, then up the Seine and the Marne. About fifty capitals of this type are known today, spread over the whole of France but most numerous in the south-west. Here, then, in Merovingian Gaul,

68

81 - JOUARRE, ABBEY. CAPITAL IN THE NORTH CRYPT.

was an industry which supplied architectural elements ready-made—'prefabricated' is the term we would use nowadays.

This in itself is proof that, after the invasions, the specialized workshops and long-distance transport system of Roman times had been successfully revived.

A similar specialization can be observed in Gaul in the seventh century for the manufacture of stone and plaster coffins. The sarcophagi found in Normandy and the Marne Valley must come from Parisian workshops, since they are made of 'vergelet' or Saint-Leu stone. Northern France and Champagne were supplied by quarries and workshops in the Dijon region. Nantes and its environs were supplied by Poitou. Coffins carved in the stone of Bourbon-l'Archambault and Coulandon are found in ancient cemeteries within the area bounded by the Loire, the Allier and the Cher, and throughout the Sologne region as well. Sarcophagi in moulded plaster made in and around Paris were shipped down the Seine to Normandy.

Coffins of this type were found at Jouarre in the funerary church which extended west of the crypts. Three stone sarcophagi have been piously preserved

83 - JOUARRE, ABBEY, NORTH CRYPT. CENOTAPH OF ST THEODECHILDE. DETAIL.

to this day in the north crypt. The magnificent carvings on them have an unfailing interest for art lovers and archaeologists. For, taken in conjunction with the oldest of the sculptured crosses in the British Isles and a small number of contemporary bas-reliefs in Lombardy and Spain, they testify, half a century before the Carolingian period, to a most remarkable renascence of religious sculpture and funerary epigraphy in barbarian Europe. The three sarcophagi at Jouarre were not carved in the same workshop, but all three alike show a feeling for monumental sculpture which seems to have been peculiar to this region of France.

In the vault made for her, the tomb of Abbess Theodechilde occupies the place of honour in the centre. It consists of the sarcophagus, in which the body was placed, surmounted by a kind of cenotaph. An inscription in Latin verse, running over both sides of the cenotaph, celebrates the virtues of the first abbess of the convent, who is described as 'blessed.' The letters of this beautifully engraved inscription are very similar to the capital letters of titles and headings in Frankish manuscripts of the first half of the eighth century. Antique art comes to life again in this splendid epitaph, which is set off by rows of admirably carved shells glittering like mirrors when their facets catch the light. This masterpiece of decorative carving far surpasses even the finest contemporary sculpture of Italy, such as that of the tomb of Theodota at Pavia.

◀ 82 - JOUARRE, ABBEY, NORTH CRYPT. CENOTAPH OF ST THEODECHILDE.

71

84 - JOUARRE, ABBEY, NORTH CRYPT. TOMB OF BISHOP AGILBERT WITH THE LAST JUDGMENT.

Another sarcophagus stands against the north wall of the crypt. Like most seventh-century sarcophagi, it is higher and wider at the head than at the foot. According to a very old local tradition, this was the tomb of Agilbert, one of the outstanding churchmen of the seventh century. Born a member of the Frankish nobility, Agilbert left his family to cross the sea and study the Scriptures in the remote fastnesses of Ireland. He was elevated to the bishopric in England and in 667 transferred to the see of Paris. A near relative of the first abbess, he is said to have retired in old age to the monastery of Jouarre. The carvings on his sarcophagus cover one of the long sides and also the short side at the head of it. On the long side is a Last Judgment which, besides being full of character, has one feature for which

85 - JOUARRE, ABBEY, NORTH CRYPT. TOMB OF BISHOP AGILBERT, DETAIL. ▶

86 - JOUARRE, ABBEY, NORTH CRYPT. TOMB OF BISHOP AGILBERT, DETAIL.

there is no parallel in any other figuration of this theme, either in sculpture or painting: the elect have their arms uplifted like the Orants in Coptic stelae of the same period.

The rugged beauty of these carvings is so unusual for the art of Merovingian Gaul that the Agilbert sarcophagus raises a knotty problem for the art historian. These outstretched hands and these faces reveal an intense feeling for life that not only has nothing in common with the academicism of Late Antique art but is also very different from the brilliant stylizations of medieval artists. In fact this sculpture of the seventh century of our era brings to mind certain images of prehistoric art —except for one thing: the burning faith that emanates from the rapt figures of this Last Judgment. This is not the embodiment of a dream but the transposition of an inner vision radiant with a hope and a conviction that nothing can frustrate.

At the head of the Agilbert sarcophagus is a figuration, no less remarkable, of Christ enthroned in a mandorla and surrounded by the four evangelist symbols.

87 - JOUARRE, ABBEY, NORTH CRYPT. TOMB OF BISHOP AGILBERT, DETAIL. ▶

89 - JOUARRE, ABBEY, NORTH CRYPT. TOMB OF BISHOP AGILBERT, SHORT SIDE: CHRIST BETWEEN THE EVANGELIST SYMBOLS.

It suggests an hypothesis concerning the origin of this image. One is struck by the fact that the symbolic animals are not looking towards Christ, as they are in all the sculptures and paintings executed in the West during the Middle Ages; instead, they turn away from Him, their forms arranged like rays projecting outward from the centre of the composition. This is a peculiarity which occurs only in an Early Christian mosaic at Salonica and in the paintings in Egyptian and Cappadocian basilicas. From this it may be inferred that the Jouarre sculptor had probably been trained in a Coptic workshop whose members fled to Europe when the Arabs invaded Egypt. A similar hypothesis has been advanced to account for the origin of the sculptured crosses of the British Isles.

◄ 88 - JOUARRE, ABBEY, NORTH CRYPT. TOMB OF BISHOP AGILBERT, SHORT SIDE, DETAIL.

90 - JOUARRE, ABBEY, NORTH CRYPT. TOMB OF ABBESS AGILBERTA.

The third of the carved sarcophagi in the Jouarre crypt is, according to tradition, that of Abbess Agilberta. It consists of two fragments fitted together which may have belonged originally to two different tombs. One piece is decorated with a Greek key-pattern frieze which recalls certain contemporary carvings in Great Britain. The style of insular sculpture is generally quite different from that of the abbey of Jouarre, but future discoveries may throw further light on their common sources.

For we know from the Venerable Bede how close were the ties between the British Isles and the monasteries founded by St Columban in the Brie region, one of which was Jouarre.

91 - JOUARRE, ABBEY, NORTH CRYPT. STELE: CENSING ANGEL AND ANOTHER FIGURE. ▶

92 - MONASTERBOICE. 'MUIREDACH' CROSS.

93 - RUTHWELL CROSS, DETAIL: HEALING OF THE BLIND MAN.

94 - BEWCASTLE CROSS, DETAIL: CHRIST.

The Celts of the British Isles were converted in the fifth century. At the time of the barbarian invasions this former Roman province, at one of the northern extremities of Europe, was left in an isolation that explains the striking originality of its art. The autonomous character of Celtic churches is one of the commonplaces of art history. By the seventh century, however, things had changed. Jouarre was one of those monasteries in the Brie region which, as Bede tells us, maintained such close relations with his country that the kings and nobles of Northumbria sent their daughters there to finish their education. The origin of the Jouarre carvings and that of the famous sculptured crosses of Northumbria and Ireland raise the same problems and—we would stress this point—the same uncertainties. Most of the crosses that have come down to us cannot be dated earlier than the ninth or tenth century, but it has been proved that this type of cross with figure reliefs goes back to the seventh century and that it played an important part as a place of station and prayer in the processions that wound their way through church cemeteries. There is an obvious connection here with similar practices on the continent. From a copy of

95 - JEDBURGH. FRAGMENT OF A CROSS. JEDBURGH MUSEUM.

96 - EASBY CROSS: CHRIST AND APOSTLES. — 97 - EASBY CROSS: DETAIL OF THE SHAFT. VICTORIA AND ALBERT MUSEUM, LONDON.

the rules of the abbey of Saint-Riquier, we learn that a procession took place every day in the large monastery church built by Angilbert at the close of the eighth century, and that the monks halted for prayers in front of panels decorated with painted carvings representing the Nativity, Crucifixion, Resurrection and Ascension. These bas-reliefs were not accompanied by altars. The Nativity stood at the church entrance, the Passion scenes in front of the east choir, between the Resurrection on the north and the Ascension on the south. Placed inside the church, these figure reliefs were made of stucco and they are described as being, each of them, a marvel of craftsmanship. The crosses of the British Isles, standing out of doors and exposed to the weather, were made of stone. They varied considerably in size and conception, but their carvings served the same purpose. They are remote ancestors of the great monumental sculpture of the Middle Ages.

98 - SAN PEDRO DE LA NAVE. EXTERIOR FROM THE SOUTH-WEST.

Far distant from Jouarre, and well beyond the frontiers of France, in regions of Spain that were conquered by the Arabs in the eighth century, several churches can still be seen which antedate the Moorish occupation. I shall discuss only those which can be certainly assigned to the seventh century: the church of San Juan Bautista de Baños in the province of Palencia, dated 661; the church of San Pedro de la Nave in the province of Zamora, not far from the Portuguese frontier; and the church of Quintanilla de las Viñas in the province of Burgos. This last has not come down to us intact. The nave goes back only to the Middle Ages, but the outer walls of the choir and transept make an unforgettable impression on all who see them, for the fine stonework of the masonry is enhanced by friezes set out on both storeys and containing exquisitely carved figures. Here the structure, which derives directly from the porticoes of the Later Empire, is as perfect in its kind as that of the Syrian churches and Byzantine edifices of the sixth century.

99 - SAN PEDRO DE LA NAVE. INTERIOR. ▶

100 - SAN PEDRO DE LA NAVE. CAPITAL: DANIEL IN THE LIONS' DEN.

None of these three churches is very large, but all are well proportioned. Their plan, which does not include an apse, is based on an ingenious arrangement of straight lines. The interior was deliberately divided up and partitioned off so as to provide support for the vaulting which partially covers the church. As in ancient buildings, the window openings are not splayed and the columns are simply backed against the walls, none of them being embedded in the masonry. But there are novel features as well, all the more striking since here they have all the air of tentative precursors of Romanesque architecture and decoration. In the church of Quintanilla de las Viñas the ornamentation and figure carvings in stone are given an exceptional prominence. A rectangular panel bears the effigy of the Saviour, somewhat naïvely represented between two angels; on another is a representation of the sun. The capitals in this church and in San Pedro de la Nave have unusually thick abaci. More remarkable is the fact that two of the sculptured capitals in San Pedro represent Old Testament scenes: Abraham's Sacrifice, Daniel in the Lions' Den. Hollowed out behind the figures, the ground produces the impression of a fresco transposed in low relief to the surface of the stone. Faint traces of colour show that these carvings

101 - SAN PEDRO DE LA NAVE. CAPITAL: THE SACRIFICE OF ISAAC.

102 - QUINTANILLA DE LAS VIÑAS, SANTA MARIA. FRIEZE: CHRIST BETWEEN TWO ANGELS.

103 - OVIEDO, SANTULLANO CHURCH. COPY OF PAINTINGS.

104 - OVIEDO, SANTULLANO CHURCH. COPY OF PAINTINGS.

105 - OVIEDO, SANTULLANO CHURCH. RECONSTRUCTION (AFTER MAGIN BERENGUER ALONSO).

were originally painted. The figures are not so expertly carved as the rinceaux of vine-patterns decorating the tops of the arches and the upper part of the walls.

The impression of beauty we get from a visit to these churches is largely due to the fineness of the masonry of both walls and vaulting. The stones, of fairly large size, are smooth and regular to a quite remarkable degree. They are given clear-cut edges and the joints are so thin that they look as if they had been bonded without cement.

Thanks to the early copies that were made of them, we can form a good idea of the wall paintings, now almost invisible, which once decorated the church of San Julian de los Prados, called Santullano, near Oviedo. The church was built about 812 by Alfonso II to serve a royal villa. Its paintings in *trompe-l'œil*, disposed on the walls like superimposed orders, attest the survival into the ninth century of iconographic practices which go back to the fourth.

89

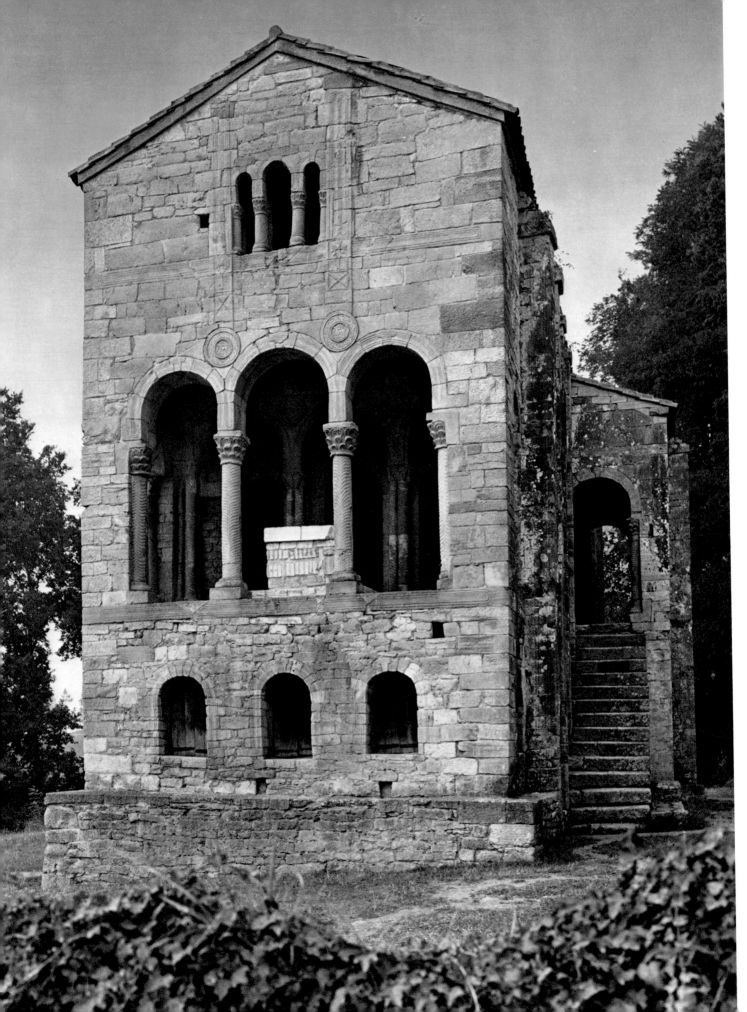

107 - SANTA MARIA DE NARANCO, PALACE. INTERIOR OF THE MAIN HALL.

Had all the religious architecture of the ancient Roman province of Spain the
same high qualities as these on the eve of the Arab conquest? We have every reason
to believe so. In Oviedo, a region where the invaders failed to set foot, the Asturian
churches of the ninth and tenth centuries and the charming little palace of Naranco,
built by King Ramiro I (842-850), have many distinctive features proving them to
be in the direct line of descent from that wonderful seventh-century Spanish architecture which was the only one in Europe that employed methods retaining something of the fine perfection of antiquity.

◄ 106 - SANTA MARIA DE NARANCO. VIEW OF THE PALACE.

108 - SANTA MARIA DE NARANCO, PALACE. GALLERY AT THE END OF THE UPPER ROOM, DETAIL.

The Arab conquest put an abrupt end to the art activities of barbarian Spain, and Spanish art exercised an influence only on Gaul, and this to a very limited extent. North of the Pyrenees, Septimania still remained an integral part of the Visigoth kingdom and it seems highly probable that the buildings erected by Desiderius, bishop of Cahors, in his see during the seventh century—notably the vaulted apartments in his episcopal palace—were the work of craftsmen brought from Spain. Somewhat later Bishop Theodulf, who came of a Gothic family settled in Spain,

109 - SANTA MARIA DE NARANCO, PALACE. EXTERNAL ARCADING, DETAIL.

enriched the Carolingian renascence with contributions deriving from the ancient Hispanic culture. But the influence of this civilization, whose architecture had been so full of promise in the seventh century, went no further. This explains why in the domains of wall painting and architecture the Carolingian renascence owed far less to Spain than to North Italy.

A startling discovery made during the last war has confirmed this, so far as painting is concerned. Some eighteen miles north of Milan, Castelseprio is no more

110 - CASTELSEPRIO, SANTA MARIA FORIS PORTAS. VIEW FROM THE SOUTH-WEST.

today than a small, out-of-the-way village situated in a hilly, thickly wooded country-side. In 1944 some soldiers amused themselves in their off hours scraping off the coat of plaster on the walls of the church and brought to light some truly remarkable paintings. Arranged in superimposed tiers, these frescoes depict the childhood and life of Christ. They represent one of the summits of religious painting of all time. The church itself, a seventh-century building, has an elegant simplicity. The walls are well constructed, with windows shaped like key-holes. This was not a mere village church but a sort of palatine chapel, for the bishops of Milan made Castelseprio their summer residence. The frescoes must have been painted a good while after the church was built, but when and by whom is a problem which still gives rise to heated controversy. Though the technique is undoubtedly Byzantine, the choice of themes and layout conform to western, not eastern, practice. Moreover one of the painted inscriptions is so faulty that it must have been written by a man of Latin origin, unfamiliar with Greek. All things considered, it would seem that these frescoes were made in the eighth or early ninth century; in other words that they were not anterior to the first productions of the Carolingian renascence. But, whatever their date, the Castelseprio paintings have an exemplary significance, for they illustrate one of the ways in which Byzantine influences took effect in the West, leading as they did to a revival of wall painting of which the pioneers of the Carolingian renascence were quick to take advantage. Byzantine influences in Italy were not confined to Rome and Ravenna. The team of Lombard craftsmen employed

111 - CASTELSEPRIO, SANTA MARIA FORIS PORTAS, EAST APSE. THE FLIGHT INTO EGYPT.

at Castelseprio had certainly been trained by Greeks, and many features of their creations pointed the way to the early ninth-century frescoes of Malles and Müstair; even to some wall paintings of the Ottonian period. (See also page 121.)

The same applies to architecture. Thus the church of Germigny-des-Prés, built by Theodulf about the year 800, reveals the Spanish background of its founder only

113 - GRENOBLE, SAINT-LAURENT. INTERIOR OF THE CRYPT.

in certain details of the mosaic decoration. Most of the distinctive architectural features of this oratory roofed with alternating domes and barrel vaults derive from a region straddling the Alps, comprising parts of present-day Switzerland, south-eastern France and upper Italy.

The edifice most typical in this respect is the one long known to archaeologists as the 'crypt' of Saint-Laurent at Grenoble on whose west side recent excavations have brought to light a number of long-buried vestiges of antiquity. This oratory (for such it was) was built in a very ancient graveyard. Given a quatrefoil plan and vaulted throughout, it is now located, cryptwise, under the nave of a church built in the early Romanesque period. Originally, however, it was at ground level and had no structure above it. Its plan and certain characteristic details of the decoration enable us to date it, without a doubt, to about the end of the eighth century. The trefoil plan of the oratory proper has exactly the same proportions and dimensions as the eastern part of a mausoleum built between 798 and 813 east of the church of Saint-Nizier at Lyons to shelter the tombs of erstwhile bishops of that city. It is

◄ 112 - GRENOBLE, SAINT-LAURENT. EAST APSE OF THE CRYPT.

115-116 - GRENOBLE, SAINT-LAURENT. CAPITALS AND ABACI IN THE CRYPT.

interesting to note that the abaci above some of the Grenoble capitals are given the characteristic form and decoration of the symbolic vase found only in sculptures of Italy and Switzerland dating to the second half of the eighth century. This proves the building to be contemporary with the beginnings of the Carolingian renascence, but it owes nothing to the art of the North. It was constructed and decorated by an indigenous team of workers whose methods linked up with those of North Italy and the south of Switzerland. The arch-stones employed are alternately of stone and brick, and the clampings of the walls and the central barrel vault are of brick. In front of the walls all is designed with an eye to spectacular effect. Columns with capitals topped by abaci carry architraves, and at the entrances of the two apses, east and west, small coupled columns placed above the architrave support the triumphal arch. The aim here is evidently to produce the illusion of a second order. The structure of the ribbed vaults of the apses is highly ingenious. These vaults rest on wall arches supported by consoles. The main apse has a decoration in stucco, with, in its upper part, a cross rising up between foliage scrolls in the

114 - GRENOBLE, SAINT-LAURENT. CRYPT, DETAIL.

117 - GRENOBLE, SAINT-LAURENT. CAPITAL AND ABACUS. — 118 - NARBONNE. SLAB: EXALTATION OF THE CROSS. MUSÉE LAPIDAIRE, NARBONNE.

Mediterranean style. In the places where the stucco does not carry decorations in relief, a sort of trellis was sketched in with a pointed instrument to simulate a decorative motif, and the small columns at the base of the springers of the wall arches were also entirely made of stucco.

On the other hand, the scrollwork on the abaci has nothing in common with that of the classical epoch or the Later Empire, but is closely affiliated to that of eighth-century North Italian closure slabs. The layout of the chancel slabs adorned with scrollwork, interlaces and rosettes suggests that this type of decoration originated, shortly before the middle of the eighth century, in the region of stone quarries lying round the meeting point of the present-day frontiers of Italy, Switzerland and Austria; thence it gradually spread west and north, at the same time as it made

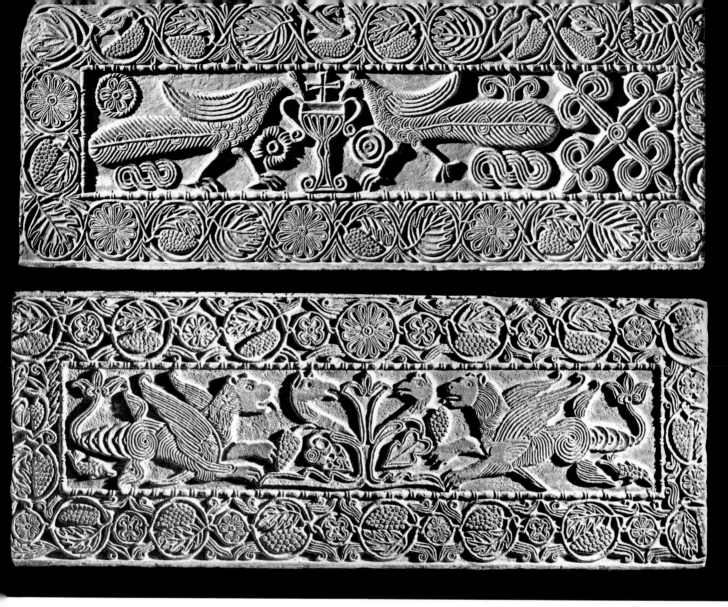

119 A AND B - PAVIA, SANTA MARIA DELLA PUSTEROLA. TOMB OF ABBESS THEODOTA. MUSEO CIVICO MALASPINA, PAVIA.

headway in the direction of central Italy. The exportation of the products of this industrial art led to the creation of local workshops in distant regions, where they were sedulously copied. The fact that the chancel slabs constituted the only decorated element in many of the smaller churches accounts for the expansion of this industry, which flourished not only in Helvetia and the Rhone Valley but also as far afield as south-western Gaul. The Narbonne panel, carrying a rather crude image of the Adoration of the Cross by two male figures, is a carving conceived and executed on the same lines as the sculpture of the Swiss closure slabs.

In drawing attention to the crypt of Saint-Laurent of Grenoble at the end of this chapter, our intention was to stress the importance of the part played by Italy and its confines at the close of the barbarian epoch, on the eve of the Carolingian

120 - READING-DESK ATTRIBUTED TO ST RADEGUND (SEEN FROM BEHIND). ABBEY OF SAINTE-CROIX, POITIERS.

renascence. Despite the widespread havoc wrought by the Lombards in the first phase of their occupation, Northern Italy continued to benefit both by the heritage of antiquity and by artistic contributions from the Byzantine provinces. At the end of the early Middle Ages this art lacked any sort of cohesion, traversed as it was by a multitude of cross-currents, but once Charlemagne set order in it and it was enriched by the manifold achievements of the art centres of Gaul during the seventh and eighth centuries, these scattered fires commingled in a flame illuminating all the West.

JEAN HUBERT

PART TWO

Book Painting

The Heritage of Antiquity

THE Carolingians owed their knowledge of antiquity to monuments of various epochs that still survived in eighth-century Italy and to their sequelae, barbarian or otherwise. Though most of these were in ruins or much changed from their original condition, they were still sufficiently evocative and numerous to enable the Franks to carry their imitation of the ancients much further than their predecessors and initiators on Latin soil, the Lombards. For, not content like the latter with merely copying, they made efforts to penetrate the underlying meaning of classical art, and succeeded in this attempt within a century. The Carolingians not only preserved the classical heritage, but in their manner ensured its continuity, and they deserve full credit for the amazing revival of European art. Wherever they made their mark, the ancient tradition was given a new lease on life, particularly in Gaul, whereas in other regions, to which they devoted less attention, that tradition tended to lose its force or fall to pieces. This was soon the case with Rome, which, however, had been the source from which they drew their knowledge of the past. It is, then, worth while trying to form a picture of the Italy they knew—or anyhow the Italy which, after twelve centuries of constant depredation, we still can conjure up. Wall paintings, mosaics, ivories and illuminated manuscripts supplied the Franks with a great diversity of forms deriving from many lands; but quite soon, perhaps even from the start, they were able to distinguish originals from copies, Mediterranean from barbarian works of art—in a word to acquire as by right the status of successors to the Empire of the West. Surprising at first sight, this phenomenon was due to the fact that they they had at their disposal the many well-trained technicians, artists and craftsmen, whom they had brought from Lombard Italy and from Rome, and, above all, that under the guidance of enlightened advisers they could select, and give employment to, the best of them.

Outstanding among the many archaeological treasures of Rome, that unique repository of art and history, is the church of Santa Maria Antiqua. Built on the north-eastern slope of the Palatine Hill, on the site of a former record-room of the Roman legions, used after that as a chapel staffed by Greek monks of the imperial

palace, and finally allowed to fall into disuse in the ninth century, this ancient sanctuary provides in superimposed fragments, like geological strata, a sort of résumé of three centuries of Christian painting; indeed there is no better place for charting its development. The successive phases of this painting, in the strongly Hellenized environment of Rome, reflect in seeming disorder the conflicting tendencies that were then operative in the Mediterranean world. A single, yet a complex world; the antinomy West-East meant nothing at this time (except as regards iconography). True, a certain image, a certain way of regarding it might belong to one region rather than to another. But the images follow a line of evolution of their own, not always coinciding with the art currents of the age. In the period when the Latin master of the world established the capital of his empire on Greek soil and became βασιλεύς των 'Ρωμαιῶν; when the Byzantine Emperor Justinian reconquered Latin Italy; when (from 642 to 752) with brief intermissions Greek and Syrian popes reigned in Rome; when the Mediterranean was a busy highway of commerce and exchanges of ideas; when, despite sometimes extremely bitter doctrinal quarrels the Empire was united by Christianity as it had never been before—throughout this period these diverse art currents proliferated in all directions, crossed and interacted. The Carolingians made their breakthrough at the heart of this complex of art trends, then took from it whatever served their turn, and it is far from easy for us today to disentangle their prototypes. Yet whether these were eastern or western, Greek or Latin, matters little; Rome and Italy supplied all alike in equal measure at the same time.

It was towards the beginning of the sixth century that Santa Maria Antiqua was given its first Christian decoration. At the time when Theodoric was ruling Italy from his headquarters at Ravenna, a 'Virgin Queen' of which large fragments have survived was painted on the west wall of the gallery. *Maria Regina* is seated frontally on a high throne, wearing a crown decked like her garment with large gems. On her knees she holds her Son, who like herself is shown full face. Her huge, staring eyes fix the beholder with a supernatural intensity. On her left an angel (only the head survives) bends towards her—a simple, natural, wholly human movement that strikes an evidently intentional contrast with the demeanour of the central group. On the right was another, matching angel, now lost. Mary and her Son, divine beings, reign in heaven; the angels are intermediate entities. This dualism in the conception of the images (it is not a mere difference of style) was stressed more and more as time went on. The picture, largely overlaid by new paintings made in the middle of the same century, was a typically Roman version of an icon which had already become widespread throughout Christendom, but in which Mary was not yet a queen; this painting is the first in which she is shown crowned, transfigured, withdrawn from the human condition, in her capacity of celestial sovereign. On the triumphal arch of Santa Maria Maggiore, among the scenes of Christ's childhood in which the mosaicist aims at conveying by the imagery the dual nature of Christ as set forth at the Council of Ephesus (431), the Son is king in Heaven as the emperor is on earth; but His royalty does not transpose Him into a world different from ours, and His Mother does not share in it. The pictures in Santa Maria Maggiore are datable at the latest to the pontificate of Sixtus III (430-440); they still derive from

HIERVSALEM

HERODES

BETHLEEM

125 - ROME, SANTA MARIA MAGGIORE, TRIUMPHAL ARCH, DETAIL. ▶

124 - ROME, SANTA MARIA MAGGIORE, TRIUMPHAL ARCH. SCENES OF THE LIFE OF THE VIRGIN AND THE CHILDHOOD OF CHRIST.

◄ 123 - ROME, SANTA MARIA MAGGIORE, TRIUMPHAL ARCH, DETAIL.

126 - ITALY. CODEX VERGILIUS VATICANUS. VATICAN LIBRARY.

the classical narrative tradition and nothing except the style differentiates them from the illustrations in early Virgil and similar manuscripts. At the beginning of the fifth century, or perhaps at the end of the fourth, a realistic art, based on the imitation of nature, was still in favour. For though Christian art made little attempt to render depth, it kept to classical procedures; only the subjects differed.

A magnificent icon in Santa Maria in Trastevere, assignable to the beginning of the eighth century, is an exact replica of the nearly two hundred years earlier Virgin of Santa Maria Antiqua. Here the two angels are raising their hands in awed amazement (*stupentes* is the term used in the inscription on the contemporary frame), as they gaze at the queenly figure, invested with a statuesque serenity. For the angels ('messengers') belong as much to earth as to heaven, they move to and fro on their errands, and are swayed by semi-human emotions, whereas the perfect symmetry of the postures of the Mother and her Son precludes any idea of movement, any trace of emotion that might ruffle the majesty implied by the crown, rich garments, and wealth of glittering jewels. Like the image in Santa Maria Antiqua, this splendid Roman icon combines the world of the unmoving with that of movement, and in it we have a perfect example of that hieraticism which was not, as is so often assumed, peculiar to Byzantium, though it was propagated by the theological capital of the East over a longer period and wider area than by any other art centre of the Empire.

Some hundred years elapsed before, about the seventh century, the *Maria Regina* in Santa Maria Antiqua was overlaid by a new painting. It represented the Annunciation and enough of the two heads (of the Virgin and the angel) has survived

127 - ITALY. CODEX VERGILIUS ROMANUS. VATICAN LIBRARY.

to show that the artist reverted to the technique of first-century Roman painting, as we see it at Pompeii, in the House of Livia, and in the Farnesina stuccoes. Hellenistic in spirit, it is characterized by sensitive, smoothly flowing, impressionist modelling. Obviously a theme of this kind had to be handled in a narrative manner, without hieratic stylization; but here the vigour, unconstraint and fluency of the style are diametrically opposed to the style of Santa Maria Maggiore, and to that of the Virgil illustrations mentioned above. This reversion after six centuries to an earlier manner might seem surprising, even inexplicable, were it really a return; in point of fact, this style never quite died out: certain techniques persisted without change for hundreds of years, and this is one of the reasons why datings are so difficult for our period. Attempts have been made to account for this putative 'return' on historical grounds, and indeed it is quite possible that the barbarian invasion of Egypt in the seventh century drove the artists westwards, leading to a rebirth of Alexandrian 'impressionism' in the West. In any case there is no question that this classical revival linked up with general conditions whose effects made themselves felt in the seventh century throughout the West, from Italy to the British Isles, by way of Gaul and Spain. The previous century was that of the Byzantine reconquest, under Justinian, then Heraclius I (610-644). Byzantium brought to the West, impoverished by the invasions, the resources of the eastern Mediterranean where the papacy, having come to terms with Constantine IV after the Council of Constantinople (681), and consolidated its political and spiritual power, was now to confront the Lombards, assume the moral governance of the western world, quell the

129 - ROME, SANTA MARIA ANTIQUA. FRAGMENT OF AN ANNUNCIATION.

Arian heresy, and unite the Church under the aegis of Pelagius II and—yet more effectively—under that of Gregory the Great (590-604). Thus the papal See attracted to itself all the most vital elements of the imperial art imported by the Byzantines and disseminated them. Of these elements the 'Alexandrian wave' formed part.

In an earlier age the mosaic-worker commissioned, about 340, to decorate the mausoleum of Constantine's daughter Constantina, now the church of Santa Costanza in Rome, had utilized for this tomb of a Christian lady a pagan repertory (at least in the decorations that have survived): garlands of vine leaves diversified with *putti*, games, children harvesting grapes, birds of various kinds, and small mythological figurations (Eros, Psyche). In the apse a double *traditio legis* (?), a very poor work, probably made much later, clashes with the otherwise wholly classical ensemble. Later, at the beginning of the fifth century, one of the vestibules in the Lateran baptistery was given decorations in the same spirit. Only a lamb surrounded by four doves, signifying the evangelists, strikes a faintly Christian note.

◄ 128 - ROME. VIRGIN OF CLEMENCY. SANTA MARIA IN TRASTEVERE, ROME.

130 - ROME, SANTA COSTANZA, VAULT, DETAIL. BACCHIC SCENES.

A century later Pope John VII (705-707), who was a Greek, son of Plato, prefect of the imperial palaces, adorned the back wall of the presbyterium (an axial chapel) in Santa Maria Antiqua with a new group of pictures. The paintings in the apse proper, at the centre of this wall, were overpainted during the pontificate of Paul I (757-768); the others, on the triumphal arch and its springers, are in the same style as the Hellenistic Annunciation described above. Despite its ruined state, this decoration constitutes a landmark in the early history of western art, for, traditional as is the execution, it points to an overall plan in which, perhaps for the first time, a painter used the lines of the architecture as guide-marks for the layout of his decorative scheme. The central axis of the arch is occupied by the figure of Christ crucified, and complementing it in the apse was that of the Virgin Queen (only a few traces remain). Crucified but living, already transmuted by earthly death into the immobility of eternity, His arms outstretched to their fullest extent, Christ dominates the scene. Standing on each side of Him are the Virgin and

116

131-132 - ROME, SANTA MARIA ANTIQUA, ARCH OF THE PRESBYTERIUM. RECONSTRUCTION—PRESENT STATE.

St John, and two groups of angels—the day hours and the night hours that mete out terrestrial time—are leaning forward, aligned to the bends of the arch on either hand. These two groups narrow down towards the centre in a movement complementary to the sweeping curve that centres on the towering, dominant mass of the body of the Saviour. A Greek inscription spans the interval between earth and sky, reminding us of the description in the Scriptures of the Redemption and Last Judgment, and lower down, at ground level are the Faithful, men and women of different walks of life and the flock of the Good Shepherd. Next we see the Popes, vicars of Christ (doubtless the founders of Santa Maria Antiqua). John VII, last on the left, is wearing a square nimbus, signifying that he was still alive. Below, we see four Greek and Latin Fathers of the Church, its 'founding fathers.' Leaning slightly forward as they walk, the Popes conform to the curve of the intrados, this movement emphasized by the book each holds out at arm's length—whereas the Fathers, shown full face, stand bolt upright like the shafts on which they figure. Here we

117

134 - CASTELSEPRIO, SANTA MARIA FORIS PORTAS. NATIVITY AND ANNUNCIATION TO THE SHEPHERDS.

have, in fact, an image of the supernal world situated outside Time and its fleeting appearances, and presided over by a Christ triumphant whom death has failed to vanquish; the tragedy of the Passion is disregarded and, protected by the Cross, the Universe is flooded with a radiant promise of redemption. When we compare this imagery with that of Santa Maria Maggiore we find it pervaded with a new spirit, the same spirit as that which bathes the face of the Virgin Queen with an otherworldly light. The scenes in the basilica are likewise strictly theological in purport, but presented separately and treated on narrative lines. Here they have been replaced by the painter of Santa Maria Antiqua with a huge synthetic decoration whose architectural disposition and compositional scheme combine to figure forth the divine plan. Medieval art has appeared.

We must not leave Santa Maria Antiqua without drawing attention to the fragments of two Annunciations originally superimposed on the left-hand pillar of the nave. They have recently been detached from each other and enable us to compare a work of the time of Pope Martin I (649-655) with a version of the same scene made fifty years later by a painter in the employ of John VII. The handling is the same in

◄ 133 - ROME, SANTA MARIA ANTIQUA. ANGEL OF AN ANNUNCIATION.

119

136 - BRESCIA, SAN SALVATORE. HEAD OF A SAINT.

both cases, impressionist, but slightly heavier in the second, in which we find some methods employed which in the first third of the ninth century Carolingian artists of the Reims school were to take over and exaggerate: zig-zag, flickering lines used to suggest the buoyancy of a garment or rapid movement, also that curious gibbosity which was to characterize the figurations of the Reims artists and of their many successors in the Romanesque epoch. These details evidence a kinship of style and technique in all the works of the period and also unmistakable affinities with those wonderful, intriguing frescoes of the small chapel of Castelseprio, near Milan.

Discovered in 1944, the Castelseprio frescoes are still something of an enigma to archaeologists. Their dating is highly conjectural; art historians have assigned them to various dates ranging from the seventh to the tenth century. They vouch for the presence in northern Italy of a Byzantine tradition as pure as that of the illuminated manuscripts made in the imperial scriptoria of Constantinople during the ninth century: a local tradition which, like many others, though driven by iconoclasm into exile or clandestinity, remained unbroken. There as elsewhere, the 'renascence' was not so much a resurrection as a restoration to the light of day. The art of the Franks had similar manifestations and practitioners. The frescoes (c. 753) recently brought to light in San Salvatore, Brescia, though differing in quality as to their finish, contain here and there sketches comparable to the Castelseprio paintings. Their affinities with the art of Cividale, which have been rightly commented on (we deal with them at a later page), go to show the active intercourse in northern Italy between art currents stemming simultaneously from East and West.

◀ 135 - CASTELSEPRIO, SANTA MARIA FORIS PORTAS. PRESENTATION IN THE TEMPLE.

At the entrance of the prothesis of Santa Maria Antiqua the spectator is confronted on the outer wall by the images of four standing saints who seem to be gazing at him across an abyss of time. These are the 'unknown martyrs,' *martyres quorum nomina Deus scit*, and their uniform faces have a strange remoteness, as if all alike were lost in an inner dream. This austere painting is datable to the period of the Greek Pope Zacharias (741-749). Its strict frontalism, the carefully calculated attitudes of the figures, the forms of the faces and the eyes have exact equivalents in the large, contemporary or near-contemporary figures adorning a small church remote from Rome, in Lombard territory, but in the vicinity of the domain of Byzantine art in Italy: the church of Santa Maria in Valle at Cividale del Friuli. Recent

139 - CIVIDALE, SANTA MARIA IN VALLE. A MARTYR.

140 - ROME, SANTA MARIA ANTIQUA. FOUR MARTYRS. ▶

137 - ROME, SANTA MARIA ANTIQUA. THE STORY OF JOSEPH (ABOVE) AND CHRIST WITH THE FATHERS OF THE CHURCH (BELOW).

research has established the date of this famous 'Tempietto' built for Desiderius, last king of the Lombards, whom Charlemagne took prisoner in 774 and who ended his days in France, at the abbey of Corbie. At Cividale, as in Santa Maria Antiqua, saints and martyrs form a line of impersonal, hieratic, little differentiated figures, and the similarity of the technique employed in the portrayal of both groups suggests that the artists concerned had been trained in the same school. Both John VII and Zacharias were Greeks, surrounded themselves with Greeks, and the Tempietto was a Near-Eastern enclave in Lombard territory. Presumably it was Pope Zacharias who had the walls of the prothesis painted with a series of images of a nature diametrically opposed to that of the preceding group. The legend of St Cyrus and his

mother Julitta, a narrative cycle treated like others in the same church deriving from
the Old and New Testaments, is set forth in rectangular pictures, painted in sweeping
brushstrokes and full of lively, gesticulating figures. For these images relate to facts
of human history, facts described in detailed legends, all of which begin with the
Latin conjunction *ubi* meaning 'at which time,' 'whenas,' followed by a verb in the
historic present, a classical Latin usage, and equating the ancient Greek word
ἔνθα used in the inscriptions on the frescoes of the nearby church of San Saba.
The same layout is employed for the tale of Joseph (painted in the time of Pope
Paul I, 757-767), while, below it, the figures of Christ and the Greek and Latin
Fathers beside Him are given the traditional hieratic alignment.

138 - CIVIDALE, SANTA MARIA IN VALLE.   A MARTYR.

It is the same with the full-page compositions in the famous seventh-century manuscript known as the Tours or Ashburnham Pentateuch, which was probably made in north-eastern Italy, somewhere near the Adriatic. In about the middle of the eighth century, it was brought to eastern Gaul; then, in the ninth, to the abbey of Saint Martin at Tours. The arrangement of the narrative scenes in this remarkable, not to say unique work, shows a departure from the normal. The images are echeloned in zones of varying sizes on the same page—almost as if pieces cut from a strip of paintings had been pasted on to the parchment. Perspective is completely vertical, the total absence of depth transforms architectural structures into flat patterns affixed to the background, and the figures, devoid of weight, seem to float in air. All the same these figures are accurately, if summarily, modelled, are given correct proportions and lively attitudes, and still conform to the classical norm. Also, the inscriptions preceded by the conjunction *ubi* keep to the traditional narrative formula. True, there is here an abundance of African details which may seem surprising: women's costumes, interminglings of whites and Negroes, camels, donkeys of a distinctively African breed, mountains of a special shape. But this is easily explicable when we remember that the Arab invasions may well have driven westwards many artists domiciled in the eastern Mediterranean area.

Of the many forms of art in northern Italy, where the Lombards caused widespread havoc before aligning themselves to the civilization they had set out to destroy, only vestiges remain. They enable us to take the measure both of the damage done and of the high artistic culture of a region in which Milan and Ravenna, West and East, joined forces; in which insular and Germanic barbarians, pouring down from the nearby Alps, were soon to establish themselves: a region rich in promise for the future. The Tempietto of Cividale and the Castelseprio decorations (whatever their exact date) testify to the presence of the tradition of the Mediterranean east on Latin soil, as do, in Rome, the superimposed paintings of Santa Maria Antiqua. Another instance of this Greco-Latin symbiosis is provided by the many bilingual manuscripts made in this part of Italy between the sixth and ninth centuries: an illustrated Psalter at Verona, the Epistles of St Paul and commentaries on the Bible at Milan, and other texts alsewhere. As capital of the western Empire from 292 to 404, religious metropolis of North Italy, residence of St Ambrose and St Augustine, yet quite near Ravenna, Milan seemed marked out to act as a sort of hinge between the two dominant trends, Latin and Hellenic, of Mediterranean culture. Here were combined both aspects of that narrative art genre which, as in certain paintings in Santa Maria Antiqua, is charged in the Castelseprio frescoes with a restless vivacity, a mannerist tension far removed from the quietude and naturalness, without a trace of hieratic rigidity, which other monuments owe to the western Roman tradition. The fragmentary fourth-century mosaics in Sant'Aquilino, Milan, have something of this nature; others, in San Vittore in Ciel d'Oro (so called after their gold grounds, soon to be adopted throughout the West), are affected by the frontalism which was something of an obsession at the time but which, here too, is tempered with a discreet feeling for supple, lifelike form. From the fourth to the tenth century a large body of wall paintings and above all illuminated manuscripts made its imprint on a vast

141 - TOURS PENTATEUCH: THE STORY OF JOSEPH. BIBLIOTHÈQUE NATIONALE, PARIS.

AMBROSIVS · MATERNVS

144 - MILAN, SANT'AMBROGIO. ST PROTASIUS, DETAIL.

145 - NORTH ITALY. ST HILARY, 'DE TRINITATE,' DETAIL. PARIS.

domain of art, extending far into the North. It was an Italo-Alpine art whose widespread success was bound up with the family relations between the Bavarian ducal house of the Agilofings and the Lombard royal dynasty: an art directly stemming from antiquity, independent both of the Carolingians (though in touch with them) and of Lombard art proper. By way of the manuscripts these illustrations were widely diffused and it was thanks to them that the imagery of North Italy crossed the Alps into the North East and the Carolingian West. Also, the art of the British Isles drew inspiration from this ancient source, some of their monks migrated to the continent, and the barbarians (last of all, the Lombards) not only settled in this part of Europe but introduced into it their techniques. Until the birth of the national Romanesque schools this Italo-Alpine art current flowed unbroken, varied only by the passing years and intercourse with neighbouring cultures. The earliest example is a book containing 'twin' texts, Greek and Latin, of the

◀ 142-143 - MILAN, SANT'AMBROGIO, CHAPEL OF SAN VITTORE. ST AMBROSE — ST MATERNUS.

146 - NORTH ITALY. GOSPEL BOOK OF ST AUGUSTINE: ST LUKE. CAMBRIDGE.

Bible. Unfortunately only two illustrations of the sixth-century Gospel Book said to have been brought to England by St Augustine of Canterbury in 596 have survived; the larger one shows St Luke seated between pilasters enframing six small scenes illustrating the text. The layout here reminds us of certain Mithraic monuments, large numbers of which existed in Italy, on which are sequences of scenes, equivalents of illustrated Bibles. Paintings of so early a date are rare and it is of interest to find a close parallel to the St Luke figure: the image of the 'Blessed Man' hymned by the psalmist, a sketch of the late sixth century in a Latin version of the Gospels made in Upper Italy and bearing contemporary annotations in Greek. Points in common are the features, the way the hair is cut, the drooping moustache and short beard, the eye with its pupil entirely surrounded with white, the similarly shaped nose drawn in side view, though the face is turned towards us. This Cisalpine,

147 - NORTH ITALY. GOSPEL BOOK OF ST AUGUSTINE: THE LIFE OF CHRIST. CORPUS CHRISTI COLLEGE LIBRARY, CAMBRIDGE. ▶

148 - ROME. DIPTYCH OF BOETIUS, INNER LEAVES. MUSEO CIVICO CRISTIANO, BRESCIA.

149 - ROME. DIPTYCH OF BOETIUS, OUTER LEAVES. MUSEO CIVICO CRISTIANO, BRESCIA.

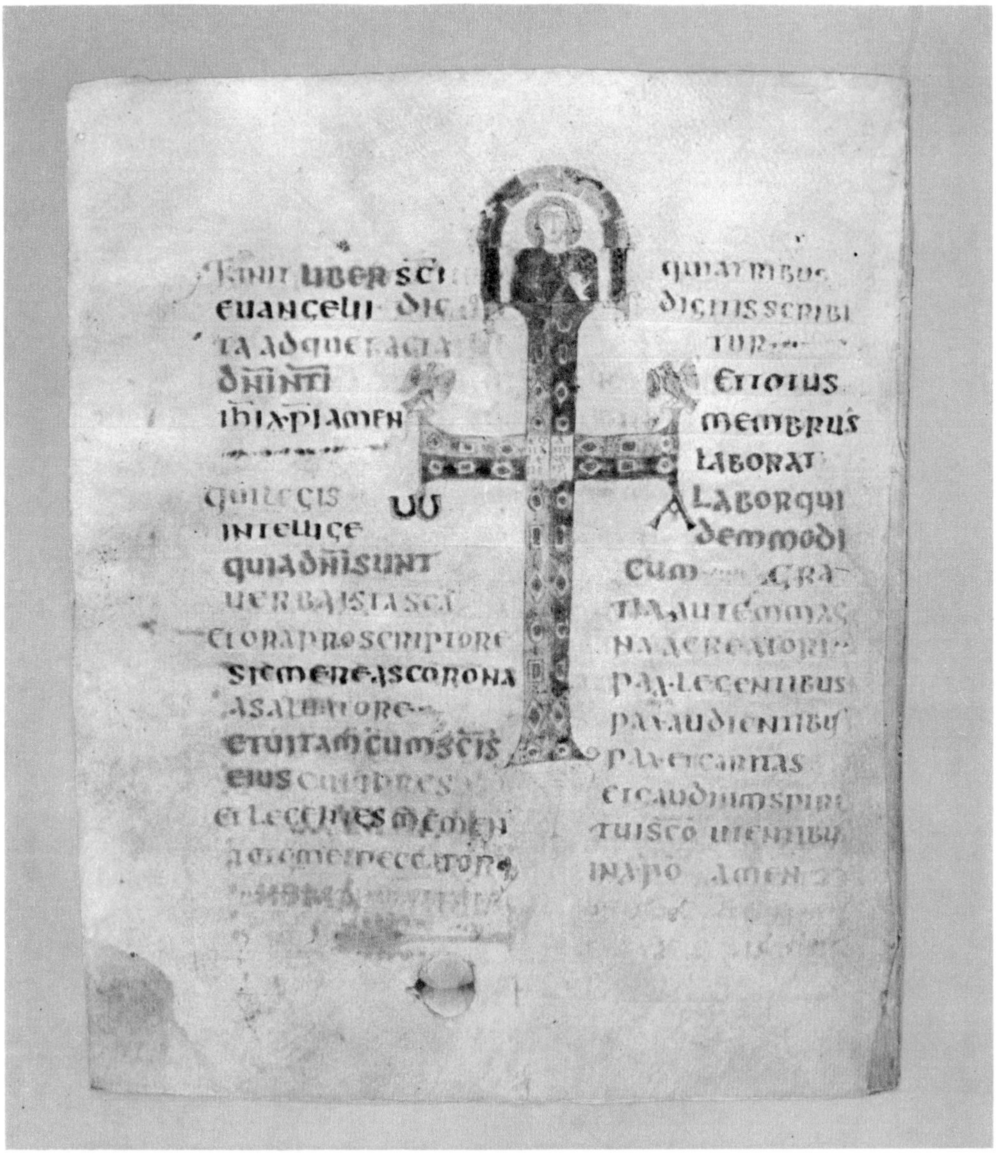

150 - NORTH-EAST ITALY. GOSPEL BOOK, SO-CALLED CODEX VALERIANUS. MUNICH, BAYERISCHE STAATSBIBLIOTHEK.

'Italo-Greek' youth was to have many descendants. In the course of the seventh century, some paintings representing Lazarus raised from the dead and several saints were inserted in an ivory diptych originally made for the Prefect Boetius (father of the famous philosopher whom Theodoric the Goth imprisoned and put to death in 524) so as to adapt it to Christian usage. Boetius has bequeathed to us a work which had far-reaching repercussions on medieval thought, his famous *De Consolatione Philosophiae*, in which the best of stoicism is blended with Christian spirituality, in much the same way as in the Brescia triptych ancient art in its Cisalpine form is combined with early intimations of medieval art. Thus from the ruins of antiquity there arose some works charged with both historic and symbolic values. A copy of the major

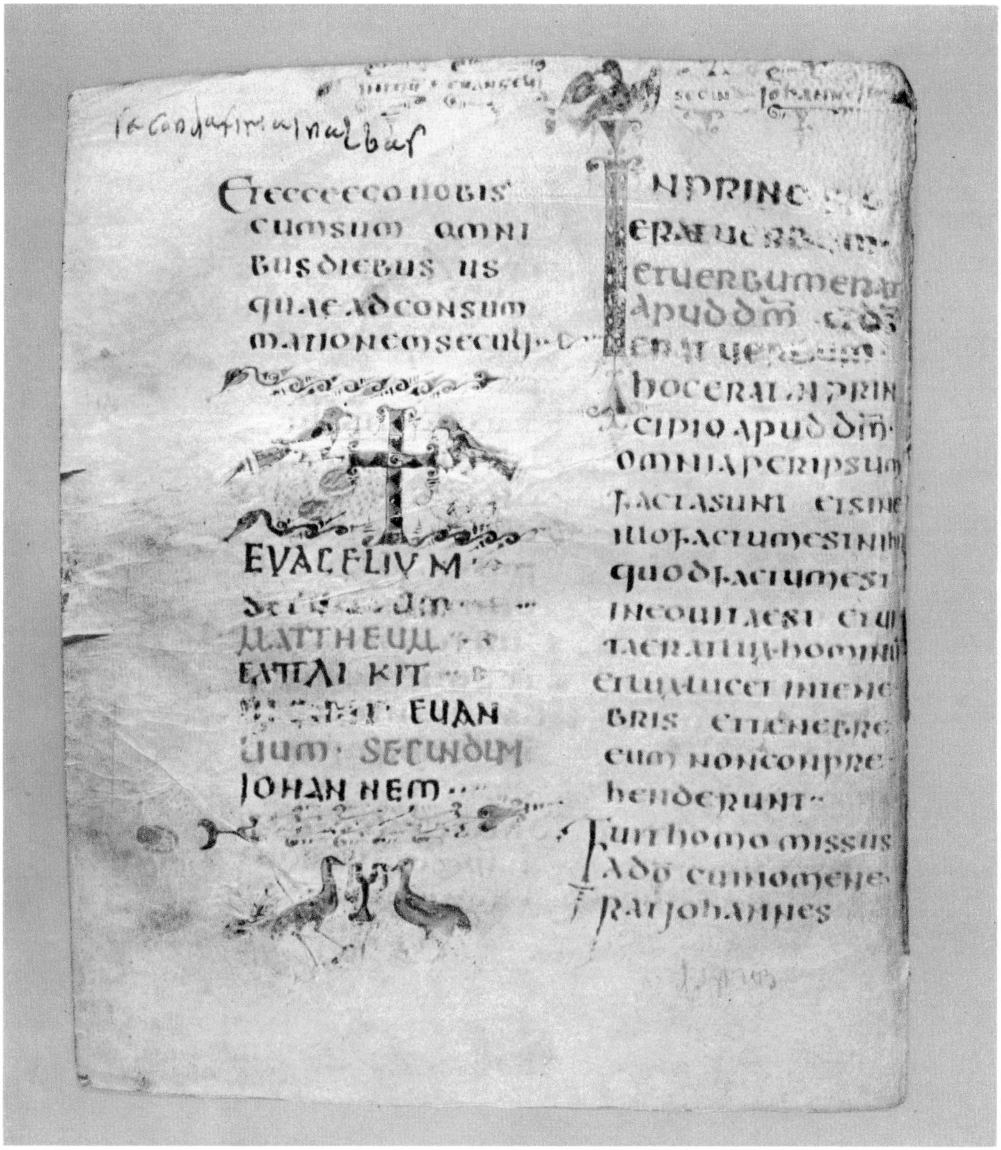

151 - NORTH-EAST ITALY. GOSPEL BOOK, SO-CALLED CODEX VALERIANUS. MUNICH, BAYERISCHE STAATSBIBLIOTHEK.

work of St Ambrose, *De Fide*, and some gospel books probably written in the same part of northern Italy by a scribe named Valerianus, have been preserved, the former at Sankt Paul im Lavanttal (Carinthia), the other at Munich, to which it was brought from Freising. Valerianus wrote in Greek characters (c. 675) the Latin names of the Gospels and their *explicits*, adorning them with scroll-work, letters embellished with palmettes or green and red geometric motifs (like those of textiles or enamels), columns, birds done from life, fishes, pendants directly borrowed from paintings, and Christian inscriptions engraved on stone or marble. His work contained all the basic elements of the decorated initial letters adopted by the Merovingian scribes and there is no need to look elsewhere for their sources. The history of the St Ambrose

152 - AUGSBURG. GOSPEL BOOK: ADORATION OF THE MAGI. MUNICH, BAYERISCHE STAATSBIBLIOTEK.

manuscript is known and from it, and others of its kind, derived the so-called
Reichenau school of Ottonian painting. At the same time as this manuscript some
Gospel Books, later in date (ninth century), but still keeping faithfully to the tradition of ancient narrative art, crossed the Alps. Each text is illustrated with pictures of the chief events described, set out on the four branches of a cross. Here we
may note the complete identity of the Massacre of the Innocents (e.g. the stance and
gestures of Herod and those of the executioners) with analogous scenes of the martyr-

153 - AUGSBURG. GOSPEL BOOK: MASSACRE OF THE INNOCENTS. MUNICH, BAYERISCHE STAATSBIBLIOTHEK.

dom of Sts Cyrus and Julitta at Santa Maria Antiqua; here, in fact, we see to full effect the persistence of the antique tradition. Also noteworthy is a book of 'homilies' written at the close of the eighth century and presented in 799 to the cathedral of Verona by Bishop Egino when he left for Reichenau. It accounts for the art associated with this abbey and also has striking stylistic resemblances with the paintings in Santa Maria Antiqua, San Crisogono and the Catacomb of Commodilla in Rome. A compendium of canon law at Vercelli, dating to the early ninth century,

154 - VERONA. CODEX EGINO: ST AUGUSTINE DICTATING TO A SCRIBE. DEUTSCHE STAATSBIBLIOTHEK, BERLIN.

155 - VERONA. CODEX EGINO: ST GREGORY. DEUTSCHE STAATSBIBLIOTHEK, BERLIN.

156 - NORTH ITALY. COMPENDIUM OF CANON LAW. BIBLIOTECA CAPITOLARE, VERCELLI.

contains crude but remarkably vivacious illustrations of the history of the various Councils. The narrative style (probably reflecting that of some earlier model) displays a keen feeling for horizontal space and natural movements, and once again we find that key word *ubi* used to designate the place and time (e.g. the scenes of the

Within the illustration:
SIHODUSHICEHI... ...HUMERUS
SCOR PATR CCCXVIII ET OMNES
SUBSCRIP
SERU
N
T
IMP
CONSTANTINUS
HERETICI
ARRIANI
DAMNATI

157 - NORTH ITALY. COMPENDIUM OF CANON LAW. BIBLIOTECA CAPITOLARE, VERCELLI.

Finding of the Cross by St Helena, Constantine's holocaust of the Arian books,
Peter and Paul commenting on the Council of Nicaea) and long explanatory texts.
At Vercelli, again, the homilies of St Gregory—these with painted illustrations—
have, like other manuscripts of the same type, affinities with the Verona group.

158-159 - NORTH ITALY. COMPENDIUM OF CANON LAW. BIBLIOTECA CAPITOLARE, VERCELLI. ▶

Theodosius iunior imp̄r sinodus effesin̄
que̅ cc sc̄i patris cū imperatore con fī m̄
strūit et subscripserunt:

VBI PETRVS ? PAVLVS +
de hocconcilio con-
FERVNT :

PAVLVS   PETRVS

SCLLCR
FERUNT.

PAVLVS

160-161 - NORTH ITALY. COMPENDIUM OF CANON LAW: APOSTLES PAUL AND PETER, DETAILS. BIBLIOTECA CAPITOLARE, VERCELLI.

162-163 - NORTH ITALY. HOMILIES OF ST GREGORY. BIBLIOTECA CAPITOLARE, VERCELLI. ▶

164 - MÜSTAIR, JOHANNESKIRCHE, NAVE. THE FLIGHT INTO EGYPT.

But it is at Müstair in the Grisons (eastern Switzerland) that we see the capital achievement of Italo-Alpine art—capital in view of its historical importance: a double sequence of frescoes almost contemporary with the church built by Charlemagne about the year 800. Scenes from the Old and New Testaments, depicted in the purest narrative style (as in San Salvatore, Brescia, and Santa Maria Maggiore, Rome), adorn the north and south walls of the nave; each of the three apses has an image of Christ in the vault, while on the walls are the lives of Sts John the Baptist, Stephen, Peter and Paul. The small church at nearby Malles Venosta belongs to the same group, both in its architecture and its decorations. The narrative style, the presentation in independent pictures and the types of figures represented link this art with that of North Italy, without surrendering to Carolingian ascendancy.

165 - MÜSTAIR, JOHANNESKIRCHE, NAVE. HEALING OF THE DEAF AND DUMB MAN, DETAIL. ▶

166 A AND B - MÜSTAIR, JOHANNESKIRCHE, NAVE. SCENES OF THE LIFE OF CHRIST.

167 A AND B - MALLES, SAN BENEDETTO.   SCENES OF SAINTS' LIVES — SCENE OF MARTYRDOM.

IMAGOLEONIS

The Barbarian Heritage

The peoples whom, following the practice of the Greeks and Romans, we call 'barbarians' put a brutal end to the ancient Mediterranean culture. This is how the epithet 'barbarian' originally meaning 'stammerer' and applied to foreigners speaking an uncouth tongue and having ways of life unlike those of the Greco-Romans, came to be a synonym for vulgar, cultureless. Long labours of archaeologists and collectors of antiquities were needed to redirect attention to the dark centuries when these peoples were active in Europe. Indeed it is only quite recently that, outside the world of specialists, any interest due to motives other than mere curiosity came to be felt in non-classical art. This explains why the term Gothic ('the art of the Goths'), invented in the seventeenth century, which today is rightly considered as descriptive of an art that was the supreme achievement of our Middle Ages, was then applied derogatively. Much the same is true of the expression 'barbarian art,' once pejorative, but which modern taste has invested with an exotic mystique, racy of the steppes and backwoods of medieval Europe. It would be wrong to see in this new vogue of the barbarians only a passing fad. It vouches for the profound affinities (deplored by some) between ourselves and that so-called backward age, and we are now able to take a juster, less biased view of it. Doubtless the barbarians speeded up the downfall of the Roman Empire, but their blows fell on a body already moribund; thanks to them, a rebirth was to follow its decease. Still, we must never overlook the immense debt this renascence owed to the culture they overthrew.

It is unlikely that these barbarians practised any sort of painting before coming in contact with the Mediterranean civilization. True, some chroniclers speak of wall paintings made between the fifth and eighth centuries in churches and palaces; Gregory of Tours of those in Gaul, Bede of those in England, Paul the Deacon of those in Lombardy. But nothing survives of these works, which were made no doubt by Gallo-Roman and Italian artists or, at least, under their supervision.

The paintings made by the barbarians were exclusively decorative and, like all the original or derivative manifestations of their art, have survived only in illus-

trated books. If any other kind existed, no trace of it remains. An art of scribes deriving from the ornamental initial letter, it arose in the mid-seventh century and developed along different lines in different regions, on the continent and in the British Isles. But the method was everywhere the same; the scribe 'read' the forms and built up from them a written text, the painter 'saw' them and imitated them.

The British Isles

Much ink was spilt, sometimes in heated polemics, over the question of the sources of the manuscripts produced in the British Isles, until the day when the discovery of manuscripts written and illuminated at Bobbio clarified and, perhaps, solved the problem. These documents, the work of Irishmen who had settled in Lombardy, prove that contemporary Irish scribes had a sense of decoration and a technical versatility enabling them to exploit certain graphic and ornamental peculiarities found *in situ* and to get from them effects that were soon carried a stage further in the striking compositions executed in the British Isles. They also show that the ornamentation of the Bobbio manuscripts was essentially Italian and their script the only Irish element. On to a script, in itself magnificently decorative, were grafted the Celtic and Germanic decorations practised to such wonderful effect on English and Irish soil by the metal-workers, and soon these motifs were completed and enriched by figural illustrations brought back from Italy by missionaries, among them Archbishop Theodore (born at Tarsus), Benedict Biscop, and St Augustine of Canterbury. Nowhere and in no other period was there so ardent a desire to produce a perfect script, worthy of the sacred text, no matter what the cost and labour this involved. Taking over the decorative elements—geometric motifs and forms adapted from the animal kingdom—used by the metal-workers practising in the British Isles, the painter developed them methodically, combined and contrasted them, giving free play to his imagination implemented by a fine sense of the appropriate colours. The drawing conformed to the structural arrangement imposed by copper or enamel work, but inevitably it lost something of its firmness in the work of subsequent, even direct, imitators, who were no longer guided by a feeling for metal and its demands. In the hands of artists who were exclusively painters, even skilful ones, the essential qualities of the insular painting tended to die out.

Insular painting can be seen at its best in four Gospel Books, named from the earliest times after the abbeys to which they are traditionally assigned: Durrow, Echternach, Lindisfarne and Kells. Their dates are spaced out from 650 or thereabouts to approximately 800. Emerging abruptly from the pictorial void of the bar-

◀ 169 - IRELAND. BOOK OF KELLS. TRINITY COLLEGE LIBRARY, DUBLIN.

barian centuries, they were the fruit of long experience in a field other than that of the book. For if we are not to be led into frequent errors, a clear-cut distinction must here be drawn between calligraphy and painting. Behind these wholly novel paintings we always sense the presence of the expert metal-worker. Moreover, the magnificent artifacts recently found at Sutton Hoo testify to the superb craftsmanship of the English metal-workers at the time of the Book of Durrow, some of whose most characteristic motifs reappear in the Sutton Hoo treasure hoard. To these motifs others were added in the later books of this group: the chessboard pattern (imitating cloisonné work), spirals, shield and trumpet forms of Celtic origin, interlaces with boat-shaped corners, paired scroll-work designs traversed by a fine-spun diagonal line, Greek key patterns. The motifs are arranged in successive bands, differentiated by their colours, which, superimposing their effects on those of the motif itself, give rise on occasion to diamond-shaped forms and zigzags. The use of several colours also served to make certain parts of a uniform ground stand out, for example the backgrounds of interlaces, and to isolate them from the rest.

Preceding each of the texts is a carpet page covered with decorative motifs. By an extraordinarily bold calligraphic transposition of an image in the Mediterranean style, the symbol of St Matthew in the Book of Durrow is represented full length, frontally, with short legs shown in side-view. He wears a flat, bell-shaped cloak adorned with elaborate geometric designs and has thick hair, parted in the middle, hanging on both sides of his head. The close-trimmed moustache and staring eyes remind us of the warrior's mask found in the tumulus of Sutton Hoo. The texts begin with the large dovetailed Irish initials created at Bobbio. Here they still are relatively simple, but they soon became intricate, reaching an extreme complexity in the last of the series, the famous Book of Kells, in which the whole page is built up of a labyrinth of spirals, zigzags and interlaces.

The same decorative programme, but with some new motifs added, was utilized for the Gospels written out and painted by Eadfrith, Bishop of Lindisfarne, between 698 and 721. The Canon Tables are placed under arches ornamented, like the columns supporting them, with a frieze of large, elongated birds nibbling each other's feet like the quadrupeds in the 'ribbon style' of the English metal-workers. This motif imported from the East and adapted by the insular craftsmen is not the only one of its kind. To a similar source may be assigned the heads of a curious animal placed at the tips of certain foliated flowers or above lettrines or elements of frames; they resemble the somewhat ovine heads with thick, puckered lips and smoothly moulded features, their outlines duplicated by deep furrows, often found in Iranian, especially Sassanian metalwork. The same applies to the capitals or stepped column-bases in these illuminations, also to the motifs imitating Greek key patterns cut in wood and the key-shaped designs we see at Bawit—some of these motifs had already been used in the Book of Durrow. But the inclusion of an evangelist portrait at the beginning of each Gospel—a portrait and no longer a symbol —was a quite new departure and this borrowing from the art of antiquity was certainly due to the contacts with that art promoted by Benedict Biscop and missionaries from Italy.

◀ 170 - IRELAND. BOOK OF DURROW. TRINITY COLLEGE LIBRARY, DUBLIN.

171 - BOOK OF LINDISFARNE. BRITISH MUSEUM, LONDON.

The Echternach Gospels, which are in the pure 'metallic' vein, owe their name to the abbey founded by St Willibrord in 698. Legend has it that they were brought by him from Great Britain on this occasion, but they may more probably be dated to around 710. Precursor at a far remove of the Carolingian Franco-insular style, their sober decoration makes a striking contrast with the exuberance of the other illuminated books. Besides the sumptuous initials they contain only the four (full page) evangelist symbols by way of decoration, but surely the man who could depict so skilfully the leaping lion of St Mark and frame it in a complex right-angled pattern designed to uphold it in the page, yet without overcrowding it, ranks among the world's greatest artists. Enclosed on all sides, the image stands out strongly on a light-hued neutral ground. In his depiction of the Man, symbol of St Matthew, the artist carries stylization to a pitch far surpassing even the boldest inventions of the Book of Durrow. Much later, the Book of Kells was to retain this lapidary rigour in renderings of the saints, the Virgin, even Christ Himself, though the margins are enlivened by small animals scampering to and fro: dogs and hares, cats and mice. The reverence felt for sacred personages ruled out their representation as ordinary mortals. This was an outcome of the assimilation of the Eternal to the immutable— of theology to cosmology—now developing throughout the world of Christendom.

172 - IRELAND. BOOK OF DIMMA. TRINITY COLLEGE LIBRARY, DUBLIN. ▶

173 - BOOK OF LINDISFARNE. BRITISH MUSEUM, LONDON

174 - ECHTERNACH GOSPELS. BIBLIOTHÈQUE NATIONALE, PARIS. ▶

162

The Continent

The adornment of pre-Carolingian initial letters had everywhere consisted for the most part of birds and fishes, some lifelike, others stylized so as to fit in with the shape of the letter and embellish it. This striking uniformity of styles in all parts of the continent was due to their common origin: the Italian method of combining script and decoration practised by the scribe Valerianus (mentioned above). This method was adopted by two Gaulish abbeys, by Luxeuil towards the middle of the seventh century, then by its daughter house, Corbie, and soon came into favour in other places. For these two abbeys, both of them active religious and intellectual centres, began to import books from northern Italy at an early date. The stylized (graphic) type was most commonly used and easiest to design (with on occasion the aid of compasses) and no animals lent themselves better than birds and fishes to emphasizing the downstrokes, upstrokes and curves of letters; all that was needed was to elongate or expand their backs and bellies. This was not a new device; in the second half of the first century Pliny the Younger speaks of its being used by Roman scribes. Besides the very early examples, we find much later cases of it, in the scripts of fifteenth-century notaries and nineteenth-century calligraphers. Throughout the ages men with a taste for fine writing have indulged in *tours de force* of the kind. This type of lettrine was in high favour in North Italy from the sixth century on, but it was the great abbey of Bobbio, a foundation of St Columban and King Agilulf, which like Luxeuil was full of Irish monks, that appears to have excelled in this style of decoration. And, as was to be expected, it was Bobbio that transmitted it to its sister house in France.

Lombard Italy gave pre-Carolingian Gaul another type of book ornament which was widely disseminated first by Luxueil, then by Corbie and nearby centres such as Laon, in ever more gorgeous forms, until the end of the eighth century. This was the frontispiece prefixed to books dealing with various subjects. It was given the form of an elongated rectangle or of a row of porticoes crowned by a gable or by a single or double arch, often enclosing a large decorated cross on whose arms sometimes figured a capital Alpha and Omega, a 'prophylactic' cross which on occasion stood alone on the page. A very early example of the portico design comes from North Italy; the cross bearing the letters A and Ω figures in a sixth-century manuscript, in uncials, hailing from Bobbio. This latter was a product of the Lombard abbey of St Columban, but its decorations are no more Irish than the script. The portico design which Luxeuil was to propagate in Gaul is, under various forms, a manuscript imitation of motifs often found in Lombard stone engravings; steles, inscriptions and a host of decorative plaques combine all its elements—even the rosettes above the cross (sc. the sun and moon of the Crucifixions) and animals, birds or quadrupeds (representing the believers) touching the cross with their beaks or tongues, an act of homage which brings to mind the cross in Narbonne Museum towards which a kneeling man is shown stretching out a finger.

◀ 175 - NORTH-EAST FRANCE. SACRAMENTARIUM GELASIANUM. VATICAN LIBRARY.

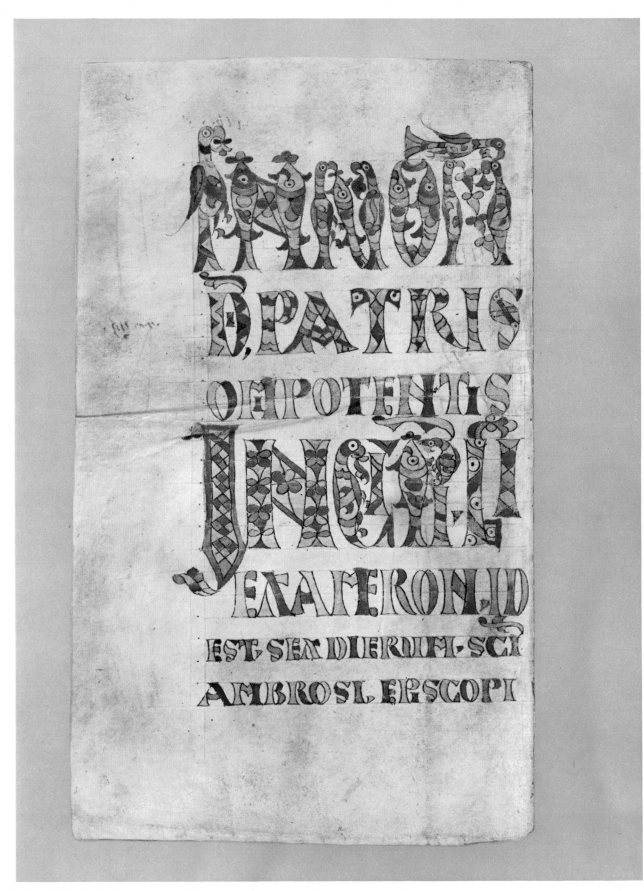

176 - CORBIE. ST AMBROSE, 'HEXAEMERON': INCIPIT PAGE. BIBLIOTHÈQUE NATIONALE, PARIS.

177 A, B, C, D - ZOOMORPHIC INITIALS. BIBLIOTHÈQUE NATIONALE, PARIS. ▶

Incipit
Silicam
Quod cantat
cu hinc loc
hic scr
quid no
MONUUL CARE.
NON EUDIE QUIOT

INCP
iuiuua
EGREDER
SONITU DNS REM
CONFERRET AUX

OST BEAT
TIONE DNI
iudaica im
INTRIDUUM POTENT
hodie dmi scorum
SACRATISSIMA ORD
utilitate nostra
Ut dum ad dno
sentix corpo
SURRECTIONIS d
muneretur, Ma
pulor corda turb
cis demissiones ps
tur

CATUS IC
ERCUIT E
EIUS AES
Sed quia
sett m
hic up
poter
sione p
Factum
AD SISTERENT COR

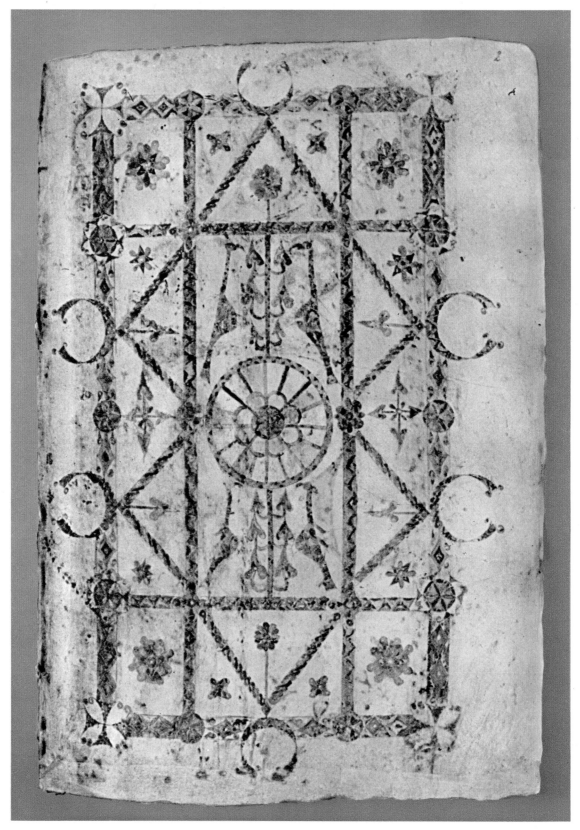

178 - LUXEUIL. ST GREGORY, EZEKIEL COMMENTARY. SALTYKOV-SHCHEDRIN LIBRARY, LENINGRAD.

179 - LUXEUIL. WORKS OF THE FATHERS OF THE CHURCH, CODEX RAGYNTRUDIS. CATHEDRAL MUSEUM, FULDA. ▶

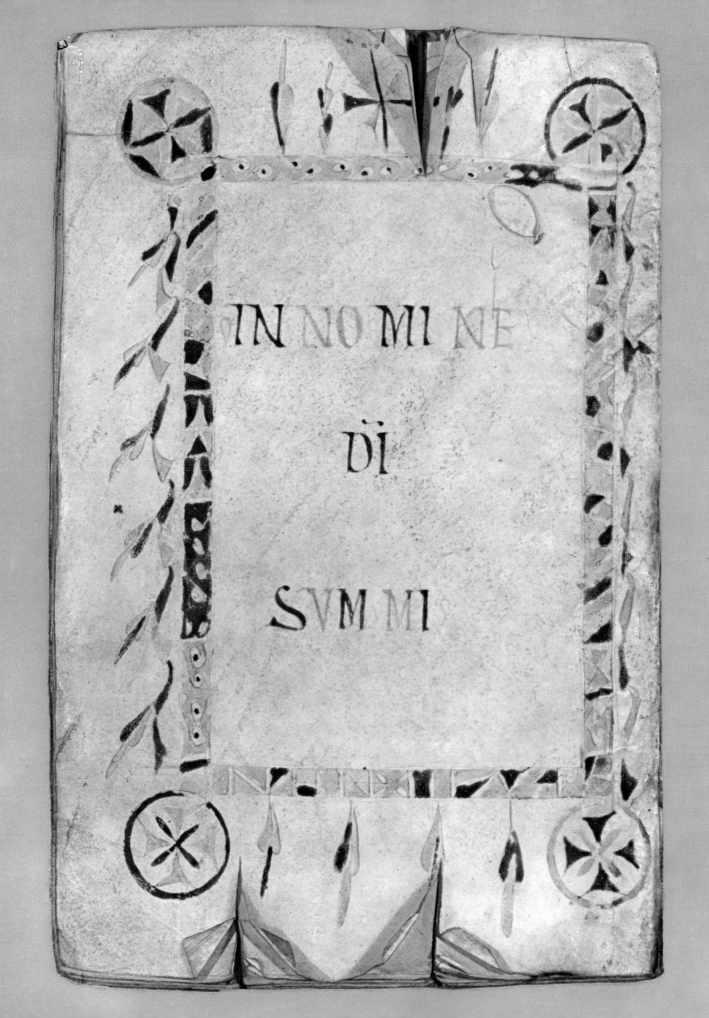

IN NO MI NE

DĪ

SVM MI

in regula sci basilij

episcopi...

180 - CORBIE. RULE OF ST BASIL. SALTYKOV-SHCHEDRIN LIBRARY, LENINGRAD.

181 - LUXEUIL. SACRAMENTARY. VATICAN LIBRARY. ▶

170

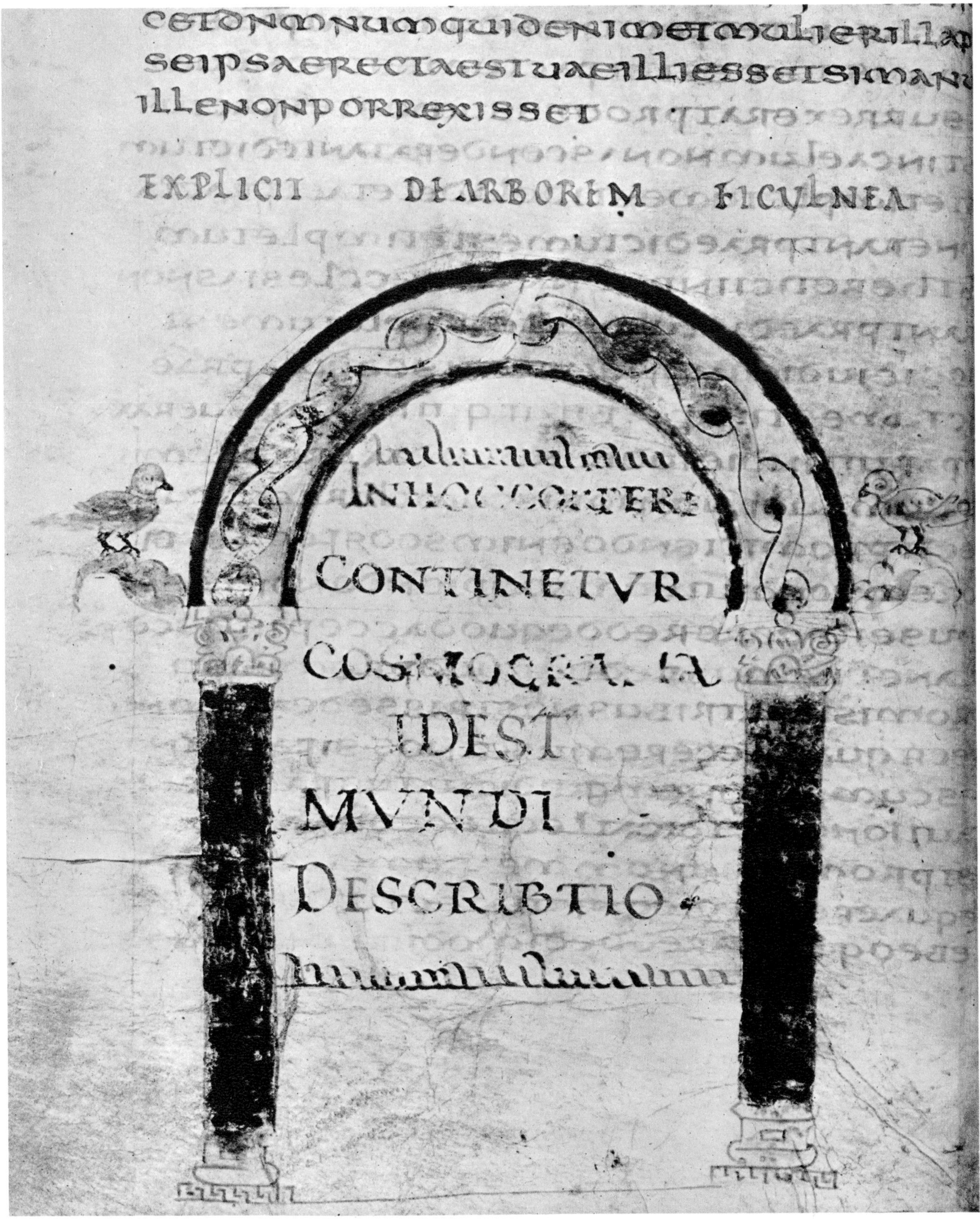

CEIDNONNUMQUIDENIMETMULIERILLA

SEIPSAERECTAESTUXEILLIESSETSIMANI

ILLENONPORREXISSET

EXPLICIT   DEARBORIM   FICULNEA

INHOCCORPERE

CONTINETVR

COSMOGRA..IA

IDEST

MVNDI

DESCRIBTIO

182 - NORTH ITALY (?). EUCHERIUS OF LYONS, 'FORMULAE SPIRITUALES,' DETAIL. BIBLIOTHÈQUE NATIONALE, PARIS.

172

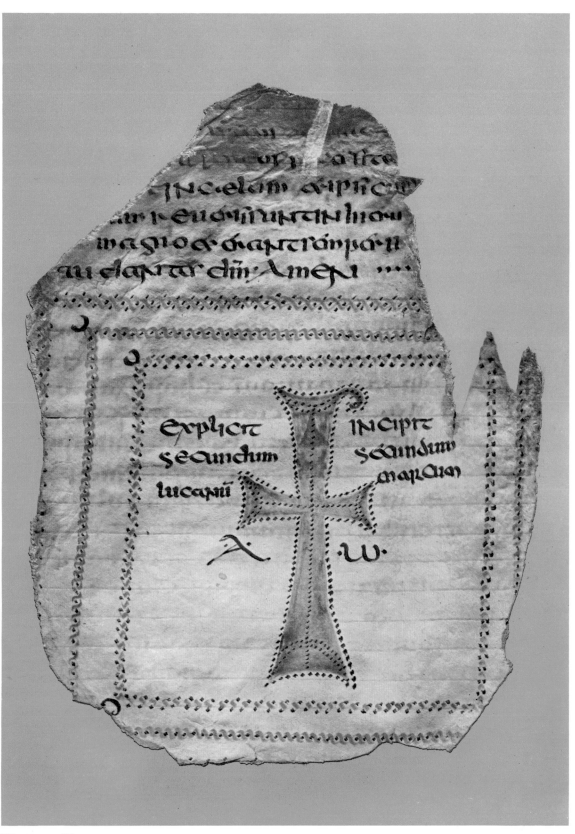

183 - BOBBIO (?). GOSPEL BOOK STYLED CODEX USSERIANUS PRIMUS. TRINITY COLLEGE LIBRARY, DUBLIN.

SOROR·MEA FLOREN
TINA ACCIPE CODICEM
QUEM TIBI COMPO
SUI FELICITER
AMEN

184 - NORTH-EAST FRANCE (?). ISIDORE OF SEVILLE, 'CONTRA JUDAEOS.' BIBLIOTHÈQUE NATIONALE, PARIS.

These porticoes and steles sometimes contain portraits of the authors, delineated with a singular clumsiness and a total incapacity for lifelikeness. For the barbarian artist has not yet learnt to 'read' forms otherwise than in terms of writing and their realities escape him.

185 - BESANÇON REGION (?). 'LEX ROMANA VISIGOTHORUM.' STIFTSBIBLIOTHEK, ST GALL. ▶

uccn dalgæ nur pæhæ

186 - NORTH-EAST FRANCE (?). ISIDORE OF SEVILLE, 'CONTRA JUDAEOS,' DETAIL. BIBLIOTHÈQUE NATIONALE, PARIS.

187 - NORTH-EAST FRANCE (?). ISIDORE OF SEVILLE, 'CONTRA JUDAEOS,' DETAIL. BIBLIOTHÈQUE NATIONALE, PARIS.

The most lavishly decorated of these porticoes and crosses are those on the frontispieces of manuscripts made in northern Gaul, in the neighbourhood of Laon and perhaps Corbie: the Sacramentarium Gelasianum (c. 750) and the near-contemporary manuscript of 'St Augustine on the Heptateuch.' The latter is more interesting since it combines motifs stemming from the eastern Mediterranean with an insular ground. It is from the East (perhaps from Coptic embroidery) that these standing quadrupeds, confronted on each side of a small tree, originate, though their wispy legs and clawlike feet are treated in the British manner. From the East come, too, the rows of large beads, palm-leaves and rosettes embellishing the portico and the big cross it surrounds, from whose arms, symbol of the time they span, hang the Alpha and Omega, terminals of a universe of which Christ is the master. On top of the cross stands an eagle, image of Christ and the Resurrection, decorated like a Merovingian fibula inlaid with cloisonné work. At the beginning of the text of this manuscript we find a curious imitation of the insular lettrines, but here, too, are some distinctively Oriental touches; the I and N in the words *In Dei Nomine* fall naturally into place in the text, but on the left the convoluted animal grappling with a sort of ribbon of interlaces merely duplicates—in a vaguely insular manner—the initial of the word *Quaestiones*, part of which is enclosed in a cartouche (this too a device characteristic of the British Isles). The insular decorators exercised, and were long to exercise, an influence on the continent justified by their talent and their inventiveness, but here the penchant for English mannerisms seems overdone.

It is possible, indeed probable, that reminiscences of the Near East and the eastern Mediterranean—Coptic textiles, above all, or other objects having the same origin—may have partially inspired these Italian prototypes. Of special interest is the fact that we find in Lombardy all the basic elements—zoomorphic initials and porticoes—of eighth-century continental book painting. Scribes and decorators of the age did not need to look far afield, for their techniques were supplied by their neighbours. Thus, as they had done already, in the domain of ancient art, the Lombards were soon to play a leading role in the Carolingian revival.

The figures decorating a Gospel Book of the second half of the eighth century, which is attributed to the abbey of Flavigny (Burgundy), though still lacking in elegance, are of a considerably higher quality than the clumsy sketches some of which we have discussed above. But the interest of this manuscript derives above all from the nature of its illustrations, wholly novel and, doubtless, unique. They consist of simple Canon Tables, their pilasters adorned with insular motifs. The first of the Tables assembles on a single page the figures that were, later, dispersed in various parts of the Carolingian Gospels: Christ to begin with, as a rule, then, at the beginning of each Gospel, the evangelist writing under the eyes of the 'living creature' of the Apocalypse that symbolizes him. (In early Carolingian times there were some exceptions to this rule.) There are also portraits of the authors, in accordance with an old tradition exemplified particularly in one of the earliest Virgil manuscripts; in short, strictly and exclusively documentary images. But in the Flavigny Gospels a different idea prevails, as is evidenced by the singular composition grouping these authors round the Master. Matthew, Mark, Luke and John are writing,

189 - NORTH-EAST FRANCE. SACRAMENTARIUM GELASIANUM. VATICAN LIBRARY.

180

190 - LAON (?). ST AUGUSTINE, 'QUAESTIONES IN HEPTATEUCHON.' BIBLIOTHÈQUE NATIONALE, PARIS.

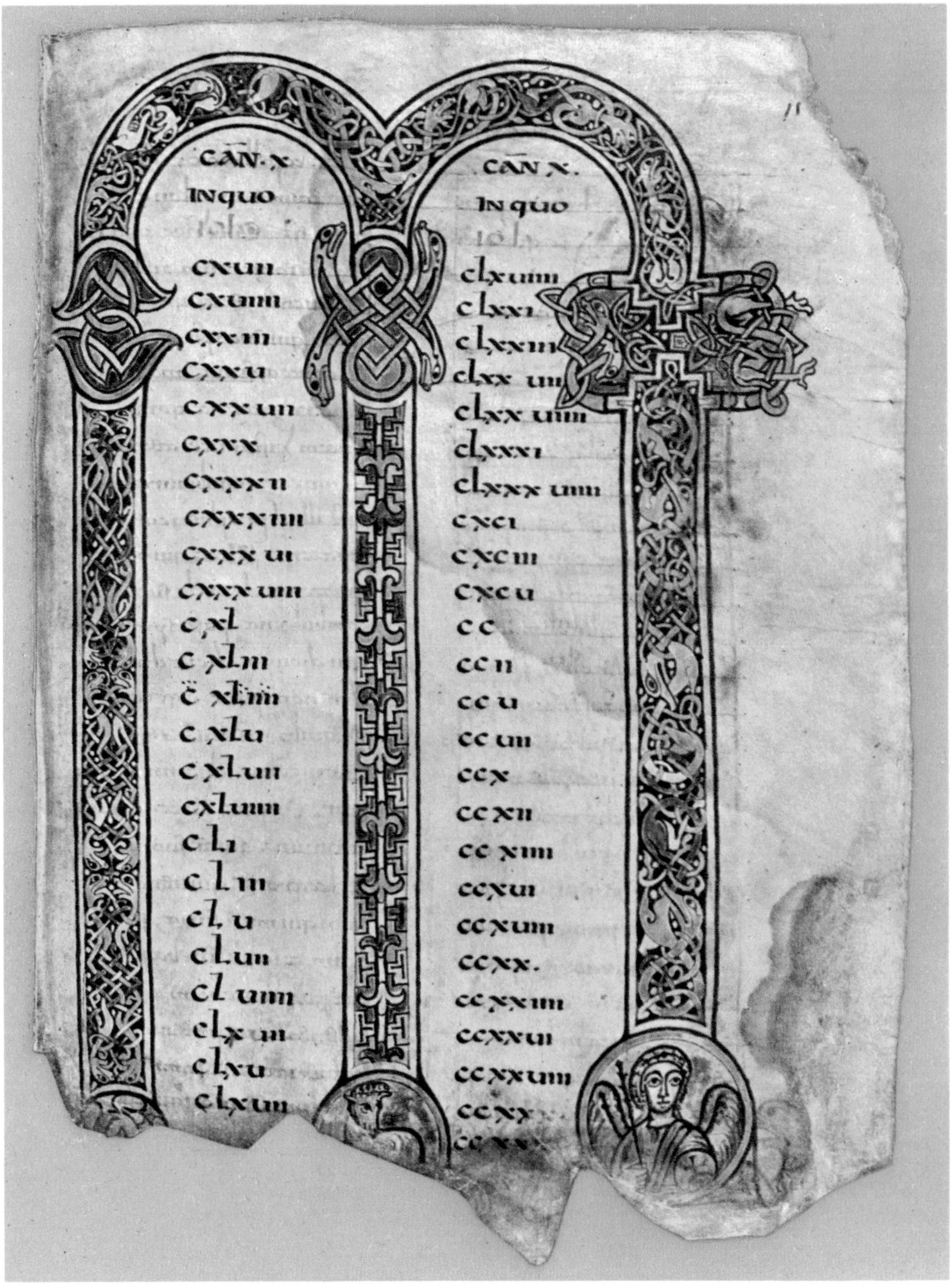

191 - FLAVIGNY GOSPELS. BIBLIOTHÈQUE MUNICIPALE, AUTUN.

looking up at their attributes, which serve as capitals and towards which, along simulated columns (each of whose bases they replace), rise verses taken from the ancient *Carmen Paschale* of Sedulius. (Here it would seem that these verses, differentiating the evangelists, engaged in their common task, in terms of their symbols, are used for the first time.) In the centre St John the Baptist, who is placed at a slightly higher level, is pointing to Christ who figures frontally, full length, at the top of the page; a text from the Gospel of St John simulates the central column, summing up in one line the message of the evangelists and the detailed account they give of the Redemption: *Ecce Dei venit Agnus peccatum tollere mundi*. Thus the entire

192 - FLAVIGNY GOSPELS. BIBLIOTHÈQUE MUNICIPALE, AUTUN.

message of the Gospels is condensed into a single image. We shall find the same synthesizing tendency operative, at about the same time, in the same part of the world, under various forms: in the illustration and structure of books, as formerly in the mural decorations of the triumphal arch of the presbytery in Santa Maria Antiqua. A fruit of theological speculation, and imbued with a certain feeling for a type of decoration foreign to classical antiquity, this synthesizing tendency was to affect medieval thought, under all its aspects, religious, philosophical, literary and artistic. True, the Carolingians, bent as they were on harking back to antiquity, lost touch with it, but it was to recur with their successors.

193 - FLAVIGNY GOSPELS, DETAIL. BIBLIOTHÈQUE MUNICIPALE, AUTUN.

184

194 - FLAVIGNY GOSPELS, DETAIL. BIBLIOTHÈQUE MUNICIPALE, AUTUN.

ΚΡωΝ ΝΚωΡΥω
ΠοϲΚΤΙΕΑΙΚΗΜ ΗΟΙΘΗ
ΡΑΠΙΚ ΗϹΤωΡΙΑω

196 - EASTERN FRANCE. CHRONICLE OF FREDEGARIUS, DETAIL. BIBLIOTHÈQUE NATIONALE, PARIS.

◀ 195 - EASTERN FRANCE. CHRONICLE OF FREDEGARIUS. BIBLIOTHÈQUE NATIONALE, PARIS.

197 - EASTERN FRANCE. CHRONICLE OF FREDEGARIUS. BIBL. NAT., PARIS.

Coptic art seems to have exercised an influence—this time a direct one—on some of the artists of northern and north-eastern Gaul in the course of the second half of the eighth century. We have in mind the textiles with figures deriving from Egypt that are obviously imitated in the curious graffiti (one can hardly call them drawings) inserted in the margins of a copy of the Chronicle of Fredegarius (c. 750). This early evidence of the artistic intercourse between East and West has an exceptional interest. A little later, shortly before 800, that famous manuscript from the neighbourhood of Meaux, the Gellone Sacramentary, was to derive the basic ideas of its initials from similar textiles. With these it intermingles reminiscences of insular art and highly ingenious lettrines of the scribe's own invention. Like his contemporary, the maker of the Corbie Psalter—though less convincingly—he makes them, so to say, grow out of the text; sometimes, we must admit, at the cost of extreme contortions. Thus a knight is made to represent the initial letter of the prayer in time of war; a huge pair of scissors cuts the incipient beard of a young monk at the opening of the prayer for novices; the Mass of the Finding of the Cross begins with an uncial capital D formed by a man digging a hole at the bottom of which are seen the crosses of Golgotha. The scene has too close a resemblance to a drawing in the Record of the Councils of Vercelli (mentioned above pages 139 ff.) not to have been copied from some picture of the same kind—therefore stemming from North Italy— which conformed to the Byzantine iconography. This procedure also inspired the painter with the idea of a simple and magnificent image, a master-piece of decorative originality and synthetic 'barbarism,' a Crucifixion in which the cross supplies the T in the *Te igitur* of the Canon: a happy inspiration that was to have many imitators.

198 - DIOCESE OF MEAUX. GELLONE SACRAMENTARY. BIBLIOTHÈQUE NATIONALE, PARIS. ▶

IN NO
MI NE
DNI NRI
IHS XPI INPI

LIBS SACRAM FR
in uigil natal dni hora
nona ad sca maria
D(eu)s qui nos redemptionis
nre annua expecta
tione letificas, presta
ut unigenitu tuu dnm redempto
re

partete illa in dni . siue quia regnat mutetur huius

leonir multifaria Inuidium; &exempla ut non uac&

dictum illud. Iuda filiur mr catulur leonir de ger-

mine. mihi ascendisti accubans dormiuit ut leo . &ric

catulur leonir quir excitauit eum díé dïac.

utsup er legit. INITIÚ e uac . sead . Lucaou

usq; PARA TR DNO plebe . ppceta . legir ad nunc

DIACONUS utsupr. Sequit . pbr his uerbir.

ucar euangelista uitulir preie gestat ad cul-

istar racluat nte . e i molatur hic enim xpi

euangeliu loquit ric coepit de zacharia &eli

sacb&h dequib; iohr baep. Insumma nature . ren&

tute . &idio lucar uitulo conparet . q; duo

cornux duo testanta Etqua tuor

pedum ungular . iiii auengelia quaer tenera firmitate

narentia inreplouir rime . continebat . Et die dia es

utsup . et leg . INITIÚ e uac . sed . ioh usq; plenú

GRATIE ET uERITATIT . legir ad nunc . dïac utsupr

pro sequitur . pbr his uerbis

ohr habet rimilitudinem aquile . eoq; d nimeral ex

petight . Ait Suim . Inprincipio e nr ther bú . &us

bum siert sunt dm . &dr siet uer bú . hoc siet

Inprincipio cepur dm . &dauid dixe dipronax

xpi renouac bir . sic aquile . iouentur tua

idest . ihu xpi domini quir uerur xdir amor tuir

ar cendir inge lor . unde iam uobir concep

tir pngnar gloriori ecclea omni festiuitate

uotorx ad nouatendir xpi ane lacir sciordi

die . ut aduenente . die . uenturir parche

lx uacr baeptir moatir renar conter ric rci

hominer miceramini cidele munur Infantie.

neribs; tuir semp por simur
CXLIIII dom.
mps sempia ds.
quinquaecenta
contineis, praef
dispsio diuisione
confersionem tui nomini

200 - DIOCESE OF MEAUX. GELLONE SACRAMENTARY. BIBLIOTHÈQUE NATIONALE, PARIS.

dié INUENTIO S
S qui
inuen
surci
praecio et
S cui cuncta o
uerbo tuo se

201 - DIOCESE OF MEAUX. GELLONE SACRAMENTARY. BIBLIOTHÈQUE NATIONALE, PARIS.

◀ 199 - DIOCESE OF MEAUX. GELLONE SACRAMENTARY. BIBLIOTHÈQUE NATIONALE, PARIS.

accedatp C...

INTERCESSIO...

ettuamnob...

&namtibice...

Munera...

utdignetur...

hermetis inte...

B qm sed...

molamu...

tui confessio...

Repleti dne...

202 - DIOCESE OF MEAUX. GELLONE SACRAMENTARY. BIBLIOTHÈQUE NATIONALE, PARIS.

203 - DIOCESE OF MEAUX. GELLONE SACRAMENTARY. BIBLIOTHÈQUE NATIONALE, PARIS. ▶

q· GRATIAS AGERE ḊNE SĊE PAɪ ȮMPS X̄ɪ̄NEDS ·
x̄p̄m ḊN̄M N̄R̄M P quem MAIESTATEM TUAM
LAUDAṄT ANGELI ADORANT DOMINA TIONIS
TREMUNT POTESTATES CÆLI CELORUM q̇ UIRTUȷ̄T
Ac BEATA SERAPHIṄ SOCIA EXULTATIONE CON
CELEBRANT CUMq̇ quɪb; ETNR̄ʌ̄S UOCES
UTAD MITTI IUBEAS DEȷ̄ICAMUR SUPPLICI COṄ
FESSIONE DICENTES· SĊS· SĊS·SĊS· ḊNS DS
CABAWΘ PΛENY·CUNT ΚEΛ UETTE[
PA ΚΛω PYΛ TUΛ WC ANNΛ YNE Z ΚΛ
SYS· BENEDYΚTUC QVY UENY·TJN NWÃ[
ANY· WC ANNΛ YNE Z ΚΛ[

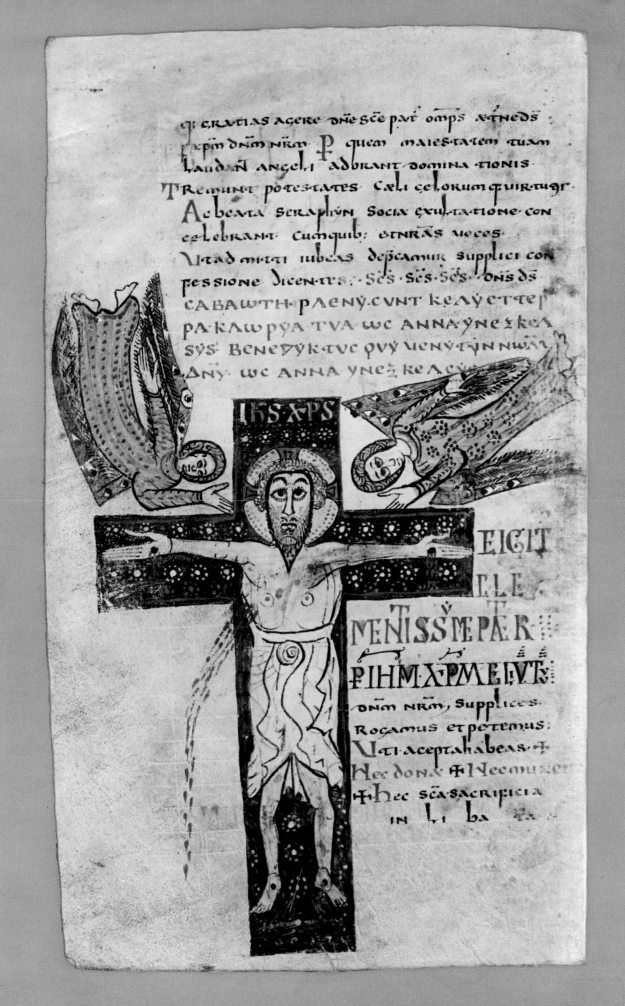

EIGIT
ELE
MENISSTMEPAER
PIHMX̄PMELVT̄
ḊN̄M NR̄M, Supplices·
ROGΛMUS ET PETIMUS·
UTI ACEPTA HABEAS· ✠
HEC DONA ✠ HEC MUNER
✠HEC SĊA SACRIFICIA
IN Li ba Ta·

These decorative initials, in which text and illustration were skilfully associated, as a century earlier architecture and decoration had been combined in the presbytery of Santa Maria Antiqua, and these synthetic initials of a new type, due unmistakably to a real confluence of Mediterranean and barbarian art currents and not, as in the past, to their mere juxtaposition—all these new developments can be seen in an illustrated Psalter made round about 800 in an abbey which then was specializing in importations of North Italian manuscripts: the abbey of Corbie. This Psalter, a work of outstanding merit, was made by a highly gifted painter whose style continued and developed, making it far more explicit (a point of prime importance) than that of the first decorated book produced under the auspices of Charlemagne. Here, though the groundwork of the decorative scheme is insular, the general atmosphere is thoroughly Iranian, as is evidenced both by the technique employed and by the number of exotic animals worked into the initials (the only decorative pages of the book): for example the *simurgh* (bird-and-dog) and the horseman wearing a long veil (a *shesh*) to protect him from the sand, of the kind still used in the desert by his modern counterparts. The flowing curves, the muscular structure emphasized by volutes and calligraphic flourishes, recall the art of ancient Persia.

First, then, we note that while some images stem from an ancient tradition, others are inspired by a commentary on the sacred text and in these everything is original, carefully thought out. Such is the initial of Psalm LII. The mighty personage seated 'in glory,' encircled by a serpent, who is being swept backwards by a monster, is Doeg the Edomite, traitor to David, and in him Cassiodorus saw an embodiment of the Antichrist. 'Thou lovest evil more than good, lying rather than to speak righteousness. Thou lovest all devouring words, O thou deceitful tongue' (Psalm LII, 3, 4). Elsewhere, in connection with Psalm XIII, a doublet of Psalm LII, Cassiodorus alludes to the serpent. The (apocryphal) Psalm CLI begins *Pusillus eram* and the capital P is shaped to represent the combat of David and Goliath (the normal illustration of this verse). God's hand is pressing back Goliath's spear. A little demon is perched on the crest of the helmet of the giant, who seems strangely inert, incapable of averting the death-dealing stone. (This adjunct to the crest of the helmet figures in other images of the same scene.) The loop of the letter P frames the picture and also serves to indicate the earth below and the heavens above. If Goliath is placed outside it, this is only to draw attention to his monstrous stature. But the initial in which we see this painter at his most brilliant is that of the Psalm of Habbakuk, in which the entire scene, a galloping horse and a sort of ship on wheels with a tiny figure riding in it, forms an uncial D. The horse's hugely elongated tail serves to define the outlines of the chariot (or ship) and tapers off to form the peaked cap of the central figure. Two long shafts, one upholding the *vexillum* of a Roman legion, the other a sceptre or a palm-branch, are bent so as to adapt themselves to the curves of the 'ship,' a turning movement continued by the hind legs of the horse. Why this curious composition seemingly so unrelated to anything in the text? A clue may be found in a commentary on the Psalms written by Theophylactos a century later than the Corbie Psalter but probably based on an earlier exegesis, in which, when discussing this Psalm, the author speaks of chariots and athletes.

204 - CORBIE PSALTER. BIBLIOTHÈQUE MUNICIPALE, AMIENS.

205 - CORBIE PSALTER. BIBLIOTHÈQUE MUNICIPALE, AMIENS.

ote eum mel[od]is &
organo ·
Laudate eum in cim
balis. benesonantib:
Laudate eum in cim
balis iubilationis om
nis sps laudet dnm.

SED HE ALXX
in quid INTER
PRETIBUS e
OICTUS EST·

hic PSALMUS
PROPRIE SCRIP
TUS DAVID ET
EXTRA CANON ee
sum:

illos era
inter fratres
meos· & adu
lescentior in
domo patris mei
pascebam oues
patris mei·
···anus meae
···ecerunt organu

p medium mare

audiui audituiratui

& timui conside

208 - CORBIE PSALTER. BIBLIOTHÈQUE MUNICIPALE, AMIENS.

There is no question that this painting was inspired by the scene, so often represented on Roman sarcophagi, of Diana ascending skywards in her chariot after a night on earth with Actaeon. But the artist entirely reconstructed his models after separating out their elements and transposing the imagery into an abstract world, as the makers of bracteates did with the ancient medals. In brief, he was a barbarian. All that old mythological apparatus—galloping horse, a veil enveloping the personification of Terra whom the goddess is about to quit—meant nothing to him, but it supplied just what he needed for his uncial D. It would be a great mistake to see in this brilliantly ingenious painter no more than a copyist; he selects, interprets, strikes out in new directions. In this context we may draw attention to the fact that a scene resembling this one (sc. the Diana motif) adorns the ancient so-called Proserpine sarcophagus at Aix in which Charlemagne was said to have been buried in 814. True, the scene here is reversed, but so expert an artist would have had no difficulty

207 - CORBIE PSALTER. BIBLIOTHÈQUE MUNICIPALE, AMIENS.

209 - CORBIE PSALTER. BIBLIOTHÈQUE MUNICIPALE, AMIENS.

in turning the Aix motif round the other way. How is this irruption at Corbie of Mediterranean art, and particularly that of the Iranian Middle East, to be accounted for? Contemporary records mention the presence of many Greeks and 'Syrians' at the Court and in Gaul, and it is interesting to find this confirmed by objects still in existence, like this Psalter. Once again it is to Lombardy we must turn for an explanation. Desiderius, the last Lombard king, had died in the abbey some years previously; and nothing approximates more clearly the art of the Psalter than that of the Cividale Tempietto in Friuli, which was built for Desiderius and adorned with brilliantly original stuccoes of which the Carolingian paintings are, in effect, the graphic counterparts. This curious fact may well throw light on the origins of the Tempietto itself. The Sassanian imprint is more deeply marked, more evident, at Corbie than at Cividale, but a great many elements of Lombard art stemmed from the Middle East and beyond it, from Iran.

210 - CORBIE PSALTER. BIBLIOTHÈQUE MUNICIPALE, AMIENS. ▶

neius,
r dia
genies
tymen.

ta in

dispsit

ntcor

otenter   dinitas seruum tu

caltauit   um dn̅e · secundum

                 uerbū tuū inpace

imple   Quia uiderunt ocu

diuites   limei · salutar & tuū ·

But such resemblances are sometimes accidental, and stylistic affinities can be misleading. Let us, then, look at the facts. When the Psalter was being made, the see of Amiens had been for some thirty years in the hands of a bishop with a Greek name, George; a reliable contemporary (early ninth century) record attributes to Bishop George the Latin version of an Alexandrian Universal Chronicle, of which a fragmentary fifth-century copy is extant. The Greek original was illustrated and the only known copy of the Latin translation, the one made by George and written at Corbie, leaves blanks in the text at the places where pictures were to be inserted. As Bishop of Ostia, George had accompanied Stephen II to France (in 754) where he became a member of the royal household of King Pepin. He was sent on several missions to the papal court by the king, and subsequently by his son Charles. In his capacity of Bishop of Amiens he was a member of the Council held in Rome, in 769, which condemned iconoclasm. In 798 he took part in the consecration of the churches of the monastery of Saint-Riquier. Of the illuminations of his Chronicle only one was brought to completion, that of the first initial letter, a P containing images of Eve, the serpent and the Fall: an appropriate beginning for a 'Universal History.' This initial, treated on synthetic lines, was the work of the same artist who illustrated the Corbie Psalter. At the time when George, the Hellenist, came from Italy to Amiens to take over the bishopric, the local scribes employed by Maurdramne, Abbot of Corbie, were gradually developing a new type of writing, the 'Caroline,' inspired by the half-uncial book-hand current in North Italy. It soon replaced the various local styles of writing, including that of Corbie, and from it come the letters of the alphabet we employ today. George held a high post in the ecclesiastical hierarchy, but in Corbie itself Adalard, who shared in the administration of the abbey during the lifetime of Maurdramne, was a cousin-german of Charlemagne. He, too, had made several long stays in Italy, where he came in touch with the monks of Monte Cassino and many prominent Lombards, beginning with King Desiderius. At his request his friend Paul the Deacon, historian of the Lombards, sent him a copy of the Letters of Gregory the Great (written in Friuli c. 787). Something of a Hellenist, and perhaps wishing to display his knowledge of the language, Adalard wrote a note in Greek on a copy of St Jerome's *Adv. Jovinianum*, to the effect that he had given the order for the book. For fifteen years or more Corbie had been gathering together—from Greece, from Roman and Lombard Italy and the British Isles as well—all that was needed for the shaping of Carolingian painting, and it was there that Charles could count on finding his first artist. There are good reasons for believing that he had already recruited scribes from Corbie. Bishop Jesse (799-831) was George's successor in the see of Amiens, and to his episcopacy dates a Gospel Book whose frontispiece shows Christ full face, surrounded by the zoomorphic evangelist symbols framed in medallions beaded in the Lombard manner. He sits under an arch in front of a curtain edged with a narrow cord like the one in a Greek copy of Dioscorides, now in Vienna, and above him is a tablet inscribed with the Greek words ΦΩΣ.ΖΩΗ with the Latin equivalents LUX-VITA flanking them. It is evident that writers and artists of this part of Gaul looked for inspiration to the eastern shores of the Medi-

Nomnem terram exiuit fonuf eorum
&infinef orbif terrę uerba eorum
Nfôleposuit taber naculum fuum
&ipfe tamquam fponfuf procedenf
dexhalamofuo
xultabit ut gigguf adcurrendā uiā fuā
Afummo egreffio eiuf
toccurfuf eiuf ufquead fummum eiuf
Neceft quife abfcondat
acalore eiuf

exdñi inmaculata conuer tenf animaf:
teftimoniumdñi fidele

mittemanum tuũdealto & eripeme &
liberame deaquis multis ·
& demanu filiorum alienorum
uorum os locutum est uanitatem ·
& dextera eorum dextera iniquitatis ;
scanticum nouum cantabo tibi ·
inpsalterio decachordo psallam tibi ;
uidas salutẽ regib; & quiredemit dauid
seruũ suũ degladio maligno eripeme ;
& erueme demanu filiorũ alienorum ·
quorũ os locutum ē uanitatem ·
& dextera eorum dextera iniquitatis ;

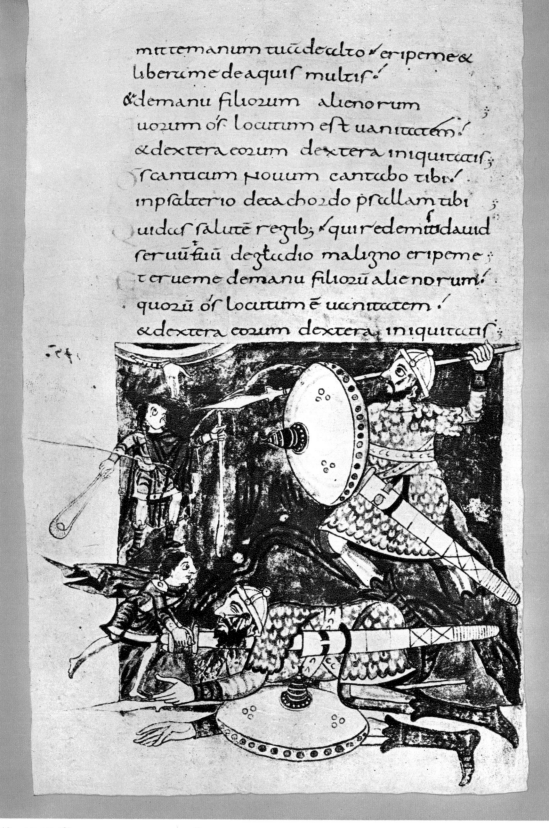

214 - SAINT-RIQUIER. PSALTER OF CHARLEMAGNE, DETAIL. BIBLIOTHÈQUE NATIONALE, PARIS.

terranean and that in the two decades 780-800 the influence of Lombard Italy, then a meeting-place of art currents stemming from the East, was paramount in their work. In eastern and north-eastern France there persisted, at the close of the eighth century, art forms that were still barbarian and akin to those of the Gellone Sacramentary (which cannot be dated earlier than 790-795) and those of early works made at Laon and Corbie. But already, as we have seen, the Gellone painter had treated in the manner of the Corbie Psalter the ideas he culled from his text. In it we have the first example of a synthetic initial letter inserted at the forefront of a chapter, like an escutcheon, a meaningful armorial bearing, or a sort of cipher, differing *toto coelo* from the narrative scenes of antiquity and their illusionist effects. The Carolingians, who looked back to antiquity for inspiration, were to eschew this form of imagery, but Romanesque art was to revert to it. None the less there co-existed another programme of images, wholly antique or Byzantine, devoid of any insular ingredients. An example is a Psalter at Stuttgart, datable some thirty years later than the Corbie Psalter. Here both pictures and narrative keep closely to the text of the Psalms and, following the so-called typological method, give special prominence to the Biblical 'types' or prefigurations of the age to come, the age of Christ. This makes it clear that from the beginning of the century on, there co-existed and persisted, alongside the courtly genre of painting and its ramifications, an art of classical, traditional inspiration.

JEAN PORCHER

PART THREE

Sculpture and Applied Arts

The Heritage of Antiquity

IN no other domain are the stylistic changes that took place in the period between antiquity and the early Middle Ages so clearly visible as in that of sculpture; in it the steady decline of the creative urge of antique art can be traced stage by stage. The period of this decline lies, approximately, between the reigns of Constantine (307-337) and Theodosius (379-395), and its effects, operative not only in the East but also in the West, can be most clearly seen in the sarcophagus reliefs and ivory carvings. The sensitive, illusionist art of antiquity gradually died out, as did all attempts to render the third dimension; stripped of its plastic values, the human figure lay solely on the surface, became purely linear, and governed by an ever more rigid symmetry.

Nevertheless, even after the fall of the Roman Empire the heritage of antiquity still bulked so large in the mentality of western Europe, and above all in that of the ecclesiastical authorities, that it held its ground, if in a latent form, throughout the following centuries. Despite the rapid permeation of the West by Oriental influences, and the driving force of a new kind of art stemming from the East and the regions north of the Alps, the classical heritage was never quite obliterated in the course of this 'dark age' among the peoples formerly incorporated in the Empire. Under different guises, however, more and more marked regional characteristics developed as time went by.

Thus in the figures of two apostles on an ivory diptych from Kranenburg (now in the Metropolitan Museum, New York), perhaps inspired originally by an effigy of Christ handing over the keys, we can sense unmistakable affinities with the Early Christian sculpture of Rome and also with the Marseilles sarcophagi: a kinship evidenced by the classical form of the garments and, from the iconographic viewpoint, by the frieze of lambs at the top of the arch. In the stiff posture of the apostles' heads and the stylized eyes we have tokens of the stylistic changes that were taking place in Gaul in the early fifth century. This impression is strikingly

◀ 215 - HEAD OF AN EMPRESS. MUSEO ARCHEOLOGICO, CASTELLO SFORZESCO, MILAN.

216-217 - GAUL. DIPTYCH: ST PETER AND ST PAUL. THE METROPOLITAN MUSEUM OF ART, NEW YORK.

218 - ITALY. PHALERA. MUSÉE ARCHÉOLOGIQUE, STRASBOURG.

confirmed when we examine the reliefs of the end of the century (c. 500) and compare *Meleager's Hunt* on the Toulouse sarcophagus with any antique hunting scene—a revealing example of the would-be literal imitation in the Gothic West of an antique prototype. The scrollwork around the hunting scene is likewise derivative from the art of antiquity. A little later a Burgundian sculptor reproduced on the buckle of St Caesarius, Bishop of Arles (d. 542), the motif of the soldiers sleeping beside the tomb that had figured on an early fifth-century Italian ivory. This use of antique motifs persisted throughout the entire course of Merovingian art. We have an interesting example of this in the silver phalerae found in the tomb of a warrior chief at Ittenheim. In these seventh-century works the figures of the warlord and the boars point unmistakably both to the influence of the toreutic art of antiquity and to their Italian origin. The fine engraved pan bearing a hunting scene and a Greek inscription on the rim, which was found at Güttingen in the tomb of a seventh-century Alamannic chief, clearly stemmed from one of the Christian communities of the East, or perhaps Ravenna. Again, further west, we have the comb of St Lupus (d. 623), now in the treasure of Sens cathedral; here the two heraldic lions leaping towards the Tree of Life reproduce a familiar motif of ancient Oriental art.

Such ancient ornamental motifs as the cymatium and acanthus leaves were retained, unaltered, in the early Middle Ages. Though often used by themselves, they were sometimes combined with elements of the new zoomorphic imagery, and on occasion with a plain band of scrollwork, as in the small Angers diptych of the late seventh century.

There is no doubt that in Gaul this antiquizing art tradition was deliberately fostered by the great senatorial families, which, even under the kings, often supplied the Church with its highest dignitaries. Thus, alongside the growing influence of the Christian East, the links with Hellenic art remained unbroken throughout the Merovingian period, and it is no less clear that the Carolingian renascence of the eighth century did not involve a break with the antique tradition.

219 - PAN WITH HUNTING SCENE AND INSCRIPTION. HEGAUMUSEUM, SINGEN.

220 - BUCKLE OF ST CAESARIUS. NOTRE-DAME-LA-MAJOR, ARLES.

221 - COMB OF ST LUPUS. CATHEDRAL TREASURE, SENS.

222 - DECORATED TABLETS. CHAPEL, INSTITUTION SAINT-MARTIN, ANGERS.

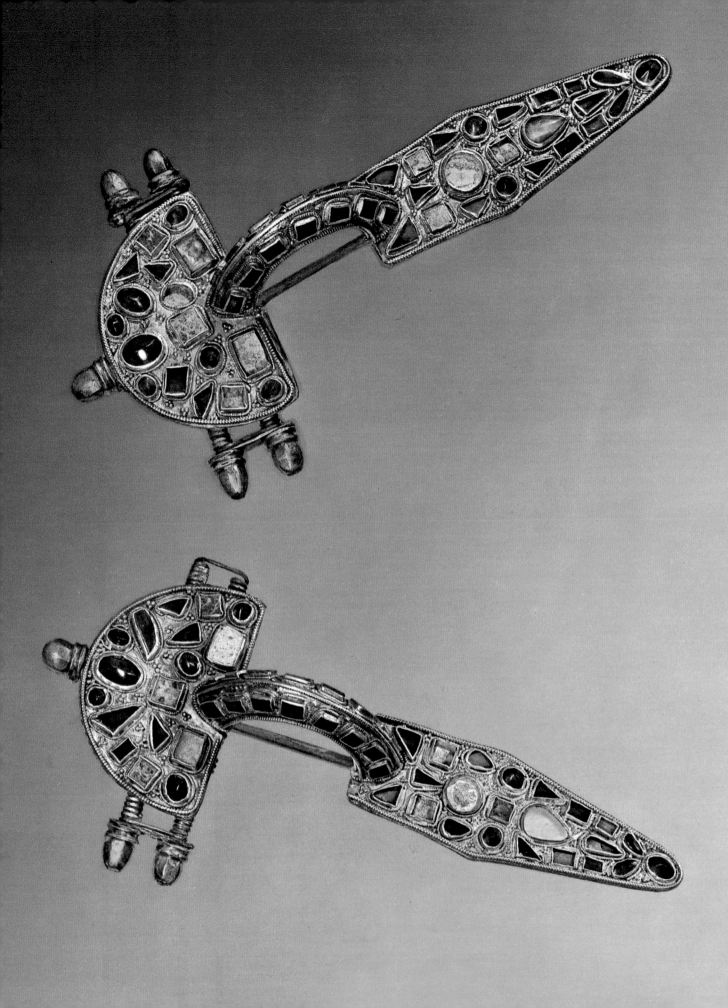

The Polychrome Style

While from the year 400 on we find a marked tendency in all the western lands to spurn the antique style and almost completely to abandon plastically modelled figurations, another tendency was making rapid headway: ornamentation became increasingly important, and there was a marked new taste for emphatic colour. Plant forms fell out of favour and artists showed a preference for geometric figures. In the domain of metalwork, this new trend is evidenced by combinations of gold with red and other colours and, in glasswork, by an extensive use of the cloisonné technique. Its earliest exponents were the peoples of the East, particularly those in the Iranian provinces and the kingdoms of the Pontus (Black Sea) area.

This art of Oriental provenance came to the West in the wake of the great migrations; also, to some extent, as a result of the direct importation of eastern artifacts. The first of these westward drives was the invasion of the East Roman Empire by the Huns in 375.

The nature of the works of art that the invaders from the East brought with them into Europe is of special interest in view of its impact on the arts and crafts of the western world. For example in Austria, at Untersiebenbrunn, some handsome fibulae stemming from the Pontus region, were discovered in a Gothic tomb; likewise some other Pontic artifacts, probably made for an Alanian burial, were found in a grave in northern France at Airan (Calvados). Other objects dating to the Hun occupation have been uncovered in the heart of the Rhineland, notably in the *Waffengrab* (weapons grave) at Altlussheim, and objects contemporary with Attila have been found at Mundolsheim in Alsace. The grave goods buried about 400 near Wolfsheim in the Rhineland comprised many gold objects and a swordbelt buckle inscribed with the name of the Persian king Ardashir I (224-241). These are but a sampling of the many Pontic, Iranian and Hunnish artifacts dating to the period of Attila that have been brought to light in Central Europe. They testify to the wealth of Oriental objects—swords, fibulae, belt buckles, etc.—that found their way to Europe in the course of the invasions.

This art had far-reaching effects on the Gallo-Roman and Germanic metalworkers, who made haste to model their own work on it. Moreover it would seem that the invaders brought with them craftsmen from the Pontus region, who continued to practise their art in the occupied territories of the West. There the amount of gold available, produce of Roman tribute or the spoils of war, must have been prodigious.

Most of the precious stones, such as the garnets used for insets, had been brought from India by the Danube route, until the time when the Arab drive westward put an end to these importations. The first great phase of the Pontic art of gem-setting ended with the crushing defeat of the Huns in 451. In the Pouan tomb was found along with other objects (now in Troyes Museum) a magnificent sword with a gold hilt dating to the time of this decisive battle.

◀ 223 - PAIR OF LOOPED FIBULAE. KUNSTHISTORISCHES MUSEUM, VIENNA.

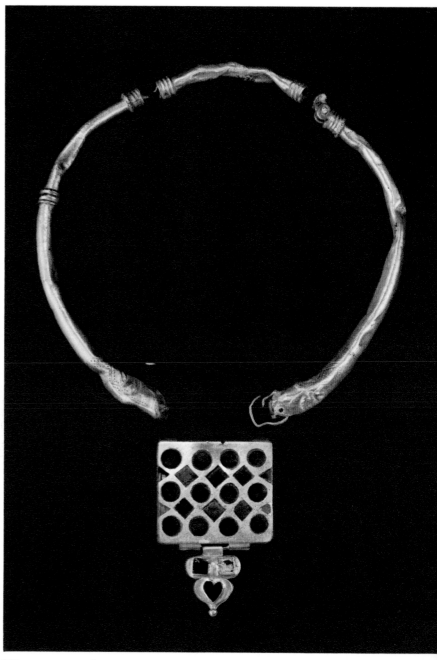

226 - **PENDANT.** STÄDTISCHES MUSEUM, WIESBADEN.

225 - SWORD. BADISCHES LANDESMUSEUM, KARLSRUHE.

◄ 224 - LARGE EAGLE-HEADED FIBULA. ACADEMIA INSTITUTUL DE ARHEOLOGIE, BUCHAREST.

In the following period—the age of Childeric—cloisonné work became at once more compact and more sumptuous. Large, symmetrically disposed coloured *cloisons* characterize the ornamental art of the East, in which any kind of figure imagery was prohibited. Examples are the works found in the Pietroasa Treasure (c. 375) now in Bucharest Museum and the cup of Chosroes II (590-628) (Cabinet des Médailles, Paris). In the West these large coloured zones were gradually reduced to narrow undulating strips setting off an elaborate central core. Only red garnets were used, to the exclusion of other coloured gems, and their lustre was intensified by a setting composed of goffered gold-leaf, the edges of which were smoothed and polished. The gems were tightly fitted into the cells, now grown thinner. The best example of this new style comes from the tomb of King Childeric (d. 481), uncovered in Tournai in 1653. Though this treasure was stolen from the Cabinet des Médailles in 1831, some fragments of it, including the King's long sword and scramasax, were discovered in the Seine. But his signet ring has never been recovered. The bees Napoleon chose for his emblem were inspired by the charming grasshoppers on a fibula from Childeric's tomb. Some other objects executed in the same cloisonné technique are so perfect in their kind that we may safely assume they were made in the royal workshops at Tournai. Since the shape of the *spathas* is typically Frankish, it is an open question whether the craftsmen who made these swords were indigenous or immigrants from the Pontus. This latter possibility must not be ruled out, for the gold wave pattern adorning them is also found on works of unquestionably Pontic origin, such as the Wolfsheim buckle and the somewhat later Apahida and Rüdern buckles (dated a little after the mid-fifth century). The only novelty here is the lavish decoration of the clasp, not found on the *spathas* with gold hilts made in southern Russia, and attributable perhaps to Nordic influences.

Until the mid-sixth century the elaborately decorated type of sword exemplified by Childeric's, made exclusively for the nobility, was being produced throughout the Frankish dominions; swords of this kind have been found in tombs at Lavoye, Flonheim and Planig. They were copied by the Alamanni, but in a simplified form, as is shown by the finds at Gültlingen, Kleinhüningen and Entringen. We find the same kind of cloisonné work, but less skilfully executed than that of the swords, on buckles and fibulae of the period, from the reign of Childeric to the sixth century. Besides red garnets, other gems of different colours were now employed, as in the handsome buckle from Tressan (in the Musée de Cluny, Paris). Here the rivets along the edges cease to serve any practical purpose and have become mere ornamental adjuncts. The indebtedness to Oriental works, especially those with embossed decorations (such as the Apahida buckle), is still evident.

In the Frankish dominion the most perfect example of the polychrome style is a small chalice and its paten discovered near Gourdon (Saône-et-Loire) in 1845. The chalice has two elegantly shaped handles and is adorned with filigree work, turquoises and glass paste; the paten has a cross in the centre and delicately wrought insets along its margins, notably on its foot. The discovery along with it of Byzantine coins (518-537) enables us to date these objects approximately, and they may well have been owned by Sigismund, King of Burgundy (d. 524). The fine-spun decor-

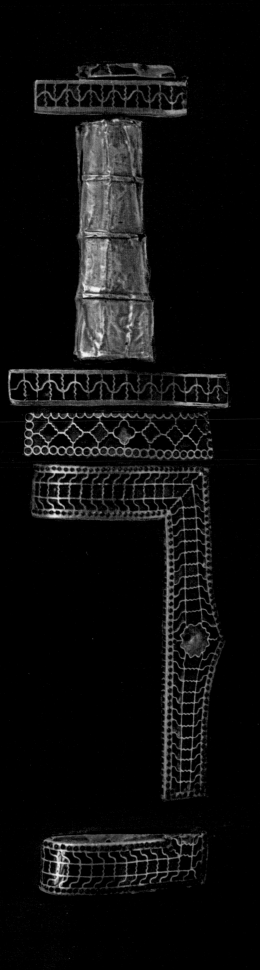

228 - RING (COPY). BIBLIOTHÈQUE NATIONALE, PARIS.

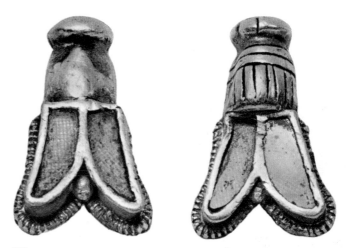

229 - PAIR OF GRASSHOPPER FIBULAE. BIBLIOTHÈQUE NATIONALE, PARIS.

230 - GRASSHOPPER FIBULA. MUSÉE DES BEAUX-ARTS, LYONS.

232 - BELT BUCKLE. MUSÉE DE CLUNY, PARIS.

233 - CHALICE. CABINET DES MÉDAILLES, BIBLIOTHÈQUE NATIONALE, PARIS.

◀ 231 - SWORD. MUSÉE DES ANTIQUITÉS NATIONALES, SAINT-GERMAIN-EN-LAYE.

ation, the filigree, the use of two colours (green and red) and the daintiness of the openwork on the foot of the paten have obvious affinities with Mediterranean art. The same association of red and green gems occurs in the first half of the sixth century on the fishes from Bülach (Zurich Museum) and those from Kleinhüningen (Basel Museum); also in the Burgundian fibulae from Jouy-le-Comte, whose technique is exceptionally proficient. The practice of combining filigree and cloisonné work, exemplified by the Gourdon chalice, was now becoming generalized, and we find it also employed in the round fibulae from Charnay-lès-Mâcon (Saône-et-Loire). Despite certain resemblances with some Scandinavian artifacts, the affinities of these objects with Ostrogothic art are unmistakable, and they are even more apparent in the pieces from Bülach and Gourdon.

So far only a small number of objects imported from the Black Sea region have been discovered in Italy, but it is known that the polychrome Oriental style was in favour there. The earliest extant example (dating most probably to the period before the invasion of the Goths) is the lamb in the central sector of a five-panelled ivory diptych in the treasure of Milan cathedral, the reliefs on which appear to have been made subsequently to 450. The serried cloisonné work in the nimbus is, despite certain differences, in the nature of the *opus inclusorium* employed in the

234 - PATEN (SEEN FROM ABOVE AND FROM THE SIDE). CABINET DES MÉDAILLES, BIBLIOTHÈQUE NATIONALE, PARIS.

so-called 'golden cuirass of Theodoric' (discussed below) formerly in Ravenna but no longer extant. (In the light of the latest excavations made at Krefeld-Gellep, it would seem that this 'cuirass' was really a plaque affixed to a horse's harness.) Since in a later period also, in the sixth century, insets of garnets are found in Italian works, such as the cover of the Gospel Book of Theodelinda in Monza and the jewelled cross (now lost) from the Sancta Sanctorum of the Vatican, it can safely be assumed that, independently of the Ostrogoths, Italian craftsmen had, on their own initiative, adopted this Oriental technique. Thus the question whether the gold portions of the Ravenna 'cuirass' were the work of Ostrogothic or of indigenous artists is of little consequence. In this domain, too, as well as in their architecture and mosaics, the Goths may well have employed local artists who had acquired these Oriental skills at the source—that is to say in the Pontus region—or, again, the 'pincer' decoration of the 'cuirass' may have been the work of some Germanic craftsman.

There is no question that when they occupied northern Italy in 488, the Ostrogoths brought with them from the Pontus the polychrome style of their home-land. The two Domagnano fibulae adorned with gold eagles (one now at Nuremberg, the other in the Marquis de Ganay Collection, Paris) are among the finest

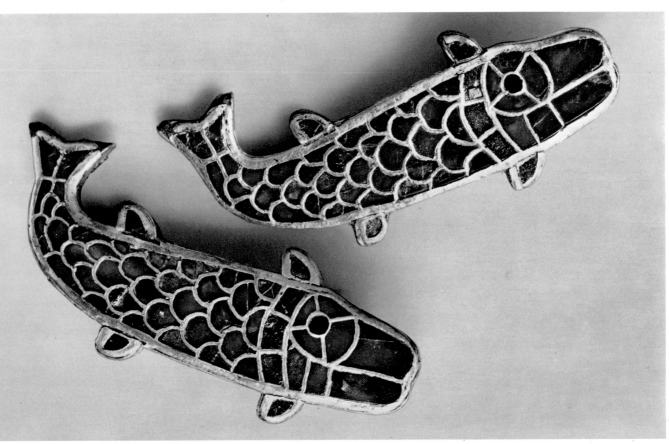

235 - PAIR OF FISH-SHAPED FIBULAE. SCHWEIZERISCHES LANDESMUSEUM, ZURICH.

236 - LOOPED FIBULA. MUSÉE DES ANTIQUITÉS NATIONALES, SAINT-GERMAIN-EN-LAYE.

240 - EAGLE-SHAPED FIBULA. GERMANISCHES NATIONALMUSEUM, NUREMBERG.

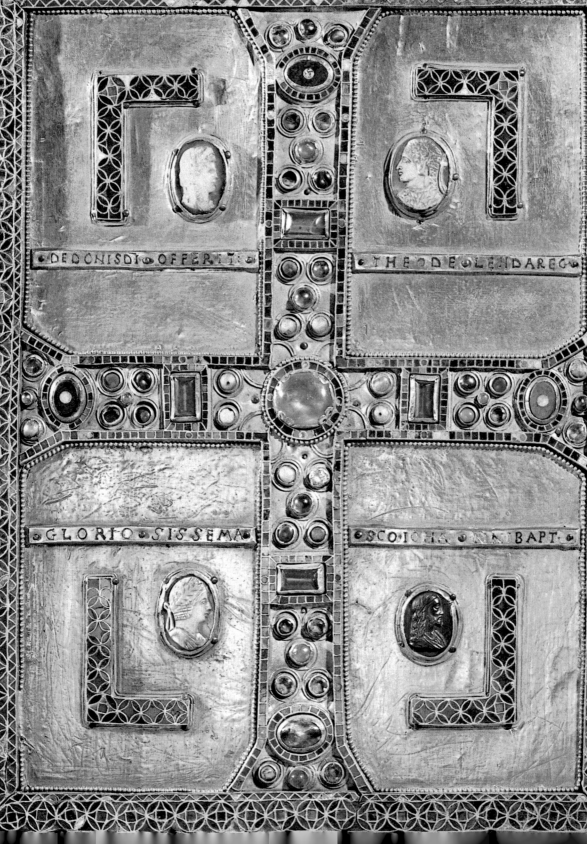

・DE DONIS DI OFFERT・   ・THEODELENDA REG・

・GLORIO・SIS SEMA・   ・SCO IOHA・NNI BAPT・

238 - FRAGMENT OF A HORSE'S HARNESS (LOST).

239 - FRAGMENT OF A HORSE'S HARNESS. KREFELD.

creations of this art and testify to the skill of the craftsman who so successfully transposed an animal motif from southern Russia into the Germanic style. Here the effect is due not only to the curiously painterly impression, as if on a flat surface, produced by the design, but also to the harmonious stylization of the ensemble. That fibulae of this type were in high favour with the Gothic nobility is proved by the quantity that have survived, among them the two examples found on the Appian Way in Rome.

The Visigoths, too, were partial to this type, but in a simplified form. Many eagle fibulae have been found in the neighbourhood of Toulouse and in Spain (e.g. those from Tierra de Barros, now in Baltimore). Those from the Ostrogoth tomb at Desana rank among the notable examples of the cloisonné work of the period. They date to about 500, when this art was at its apogee. Noteworthy is a pair of fibulae inset with red and green stones, some flat, some faceted, the upper edge adorned with birds' heads. These heads resemble those on a fibula from Fano and on the handsome Gothic buckles (with a more distinctively Oriental form) in the Berlin and Karlsruhe museums and also at Norcia, whose lower edges already carry strips of interlaces. All are assignable to the Pontic heritage of Gothic art. The cloisonné-work pieces of the late Ostrogothic period are less ornate. Most

◄ 237 - DIPTYCH, DETAIL OF THE CENTRAL ELEMENT. CATHEDRAL TREASURE, MILAN.

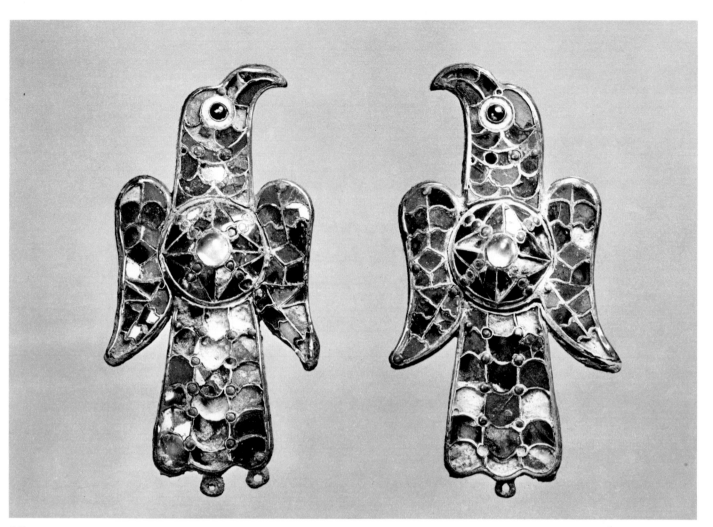

242 - PAIR OF EAGLE-SHAPED FIBULAE. THE WALTERS ART GALLERY, BALTIMORE.

are in bronze, a few in silver, and gems are now more sparingly used. The large belt buckle at Pavia illustrates this trend and the most striking examples of it are to be found in Hungary. True, these latter are lavishly decorated, but their cuneiform ornamentation and the birds' heads on the edges show a marked deterioration and are at a far remove from the achievements of Ostrogothic art in its glorious heyday in Pannonia.

When the Ostrogothic empire fell to pieces in 553, the Byzantine emperor regained possession of Ravenna. Then came the Lombard invasion of 568. But, despite Lombard domination, Byzantium lost none of its prestige in Italy; indeed its art enlarged its sphere of influence, spreading across the Italian frontier into western Europe. Expelled from Alexandria and Constantinople by religious feuds, many monks and high-ranking prelates sought refuge in the West. Soon, and for a relatively long period, Oriental popes sat on St Peter's throne and promoted in Rome the arts of their mother countries. As early as the pontificate of Hormisdas

◀ 241 - ROME (?). COVERS OF THE GOSPEL BOOK OF QUEEN THEODELINDA. CATHEDRAL TREASURE, MONZA.

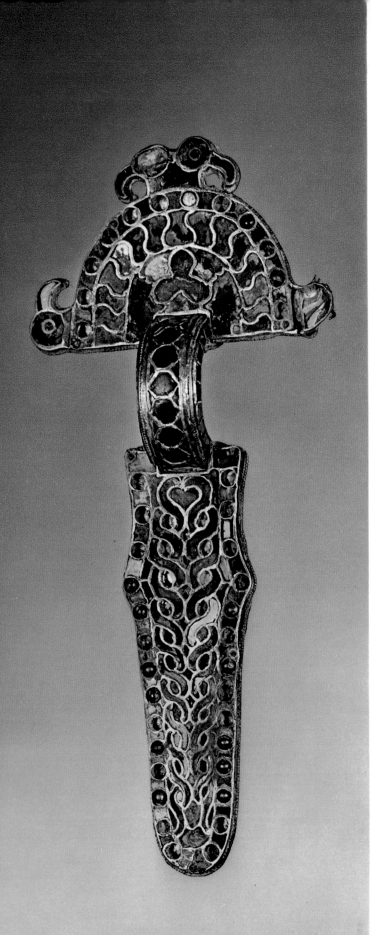

244 - BELT BUCKLE. BADISCHES LANDESMUSEUM, KARLSRUHE.

245 - BELT BUCKLE. MUSEO CIVICO, PAVIA.

◀ 243 - LOOPED FIBULA. MUSEO CIVICO D'ARTE ANTICA, TURIN.

(514-523) there were signs in Rome of this infiltration of eastern art forms, while such Byzantine outposts as Ravenna, Grado and Parenzo became active art centres. We have only to read the Liber Pontificalis to see how rich were the Roman churches in works of art, precious fabrics, gold and jewellery imported from the East.

After a brief eclipse, works in the Oriental polychrome style returned to favour in the seventh century. One of the best examples is the famous cover of the Gospel Book of Theodelinda, evidently one of the gifts which Gregory the Great (d. 604) made in 603 to the sovereigns at Monza. (This binding is probably to be identified with the 'Theca Persica' mentioned in the list of presents.) That an awareness of the Oriental origin of the technique of glass inlays persisted is proved by a passage in the chronicle of Theophylactus of Simocatta where he speaks of 'a Hunnish binding with both covers bedecked with gold.' On the binding of the Theodelinda Gospels a large cross studded with coloured gems is surrounded by a frame enriched with inlays. (Similar corner decorations are found on antique cameos between the upright of a cross and the edges.) In this finely executed work, garnets are inset in rows of circles with segments of circles engraved within them. The clear-cut, near-classical layout of the covers of this Gospel Book suggests that it was made in an Italian workshop and its dedicatory inscription in Latin points to Rome.

The same technique was employed in the jewelled cross, now lost, that was once in the Sancta Sanctorum, of the Vatican. Alongside rows of large, uncut stones there was an ornamental border of cloisonné work executed in the same manner. This reliquary cross may, too, have been made in a Roman workshop. The widespread influence of this style is demonstrated by the similarly inset decoration of the gold votive crown of the Visigoth king Recceswinth (649-672) which formed part of the treasure hoard from Fuente de Guarrazar, near Toledo, now in Madrid. The protruding vertical arrangement of the gems on this crown obviously affiliates it to the decorative technique of such Italian works as the crown of Theodelinda found at Monza.

When the technique of Visigoth metalwork is examined closely and compared with pieces of the same kind made in Italy, it is seen to be of markedly inferior quality. Many pieces have close affinities with the works of Lombard courtly art that have been discovered in quantities of tombs, some far north of the Alps; for example the royal tombs dating to the first half of the sixth century at Saint-Denis, Cologne and Krefeld-Gellep. They demonstrate the minute attention that the Lombard craftsmen gave to this technique. Some S-shaped fibulae, inset with garnets, are technically akin to the circular fibulae, incrusted with gems, which have been discovered in large numbers in the graveyards of Nocera Umbra and Castel Trosino. A piece from Lingotto, now in Turin Museum, illustrates the extreme delicacy of this cloisonné work at its best; while its oval cells testify to the continuity of the Ostrogoth tradition. An exceptionally beautiful round fibula, with blue stones alternating with garnets, was found in a tomb at Parma. Its kinship with the circular Anglo-Saxon fibulae in the same technique, such as the one discovered at Kingston in Kent, is plain to see. Like the fibula from Lingotto it has a central boss, but it differs from Lombard fibulae in its more elaborate filigree work and its use of animal forms.

246 - JEWELLED CROSS (LOST). FORMERLY IN THE TREASURE OF THE SANCTA SANCTORUM, VATICAN CITY.

247 - BELT BUCKLE. MUSEO ARQUEOLOGICO, MADRID.

248 - JEWELLED CROWN OF KING RECCESWINTH. MUSEO ARQUEOLOGICO, MADRID. ▶

249 - ORNAMENTS OF QUEEN ARNEGONDE. DIRECTION DES ANTIQUITÉS HISTORIQUES, PARIS.

That there was a close connection between Lombard and Anglo-Saxon art is evident—the technique of the magnificent artifacts (British Museum) found in the royal tomb at Sutton Hoo, dating to about 650, proves its existence—but how this came about, how these exchanges of ideas between the islands of the north and the Mediterranean lands took place there is no knowing. Comparing the two groups of works, Nordic and Mediterranean, we get an impression that the Lombards gave more than they received. Anyhow there can be no question that the various types of fibulae inlaid with gems found in Frankish and Alamannic tombs were imported from Italy. Moreover many of the works discovered are obvious imitations of Italian prototypes. For example the round fibulae found in a mid-seventh century Frankish tomb at Soest, in Westphalia, at Pfullingen (now in Stuttgart) and at Charnay (now at Saint-Germain-en-Laye) have close affinities with such Lombard works as the fibulae of Castel Trosino. The superb piece from Schretzheim, however, was probably an Alamannic production; the seething mass of animals, arranged in the form of a swastika (formerly containing cloisonné work) points to a convergence of elements stemming from Lombardy and northern Germany. But some fibulae, such as the silver one with handles found at Wittislingen, adorned with filigree work and inset gems, display equally close affinities with Lombard originals, though alongside these marked similarities we find no less clear associations with Nordic, in particular Frisian works.

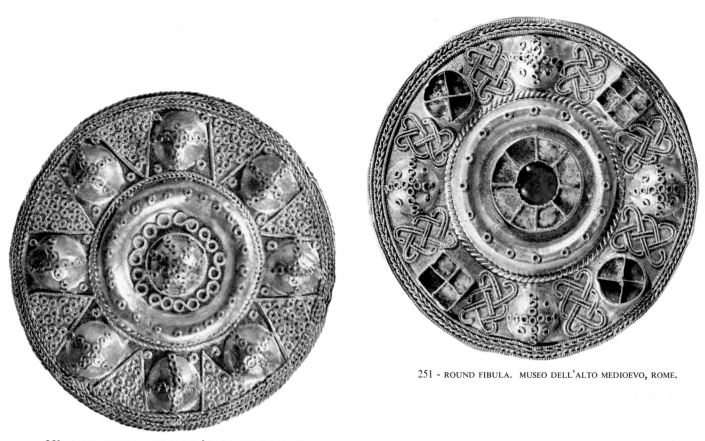

250 - ROUND FIBULA. MUSEO DELL'ALTO MEDIOEVO, ROME.

251 - ROUND FIBULA. MUSEO DELL'ALTO MEDIOEVO, ROME.

252 - LOOPED FIBULAE. RÖMISCH-GERMANISCHES MUSEUM, COLOGNE. — 253 - S-SHAPED FIBULA. WÜRTTEMBERGISCHES LANDESMUSEUM, STUTTGART.

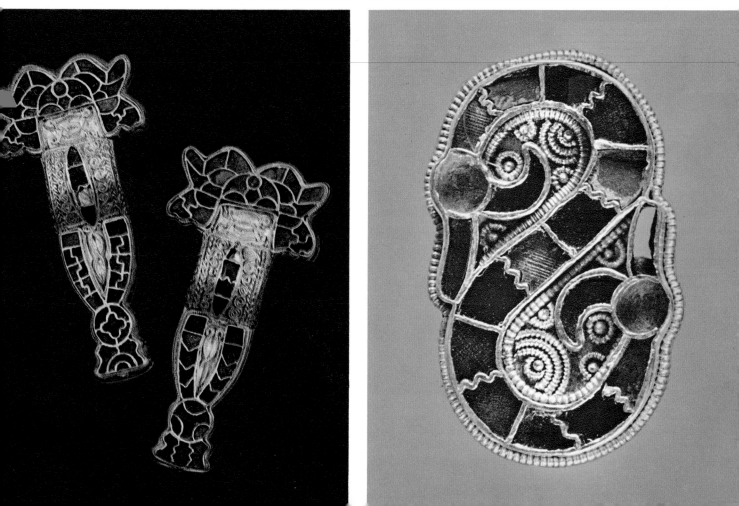

254 - ROUND FIBULA. CITY OF LIVERPOOL MUSEUMS.

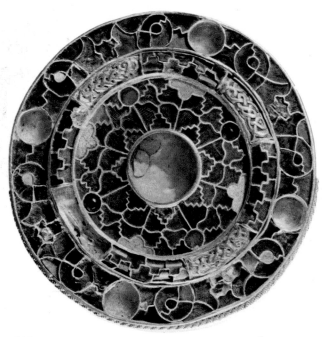

255 - ROUND FIBULA. MUSEO NAZIONALE DI ANTICHITÀ, PARMA.

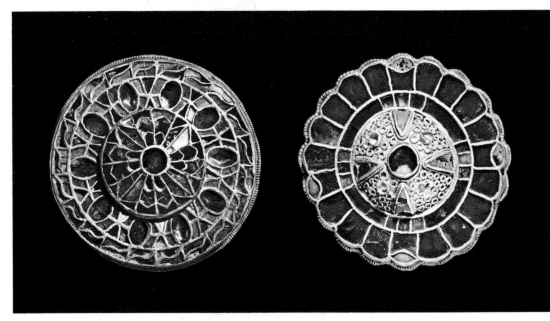

256-257 - ROUND FIBULAE. MUSEO ARCHEOLOGICO, TURIN AND RÖMISCH-GERMANISCHES MUSEUM, COLOGNE.

258 - ROUND FIBULA. MUSÉE DES ANTIQUITÉS NATIONALES, SAINT-GERMAIN-EN-LAYE.

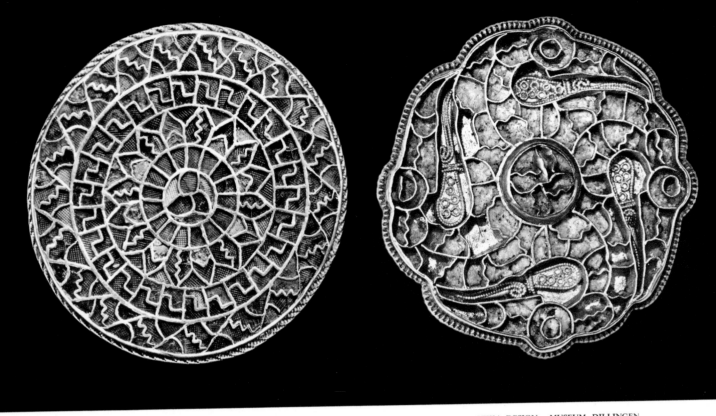

259 - ROUND FIBULA. LANDESMUSEUM, MÜNSTER. — 260 - ROUND FIBULA WITH SWASTIKA DESIGN. MUSEUM, DILLINGEN.

In view of the exceptional technique, all these fibulae may safely be assigned to the latter half of the seventh century.

The workshop of Wigerig, the craftsman who signed the Wittislingen fibula, may well have been in the Rhineland. Representative of the final phase of the cloisonné technique, as evidenced in grave goods of the end of the century, is the large round fibula from a woman's grave at Wittislingen, executed in a technique markedly differing from that of its precursors. On it four interlacing animals project in bold relief from a hollowed-out ground of filigree work. The workshop where this magnificent piece was made has not so far been located, but there are good reasons for believing it was somewhere in south-western Germany, in Alamannic territory; this would also account for the evident influence of Lombard art and the presence of animal ornaments.

During the final phase the technique of cloisonné work developed on independent lines in the western territories of the Frankish kingdom. We find an indication of the shift from the style of work produced in south-western Germany (such as the Täbingen and Pfullingen fibulae) to that of the works produced in France, in the fibula inset with garnets and with a *solidus* of the Emperor Justinian in the centre, which figures on the narrow side of the reliquary of St Andrew in the treasure of Trier cathedral.

West Frankish art came to its full flowering chiefly in the workshops attached to the court of King Dagobert (628-638) in Paris, but there were also flourishing centres at Limoges, Metz, Arras, Lyons. St Eloi (Eligius), who was not only the king's

261 - LOOPED FIBULA. PRÄHISTORISCHE STAATSSAMMLUNG, MUNICH. ▶

262 - ROUND FIBULA. PRÄHISTORISCHE STAATSSAMMLUNG, MUNICH.

minister but comptroller of the royal mint, was an enthusiastic patron of the crafts of gold-and-silver-work and a vast number of pieces, most of which have disappeared, are said to have been commissioned by him. They were preserved in the treasures of great French churches, Notre-Dame of Paris, Saint-Denis, Saint-Loup of Noyon, Saint-Martin of Limoges, the Abbey of Chelles, and others. The most famous work of the period, the large gold chalice of Chelles, ornamented with garnets and blue, white and green gems, was destroyed during the Revolution; it is known today only by a sketch of it made in 1653. The plain, clear-cut geometric layout of the decoration is reminiscent of the Gourdon paten and the partition lines inset with garnets between its sections remind us of the so-called 'cuirass of Theodoric' which, judging by the objects recently discovered at Krefeld-Gellep, more probably formed part of a horse's trappings. In fact this chalice, too, has evident affinities with the Italian inlaid metalwork described at an earlier page and goes to show that the Mediterranean tradition was still active in France in the mid-seventh century. There is every likelihood that Count de Montesquiou-Fezensac was well-advised in identifying a fragment preserved in the Cabinet des Médailles as being part of the cross of St Eloi (Eligius) in Saint-Denis. This fragment, worked in an austere geometric style, carries a pattern of circles, ovals and rectangles alternating with spheres and truncated arcs—a design that figures in a more elaborate form on Ostrogothic fibulae (e.g. the Lingotto fibula) and on the Visigoth crown from Guarrazar.

264 - CHALICE OF ST ELIGIUS. DRAWING OF 1653.

263 - PORTABLE ALTAR OF ST ANDREW. CATHEDRAL TREASURE, TRIER.

265 - CROOK OF ST GERMANUS, DETAIL. DELÉMONT. ▶

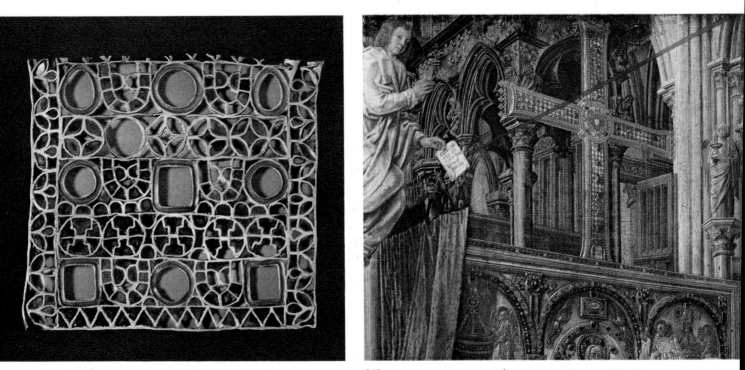

266 - FRAGMENT OF THE CROSS OF ST ELIGIUS. BIBL. NAT., PARIS. — 267 - 'THE CROSS OF ST ELIGIUS.' NATIONAL GALLERY, LONDON.

268 - RELIQUARY CASKET OF TEUDERIGUS. TREASURE, SAINT-MAURICE-D'AGAUNE.

Though it is not absolutely certain that this fragment actually figured on the great cross above the high altar of Saint-Denis, known to us by a fifteenth-century painting in the National Gallery, London, it certainly formed part of the St Eligius imagery and, since the superb cross itself was dismantled or destroyed during the French Revolution, it constitutes one of the most revealing vestiges of what was clearly a *magnum opus* of the seventh century.

Representative of the last phase of cloisonné work is the reliquary casket at Saint-Maurice d'Agaune, made by Undiho and Ello for the local priest Teuderigus. The place of origin and date are not definitely established but a comparison with similar pieces justifies us in believing that this casket was made in the second half of the seventh century, perhaps in one of the abbey workshops. The curiously erratic disposition of the insets rules out any question of a pre-determined structural plan, and chalice-shaped cells of this type are not found on any Lombard model. On the other hand the layout of the planes recalls the ornamental art of certain early round Lombard fibulae, for example those from Pfullingen and Nocera Umbra. But here the technique of the models is carried a stage further and the exceptional size of the flat surfaces tends to create an illusion of infinite space. Stylistically, this casket shows affinities with a later work, the abbatial crook of St Germanus at Delémont (canton of Berne). Here the inlays are limited to S-shaped animal forms arranged in pairs, in combination with the filigree and repoussé work. The year of the foundation of the abbey (c. 640) gives a clue to the dating of this crook—some time in the second half of the seventh century. It was certainly made in a provincial workshop situated on the Alamannic-Burgundian frontier. We can trace in such objects the transition to Carolingian art, chiefly in the crosswise arrangement of large stones, of which we shall find a later example in the Enger reliquary (in Berlin). Here, too, we see in action a new art trend which, though the means employed are somewhat rudimentary, seeks to render plastic form. But the technique of incrustation of polychrome glass was dying out; two hundred years later the author of the *Gesta Dagoberti*, when giving a list of the St Eligius artifacts, observes that 'this technique is no longer employed.'

The Figure Style

Towards the end of the fifth century the infiltration of Oriental, in particular Byzantine art into all the lands of the West and the gradual abandonment under its influence of the realistic style is evident in the renderings of both human figures and animals. There had been premonitory signs of this break with the past even before the Byzantine invasion (c. 540) in Justinian's reign, not only in Ravenna but in the rest of Italy. Its effects were so rapid and so widespread that soon the new 'Byzantine style' came to be regarded as basic to the national art of all the territories of the former Roman Empire. It is not always easy to distinguish the part played by the Germanic invaders in this drastic change-over to a new form of art. In any case the Mediterranean element predominated, especially in Italy (as has been demonstrated in the magisterial studies of Cattaneo, Mâle, Wulff and Toesca). Byzantine works of art found their way into all the western lands and indigenous artists hastened to draw inspiration from the ivories, the silver dishes adorned with ancient motifs and above all the precious silks imported in large numbers, many of which are still preserved in the treasures of Roman churches, in the cathedrals of Sens and Cologne and in several museums. The feeling for plastic values dwindled in all these lands at approximately the same speed, reliefs became steadily flatter, more purely linear. Perspectival effects were eliminated, movement was arrested. Human and animal forms tended more and more towards abstraction and were symmetrized as far as possible, with the result that by the end of the eighth century illusionist effects had been suppressed *in toto*.

Characteristic of the age is the marked predilection for toreutic art. But stone and marble carving now fell out of favour. Art and all its manifestations were aligned to the requirements of the Church. This is why most of the reliefs of this age represent scenes concerned with Christ and the lives of the saints. Secular works are the exception; most interesting among them is the golden hen and her seven chickens, in the Monza treasure. The style of this work seems too advanced for it to be assigned to the time of Theodelinda and we are inclined to date it to a later period (it may even be an Islamic work).

Stone was almost always reserved for architecture in the early Middle Ages and was employed throughout this period almost exclusively for the capitals of pillars, pulpits, choir stalls, ciboria and sarcophagi. Metalwork was employed for the adornment of altar frontals, ciboria, candelabra, chalices and patens. The ever-increasing cult of relics called for sumptuous reliquaries. Only a small proportion of these finely wrought works of art has come down to us, but the treasures of abbeys and monasteries still contain some admirable pieces which have escaped the ravages of pillagers—and ill-advised attempts to modernize. By dint of an intensive study of ancient documents—this has been undertaken in France by Paul Deschamps, Bréhier and Ebersolt—it should be possible to compile an almost complete

◄ 269 - EMPERORS HUNTING. MUSÉE HISTORIQUE DES TISSUS, LYONS.

description of the metalwork of the early Middle Ages. Of no less interest for the light they throw on the history of medieval style are the smaller objects, such as the buckles and fibulae discovered in sixth-century tombs.

Though artistically inferior to the works made in the ateliers under royal patronage and those of the monasteries, these objects keep well abreast of the widespread progress of the decorative arts. But in the eighth century this progress seems to have taken a different turn. Thus hardly any objects are now found in the tombs and such few as have survived derive from workshops maintaining an exceptionally high standard. The transition from the classic-Byzantine style of the sixth century to an ever-increasing stylization can be seen most clearly in Italy, in the art

270 - HEN AND SEVEN CHICKS. CATHEDRAL TREASURE, MONZA.

271 - FRONTAL PLAQUE OF A HELMET. BARGELLO, FLORENCE.

of Ravenna. Whereas in the confronted peacocks among vineshoots facing the monogram of Christ on the sarcophagus of Archbishop Theodore (a fifth-century work) we still find a concern for plastic values, the change that came over art in the next century is evidenced by the sarcophagus of St Ecclesius in San Vitale on which the peacock motif recurs, but treated calligraphically, without the least hint of depth. The style adopted here resembles that of another sixth-century work, the ambo of Archbishop Agnellus (556-569) in the cathedral. From the iconographic viewpoint the gilt-bronze helmet front discovered at Val di Nievole, near Lucca and bearing the effigy of King Agilulf (591-615) enthroned, recalls the effigies of the emperors made in late antiquity. This, the earliest representation of a Germanic monarch seated on his throne that has come down to us, illustrates a new form of barbarian stylization. And, comparing it with the portrait of the Emperor Theodosius on a *missorium* at Madrid, we can see how far the art of the first period of the Middle Ages has departed from its prototypes.

Further east, another active centre of Lombard stone carving flourished in the Friuli district, chiefly at Cividale. A number of striking works from this region have been preserved, among them the animal figures, representations of peacocks, sea monsters, griffins and stags, in which the School of Cividale excelled. They adorned seven archivolts of the octangular ciborium above the font, originally in the baptistery, now housed in the cathedral of Cividale. They have close affinities with the reliefs at Pavia and with the one bearing the name of Bishop Lopicenus in Modena museum, though they do not attain the same high quality. The ciborium dates to the time of the patriarch Callistus, who supervised the building of the baptistery (c. 730). Thus this work is contemporary with the altar of San Martino, which was

272 - FRONTAL PLAQUE OF A HELMET, DETAIL: KING AGILULF ON HIS THRONE. BARGELLO, FLORENCE.

built by Duke Ratchis (from 734 on) thanks to donations made by Count Pemmo, and completed about 737. On the front is an effigy of Christ in Majesty and on the sides are represented the three Kings of the East and the Visitation of the Virgin. Though the iconography clearly derives from the East, no trace of Oriental influence can be detected in the style. Here the abstraction of the human figure and the systematic rejection of any attempt to render space are carried to the highest possible pitch; bodies are treated as mere ornaments, little more than symbols. The plaque representing two evangelist symbols—this motif was reproduced on the balustrade of the baptistery of San Callisto—has suffered greatly from the ravages of time; it belongs to a late phase of Cividale sculpture, whereas the triple cable moulding of the upper string-course is inspired by earlier models. The two evangelist symbols, which are treated with an even greater spareness, point the way to one of the outstanding, and latest, works of this group: the plaque representing the evangelists, utilized later as a baldachin in the baptistery. This piece is dated by an inscription on which can be deciphered the name of the prelate commissioning it, the patriarch Sigualdus (762-776).

Soon after this came one of the most remarkable and most discussed works of the period: the stucco decorations of the so-called Tempietto (Santa Maria in

273 - CIVIDALE, SANTA MARIA IN VALLE. ENTRANCE WALL. ▶

Valle) at Cividale. They have been assigned to various periods ranging from the eighth to the thirteenth century. After a close examination of the structure of the edifice and the nature of the decorations E. Dyggve has been convinced that the stuccoes date to the eighth century; they were added to an already existing building, and the paintings were made later. Only one part of the decoration has survived, that on the entrance wall. The upper register, on either side of a window whose arch is adorned with plant motifs, contains six figures of saints in relief. In the lower portion of the wall a relatively large portal lunette is lavishly decorated with palmettes, vineshoots and bunches of grapes, also in relief. Two friezes of rosettes separate the upper from the lower register. When we observe the ample modelling of the reliefs, the hieratic postures of the figures and their ceremonial garments (in the Byzantine style) we cannot fail to be surprised by the differences between this work and its immediate predecessors, for example the Pemmo altar. It is easy to see why some authorities, among them Geza de Francovich, have assigned these reliefs to a later (the Ottonian) period. Nevertheless, a comparison of them with Byzantine reliefs such as the ivory plaque representing a female saint from Sant' Ansano, Fiesole, suggests that these stuccoes may very well have been made about the year 800 or a little earlier.

The same applies to the decorations and ornamentations, characterized by an exceptional feeling for strong effects of light and shade, which led Strzygowski to see in them signs of Oriental (chiefly Syrian) influences. Indeed the differences from all previous Lombard works, both in their technique and in the maker's lively sense of plastic values, are so pronounced that, like Cattaneo, we can hardly fail to see in these works the hand of Oriental artists. There is no knowing if these were Byzantine artists expelled from the East who had made their way to Cividale as a result of the iconoclast controversy. In any case there can be no doubt of the basic affinities between their work and the Castelseprio frescoes. This drastic break with tradition might also be accounted for by a difference in the taste of the new Frankish overlords, a predilection for a classicism resembling that which was making headway in the north at the Palace School of Charlemagne. On the other hand, there are conspicuous differences between the stucco reliefs at Cividale and Ottonian reliefs, for example those of the ciborium of Sant'Ambrogio, Milan, or the representation of the sun at Solnhofen (Bavaria)—works that are datable to about the year 1000 or even later. And, stylistically, the stuccoes in San Pietro al Monte at Civate, near Como, and those at Müstair in the Grisons (Switzerland) are still more different. Here Byzantine influences, though still perceptible, are already losing ground in this late period.

In central Italy figure sculpture underwent much the same changes as in northern Italy, and differed only in its more primitive handling of forms. Traces of Lombard elements have almost completely disappeared. The few representations of human figures and above all those of animals have an unquestionable kinship with Oriental art. Of the works that have survived, the altar of Magister Ursus (San Pietro in Valle, near Ferentillo) commissioned by Duke Hilderic Dagileopa of Spoleto (after 739) is a typical example.

274 - CIVIDALE, SANTA MARIA IN VALLE. ENTRANCE WALL, DETAIL: THREE HOLY WOMEN. ▶

275 - CIVIDALE, SANTA MARIA IN VALLE. ENTRANCE WALL, DETAIL.

276 - CIVIDALE, SANTA MARIA IN VALLE. ENTRANCE WALL, DETAIL.

277 - ALTAR OF DUKE RATCHIS: CHRIST IN MAJESTY. CHAPTER ROOM, SAN MARTINO, CIVIDALE.

278 - ALTAR SLAB OF MAGISTER URSUS. SAN PIETRO, FERENTILLO.

279 - ALTAR OF DUKE RATCHIS: ADORATION OF THE MAGI. CHAPTER ROOM, SAN MARTINO, CIVIDALE.

280 - ALTAR OF DUKE RATCHIS: ADORATION OF THE MAGI, DETAIL. SAN MARTINO, CIVIDALE.

281 - ALTAR OF DUKE RATCHIS: THE VISITATION. CHAPTER ROOM, SAN MARTINO, CIVIDALE.

In its handling of linear relief, without recourse to any effects of plasticity, eighth-century art was brought here to a perfection never attained elsewhere, not even in northern Italy. Beneath three cruciform disks stand Ursus and another man, both treated as purely ornamental motifs. This abstract style prevailed in central Italy over a long period, and was especially appreciated at Rome, as is evidenced by the reliefs with hunting scenes in San Saba in Rome and at Civita Castellana. Only a few examples of the pre-Carolingian art that flourished in art centres in Campania have been preserved in Naples and Cimitile. However, such works of a high artistic quality as have come down to us show that in this region Oriental and above all Byzantine influences were of paramount importance. Nevertheless the art of antiquity was by no means extinct: copies of antique bas-reliefs were still being made.

Germanic elements played a very minor role, even in the works adorning the residences of the Lombard aristocracy at, for example, Capua, and their courtly art was tributary in the main to Byzantine-Italian influences. Still there were some exceptions, for instance two interesting, if rather perplexing bas-reliefs representing animals and a knight fighting a dragon, in the cathedral of Aversa. Stylistically this relief pertains to the Lombard art of northern Italy, whereas its theme seems to derive from Nordic models. But on another part of the same plaque, where elephants and other animals are grouped in a circle, we can see unmistakable reminiscences of Byzantine and Islamic textiles.

The same is true of a curious altar screen in Sant'Aspreno, Naples, decorated with fabulous animals. The carvings in San Felice at Cimitile, near Nola, are datable to approximately the same period (from 700 on) as these pieces in southern Italy: the period when Bishop Leo III had the old church rebuilt and its woodwork and pillars decorated in the Oriental manner.

The contemporary figure sculpture of the Visigoth empire followed the same course as Italian art; its Mediterranean connections are evident. After the break-up, in 507, of the kingdom of Toulouse, the transfer of the capital to Toledo, and the achievement of religious unity under King Reccared, the fusion of Visigoth and Italic elements was carried a stage further. Here, too, at the end of the sixth century, Byzantine art firmly established itself. Soon the new forms imported by the sea routes from Egypt, North Africa, Italy and Sicily became the order of the day. The carvings and, above all, the many objects in bronze that have been discovered, buckles and fibulae, testify to a progressive decline of the Visigothic style down to the time (c. 711) when it was totally extinguished by the Arab invasions. As in Italy, figure carving was almost exclusively restricted to monumental sculpture; hardly any free-standing statuary has come down to us.

Even in the kingdom of the Franks it is extremely hard to trace the evolution of figure art in the pre-Carolingian period. Political upheavals, wars and famines account for the disappearance of all but a few examples of it. To make things worse, recurrent changes and cleavages at every level of the social system impeded any orderly development.

283 - HELMET OF A PRINCE. ALTERTUMSMUSEUM, MAINZ.

◄ 282 - KNIGHT FIGHTING A DRAGON. CATHEDRAL, AVERSA.

284 - BELT BUCKLE. MUSEO ARQUEOLOGICO, BARCELONA.

Whereas the Gallo-Roman substratum of the population remained obstinately attached to the art traditions of antiquity, the new overlords, scions of the Frankish nobility, did their utmost to promote an aristocratic art congenial to their status, while the Frankish peasantry was in course of creating a popular art stemming from more distinctively Germanic sources. Many examples of this peasant art have been found in the tombs in public graveyards. To the Gallo-Roman population must be added the many foreigners, mostly engaged in trade and commerce, who had poured in from Syria, Egypt and India. In 585 King Gontran was welcomed at Orleans by three races: Latins, Syrians and Jews. These were certainly the men who, along with the pilgrims, introduced Oriental works of art into Gaul. There are innumerable references to these works in contemporary records.

Several manuscripts, one of them the *Gesta Dagoberti*, also contain references to precious fabrics adorning the walls, pillars and vaults of churches. It is round about the year 500 that we find the first figurative motifs inspired by Oriental models. These are the adornments of the warriors' helmets specially made to be buried in princely tombs. Mention may be made in this context of the recent finds in

285 - BELT BUCKLE. MUSÉE DE CLUNY, PARIS.

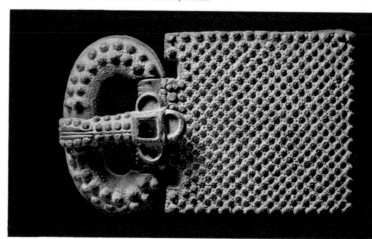

286 - CLASP FOR A BAG. MUSÉE DES ANTIQUITÉS NATIONALES, SAINT-GERMAIN-EN-LAYE.

the royal graves at Morken and Krefeld-Gellep (Rhineland) and the helmet of the 'Young Prince' in Cologne cathedral. The fronts of all these helmets were adorned with a profusion of figural elements, either stamped or engraved. Two such helmets are in an exceptionally fine state of preservation: one at Chalon-sur-Saône, decorated with scenes of fighting animals, the other, found at Planig near Mainz, with birds pecking at grapes.

Both these decorative motifs are Oriental; they are often found in Syrian mosaics and Coptic textiles. Quite possibly these helmets were imported from the Ostrogothic domain, but their widespread popularity in the Frankish empire proves that they answered to the taste of the great feudal lords of western Europe.

Two highly interesting works dating to about this period are a bronze flagon from a tomb at Lavoye and a gold clasp (for a bag inset with garnets) which was found along with it; both are now in the Musée des Antiquités Nationales at Saint-Germain-en-Laye. The flagon, which is decorated with Christological scenes stamped in relief, points to a change of attitude on the part of the Franks *vis-à-vis* the productions of the early Christian age. True, the decorations on the rim still resemble those of the pottery of the post-Roman period, but the stylization of human forms has been carried much further. And on other cult objects of the same type, such as the piece (now lost) from Miannay (Somme) and the one from Wiesoppenheim, near Worms, the human form has undergone a still greater transformation. Yet even here we can discern reminiscences of ancient models. This becomes evident when we compare them with early Christian (fifth-century) bronze reliefs such as those from Vermand, Mainz and Trier.

287 - FLAGON WITH CHRISTOLOGICAL SCENES. SAINT-GERMAIN-EN-LAYE. ▶

289 - LEAF OF THE SAINT-LUPICIN DIPTYCH, DETAIL. PARIS. — 290 - LEAF OF A DIPTYCH. THE METROPOLITAN MUSEUM OF ART, NEW YORK.

Though in these works traces of antique art are still discernible, the break with western tradition in the treatment of figures was a *fait accompli* after the middle of the sixth century. Henceforth the iconography of the Eastern Church and its art style were paramount throughout the West. The ecclesiastical authorities in particular enjoined the use of eastern models for the works they commissioned, and to such effect that it is often hard to say if a given work is of eastern or of local provenance. An example is the Saint-Lupicin ivory diptych in five panels now in the Bibliothèque Nationale, Paris, on which figure Mary and the Christ-child, with scenes from the life of Christ on the edges. Its kinship with the diptych

288 - BOOK COVER, DETAIL. TREASURE OF SAINT-ANDOCHE, SAULIEU.

291 - CLOSURE SLAB: CHRIST BENEATH AN ARCH. MUSÉE CENTRAL, METZ.

from Echmiadzin, which was certainly made in the eastern part of the Byzantine empire, is unmistakable. And its close affiliation to the ivory throne of Bishop Maximian at Ravenna enables us to date this diptych a little after 550. Here the clumsiness of the bodies, as compared with those on authentically Byzantine reliefs, and the decline in the quality of the composition are so marked that we are tempted to assign it to a workshop in Gaul. This view is supported when we compare it with the book covers representing Christ and the Madonna, now at Saulieu, in which we see the barbarization of the forms of the large diptych carried a stage further. The over-large heads, the stiffness of the folds of garments and the squat bodies are typically Gallo-Roman. Another group of works, assignable to the end of the Merovingian period and preserved in what was then north-eastern Gaul—the apostle figures from Trier, Tongres and Mettlach—evidence a still more complete disintegration of forms. When, for example, we compare the Mettlach St Peter (Metropolitan Museum) with analogous reliefs in the cathedral of Ravenna, it is clear that, though the iconography has not changed, the process of 'disincarnation' has been carried to its extreme limit. The development of Frankish art, which always kept in touch with the royal courts, was not wholly uniform. In it we find extraneous elements, sometimes hard to identify, intermingling with the 'Byzantine' style. Moreover local schools seem to have played a much greater part in it. But the examples that have survived are too few and too fragmentary for us to differentiate between the various ateliers.

Such works from the east of the Frankish kingdom as have come down to us are of poor quality and their style, as compared with that of the eastern Mediterranean, is patently Germanic. Thus, on the chancel slabs of Saint-Pierre at Metz, a typically Germanic decoration of animals and interlaces figures beside Oriental palmettes resembling those on early Aquitanian sarcophagi. The representation of Christ under an arcade has much in common with a stucco bas-relief in the Orthodox Baptistery at Ravenna and sarcophagus reliefs of the south of France. This curious mixture of Mediterranean human and animal forms is also found in works of smaller dimensions, such as Burgundian 'Daniel' and Orant buckles, and the gold fibula from Limons studded with small garnets, in which a circular faceted band entirely made in openwork and shaped like a nimbus surrounds the Holy Face.

Some large stone monuments were set up in the heart of the Rhineland, not far from Andernach. They are now preserved in Bonn. On one of them, a tomb stele from Gondorf on the Moselle, figures the bust of a bearded man holding a book and clad in a tunic and pallium. This may well be an image of Christ, a *Majestas Domini*, since two doves perch on the man's shoulders. In this relief the influence of Mediterranean models is evident, even more than in the chancel slabs of Metz. On the tomb stele in the Christian-Frankish cemetery of Niederdollendorf Germanic idiosyncrasies are still more pronounced; nonetheless it may have been made in one of the same workshops.

The dead man is shown on the front of the stele, armed with his Breitsax (broadsword) in a sheath of riveted leather—a type form widely current in the

292 - BELT BUCKLE. MUSÉE D'ART ET D'HISTOIRE, GENEVA. — 293 - ROUND FIBULA. BIBLIOTHÈQUE NATIONALE, PARIS.

295 - TOMB STELE (FRONT AND BACK). RHEINISCHES LANDESMUSEUM, BONN.

last three quarters of the seventh century. The warrior is combing his hair and above him swoops a serpent—symbol of death—seeking to devour him. On the back Christ is shown in kingly mien carrying a spear. The old-fashioned technique of this stele recalls that of the early wood carvings. Stylistically, a contemporary stele from Moselkern (near Kochem) has affinities with it; on it, too, figures an image of Christ on the Cross, treated however in the Christian spirit. Here the artist seems to have taken guidance from insular as well as from Mediterranean prototypes.

The last phase of this progressive stylization can be seen in motifs of the reliefs (now in a fragmentary state) on the large reliquary casket in the church of Essen-Werden. As on the Niederdollendorf stele the figure of Christ crucified between two angels on the front is designated 'REX'. The animals on the lid are reminiscent of Mediterranean and Oriental models. Here we can gauge the extent to which the feeling for plastic values had died out in the Frankish art of the

◀ 294 - RELIQUARY CASKET. CHURCH OF ST LIUDGER, ESSEN-WERDEN.

Rhineland during the eighth century. An enormous number of small articles adorned with figure motifs have been brought to light by excavation. The bulk of the works of art found in graveyards of the late sixth and the seventh century consisted of objects in repoussé-work or moulded: buckles, fibulae, ornamental disks. Far fewer eighth-century works have been found, since the dead were then no longer buried in cemeteries containing several rows of graves. With the spread of Christianity more and more burials were made near churches and no grave goods were placed in the coffins.

The coins which have been found in a great many tombs enable us to date their contents. When these finds are classified and compared it becomes clear that the cultural evolution of all the Germanic tribes did not proceed everywhere on the same lines. The various communities can be clearly distinguished not only by the shapes of their buckles and fibulae but also by the nature of the figure motifs. Nothing definite is known as yet about the workshops where they were made, but it seems safe to assume that most of the goldsmiths and metalworkers lived in the larger towns and that they belonged to and catered for different social classes. The mass-produced objects made for the humbler walks of society differed greatly from those intended for the nobility. Ancient models were imitated, but given cruder forms, and this 'popular art' incorporated a larger number of purely Germanic elements. But often the objects made for the upper classes too were, stylistically speaking, barbarized.

For the cheap, mass-produced objects, the process usually employed was that of stamping. As early as the fifth century copies were made in the northern lands of the medallions of Roman emperors and this led to the large-scale manufacture of gold bracteates, stamped medallions which to begin with exactly reproduced the ancient prototypes. Before long, however, they became completely stylized. These imitations of ancient models made their appearance on the continent at an early date. The effigy of 'Rome enthroned,' adapted to the Germanic taste, figures on pieces found in women's graves at Andernach, at Dotzheim (near Wiesbaden) and also in France, at Maizières-le-Vic (near Nancy). Elsewhere, in tombs at Monceau-le-Neuf and La Sablonnière, we see the emperor riding in his triumphal chariot.

It is quite possible that the populace at large regarded these ornaments as prophylactic amulets. That is certainly true of the pieces bearing religious images: the Adoration of the Magi, warrior saints or knights in prayer. Pagan and Christian images, such as a representation of the Roman emperor and that of St George slaying the dragon, are sometimes combined on the same piece—as on the Ennabeuren reliquary, made in a workshop of south-west Germany active in the seventh century. To the same century is to be assigned the bronze disk representing the Adoration of the Magi found at Minden (near Trier). Here, again, we have an obvious imitation of Mediterranean models of the fifth or sixth century, made in bronze in Rome and in stamped gold in southern Italy. The fact that bronze was always used for copies of this kind made in northern Europe is easily accounted for by the shortage of precious metals in the seventh century.

296 - TOMB STELE: CHRIST (?). RHEINISCHES LANDESMUSEUM, BONN.

297 - RELIQUARY CASKET: A HOLY KNIGHT AND DANIEL IN THE LIONS' DEN. CHURCH OF ENNABEUREN.

298 - ROUND FIBULA. RHEINISCHES LANDESMUSEUM, TRIER. — 299 - DISK. MUSEO ARCHEOLOGICO NAZIONALE, CIVIDALE.

One of the images most in favor with the Germanic cultural élite was that of the 'holy knight,' appealing as it did both to Christian and to pagan sentiment. A leitmotiv of (pagan) Germanic symbolism, it figures on many Nordic works, such as the helmets from Wendel and Sutton Hoo and, later, on the Hornhausen tombstone (Halle Museum). A survey of all the antecedents of the knight image in antiquity and its syncretic derivatives in early Christian art would take us too far afield. These seventh-century figurations were certainly inspired by fibulae imported from the East, and the same is true of those of La Copelanz, Güttingen and Strasbourg. The motif was also very popular in the Lombard region, where we find the same knight represented on a stamped gold disk found at Cividale, but under a barbarized aspect, carrying a shield and spear. Here the style has been completely transformed and the image of the dragon-slayer of late antiquity, surrounded by elaborate strapwork, is barely recognizable. In view of its distinctively 'period' style this disk is reminiscent of the stamped gold cross adorned with heads found in the tomb of Gisulf at Cividale. The figure has been identified by some authorities as the Duke of Friuli, killed in a battle with the Avars in 611. But, given the fact of the affinity between its style and that of the late seventh-century stone carving at Cividale (e.g. the stele of Sigualdus), this work might equally well be dated later, to the second half of the seventh century. The Cividale disk also

300 - JEWELLED CROSS ADORNED WITH EIGHT HEADS. MUSEO ARCHEOLOGICO NAZIONALE, CIVIDALE.

recalls the effigy (in lead) of Christ crucified from Paspels which is now in Chur cathedral (Grisons, Switzerland).

Related to this is the work (now in the Stuttgart museum) in stamped iron gilt stemming from the Alamannic regions, which was found at Pliezhausen. On comparing it with the Cividale disk, we find the stylistic mutation carried a stage further. The horseman, pursued doubtless by a demon and brandishing his lance, is riding in a manner that recalls the figurations on the helmet from Sutton Hoo; stretched on the ground beneath him lies a foeman who is thrusting his sword into the horse's breast. Quite possibly this Alamannic bracteate worked in the manner of a fibula derived from Lombard prototypes and not directly from Roman imperial medallions or from gravestones. The motif of symmetrically disposed lions above the horseman's head tends to confirm this view.

The horseman with lowered lance, cast in bronze and gilt, which was found near Stabio (Ticino, Switzerland) more resembles a *venatio*. It served as a decoration on a circular Lombard shield and was made in the seventh century in the same atelier as the Pliezhausen horseman. The other appliques on this shield, two dogs

301 - ORNAMENTAL PLAQUE FROM A SHIELD. HISTORISCHES MUSEUM, BERNE.

302 - ORNAMENTAL PLAQUE FROM A SHIELD. HISTORISCHES MUSEUM, BERNE.

and a tree, show that it is a hunting scene like the ones often represented in late antiquity on textiles, mosaics and metal objects (e.g. the silver plate in the Vatican and the Ittenheim phalera). Its verve and the frankly realistic presentation of horse and rider have exact parallels in certain works of late antiquity, such as the silver disks in the Vatican, Perugia and Verona. Thus we are justified in assigning this piece to an Italian armourer's workshop patronized by the Lombard nobility. The pendant of the Stabio horseman, made in the same workshop, is in the Museo Nazionale, Florence. On the other hand it seems likely that some other figure adornments of Lombard shields were made by Germanic craftsmen. The gilt eagle in the Musée de Cluny, Paris (which may have figured on the same shield as the two other applied ornaments in Munich) is a striking example of this; it is wholly Nordic both in conception and in its thoroughgoing stylization.

In the Alamannic domain, this horseman image developed into a more specific type, representative of which are some openwork disks found in women's tombs of the seventh century. An excellent specimen is the one discovered at Bräunlingen and now in Karlsruhe museum. On all these disks the rider is presented realistically, with his spear pointing downwards. Whether these works were of pagan or Christian provenance is still an open question. However this may be, it is clear that they had a symbolic value. This is confirmed by the fact that their equivalents, the openwork disks in bronze, equally numerous, made in the Frankish and (to a lesser extent) in the Burgundian domains, always show the horseman in

303 - ORNAMENTAL PLAQUE FROM A SHIELD. PRÄHISTORISCHE STAATSSAMMLUNG, MUNICH.

304 - OPENWORK DISK. ESSLINGEN.

◄ 305 - BELT BUCKLE. LAUSANNE.

the Orant attitude. Quite possibly this motif was borrowed directly from Coptic originals, such as the wooden combs on which an Orant rider often figured.

Typical of the art of the Burgundian region are the bronze buckles, representing Daniel in the lions' den, produced in large numbers in the neighbourhood of the Lake of Geneva. In them the Christian significance of the motif and its derivation from Early Christian prototypes are particularly evident. Quite possibly Irish monks, in close contact with the Egyptian monasteries, introduced it into the Rhone region. In the Germanic countries it seems to have been regarded as a talismanic symbol, averting evil from its owner. The earliest of these buckles, dating to about the year 600, such as those from Daillens, Lavigny and Chalon-sur-Saône, while still inspired by models made in the Christian East, were barbarized versions, executed in a purely linear style.

The changes that came over this type form are of much interest to the art historian. In the first half of the seventh century the purport of the theme grew

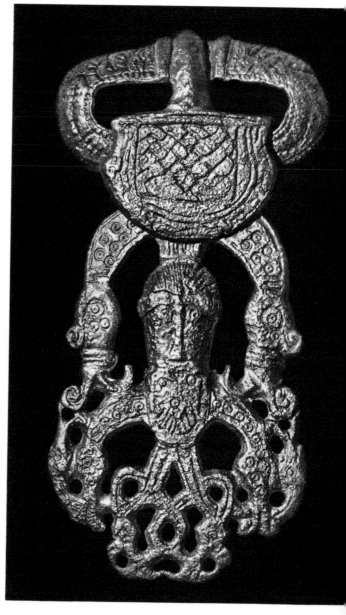

306 - OPENWORK DISK. FÜRSTLICH HOHENZOLLERNSCHES MUSEUM, SIGMARINGEN.

307 - BELT BUCKLE. MUSÉE DES ANTIQUITÉS, ROUEN. ▶

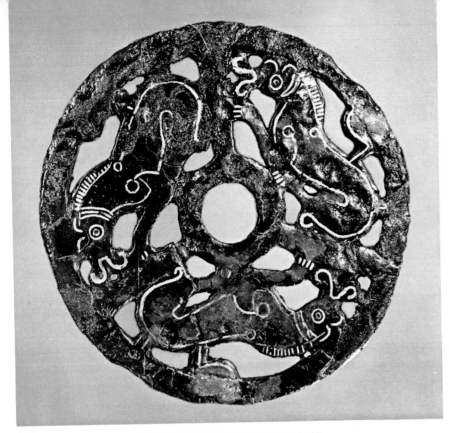

308 - OPENWORK DISK. PRÄHISTORISCHE STAATSSAMMLUNG, MUNICH.

less and less distinct, until finally, under the influence of Animal Style II, the lions become mere heraldic emblems and Daniel's face and body dwindle almost out of recognition, as on a buckle from Yverdon (Switzerland). In the Visigoth domain, however, the Daniel theme was treated in a different manner, dominated by Byzantine influences, as is evidenced by a buckle in the Berlin Museum on which the prophet is represented half-length, without any trace of Germanic stylization.

When the motif on the buckle plaque is presented vertically, the animals flanking the main figure are omitted and all that remains is a man in the Orant posture. But, as is shown by a buckle from La Balme, now in the Geneva Museum, the figure soon underwent a stylization, a regression to a primitive type of imagery. All the works of this group have such a pronounced family likeness, even in technique, that we believe they were made in the same workshop, located quite likely in Geneva. We see a west Frankish variant in an openwork belt buckle found at Criel, now in Rouen Museum; it represents a demon, its dangling arms tipped with birds' heads pointing downwards, beneath a two-headed snake. This device had clearly a protective, evil-averting function and the same applies to the Alamannic openwork disk from Gammertingen. The central figure, a crouching bearded demon, probably represents Hercules, club in hand, and is surrounded by a circle of eagles' heads. Other Burgundian buckles are adorned with motifs stemming from the Christian East, such as Christ's Entry into Jerusalem and the Three Youths in the Fiery Furnace. But an imperfect understanding of the basic themes has led not only to the transformation of the figures into mere ornaments but to

278

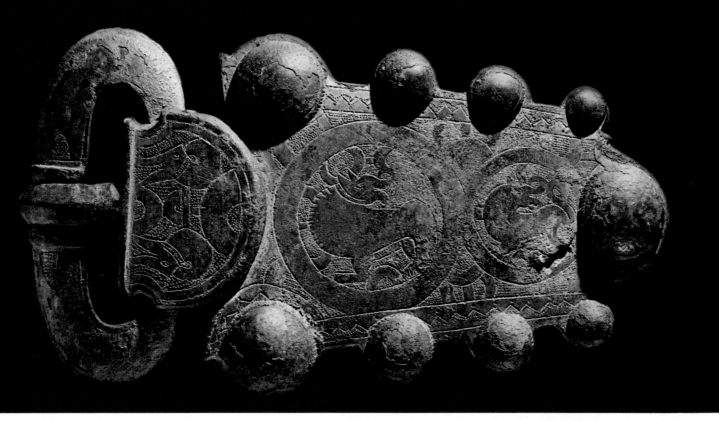

309 - BELT BUCKLE. MUSÉE DES BEAUX-ARTS, TROYES.

an illogical multiplication of their original number. Sometimes, on the belt buckles, paired heraldic animals are combined with such ancient Oriental motifs as the Tree of Life and the Fountain of Youth. This imagery is found both on Visigothic openwork buckles and on the more diversified buckles of the Burgundian domain. Also to the Germanic Merovingian milieu are assignable the openwork disks mentioned above, most of which are adorned with geometric designs, but some with figures. We have an example of this latter class in a group (whose theme is obscure) of two warriors fighting and a man and woman. A circular ornament in wrought iron, unique of its kind, was discovered in a Bavarian tomb at Mühltal and is now preserved in the Munich museum. It contains figurations of three squatting winged horses (or griffins) of the Burgundian type arranged wheelwise, so that spun round it would give an effect of animals in movement. (The Tree of Life is not included.) Though Oriental influences can be seen in the surviving Burgundian and Visigothic works, they are still more evident in the massive belt buckles made in a Frankish workshop active in Aquitaine. Here the fabulous animals, usually gazing backwards, set out in rows or isolated in medallions, show marked divergences from their equivalents in the Germanic lands. Both the technique, of large empty spaces telling out on a profusely chiselled ground, and the style, in which we sense a lively feeling for natural forms, are quite different. The backward-gazing animal had already made its appearance in the north of France in the sixth century but under a modified form, in which filigree work and inset gems played a considerable part. An example is the large belt buckle, in fine condition, now in the museum of Troyes.

310 - SCABBARD (LOST).

From the technical viewpoint the stamped reliefs on a silver scabbard that was found at Gutenstein in an Alamannic tomb of the second half of the seventh century are akin to those on the horseman disk from Pliezhausen. The imagery on it reflects the religious conceptions and practices of the northern Germanic races and might indeed be described as a sublimation of their theogony. Similar images, executed in the same technique, figure on the sumptuous helmets found in the graves of Anglo-Saxon and Scandinavian princes and on the stamped bronze objects from Torslunda and the embossed helmet decorations from Sutton Hoo. The figures, especially those of the two warriors wearing wolf masks, carrying sword, spear and quiver, and the surging throng of capering animals, are treated in a typically Germanic spirit, as is the man in combat with two confronted animals.

This use of figural representations executed in the repoussé technique was not

311 - RELIQUARY CASKET OF MUMMA. ABBEY CHURCH, SAINT-BENOÎT-SUR-LOIRE. ▶

confined to the adornment of such objects as helmet plaques, weapons and fibulae. We find the same technique employed in a large group of Merovingian reliquaries, some of them made to be hung at eye level. The house shape given these objects recalls the far more sumptuous reliquary embellished with precious gems from Saint-Maurice-d'Agaune, whereas the much less elaborate execution of the Merovingian reliquaries produces the effect of a relatively inexpert imitation. Some, for example those of Chur and Andenne (at Namur), are adorned merely with an interlace, while others carry embossed figurative stamped designs and still show affinities with the Ennabeuren casket. The execution is so primitive in places as to rule out any reliable dating. Hence the importance of the Saint-Benoît-sur-Loire reliquary, since it is known to have been presented by a lady named Mumma to the abbey of Fleury-sur-Loire, the date of whose foundation (651) is established. The effigies of the six half-length angels (or apostles) on the lid are stylized, purely linear. Other reliquaries of the same type, in copper repoussé-work, keep to this same primitive

312 - RELIQUARY CASKET: VIRGIN AND CHILD BETWEEN ST PETER AND ST PAUL. MUSÉE DE CLUNY, PARIS.

style; for example the caskets adorned with two busts at Saint-Bonnet-Avalouze, the more elaborate reliquary shrine in the Musée de Cluny, Paris, on which are represented the Virgin and Child between Sts Peter and Paul, and above all the chrismal reliquary in the church of Saint-Evroult at Mortain. Reliquaries of this type persisted until the beginning of the Carolingian period, when a new, more realistic

313 - RELIQUARY CASKET. TREASURE OF SAINT-EVROULT, MORTAIN. ▶

314 - RELIQUARY CASKET OF PEPIN OF AQUITAINE. TREASURE OF SAINTE-FOY, CONQUES.

315 - RELIQUARY CASKET OF BISHOP ALTHEUS. CATHEDRAL TREASURE, SION.

style came into vogue. The most significant examples of this change are a reliquary from Enger (Westphalia), now in Berlin, and the one commissioned by Bishop Altheus (died 799 at Sion), dating to about the same time. Similar in conception is the famous reliquary said to have been presented by Pepin of Aquitaine (died 838) to the monastery of Conques. We must not, however, overlook the fact that when it was restored in 1955, it seemed that only the form of the original reliquary and some small enamel plaques had survived unchanged. The image of Christ crucified, between the Virgin and St John (found inside it) and its filigree ornamentation enhanced with gems and intaglios belong in part, already, to the Romanesque period.

W. F. VOLBACH

316 - RELIQUARY CASKET. STAATLICHE MUSEEN, BERLIN.

Conclusion

THE authors of this volume have collated a variety of data—facts and documents—bearing on the period it covers. They have abstained from reviving or discussing the often heated controversies which formerly loomed large in studies of European art of the period following the capture of a portion of the Roman Empire by the barbarians. These controversies had their point when they arose but they now seem sadly antiquated. Yet there is no question that by passionately taking sides for or against Rome, for or against the barbarians, those early writers, whether romantics or classicists, rendered no mean service to art history, for these conflicts of ideas stimulated the intensive research whose fruits we reap today.

One of the objects the present work achieves is to demonstrate and illustrate the beauty and originality of the so-called 'barbarian' metalwork. That traditional epithet is justified by the fact that this fascinating art, which reigned supreme in all the new states founded by the invaders, owed much to craftsmen hailing from northern and eastern Europe. However, recent research has made it clear that this 'barbarian' metalwork derived the best elements of its style and some of its techniques from contacts with the arts of the Mediterranean basin. Nor must we forget that, during the first part of the early Middle Ages, there was no change from the methods current in the Late Empire so far as stone-built architecture and marble sculpture were concerned.

Until the violent upheavals due to the conquest and occupation of a large part of the Roman world by the barbarians, Christian art had displayed a remarkable unity. This was shattered by the great invasions. In the sixth century Syria, Byzantium and the ancient provinces of the Roman Empire contained, like Italy, Spain and Gaul, schools of religious architecture which, though each had characteristics wholly peculiar to itself, had also certain similarities testifying to their common origin. In the religious architecture of some countries, there was a very real decadence, while in that of others the old standards were faithfully maintained. The latter was the case with those parts of the Empire in which the barbarians had failed

287

to secure a foothold; for example Byzantium and Syria. The same course was followed by the minor arts. For many centuries the great cities of the East, Constantinople, Antioch and Alexandria, remained intact, and their populations were swelled by refugees. On the other hand, there was a steady decline in the population of Rome, then passing through her darkest hour. The larger eastern cities maintained the schools, factories and workshops to which they owed their wealth and thanks to which they now were in a position to export more luxury goods than ever—textiles, ivories, bronzes and other metal objects, papyri and spices—to the ancient Roman towns of the West, now overrun by the invaders. In these towns, trade was in the hands of Orientals, mostly Jews and Syrians. The old organization of commerce and long-distance traffic had survived the collapse of the Empire, but the main axis of the new Roman world had shifted eastwards. It still ran principally between Greece and Asia Minor even after Justinian's reconquest in 534 of south Italy and part of North Africa. Thus the East and its specific art forms enjoyed a certain ascendancy over a considerable period, as a result of the historical situation. Meanwhile, however, another change was in progress. The Nordic peoples, whom the Romans had failed to colonize, took steps to develop their overseas commerce and with this in view, introduced a common coinage, while their ships plied a busy trade along the coasts. Nonetheless the Mediterranean remained over a long period the one true seminal centre of western civilization.

Had it not been that barbarian Gaul took over from Rome the custom of honouring the dead by decking them with jewels and burying them in finely carved sarcophagi stored in the safe recesses of a vault, we should know but little of the Merovingian civilization. Thus we are limited to vague conjectures as to the origins of the remarkably expert carvings on the stone crosses of the British Isles, dating to the early Middle Ages. However, these are works of high quality and it is evident that by some channel Mediterranean skills found their way to this barbarian culture of the North. In short, there are enormous gaps in our knowledge of the period. Nevertheless, in the light of such historical data as are now available, there can be no question of the high importance, for the development of art in Europe, of the three centuries previous to the rise to power of Charlemagne.

After the ill-starred reigns of the last Merovingian kings, the Carolingian renascence, viewed in historical perspective, presents itself as the triumph of order over disorder, with a well-organized, sagacious administration putting a stop to anarchy. This view is correct up to a point, but it calls for an important qualification. As readers of this volume will have noted, we can trace to approximately the second half of the sixth century the beginnings of that gradual advance in the quality of art which, with occasional setbacks, continued until the end of the eighth century and led directly to the renascence of the age of Charlemagne. And all the progress that was made in the Merovingian period has this distinctive feature: it was not due to kings or bishops, but to an institution which then was taking a new form, the monastic system.

The monk (*monachos*) was, to begin with, as his name denotes, a solitary. In the countrysides of the West as in the eastern deserts, the first *laurae* were occupied by hermits living in grottoes or isolated cells. Then, like the monks assembled by St Martin of Tours at Marmoutier, a colony of several hundred monks and nuns established itself at the end of the fifth century in the vicinity of Condat (now Saint-Claude) in the forests of the Jura. When the group of wooden huts they occupied was burnt down, their abbot, Eugende, prudently decided to replace these by stone buildings. Many religious edifices of this type were built in the following century. There was no uniformity in their plans. Even their churches were given different orientations, as has been demonstrated by Jacques Mertens' recent excavation of the monastery, founded in the seventh century, at Nivelles in Belgium. To the best of my knowledge, we have the first indication of a systematized arrangement of the elements of a monastery, foreshadowing the almost geometric symmetry of the medieval abbeys, in the monastery of Manglieu in Auvergne (c. 700). Only some vestiges survive, but a description by a contemporary has come down to us. Excavations made in the last century showed that the first monastery founded (in 763) at Lorsch near Mainz had a plan of an even stricter regularity, with the communal buildings and church aligned round a square court bordered with porticoes. These facts carry all the more weight since they are not the only ones testifying to the part played by the monastic orders in the pre-Carolingian period as promoters of good order and disciplined activity in a still anarchic age. In 754 Chrodegang, bishop of Mainz, enjoined on the prelates of his cathedral the monastic way of life. And soon afterwards Charlemagne sought to impose the new Rule on all the episcopal churches of the kingdom. We have a striking example of the reform of ancient practices in another domain, that of sepulchral inscriptions. In the famous Jouarre crypt, the tomb of the first abbess, St Theodechilde (early eighth century), is noteworthy not only for its decorations (rows of sea shells) but also for a long metrical epitaph, whose characters, while retaining some of the peculiarities of the Merovingian hand, point the way to the fine engraved inscriptions, modelled on the classical script, of the Carolingian renascence. From the beginning of the eighth century on, similar changes were made in the lettering of the rubrics of manuscripts. Thus antique culture had been resuscitated in the shadow of the cloisters before its 'official' re-integration at the court of Charlemagne.

Building in wood goes back to time immemorial, and it is often assumed that this was the major art of the barbarian epoch. If our readers have found few references to it in the preceding pages, this is because an archaeologist is concerned, strictly speaking, only with what he can see, analyse and measure, and not one of the wooden buildings previous to the Carolingian epoch has survived. But as there are frequent mentions of them in ancient chronicles, we set forth here what has been surmised on the subject, chiefly in the light of what is known today of the wooden buildings of the immediately succeeding period.

The reliefs of Trajan's column include representations of Nordic huts built with large logs or ingeniously assembled planks. During the same period there existed in Roman Gaul, at Strasbourg in particular, buildings of wood and pisé, traces of which have been brought to light by excavations. Excavations have also enabled us to make graphic reconstructions of the wooden buildings erected in various parts of Europe in the early Middle Ages; holes in the earth reveal the shapes and sizes of the supporting posts. Two points call for mention. These buildings are never large ones. The posts are always relatively close to each other, since the only material used was wood and this ruled out long spans between them. This also applies to the churches in wood and pisé built in the south of the Champagne region at the close of the Middle Ages; such as have survived display the same characteristics. The result is a marked predominance of vertical lines. If the Gothic art of northern France follows suit, have we not here a transposition into stone of the wooden architecture of the earlier age? This view has often been expressed and has, in my opinion, much to commend it. But we must not overlook the fact that between the barbarian and the Gothic period timber architecture was also put to new uses and adapted in the tenth and eleventh centuries to the construction of vast fortified enceintes, strongholds several storeys high, barracks and engines of war. It is certain that nothing of this kind existed in the Europe of the invasions, submerged in the dark tide of an uncharted past, whose intriguing vestiges have never ceased to fire the imagination of succeeding generations.

JEAN HUBERT

PART FOUR

General Documentation

CLÉMENCE DUPRAT ably and actively assisted the general editor GEORGES SALLES from the very beginning of the ARTS OF MANKIND series. This volume was the last to have the benefit of her collaboration before her premature death. It is fitting that tribute should be paid to her here.

SCIENTIFIC ADVISOR MADELEINE DANY

Plans

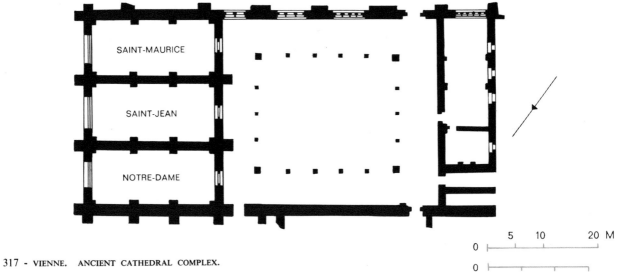

317 - VIENNE. ANCIENT CATHEDRAL COMPLEX.

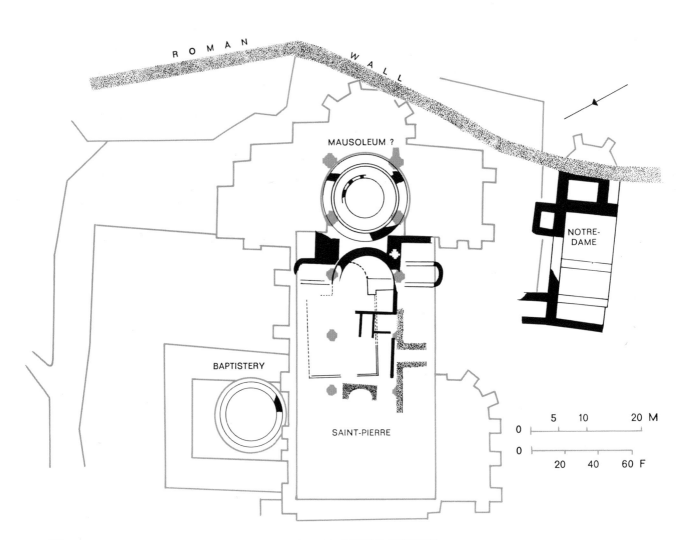

318 - GENEVA. ANCIENT CATHEDRAL AND BAPTISTERY, WITH ADJOINING BUILDINGS.

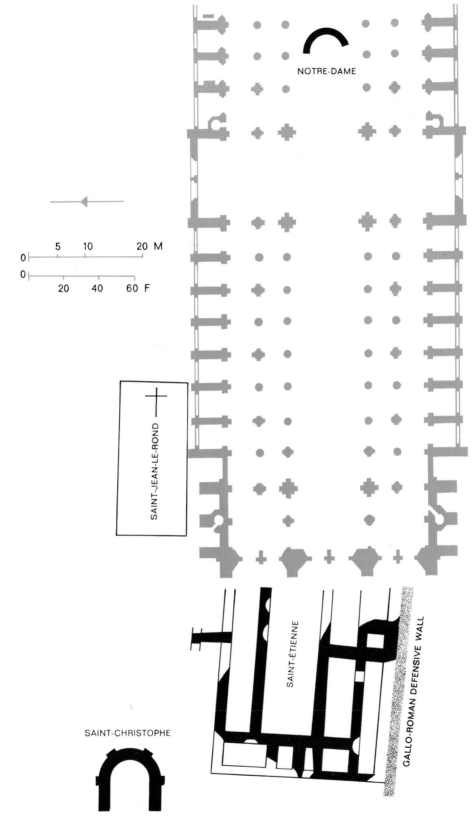

NOTRE-DAME

SAINT-JEAN-LE-ROND

5   10   20 M
0 |——|——|——|——|

0 |——|——|——|——|
20   40   60 F

SAINT-ÉTIENNE

GALLO-ROMAN DEFENSIVE WALL

SAINT-CHRISTOPHE

319 - PARIS. ANCIENT CATHEDRAL COMPLEX.

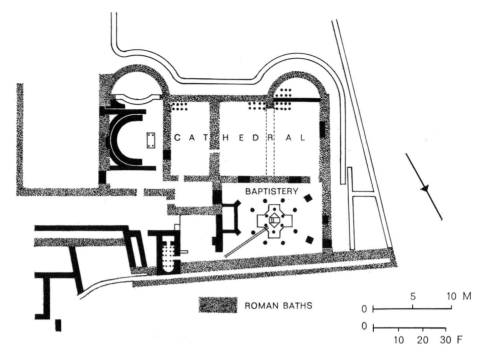

ROMAN BATHS

5   10 M
0

0
10 20 30 F

320 - NICE (CIMIEZ).   ANCIENT CATHEDRAL AND BAPTISTERY.

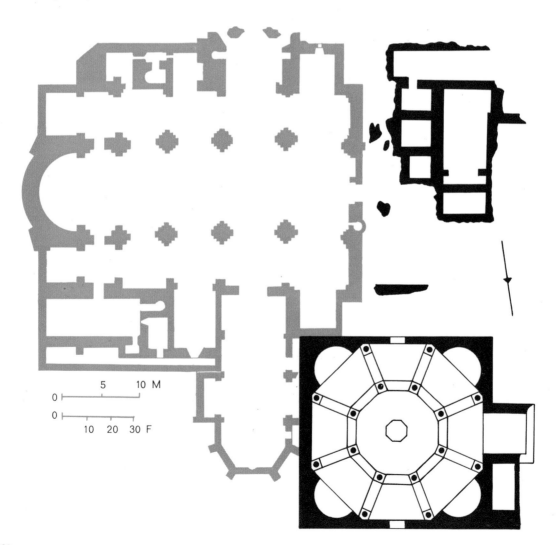

5   10 M
0

0
10 20 30 F

321 - MARSEILLES.   ANCIENT CATHEDRAL COMPLEX AND BAPTISTERY.

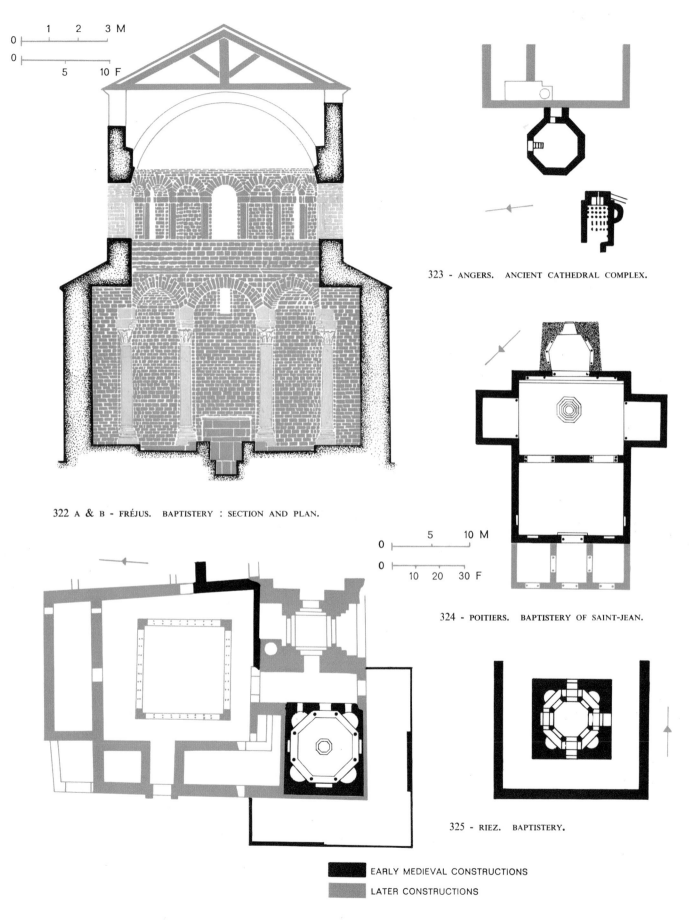

1 2 3 M
0
0
5 10 F

322 A & B - FRÉJUS. BAPTISTERY : SECTION AND PLAN.

323 - ANGERS. ANCIENT CATHEDRAL COMPLEX.

5 10 M
0
0
10 20 30 F

324 - POITIERS. BAPTISTERY OF SAINT-JEAN.

325 - RIEZ. BAPTISTERY.

EARLY MEDIEVAL CONSTRUCTIONS

LATER CONSTRUCTIONS

297

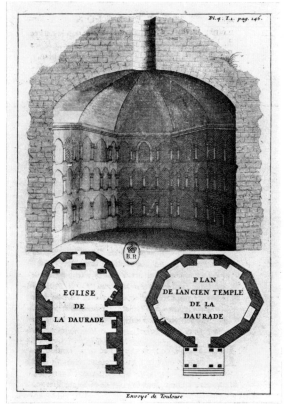

326 - TOULOUSE.   NOTRE-DAME-DE-LA-DAURADE : ELEVATION AND PLANS.

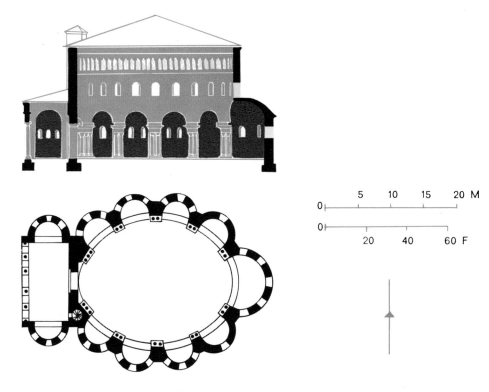

327 A & B - COLOGNE.   ST GEREON : SECTION AND PLAN.

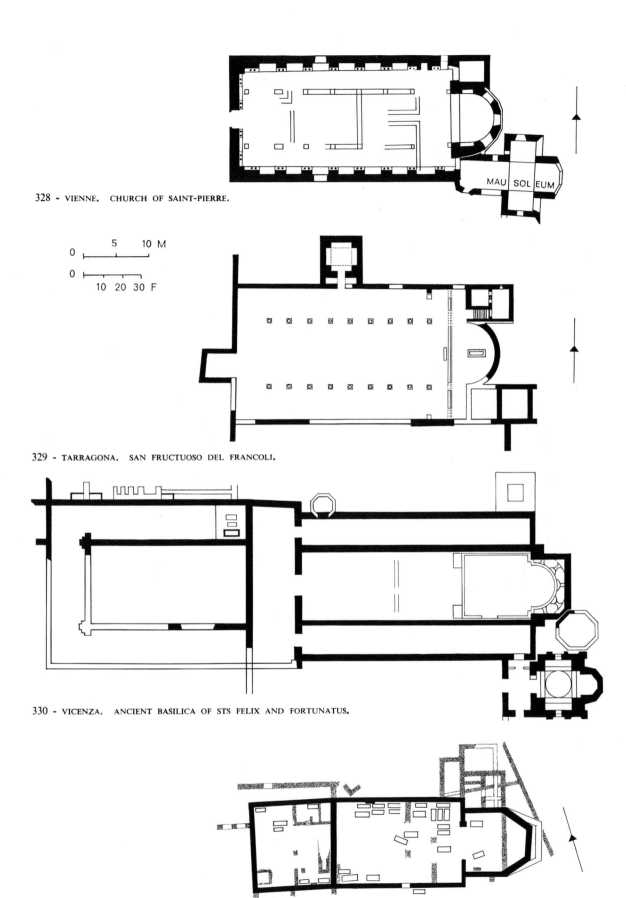

328 - VIENNE. CHURCH OF SAINT-PIERRE.

329 - TARRAGONA. SAN FRUCTUOSO DEL FRANCOLI.

330 - VICENZA. ANCIENT BASILICA OF STS FELIX AND FORTUNATUS.

331 - SAINT-BERTRAND-DE-COMMINGES. FUNERARY BASILICA.

299

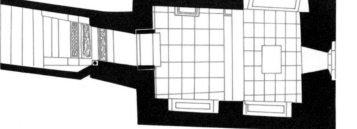

332 A & B - POITIERS. HYPOGEUM ('HYPOGÉE DES DUNES') : SECTION AND PLAN.

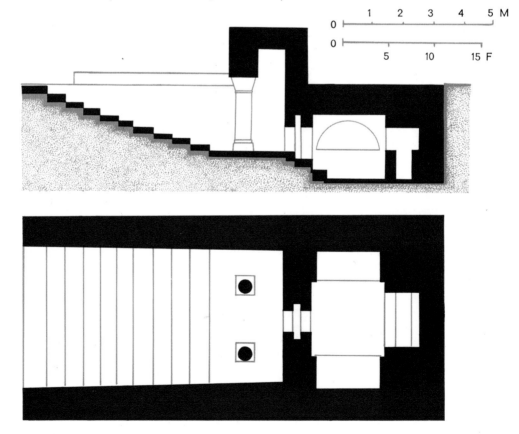

333 A & B - MUJELEIA. BURIAL VAULT : SECTION AND PLAN.

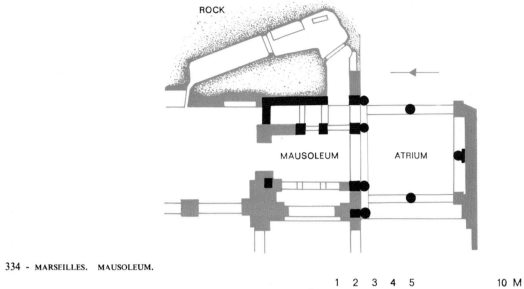

ROCK

MAUSOLEUM   ATRIUM

334 - MARSEILLES.   MAUSOLEUM.

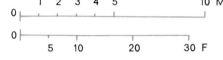

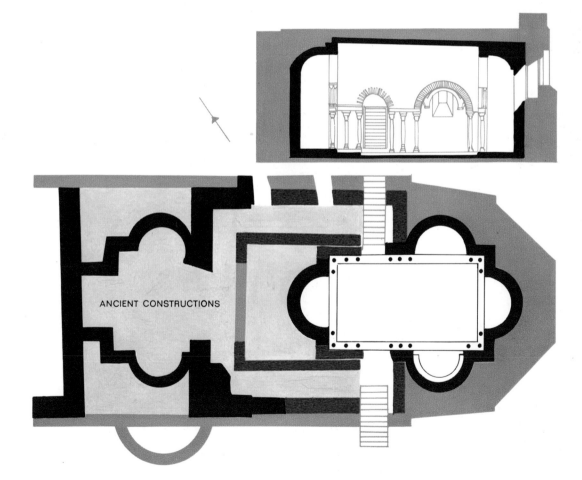

ANCIENT CONSTRUCTIONS

335 A & B - GRENOBLE.   'CRYPT' OF SAINT-LAURENT : SECTION AND PLAN.

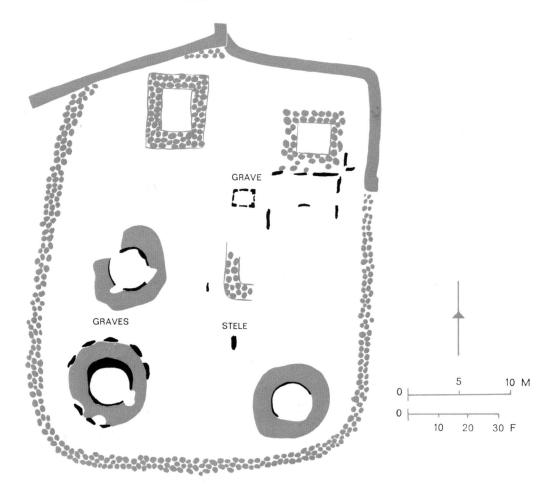

336 - KILDRENAGH.   MONASTERY.

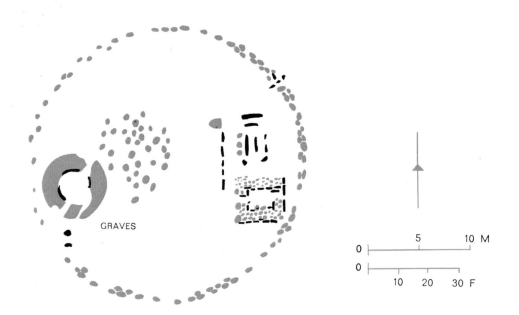

337 - WEST FEAGHMAAN.   MONASTERY.

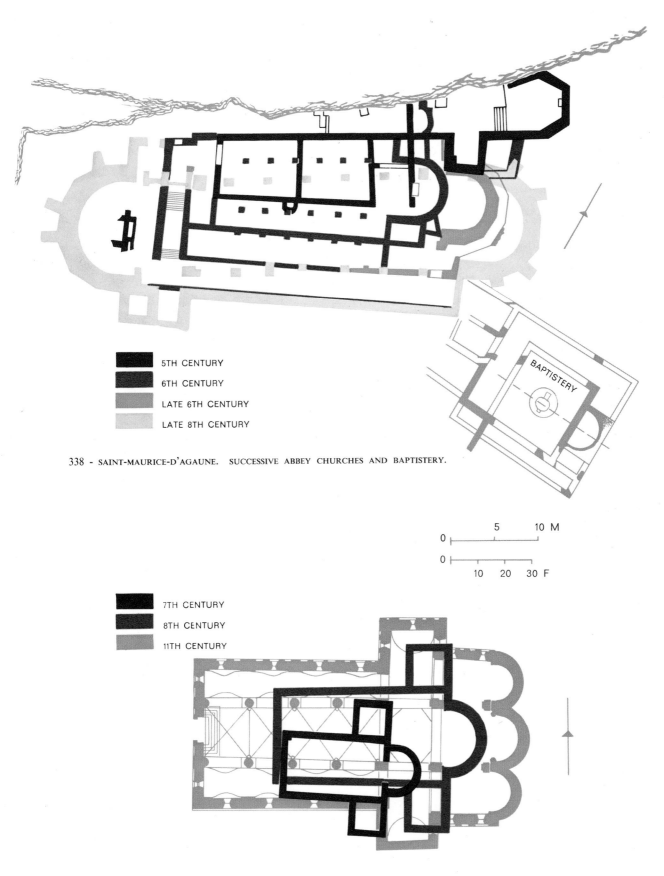

5TH CENTURY
6TH CENTURY
LATE 6TH CENTURY
LATE 8TH CENTURY

BAPTISTERY

338 - SAINT-MAURICE-D'AGAUNE.   SUCCESSIVE ABBEY CHURCHES AND BAPTISTERY.

5   10 M
0
0
10   20   30 F

7TH CENTURY
8TH CENTURY
11TH CENTURY

339 - ROMAINMOTIER.   SUCCESSIVE CHURCHES OF THE MONASTERY.

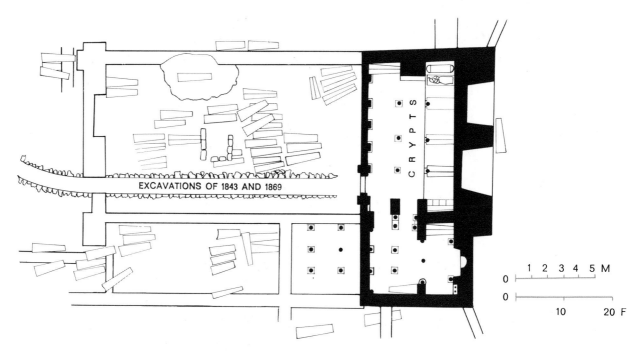

340 A & B - JOUARRE. CEMETERIAL CHURCH (ABOVE) AND ANCIENT CHURCHES OF THE ABBEY (BELOW).

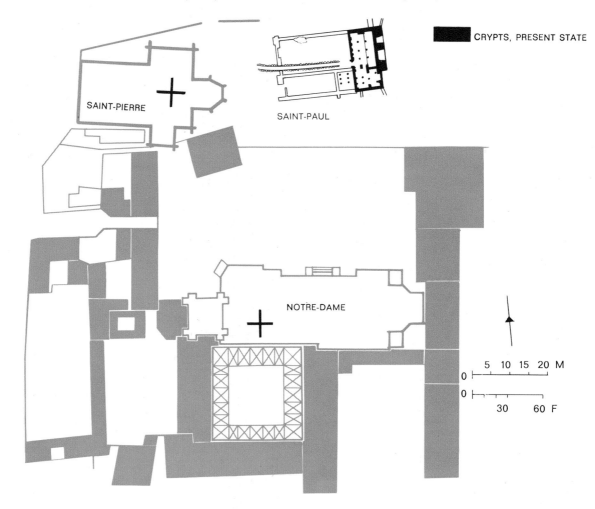

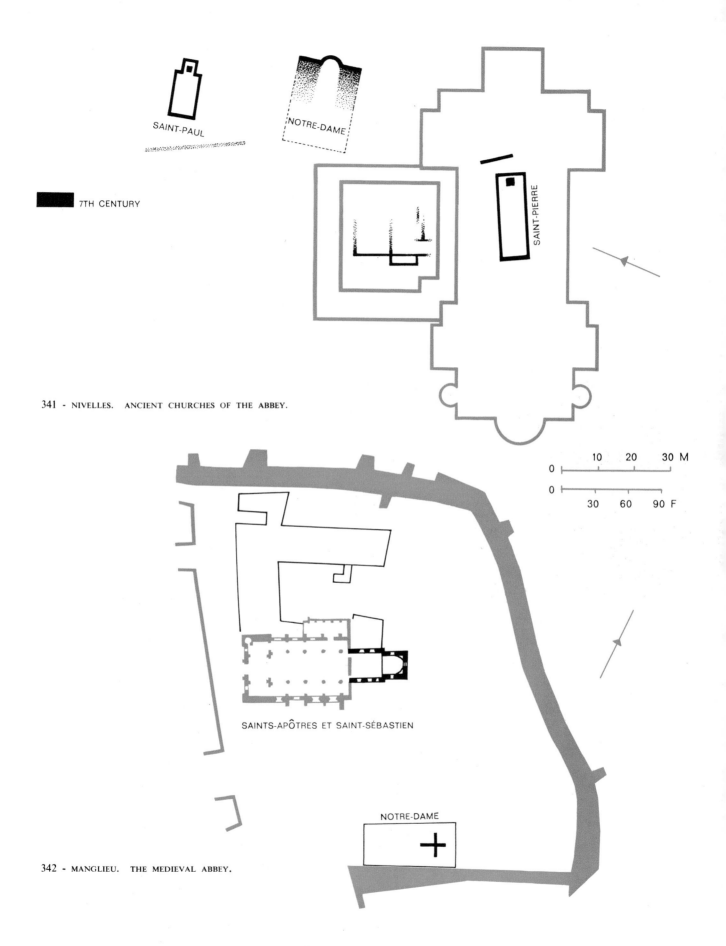

SAINT-PAUL

NOTRE-DAME

SAINT-PIERRE

7TH CENTURY

341 - NIVELLES. ANCIENT CHURCHES OF THE ABBEY.

10   20   30 M
0

0
30   60   90 F

SAINTS-APÔTRES ET SAINT-SÉBASTIEN

NOTRE-DAME

342 - MANGLIEU. THE MEDIEVAL ABBEY.

305

BASILICAS WITH SIDE PORCHES

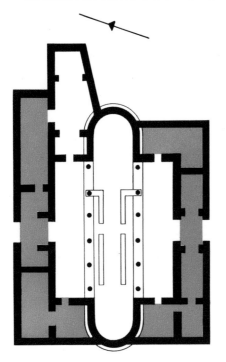

343 - CASA HERRERA. BASILICA.

344 - SILCHESTER. CHURCH.

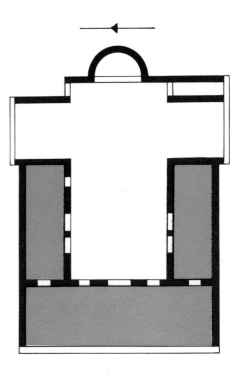

345 - COMO. HOLY APOSTLES.

SIDE PORCHES

5   10 M
0
0
10   20   30 F

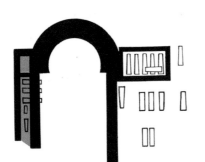

346 - ALBON. ANCIENT CHURCH.

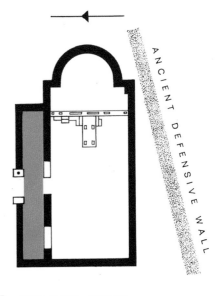

ANCIENT DEFENSIVE WALL

347 - SAINT-BLAISE. BASILICA.

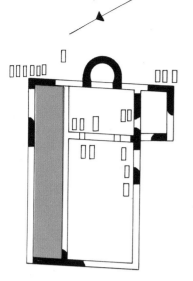

348 - ANGERS. SAINT-MARTIN.

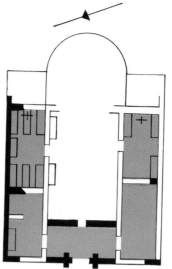

349 - CANTERBURY. STS PETER AND PAUL.

350 - RECULVER. ST MARY'S.

SIDE PORCHES

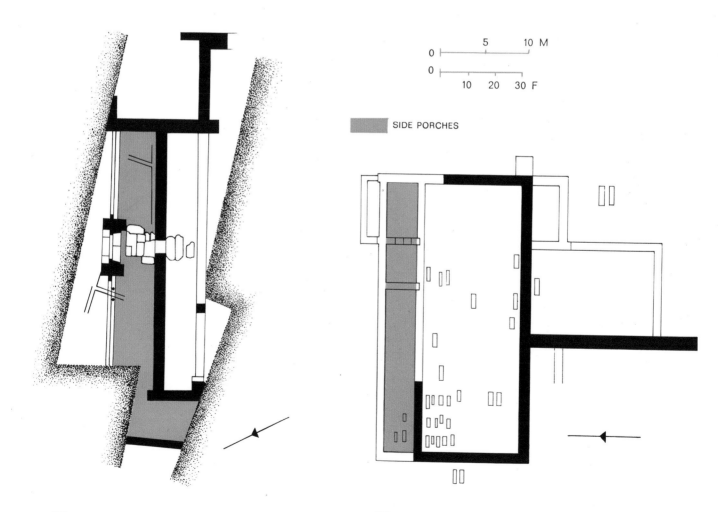

351 - LYONS. SAINT-LAURENT.

352 - SAINT-AMBROIX. MONASTERY.

List of Manuscripts Reproduced

The numbers in italics refer to the illustrations in this book.

AMIENS
Bibliothèque municipale
ms. 18 — *204-210.*

AUTUN
Bibliothèque municipale
ms. 4 — *191-194.*

BERLIN
Deutsche Staatsbibliothek
ms. Phill. 1676 — *154, 155.*

CAMBRIDGE
Corpus Christi College Library
ms. 286 — *146, 147.*

DUBLIN
Trinity College Library
ms. 55 (A.IV.15) — *183.*
ms. 57 (A.IV.5) — *170.*
ms. 58 (A.I.6) — *169.*
ms. 59 — *172.*

FULDA
Landesbibliothek (Domschatz)
ms. Cod. Bonif. 2 — *179.*

LENINGRAD
Saltykov-Shchedrin State Library
ms. lat. Q.v.I.N.14 — *178.*
ms. lat. F.v.I.N.2 — *180.*

LONDON
British Museum, Cotton
ms. Nero D.IV. — *171, 173.*

MUNICH
Bayerische Staatsbibliothek
ms. CLM 6224 — *150, 151.*
ms. CLM 23631 — *152, 153.*

PARIS
Bibliothèque nationale
ms. lat. 1732 — *177 B.*
ms. lat. 2630 — *145.*
ms. lat. 2769 — *182.*
ms. lat. 9389 — *168, 174.*
ms. lat. 10910 — *195-197.*
ms. lat. 12048 — *198-203.*
ms. lat. 12135 — *176.*
ms. lat. 12168 — *188, 190.*
ms. lat. 13159 — *214.*
ms. lat. 13396 — *184, 186, 187.*
ms. Nouv. acq. lat. 1598 — *177 A, 177 C.*
ms. Nouv. acq. lat. 2061 — *177 D.*
ms. Nouv. acq. lat. 2334 — *141.*

POITIERS
Bibliothèque municipale
ms. 17 — *211.*

ST GALL
Stiftsbibliothek
ms. 731 — *185.*

STUTTGART
Württembergische Landesbibliothek
ms. Bibl. fol. 23 r° — *212, 213.*

VATICAN CITY
Biblioteca Apostolica
Vat. ms. lat. 3225 — *126.*
Vat. ms. lat. 3867 — *127.*
Vat. ms. Reg. lat. 316 — *175, 189.*
Vat. ms. Reg. lat. 317 — *181.*

VERCELLI
Biblioteca Capitolare
ms. CLXV — *156-161.*
ms. CXLVIII — *121, 162, 163.*

353 - FIBULA. HESSISCHES LANDESMUSEUM, DARMSTADT.

Note on Ornament

The history of ornament from antiquity to the Carolingian age throws light on the aesthetic evolution which led up to the decorative art of the Early Middle Ages. Vegetable motifs, vineshoots in particular, always had a large part in it, despite changes of style and persistent geometrization. Incised geometric decoration, in the later period, struck out in a new direction concurrently with the interlace, brought to artistic perfection by the Easterners. It was already widely practised in the fifth century throughout the western half of the Empire.

During the sixth and seventh centuries motifs of the early Byzantine period still prevailed in Italy. The most striking examples that have survived come from the exarchate of Ravenna. Not only the 'Christian' kinds of animals (peacocks, lambs and so forth) were re-adopted—and transformed—, but also the acanthus patterns with lobate half-leaves, or leaves curled into spirals (San Vitale), borders and motifs of bunches of grapes (sarcophagus of St Theodore in Sant'Apollinare in Classe), palmettes, trefoils *et al.* This increasingly geometric stylization of vegetable forms in the seventh century can be clearly seen in the acanthus borders and half-palmettes, of Byzantine origin, on the gold cross of Stabio (Ticino, Switzerland) which belongs to the domain of Lombard art. The half-palmettes on the mounts of the dagger from Castel Trosino (in Rome) show a further step in this progressive stylization. This is not the case with the gold saddle ornaments, in which can he detected Oriental, perhaps Iranian, influences in the 'Byzantinizing' milieux of Lombard Italy. We have already drawn attention to the fact that the decorations on the surrounds of the arches in the Tempietto at Cividale are purely Oriental in conception.

North of the Alps, these vegetable forms are sometimes found combined on the same monument with Germanic zoomorphic imagery. A striking example is the Beromünster reliquary of Warnebertus, doubtless to be identified with the seventh-century bishop of Soissons (died c. 676). Here the palmette motifs on the front are somewhat more elaborately developed than in Italy and the ornamental border formed by them links up with a running or intermittent pattern of vine-tendrils. It is not surprising that these finely conceived and superbly executed works had a decisive influence not only on the art of the lands north of the Alps but on Visigothic art as well.

The group of Visigothic works in Spain, in which the Oriental element is most prominent, consists of lyre-shaped belt decorations whose outlines have an almost Baroque elegance. Deriving directly from Byzantine prototypes wrought in gold, they make their first appearance here not earlier than the seventh century. The ornamented surfaces, like those of their models, are divided into compartments and usually filled with spirals of stylized S-shaped palmettes whose extremities are given the form of animals' heads—an Iranian device. A typical example of this is the central portion of the 'Byzantine' saddle ornament from Castel Trosino described at an earlier page.

From the seventh century on, one of the ornamental patterns most in favour both in Italy and north of the Alps was the interlace. We find it recurring, built up of a great variety of motifs, on a large number of stone carvings and smaller artefacts. In the form of a simple braid or cable moulding, quadrangular or circular, this widely employed motif underwent many transformations in the course of the succeeding centuries and was utilized in manners varying with the provinces concerned.

Around the year 300, within the territories of the Roman Empire, the decline of the realistic style and the prejudice against anthropomorphic imagery led to an increasing use of the interlace, chiefly in the East. Interesting examples of this new development are found in the Coptic purple textiles, also in Syrian and Palestinian mosaics. At Ravenna, from the sixth century on, these Byzantine motifs were widely employed on choir-screens, capitals and other architectural elements. Thereafter they were adopted and elaborated in all parts of Italy during the eighth century. The ornamentation of the Valpolicella ciborium (c. 712) exemplifies the early use of a simple interlace pattern, and almost all sepulchral monuments of the end of the eighth century are adorned with this motif. At Rome it was given logical developments. The interlaces became more intricate and their original forms were greatly modified in the course of the ninth century. They evolved along similar lines in the lands north of the Alps, to which they had been transmitted from the Mediterranean region. The interlace had nothing in common with the spirit of Germanic art. This can be clearly seen in the art of the Aquitanian province of southern Gaul whose Roman population made a practice of adorning their belts with a profusion of interlaces of varied shapes and sizes. Among the inhabitants of the former Gallo-Roman zone between the Seine and the Loire, and most notably in the Burgundian domain on the banks of the Rhone, there was a marked preference for motifs of an Oriental nature, composed exclusively of interlaces, for the adornment of the surfaces of their tinned and silver-plated belts.

Whereas the channel through which these peoples of Germanic origin became acquainted with this West-Mediterranean type of ornament was undoubtedly the Rhone, the Lombards, after their incursion into Italy (568) came into more direct contact with the Mediterranean interlace. This is particularly evident in a group of seventh-century gold-leaf crosses decorated with interlaces of various kinds, and they show that this type of ornament, much used in (though not peculiar to) North Italy, was adopted by the Lombard metalworkers. Examples of it are the crosses from Fornovo di San Giovanni (now in Milan) and from Andelfingen (now in Stuttgart). Clearly there is nothing in common between the stamped decorations in favour with the Lombard metalworkers and the Ostrogothic moulded fibulae and belt buckles of the previous century (up to 550). These latter were adorned with edgings of quite simple braids, doubtless inspired by Late Antique mosaics of the Adriatic region.

The purely Germanic element in Lombard metalwork can best be seen in the interlaces consisting in the main of representations of animals, treated at first as isolated units. These led up to the use of animal ornament covering entire surfaces. This method was employed in a number of stamped gold crosses made for the most part in North Italy, such as the pectoral cross from Floro, in Brescia, and also in the looped fibulae made north of the Alps in regions strongly exposed to Lombard influence. Examples are the fibula from Nocera Umbra and the magnificent pieces from Soest, now in Münster, and from Heidingsfeld, now at Würzburg. The belt adornment stamped in gilt iron from Trebur in the Städtisches Museum, Mainz, carries an animal interlace of the same type. Given its distinctive shape and closed recesses, it can safely be assigned to a Lombard workshop. This is borne out by a similar ornament from Nocera Umbra. There have been lengthy controversies about the origins of this type of ornament, but no wholly satisfactory answer has so far been given. It is, however, generally accepted today that the sources of its original components can be traced to the Mediterranean interlace and that the Lombards skilfully combined with this selected elements of the animal art of the Germanic North. It was as a sequel of their many incursions into central Europe that they imported these Nordic animal figures into Lombardy. This is why we find on some early Lombard fibulae, from Friuli and Central Italy, a pair of fully articulated animals in the upper and lower segments. Bernhard Salin has named this class of ornamentation Animal Style I. Needless to say the various theories advanced regarding the evolution of Lombard art take into account its much earlier and, geographically, remoter antecedents. Thus the Scandinavian branch of the Germanic race took over the squatting animals along the borders from the group of cuneiform bronzes datable to late antiquity produced in northern Gaul and transmuted them into isolated figurations, in accordance with the tendency we find in all Germanic art to fragmentate the antique naturalistic imagery. This is apparent when we compare the Late Antique belt ornaments at Saint-Quentin (Aisne) and at Namur with the large silver-gilt, looped fibula from Gummersmark, now in Copenhagen. On the Continent this stage of assimilation is evidenced by fibulae of the type of those presumably imported from England: the Engers fibula in Bonn and the one from Täbingen in Stuttgart Museum.

In the North Germanic centres, the Late Antique emperor image was split into separate elements, as on the upper plaque of the Gummersmark fibula, on the sides of the clasp. The Germanic settlers on the banks of the Rhine and the Danube did not confine their borrowings to the ornamental animal figures on engraved Late Antique bronzes; they also took over the elaborate spirals and crossed angles forming the decorative motifs of their models. It was in the mid-sixth century that a team of Lombard craftsmen successfully adapted the Late Antique system of spirals and meanders to the decoration of a group of fibulae. The skill and sensitivity they brought to the venture is brilliantly indicated by a fibula of the period now in Berlin. By the year 600, many elements of the decorative art of late antiquity—intaglio work, the spiral, the components of the emperor image—had struck root so deeply in Germanic ornamental art (Style I) that they ceased to be regarded as independent or imported decorative motifs. During the seventh century the creative genius of the Germanic peoples was oriented chiefly towards the development of what is known as Animal Style II, examples of which, on Lombard monuments and more especially the gold crosses, have been cited and discussed at an earlier page. Distinctive of this art of animal ornament, at its acme, is its rhythmic, strictly symmetrical composition. North of the Alps, its best examples are large Burgundian belt adornments, of the type of the plaques from Fétigny, now at Fribourg (Switzerland). It is worth noting that in this same cemetery, alongside pieces decorated in the purest Germanic style, variants were also found, pieces whose decoration was restricted to such Mediterranean Christian motifs as the Greek cross and fishes, with an infrastructure resembling that of antique sarcophagi. The surface of these objects is covered with a coat of silver foil in which the ornament is incised, whereas in those with animal decorations, the bodies of the animals are usually shown in fairly high relief. In contrast to these objects of an exclusively Burgundian type, we find in the regions adjoining the Alamanno-Burgundian frontier, belt adornments with clear-cut outlines divided in three parts; these show that Lombard influences predominated among the Alamanni and Bavarians of South Germany. The above example shows how the zoomorphic style has been given greater flexibility, but without detriment to the feeling for organic rhythm characteristic of this group of works. Around the year 700 this tendency reached its peak on the Continent, where motifs in the form of edgings of braids, devoid of animal figures, make their reappearance.

The long development of Merovingian art came to a halt in all domains at the beginning of the eighth century. Influences of Late Roman art, of Oriental cultures and the adoption of new motifs from Italy and the North had combined to create an art which achieved cohesion on the Continent above all in the Merovingian period. The technique of cloisonné jewellery had almost died out, after the Arab invasion had all but cut off the importation of gold and precious stones. An equilibrium was struck between the Mediterranean and the Germanic art currents round about the year 700, when the arts of ornamentation were systematized. Henceforth surfaces were given more harmonious layouts, discrepancies of style reduced to a minimum, and gems and cloisonné enamelwork became indispensable elements of the overall effect. The fibula from Molsheim near Worms, now at Darmstadt, illustrates the ultimate development of this style. On comparing it with earlier gold fibulae of the Rhineland, such as the one from Kärlich, we cannot fail to be struck by the vast improvement in the arrangement of surfaces and the craftsman's feeling for tectonic unity. Here the plastic handling of the symmetrically disposed stones and the superb cameo in the centre are at a far remove from earlier fibulae of the same class. This work points the way to the lucid, skilfully planned structuration of such Carolingian works of art as the 'Cross of the Ardennes' (Nuremberg), and of the cabochons on the rim of the Saint-Denis paten (Louvre).

W.F. VOLBACH

Chronological Table

	ITALY	GAUL	SPAIN
200			
250		250 and 258. Invasion of Gaul by Germanic tribes.	
	272-279. Construction of Aurelian's wall at Rome.		259. Martyrdom of Fructuosus, Bishop of Tarragona, with two of his deacons.
		276. Gaul devastated by Franks and Alamanni.	
		276 to about 320. As a measure of defence, about fifty of the main towns of Gaul are transformed into strongholds or citadel towns.	
300			304. During the persecutions of Diocletian, St Eulalia is martyred at Merida, St Vincent at Saragossa, St Felix at Gerona.
		314. Council of Arles.	Before 314. Church council at Elvira, attended by 19 bishops and 24 priests.
	About 319. Death of Bishop Theodore, builder of Aquileia Cathedral.		
	About 320. Basilica of St Peter's erected in Rome, on the Vatican Hill.		
	After 326. The Lateran church erected in Rome.		
	337. Baptism of Constantine.		
350	About 356. Pagan temples officially closed and sacrifices prohibited.	355 & 364. New Germanic invasions.	
	366. Pope Damasius (366-384).	355 & 367. Apologetical activities of St Hilary, Bishop of Poitiers.	
	374-397. St Ambrose bishop of Milan.	371. *Mosella*, a descriptive poem on the Moselle, by Ausonius.	
	380. Edict of Theodosius proclaiming Christianity the state religion.		
	About 382. Church of the Holy Apostles (San Nazzaro), Milan.		
	383. Basilica of the Martyrs (Sant' Ambrogio), Milan (383-386).		
	384. San Paolo fuori le Mura erected in Rome by the emperors Valentinian II, Theodosius and Arcadius.		384. Priscillian, condemned as a heretic but defended by St Martin, appeals to the Emperor Maximus at Trier—in vain, and he was burned alive in 385.
		About 390. Death of Concordius, Bishop of Arles: he is buried in a marble sarcophagus from Italy.	
		About 395. The praetorian prefecture transferred from Trier to Arles.	
	Late 4th century. Christian churches recognized as a place of asylum.	397. Death of St Martin, Bishop of Tours, founder of the monasteries of Ligugé and Marmoutier.	
	Late 4th century. Compilation of the extant text of the *Notitia dignitatum*.		
400	401. Alaric, King of the Goths, in Italy. Driven back in 402 by Stilicho.	403. Journey to Rome of Victricius, Bishop of Rouen.	400. First Council of Toledo.
	404. Ravenna capital of the West Roman Empire (404-476).	Before 405. Death of Delphinus, Bishop of Bordeaux, whom Paulinus of Nola regarded as the peer of St Martin.	
	408. Alaric reappears in Italy, has Attalus proclaimed emperor (409-410) and captures Rome (410).	406-407. Invasions of the Vandals and Suevi.	About 406. Death of the Christian poet Prudentius.
		About 410. St Honoratus withdraws to the monastery of Lérins.	409. The Vandals and Suevi gain control of Spain.

BRITISH ISLES	EAST ROMAN EMPIRE AND BYZANTIUM	ISLAM	
	About 200. Christian church of Dura-Europos, on the Euphrates.		200
	245-256. Wall paintings in the synagogue of Dura-Europos.		250
			300
	About 315. Churches of Golgotha erected in Jerusalem by Constantine. Church of the Nativity erected in Bethlehem by St Helena.		
	318. Beginning of the Arian heresy.		
	About 320. First monastery founded by St Pacomius.		
	About 320. Arian heresy condemned and Arius driven out of Alexandria.		
	325. Council of Nicaea.		
	330. Founding of Constantinople.		
	356. Death of St Anthony.		350
	About 378. Church of the Ascension at Jerusalem.		
	395. Arcadius Emperor of the East.		
397. St Ninian founds a church at Whithorn, Scotland, and dedicates it to St Martin of Tours.			
	About 400. Second basilica of St Menas, near Alexandria.		400
408. The Saxons invade Britannia and the last Roman troops withdraw from the island.			
	413-440. Construction of the great wall of Constantinople.		

ITALY	GAUL	SPAIN
414. Ataulf, Alaric's brother-in-law, marries Galla Placidia, daughter of Theodosius the Great.		414. Ataulf succeeds Alaric as king of the Visigoths.
418. Pelagius condemned by Pope Zosimus.	418. Assembly of the Gauls held at Arles.	415. Assassination of Ataulf. His successors wage war against the Alans and Vandals.
	418. Honorius yields Aquitaine to the Arian Visigoths of Spain, who remained masters of Toulouse until 507.	
	About 418. Cassianus founds the monastery of St Victor at Marseilles.	
	420. Death of Sulpicius Severus.	
	428. Aetius drives the Franks back across the Rhine.	428. Seville and Carthagena taken by the Vandals.
431. Death of St Paulinus of Nola.		429-430. The Vandals land in North Africa.
432. Pontificate of Sixtus III (432-440). who rebuilds the basilica of Santa Maria Maggiore and the Lateran baptistery in Rome.		
	About 441. The Britons begin to settle in Armorica.	
	443. The Burgundians settle on the upper Rhone, between the Alps and the Jura.	
About 450. Mausoleum of Galla Placidia and Orthodox Baptistery in Ravenna.	About 450. Building of the cathedral of Clermont.	
	451. Attila invades Gaul. Defeated at Campus Mauriacus by Aetius and the Visigoths.	
452. Attila in Italy.		
455. Genseric, king of the Vandals, in Italy. Capture of Rome.	About 455. The Ripuarian Franks advance as far as Trier.	
	About 460. The Alamanni settle in Alsatia.	
	460-491. Perpetuus Bishop of Tours, He builds the basilica of St Martin.	
	Before 463 to about 475. Mamertus Bishop of Vienne. He builds the basilica of the Holy Apostles.	
	463-471. The Burgundians occupy the area between the Durance and the plateau of Langres.	
	468-476. Part of Gaul occupied by the Visigoths under Euric. The Burgundians establish themselves in Lugdunensis Prima.	
476. End of the Roman Empire of the West. Genseric surrenders Sicily to Odoacer, chief of the Heruli.		
481. Odoacer seizes Dalmatia.	481. Reign of Clovis begins.	
488. Zeno gives Italy to Theodoric the Great, king of the Ostrogoths, who triumphs over Odoacer in 493.	486-496. Syagrius defeated at the battle of Soissons. Clovis occupies the area between the Seine and the Loire.	
	About 488. Death of Sidonius Apollinaris.	
	About 490-about 525. St Avitus Bishop of Vienne.	
	About 493. Marriage of Clovis and Clotilde. Basilica of St Germanus erected at Auxerre by Clotilde.	
	About 494. Clovis extends his dominion south of the Loire.	
	About 496. Conversion of Clovis.	

450

BRITISH ISLES	EAST ROMAN EMPIRE AND BYZANTIUM	ISLAM	
	418. Church of Dar Kita in Syria.		
	420. Death of St Jerome in Bethlehem.		
429. Mission of St Germanus, Bishop of Auxerre, against the Pelagians.			
432. St Patrick begins the conversion of Ireland.			
441-450. The Angles and Saxons complete the conquest of the southern and eastern parts of England. The Christian Britons withdraw into the west of England and into Ireland and Armorica. The Picts and Scots hold their own in Scotland.			
			450
	459. Death of St Simeon Stylites.		
461. Death of St Patrick.			
	About 480-about 500. Church of Mount Garizim in Palestine. Church and monastery built in memory of St Simeon Stylites at Kalat Seman, near Antioch. Painted illustrations in the Dioscorides manuscript now preserved in the Nationalbibliothek, Vienna.		

	ITALY	GAUL	SPAIN
500		500. Clovis defeats the Burgundians near Dijon.	
		503-543. St Caesarius Bishop of Arles.	
			506. *Breviary of Alaric.*
		507. Clovis defeats the Visigoths at Vouillé. He receives a Byzantine embassy. He builds the basilica of the Apostles (later called St Genevieve) in Paris.	
		509-531. The Visigoths settle in Spain; their last remaining possession in Gaul is Septimania.	
		About 510. Publication of the Salic law.	
		511. Death of Clovis. Council of Orléans. Reign of Childebert I (511-558).	
		515. Monastery of Saint-Maurice d'Agaune founded by Sigismund, son of Gondebaud, king of the Burgundians, whom Sigismund succeeds in 516.	
	About 520. Completion of Sant'Apollinare Nuovo in Ravenna.	523-524. Burgundians crushed by the Franks. Death of Sigismund.	
	524. Boethius executed by order of Theodoric.		
	Before 526. Mausoleum of Theodoric the Great in Ravenna.		
		531-534. The Franks conquer Thuringia and drive the Visigoths into Spain.	
	After 534. The Rule of St Benedict drawn up.		
		536-537. The Franks in Provence.	
	537. Rome besieged by the Goths.	538. Birth of Gregory of Tours.	
	539. The Franks in Italy.		
	540. Ravenna recaptured by the Byzantines.		
		541-542. Campaign of Childebert I in Spain against the Visigoths. He seizes Pamplona, besieges Saragossa, and on his return to Gaul, before 558, the year of his death, founds the basilica of the Holy Cross and St Vincent (later Saint-Germain-des-Prés) in Paris and the basilica of St Eusicius at Selles-sur-Cher.	
		543. Death of St Caesarius, Bishop of Arles. His leather belt, with a carved ivory buckle, was found in his tomb and has been preserved.	
	546. Rome taken by Totila, king of the Ostrogoths. Maximian Bishop of Ravenna (546-566). Carved ivory throne bearing his monogram.		
	547. Consecration of the basilica of San Vitale in Ravenna.		
	549. Consecration of the basilica of Sant'Apollinare in Classe, Ravenna.		
550	About 550. Death of Bishop Eufronius, builder of the cathedral of Parenzo.		
	550. Totila again seizes Rome after it had been occupied by Belisarius.		
	553. Franks and Alamanni in North Italy.	About 555. St Radegund, wife of Clotaire I, founds the monastery of the Holy Cross at Poitiers where a carved wooden reading desk, thought to have been hers, is still preserved.	
	557. Agnellus Bishop of Ravenna (556-about 569). Stone ambo bearing his name.		

BRITISH ISLES	EAST ROMAN EMPIRE AND BYZANTIUM	ISLAM	
			500
	527. Beginning of the reign of Justinian (527-565).		
	534. The Byzantine armies reconquer North Africa.		
	535. Beginning of the reconquest of Italy by the Byzantines.		
	536-546. Church of the Holy Apostles in Constantinople.		
	537. Dedication of St Sophia in Constantinople.		
	About 540. Church of Sts Peter and Paul at Gerasa, Palestine.		
	541. The Persians invade the eastern provinces of the Empire.		
	542. Justinian calls for the conversion of all pagans.		
550. The Anglo-Saxons resume the offensive.	About 550. The *Topographia Christiana* of Cosmas Indicopleustes.		550
	552. Salonica threatened by a Slav invasion.		

ITALY	GAUL	SPAIN
558. Dedication of the church of Sant' Apollinare Nuovo in Ravenna.	558. Death of King Childebert I. About 558. Consecration by the bishop St Felix of Nantes Cathedral, begun before 548 by Bishop Eumerius. Some of its marbles and capitals have been preserved.	
		560. Conversion of the Suevi by Martin of Braga. The Byzantines, having retaken North Africa from the Vandals, occupy the Balearic Islands and the Mediterranean coast of Spain from Valencia to Malaga, in addition to the cities of Murcia, Cordova and Carthagena. The Visigoth king Athanagild moves his capital inland to Toledo.
	565. The poet Fortunatus in Gaul. 567. Chilperic I marries Fredegond.	
568. The Lombards invade North Italy.		
		572. The Visigoths under Leovigild recapture Cordova and Malaga from the Byzantines.
	573. Episcopate of St Gregory of Tours (573-584), author of the *Historia Francorum*. 575. Murder of Sigebert I.	
	578-579. The Britons take Vannes and invade the region of Rennes and Nantes.	579. Hermenegild, son of Leovigild, converted to Catholicism, takes refuge at Seville with Archbishop Leander, brother of Isidore of Seville.
584. The Exarch of Ravenna begins the struggle against the Lombards. The Franks in Italy.		
		585. The kingdom of the Suevi annexed to the Visigothic kingdom.
586. Completion of the cathedral church of Santa Maria delle Grazie at Grado.	587. Death of St Radegund. The Gascons settle in Aquitaine. 589-600. Brunhilda, widow of Sigebert I, founds the monastery of St Martin at Autun.	586. Death of Leovigild, succeeded by Reccared. 587. Conversion of Reccared and the Visigoths to Catholicism.
590. Pontificate of Gregory I the Great (590-604).	590. St Columban founds the monastery of Luxeuil.	
591. Agilulf, king of the Lombards (591-615/616), represented on a helmet found at Nievole (Museo Nazionale, Florence). 593. Siege of Rome by the Lombards. 596. Ambo of the former church of Sts John and Paul (Museo Arcivescovile, Ravenna).	597. Death of Queen Fredegond.	
	After 600. Death of Fortunatus, Bishop of Poitiers. About 601. Death of St Martin, founder of the abbey of St John the Baptist (now St Martin) at Vertou. Some of its capitals and terracottas extant. 601-622. Gold and silver monument erected at Auxerre over the tomb of St Germanus by King Clotaire II and Bishop Lupus. 604. Tomb of Bishop Boethius at Venasque.	
About 609. Pope Boniface IV, with the consent of the Emperor Phocas, dedicates the Pantheon in Rome to the Virgin of the martyrs.		

600

BRITISH ISLES	EAST ROMAN EMPIRE AND BYZANTIUM	ISLAM	
563. St Columban founds the monastery of Iona, off the west coast of Scotland: from here he began the evangelization of the Scots and Picts.			
		About 570. Birth of Mohammed.	
	575. Persians defeated at Melitene.		
	580. The Slavs occupy Thrace and Macedonia.		
	584. The Emperor Maurice allied with the Franks.		
590. St Columban and his monks go to the continent where they found the monastery of Luxeuil, among others, and evangelize the Rhineland.	591. Victorious peace with Persia.		
596-597. Pope Gregory the Great sends St Augustine to evangelize England.			
597. Conversion of Ethelbert, king of Kent, at Canterbury.			
	About 600. Church of St Catherine on Mount Sinai.		600
601-604. Augustine primate of England. On his death, he is buried in the basilica of Sts Peter and Paul at Canterbury, founded as the royal necropolis by Ethelbert.	602. Murder of the Emperor Maurice.		
		605. The Arabs crush the Persians at Dhonkar.	

ITALY	GAUL	SPAIN
615. Death of St Columban at the monastery of Bobbio.	613. Queen Brunhilda put to death.	
		621. *Historia de regibus Gothorum, Wandalorum et Suevorum* by Isidore of Seville (621-631).
	629-639. Reign of King Dagobert I.	629. The Visigoth king Swinthila drives the Byzantines out of Spain, but is dethroned in 633 by the fourth council of Toledo, presided by Isidore of Seville, which makes the monarchy elective.
	630-655. St Desiderius (Didier) Bishop of Cahors.	
	About 630-680. Founding of Jouarre and many Columbanian monasteries in the north and east of Gaul. The Rule of St Benedict taken up in Gaul.	
		636. Death of Isidore of Seville.
	641-660. St Eligius (Eloi) Bishop of Noyon.	
653. The Lombards converted to Christianity.	About 650. Shrine of Teuderigus at Saint-Maurice d'Agaune. Founding of the abbey of Fontenelle (Saint-Wandrille) in Normandy.	
	654. Founding of the abbey of Jumièges in Normandy.	
	About 660. *Chronicle* attributed to Fredegarius.	661. Reccesvinth consecrates the church of San Juan de Baños. A crown bearing his name was found in the Guarrazar Treasure.
	663-about 679. St Leger Bishop of Autun.	
	673. Revolt of the nobles.	
	After 673. Death of Agilbert, Bishop of Paris, in retirement at Jouarre, where he was probably the builder of the funerary crypt of the abbey.	
	675. Murder of Childeric II.	
	675. Revolt of the Aquitanians.	

650

BRITISH ISLES	EAST ROMAN EMPIRE AND BYZANTIUM	ISLAM	
		About 610. Mohammed preaches at Mecca.	
616. Death of King Ethelbert, followed by a pagan reaction.			
617. Edwin, King of Northumbria, an avowed pagan, dominates England.	617. Egypt occupied by the Persians.		
	623. Slavs in Crete.	622. Flight (Hegira) of Mohammed to Medina.	
627. Edwin converted to Christianity.	629. The Persians, weakened by internal strife, evacuate the Empire.		
		630. Battle of Mut, the first engagement between Byzantines and Muslims. Islam becomes the religion of Arabia.	
		632. Death of Mohammed.	
634. St Oswald, his successor, defeats the Britons.			
635. Founding of the monastery of Lindisfarne, in Northumbria, by Irish monks.		636. Conquest of Syria.	
		637-638. Taking of Jerusalem and Antioch.	
		639-644. Conquest of Egypt.	
642. St Oswald defeated and killed by the pagan king of Mercia, Penda. Mercia prevailed over Northumbria until the end of the 8th century.			
		About 646-653. Writing of the Koran.	
		647. The Arabs move into North Africa.	
			650
		651. The Arabs complete the conquest of Persia.	
655-656. Aethelhere, King of the Angles, an ally of Penda and like him a pagan, is killed in combat. The tumulus in which the Sutton Hoo ship treasure was found in 1939 may have been his tomb.			
		661. Beginning of the Omayyad dynasty of caliphs.	
663-664. Synod of Whitby where Agilbert, later Bishop of Paris, imposes the authority of Rome on the Britons, represented by Colman, abbot of Lindisfarne.			
668-690. Theodore of Tarsus, becoming Archbishop of Canterbury, imposes the Roman rites. Theodore brought to England his friends Hadrian of Niridanum, an African, and Benedict Biscop, a Northumbrian who for some years was a monk at Lérins.	670. The Arabs in Thrace.	671. Founding of Kairouan, in Tunisia.	
		671-675. Building of the great mosque of Kairouan.	
672-735. The Venerable Bede, author of the *Ecclesiastical History of the English Nation*.			
About 673-754. St Boniface, martyred in Friesland and buried at Fulda.	673. Siege of Constantinople, by land and by sea. The siege is not lifted till 677.		
674. St Benedict Bishop founds the monastery of Wearmouth and, in 682, Jarrow, providing them with manuscripts from Rome, in particular the works of Cassiodorus.			

	ITALY	GAUL	SPAIN
		680. Pepin of Heristal, mayor of the palace in Austrasia. About 683. Murder of Ebroin, mayor of the palace in Austrasia.	
		About 695. Pepin drives the Frisians back across the Rhine.	
700		About 700. *Lectionary* of Luxeuil.	
		709. Pepin's expedition against the Alamanni.	711. Arab invasion.
	712. Ciborium of Valpolicella. 713-744. Tomb of Bishop Cumian at Bobbio.	716-719. Charles Martel victorious over the Neustrians. 717-725. Septimania occupied by the Saracens. 719-738. Campaign of Charles Martel against the Saxons.	
	720. Sarcophagus of Abbess Theodota at Pavia. 725. Sarcophagus of Bishop Felix at Ravenna.	720. Victory of Charles Martel over the Aquitanians.	722. Beginning of the Reconquest in the Asturias.
	727. The edict of the Byzantine emperor Leo III the Isaurian against image worship (726) is denounced as impious by Pope Gregory II.	728. Charles Martel conquers Bavaria.	
		732. The Saracens defeated at Poitiers. 733. Conquest of Frisia by Charles Martel. 734. Provence invaded by the Saracens.	
	737. Baptistery of Callistus at Cividale.		
	739. Siege of Rome by Liutprand, king of the Lombards. 740. Altar of St Martin at Cividale, carved by order of Duke Ratchis.	741. Death of Charles Martel. 742. Pepin and Carloman subjugate the Aquitanians and the Alamanni.	739-757. Reign of King Alfonso I.
	744. Ratchis succeeds Liutprand.	744. Surrender of the Bavarians. Revolt of the Alamanni, put down in 745.	
750	750. Closure slab at Modena bearing the name of Bishop Lopicenus. 751. Capture of Rome by the Lombards.	752-759. Septimania reconquered by Pepin. 753. Pope Stephen II in Gaul.	
	754. Pepin in Italy.	754. Second crowning of Pepin by the pope, who consecrates the high altar of the basilica of Saint-Denis.	
	760. Consecration of the church of St Sophia at Benevento. About 760. Carved panel at Ferentillo bearing the name of Duke Hildericus. 762. Sigvald, patriarch of Aquileia (762-about 786). Bas-reliefs with his name in the cathedral of Cividale.		755-756. Abd er-Rahman conquers a large part of southern Spain and establishes himself at Cordova as Emir.
		768. Submission of Aquitaine. Death of Pepin, succeeded by Charles (Charlemagne) and Carloman. 771. Charles (Charlemagne) reigns alone.	

BRITISH ISLES	EAST ROMAN EMPIRE AND BYZANTIUM	ISLAM	
678. Wilfrid of York evangelizes Friesland.			
687. Death of St Cuthbert, Bishop of Lindisfarne (wooden coffin decorated with incised designs).		688-691. Building of the Mosque of Omar at Jerusalem.	
About 688. St Kilian, apostle of Thuringia, martyred at Würzburg.			
690. Echternach Gospels.		695. First Arab occupation of Carthage.	
697. After long resistance, the Irish finally accept the Roman computation of Easter.			700
About 700. Epic poem of *Beowulf* written in Old English.			
709. Death of St Aldhelm, scholar and Bishop of Sherborne.		708. Building of the great mosque of Damascus.	
		711-713. Arab conquest of Spain.	
	717-718. The Arabs besiege Constantinople for the second time, but are defeated by Leo III the Isaurian.		
		720-721. The Arabs besiege Toulouse.	
		725-731. They take Carcassonne and sack Autun.	
	726. Beginning of the iconoclast controversy.		
	727. Pope Gregory II condemns iconoclasm.		
	730. Edict forbidding the use of images in churches.		
	731. Pope Gregory III also condemns iconoclasm.	732. Arabs driven out of Gaul.	
		737. Charles Martel defeats the Arabs near Narbonne.	
738. Death of St Willibrord, who evangelized the Frisians and founded the bishopric of Utrecht (696) and the abbey of Echternach (698).			
740. Death of St Acca, Bishop of Hexham, who erected one of the oldest surviving stone crosses, decorated with vine shoots imitated from the antique.			750

Bibliography

1. ABERG (Nils), *Die Franken und Westgoten in der Völkerwanderungszeit,* Uppsala, 1922.

2. ABERG (Nils), *Die Goten und Langobarden in Italien,* Uppsala, 1923.

3. ABERG (Nils), *The Occident and the Orient in the Art of the Seventh Century:* I, *The British Isles,* Stockholm, 1943; II, *Lombard Italy,* Stockholm, 1945; III, *The Merovingian Empire,* Stockholm, 1947. Kgl. Vitterhersts hist. och antiqvitets Akademiens Handlingar, 1943-1947.

4. ALFÖLDI (András), *Funde aus der Hunnenzeit und ihre ethnische Sonderung,* in *Archaeologia Hungarica,* IX, Budapest, 1932, p. 26 sq.

5. ALFÖLDI (András), *Eine spätrömische Helmform und ihre Schicksale im germanisch-romanischen Mittelalter,* in *Acta archaeologica,* V, Copenhagen, 1934, p. 99 sq.

6. ALFÖLDI (András), *Die Kontorniaten,* Budapest, 1942-1943.

7. ALMAGRO (Martin), *Algunas falsificaciones visigodas,* Ampurias, III, 1941, p. 3.

8. ANNIBALDI (G.) and WERNER (Joachim), *Ostgotische Grabfunde aus Acquasanta (Provinz Ascoli Piceno),* in *Germania,* XLI, 1963, p. 356 sq.

9. ARBMAN (Holger), *Les Épées du tombeau de Childéric,* in *Meddelanden fran Lunds Universitets Historiska Museum,* Lund, 1948, p. 97 sq.

10. ARBMAN (Holger), *Verroterie cloisonnée et filigranée,* in *Meddelanden fran Lunds Universitets Historiska Museum,* Lund, 1950, p. 160 sq.

11. ARENS (Fritz Victor), *Funde in der St. Johanneskirche zu Mainz,* in *Mainzer Zeitschrift,* LIII, Mainz, 1958, p. 21 sq.

12. *Ars Hispaniae. Historia universal del arte hispanico,* II, Madrid, 1947.

13. *Ars sacra. Kunst des frühen Mittelalters,* Bayerische Staatsbibliothek, Munich, 1950. (Exhibition.)

14. ARSLAN (Edoardo), *La pittura e la scultura veronese, dal secolo VIII al secolo XIII,* Milan, 1943.

15. ARSLAN (Edoardo), *Remarques sur l'architecture lombarde du VIIe siècle,* in *Cahiers archéologiques,* VII, 1954, pp. 129-138.

16. *Art du haut Moyen Age dans la région alpine,* in *Actes du IIIe Congrès international pour l'étude du haut Moyen Age, 1951,* Lausanne, Urs Graf Verlag, 1954.

17. *Art in the Dark Ages,* Burlington Fine Arts Club, London, 1930.

18. *Arte del primo millennio. Atti del primo convegno per lo studio dell'arte dell'alto medio evo tenuto presso l'Università di Pavia (1950),* Turin, Viglongo, 1952.

19. *L'Art mérovingien,* Musées royaux d'Art et d'Histoire, Brussels, 1954. (Exhibition.)

20. *Atti dell'ottavo congresso di studi sull'alto medioevo :* I, *Stucchi e mosaici alto-medioevali;* II, *La chiesa di S. Salvatore in Brescia,* Milan, Ceschina, 1962.

21. AURENHAMMER (Hans), *Lexikon der christlichen Ikonographie,* Vienna. (In course of publication since 1959.)

22. AVERY (Myrtilla), *The Alexandrian Style at Santa Maria Antiqua, Rome,* in *The Art Bulletin,* VII, 1925, pp. 131-149.

23. BABELON (Ernest), *Le Tombeau du roi Childéric et les origines de l'orfèvrerie cloisonnée,* in *Mémoires de la Société nationale des Antiquaires de France,* LXXVI, Paris, 1924.

24. BARRIÈRE-FLAVY (C.), *Études sur les sépultures barbares du Midi et de l'Ouest de la France. Industrie wisigothique,* Toulouse-Paris, Leroux, 1893.

25. BARRIÈRE-FLAVY (C.), *Les Arts industriels des peuples barbares de la Gaule, du Ve au VIIIe siècle,* Toulouse-Paris, Picard, 1901, 3 vols.

26. BARSALI (Isa Belli), *Corpus della scultura altomedievale,* I, *La diocesi di Lucca,* Spoleto, Centro italiano di studi sull'alto medioevo, 1959.

27. BAUDOT (Henri), *Mémoire sur les sépultures des Barbares de l'époque mérovingienne, découvertes en Bourgogne,* Mémoire de la Commission archéologique de la Côte-d'Or, Dijon-Paris, 1860.

28. BAUM (Julius), *Frühchristlicher Bischofsstuhl in Trier,* in *Pantheon,* IV, 1929, p. 374.

29. BAUM (Julius), *Die Malerei und Plastik des Mittelalters,* II, *Deutschland, Frankreich und Britannien,* Potsdam, 1930.

30. BAUM (Julius), *Zu den Hornhauser Steinen,* in *Schumacher Festschrift,* Mainz, 1930, p. 351 sq.

31. BAUM (Julius), *La Sculpture figurale en Europe à l'époque mérovingienne,* Paris, 1937.

32. BAUM (Julius), *Das Warnebertusreliquiar,* in *Zeitschrift für schweizerische Archäologie und Kunstgeschichte,* VIII, 1946, p. 206 sq.

33. BAUM (Julius), *Darstellungen aus der germanischen Götter und Heldensage in der nordischen Kunst,* in *Eranos Jahrbuch,* Zurich, 1950.

34. BAUM (Julius), *Die Flechtwerkplatten von St. Aurelius in Hirsau,* in *Zeitschrift für württembergische Landesgeschichte,* XVII, 1958, pp. 241-252.

35. *Bayerische Frömmigkeit. 1 400 Jahre christliches Bayern,* Stadtmuseum, Munich, 1960.

36. BECATTI (Giovanni), *Oreficerie antiche, dalle minoiche alle barbariche,* Rome, 1955.

37. BEHRENS (Gustav), *Aus der frühen Völkerwanderungszeit des Mittelrheingebietes,* in *Mainzer Zeitschrift,* XVII-XIX, Mainz, 1921-1924, p. 73 sq.

38. BEHRENS (Gustav), *Merovingische Pressblechscheibenfibeln,* in *Mainzer Zeitschrift,* XXXIX-XL, Mainz 1944-1945, pp. 17-21.

39. BEHRENS (Gustav), *Merovingerzeit,* Katalog 13 des Römisch-Germanischen in Zentralmuseum Mainz, Mainz, 1947.

40. BENOIT (Fernand), *Les Cimetières suburbains d'Arles dans l'antiquité chrétienne et au Moyen Age,* Paris-Rome, Institut pontifical d'archéologie chrétienne, 1935. (Studi di antichità cristiana, XI.)

41. BENOIT (Fernand), *L'Abbaye de Saint-Victor et l'église de la Major à Marseille,* Paris, Laurens, 1936. (Petites monographies des grands édifices de la France.)

42. BENOIT (Fernand), *Les Reliques de saint Césaire, évêque d'Arles,* in *Cahiers archéologiques,* I, 1945, pp. 51-62.

43. BENOIT (Fernand), *Les Cimetières paléochrétiens de la Provence,* in *Cahiers archéologiques,* II, 1947, pp. 7-15.

44. BENOIT (Fernand), *Sarcophages paléochrétiens d'Arles et de Marseille*, Suppléments à *Gallia*, v, Paris, 1954.

45. BENOIT (Fernand), *La Basilique Saint-Pierre-et-Saint-Paul à Arles. Étude sur les cancels paléochrétiens*, in *Provence historique*, vii, 1957, pp. 8-21.
Closure slabs of the 5th to the late 8th century.

46. BENOIT (Fernand), *Le Baptistère de Cimiez*, in *Atti del VI congresso internazionale di archeologia cristiana*, 1962, pp. 147-168.

47. BENOIT (Fernand), *L'Origine de l'abbaye de Saint-Victor révélée par les fouilles*, in *Marseille*, 60, 1965, pp. 1-11.

48. BENOIT (Fernand), *Le Martyrium rupestre de l'abbaye Saint-Victor*, in *Comptes rendus de l'Académie des inscriptions et belles-lettres*, 1966, pp. 110-125.

49. BENOIT (François), « L'Architecture ». *L'Occident médiéval du romain au roman*, Paris, Laurens, 1933. (Manuels d'histoire de l'art.)

50. BERNHEIMER (R.), *A Sassanian Monument in Merovingian France*, in *Ars Islamica*, v, 12, 1938, p. 222 sq.

51. BESSE (Jean-Martial), *Les Moines de l'ancienne France. Période gallo-romaine et mérovingienne*, Paris, Poussielgue, 1906.

52. BESSON (Marius), *Antiquités du Valais*, Fribourg (Switzerland), 1900.

53. BESSON (Marius), *L'Art barbare dans l'ancien diocèse de Lausanne*, Lausanne, 1909.

54. BESSON (Marius), *Tombes mérovingiennes découvertes à Corcelles*, Musée neuchâtelois, Neuchâtel, 1916.

55. BISCHOFF (B.), *Das griechische Element in der abendländischen Bildung des Mittelalters*, in *Byzantinische Zeitschrift*, xliv, Munich, 1951, pp. 27-55.

56. BISCHOFF (B.), *Die kölner Nonnenhandschriften und das Skriptorium von Chelles*, in *Karolingische und ottonische Kunst, Forschungen zur Kunstgeschichte und christliche Archäologie*, iii, Wiesbaden, 1957, p. 395 sq.

57. BISCHOFF (B.), *Die südostdeutschen Schreibschulen und Bibliotheken in der Karolingerzeit*, i, *Die bayerischen Diözesen*, Wiesbaden, 1960.

58. BLANCHET (Adrien), *Les Trésors de monnaies romaines et les invasions germaniques en Gaule*, Paris, Leroux, 1900 [1899].

59. BLANCHET (Adrien), *Les Enceintes romaines de la Gaule. Étude sur l'origine d'un grand nombre de villes françaises*, Paris, Leroux, 1907.

60. BLONDEL (Louis), *Les Premiers Édifices chrétiens de Genève de la fin de l'époque romaine à l'époque romane*, in *Genava*, n. s., xi, 1933, pp. 77-101.

61. BLONDEL (Louis), *Carouge, villa romaine et burgonde*, in *Genava*, n. s., xviii, 1940, pp. 54-68.

62. BLONDEL (Louis), *Les Origines de Lausanne et les édifices qui ont précédé la cathédrale actuelle*, Lausanne, Rougé, 1943.

63. BLONDEL (Louis), *Les Anciennes Basiliques d'Agaune. Étude archéologique*, in *Vallesia*, iii, 1948, pp. 9-57.

64. BLONDEL (Louis), *Le Baptistère et les anciens édifices conventuels d'Agaune [à Saint-Maurice en Valais]*, in *Vallesia*, iv, 1949, pp. 19-28.

65. BLONDEL (Louis), *Aperçu sur les édifices chrétiens dans la Suisse occidentale avant l'an mille*, in *Art du haut Moyen Age dans la région alpine*, Lausanne, 1954, pp. 371-407.

66. BLONDEL (Louis), *Le Temple de l'Auditoire, ancienne église Notre-Dame-la-Neuve*, in *Genava*, n. s., v, 1957, pp. 97-128. *Excavations of the 5th century church which formed with Saint-Pierre the double cathedral of Geneva.*

67. BLONDEL (Louis), *Église de Saint-Germain à Genève. Pierres sculptées paléochrétiennes*, in *Genava*, n. s., viii, 1960, pp. 153-160.

68. BLONDEL (Louis), *L'Abbaye de Saint-Maurice d'Agaune et ses sanctuaires. Une ville sainte*, in *Revue suisse d'art et d'archéologie*, xxii, 1962, pp. 158-164.

69. BOECKLER (Albert), *Abendländische Miniaturen bis zum Ausgang der romanischen Zeit*, Berlin-Leipzig, Lietzmann, 1930.

70. BOECKLER (Albert), *Bildvorlagen der Reichenau*, in *Zeitschrift für Kunstgeschichte*, xii, Munich-Berlin, Deutscher Kunstverlag, 1949, pp. 7-29.

71. BOECKLER (Albert), *Deutsche Buchmalerei vorgotischer Zeit (Die Blauen Bücher)*, Königstein im Taunus, 1952.

72. BOECKLER (Albert), *Malerei und Plastik im ostfränkischen Reich*, in *Settimane di studio del Centro italiano di studi sull'alto medioevo*, Spoleto, 1954, p. 173 sq.

73. BOGNETTI (Gian Piero), *Storia di Milano*, ii, *L'alto Medio Evo (493-1002)*, Milan-Rome, Fondazione Treccani degli Alfieri per la storia di Milano, 1954.

74. BOGNETTI (Gian Piero), *Un nuovo elemento di datazione degli affreschi di Castelseprio*, in *Cahiers archéologiques*, vii, 1954, pp. 139-156.

75. BOGNETTI (Gian Piero), *Sul tipo e il grado di civiltà dei longobardi in Italia, secondo i dati dell'archeologia e della storia dell'arte*, in *Frühmittelalterliche Kunst in den Alpenländern*, Olten-Lausanne, 1954, pp. 41-76.

76. BOGNETTI (Gian Piero), CHIERRICI (Gino) and DE CAPITANI D'ARZAGO (Alberto), *Santa Maria di Castelseprio*, Milan, Fondazione Treccani degli Alfieri per la storia di Milano, 1948.

77. BOGYAY (T. von), *Zum Problem der Flechtwerksteine, in karolingischer und ottonischer Kunst*, in *Forschungen zur Kunstgeschichte und christlichen Archäologie*, Wiesbaden, 1957, p. 262 sq.

78. BÖHNER (Kurt), *Das Langschwert des Frankenkönigs Childerich*, in *Bonner Jahrbücher*, Bonn, 1948, pp. 218-248.

79. BÖHNER (Kurt), *Les Monuments lapidaires de l'époque franque au Musée régional rhénan de Bonn*, in *Mémorial d'un voyage d'études de la Société nationale des Antiquaires de France en Rhénanie (1951)*, Paris, 1953, pp. 83-90.

80. BÖHNER (Kurt), *Das Grab eines fränkischen Herren aus Morken im Rheinland*, in *Neue Ausgrabungen in Deutschland*, Berlin, 1958, pp. 432-468.

81. BÖHNER (Kurt), *Die fränkischen Altertümer des Trierer Landes*, in *Germanische Denkmäler der Völkerwanderungszeit*, i-ii, Berlin-Leipzig, 1958.

82. BONICATTI (M.), *Aspetti dell'industria libraria media-bizantina negli 'scriptoria' italogreci, e considerazione su alcuni manoscritti criptensi miniati*, in *Atti del III° congresso internazionale di studi sull'alto medioevo*, Spoleto, 1959, pp. 341-364.

83. BOTT (Hans), *Bajuwarischer Schmuck der Agilolfingerzeit. Schriftenreihe zur bayerischen Landegeschichte*, vol. XLVI. Munich, 1952.

84. BOÜARD (Michel de), *Le Baptistère de Port-Bail (Manche)*, in *Cahiers archéologiques*, IX, Paris, 1957, pp. 1-22.

85. BOUBE (Jean), *Les Sarcophages paléochrétiens de Martres-Tolosane*, in *Cahiers archéologiques*, IX, Paris, 1957, pp. 33-72.

86. BOUFFARD (Pierre), *Nécropoles burgondes de la Suisse. Les garnitures de ceinture. Cahiers de préhistoire et d'archéologie*, Geneva-Nyon, 1945.

87. BOULANGER (Camille), *Le Mobilier funéraire gallo-romain et franc en Picardie et en Artois*, Paris, 1902-1905.

88. BOULANGER (Camille), *Trois Cimetières mérovingiens : Cléry, Maurepas et Corbie*, in *Bulletin archéologique*, Paris, 1907, p. 18 sq.

89. BOULANGER (Camille). *Le Cimetière franco-mérovingien et carolingien de Marchélepot (Somme)*, Paris, 1909.

90. BRÉHIER (Louis), *L'Art en France, des invasions barbares à l'époque romane*, Paris, 1930.

91. BRENK (Beat), *Marginalien zum sogenannten Sarkophag des Agilbert in Jouarre*, in *Cahiers archéologiques*, XIV, Paris, 1964, p. 95 sq.

92. BREUER (J.) and ROOSENS (Heli), *Le Cimetière franc de Haillot*, in *Annales de la Société archéologique de Namur*, XLVIII (1956), Brussels, 1957, pp. 171-376.

93. BRIESENICK (B.), *Typologie und Chronologie der südwest-gallischen Sarkophage*, in *Jahrbuch des Römisch-Germanischen Zentralmuseums in Mainz*, IX, 1962-[1964], p. 76 sq.

94. BROZZI (M.) and TAGLIAFERRI (A.), *Arte longobarda*, I, *La scultura figurativa su marmo*, Cividale, 1960.

95. BRUCKNER (Albert Theophil), *Scriptoria medii aevi helvetica*, I-X, Geneva, 1935-1964.

96. BRUSIN (G.) and ZOVATTO (P.L.), *Monumenti paleocristiani di Aquileia e di Grado*, Udine, 1957.

97. BYVANCK (A. W.), *Les Principaux Manuscrits à peintures conservés dans les collections publiques du royaume des Pays-Bas*, XV, Paris, Société française de reproduction de manuscrits à peintures, 1931.

98. CABROL (F.), LECLERCQ (H.) and MARROU (H.I.), *Dictionnaire d'archéologie chrétienne et de liturgie*, Paris, 1908-1953, 15 volumes.

99. CALDERINI (Aristide), CHIERICI (Gino) and CECCHELLI (Carlo), *La basilica di S. Lorenzo Maggiore in Milano*, Milan, Fondazione Treccani degli Alfieri per la storia di Milano, 1951.

100. CATTANEO (Raffaele), *L'architettura in Italia dal secolo VI al mille circa*, Venice, 1888. (English edition: *Architecture in Italy from the Sixth to the Eleventh Century*, T. Fisher Unwin, London, 1896.)

101. CECCHELLI (Carlo), *I monumenti del Friuli dal secolo IV all XI*, I, *Cividale*, Milan-Rome, 1943.

102. *Charlemagne, œuvre, rayonnement et survivances*, Aix-la-Chapelle, 1965. (Exhibition catalogue.)

103. CHARTRAIRE (Chanoine), *Les Tissus anciens du trésor de la cathédrale de Sens*, in *Revue de l'art chrétien*, 1911, pp. 20-118.

104. CHAUME (Maurice), *Les Origines du duché de Bourgogne*, Dijon, Rebourseau, 1925-1937, 4 vols.

105. CHENET (G.), *La Tombe 319 et la buire chrétienne du cimetière mérovingien de Lavoye (Meuse)*, in *Préhistoire*, IV, Paris, 1935, pp. 34-118.

106. CHIFLET (J.), *Anastasis Childerici I, Francorum regis, sive Thesaurus sepulchralis Tornaci Nerviorum. Effusus et commentario illustratus*, Antwerp, 1665.

107. CHRIST (Yvan), *Les Cryptes mérovingiennes de l'abbaye de Jouarre*, Paris, Éditions d'art et d'histoire, 1955.

108. CIBULKA (Josef), *Grossmährische Kirchenbauten*, in *Sancti Cyrillus et Methodius Leben und Wirken*, Prague, 1963, pp. 49-117.

109. CLAPHAM (Alfred William), *English Romanesque Architecture before the Conquest*, Oxford, Clarendon Press, 1930.

110. COCHE DE LA FERTÉ (Étienne), *Bijoux du haut Moyen Age*, Lausanne, Payot, n.d. [1960]. (Orbis Pictus series, 34.)

111. COCHE DE LA FERTÉ (Étienne), *Art paléochrétien*, in *Histoire de l'Art*, II, *L'Europe médiévale*, Paris, Gallimard, 1966. (Encyclopédie de la Pléiade.)

112. COLETTI (Luigi), *Il tempietto di Cividale*, Rome, 1952.

113. CONWAY (M.), *Burgundian Buckles and Coptic Influences*, in *Proceedings of the Society of the Antiquaries of London*, 2nd series, XXX, London, 1917-1918, p. 65 sq.

114. COSSERAT (Lucien), *Le Cimetière mérovingien d'Andrésy (Seine-et-Oise)*, Paris, 1891.

115. COSTA (Dominique), *Nantes. Musée Th. Dobrée. Art mérovingien*, Paris, Ed. des Musées nationaux, 1964. (Inventaire des collections publiques françaises, 10.)

116. COUFFON (R.), *Essai sur l'architecture religieuse en Bretagne du Ve au Xe siècle*, Rennes, 1943. (Offprint from *Mémoires de la Société d'histoire et d'archéologie de la Bretagne*, 1943.)

117. COURAJOD (Louis), *Leçons professées à l'École du Louvre (1887-1896)*, I, *Origines de l'art roman et gothique*, Paris, 1899.

118. COURCELLE (Pierre), *Histoire littéraire des grandes invasions germaniques*, Paris, Études augustiniennes, 1964, Hachette (3rd ed. Many illustrations).

119. COUTIL (Léon), *L'Art mérovingien et carolingien*, Bordeaux, 1930.

120. CREMA (Luigi), *Osservazioni sull'architettura tardo-romana*, in *Studi in onore di Aristide Calderini e Roberto Paribeni*, III, 1956, pp. 569-592.

121. CREMA (Luigi), *L'Architettura romana*, Turin Società editrice internazionale, 1959. (Enciclopedia classica, III, 12.)

122. DANIÉLOU (Le Père Jean), *Sacramentum futuri, Études sur les origines de la typologie biblique*, Paris, Beauchesne et ses fils, 1950. *Studies in historical theology*.

123. DANNHEIMER (H.), *Die germanischen Funde der späten Kaiserzeit und des frühen Mittelalters in Mittelfranken*, in *Germanische Denkmäler der Völkerwanderungszeit*, Series A, Vol. VII, Berlin, 1962.

124. DANNHEIMER (H.) and LENZ KRISS-RETTENBECK, *Die Eininger Eisenkreuze, ihre Deutung und Datierung*, in *Bayrische Vorgeschichtblätter*, XXIX, 1964, p. 192 sq.

125. *The Dark Ages*, Worcester Art Museum, Worcester (Mass.), 1937.

126. DASNOY (Albert), *Le Reliquaire mérovingien d'Andenne*, in *Annales de la Société archéologique de Namur*, XLIX, Brussels, 1959, p. 41 sq.

127. DAVIES (G. G.), *The Origin and Development of Early Christian Architecture*, London, 1952.

128. *De l'art des Gaules à l'art français*, Musée des Augustins, Toulouse, 1956.

129. DE BERNARDI FERRERO (Daria), *Le cripte di Jouarre*, Turin, 1959.

130. DE CAPITANI D'ARZAGO (Alberto), *Architettura dei secoli quarto e quinto in alta Italia*, Milan, 1944, (21 plates with plans.)

131. DÉCHELETTE (Joseph), *Manuel d'archéologie préhistorique et celtique*, Paris, 1908-1928, 4 vols.

132. DEGANI (M.), *Il tesoro romano barbarico di Reggio Emilia*, Florence, 1959.

133. DEGEN (K), *Frühmittelalterliches Kunsthandwerk*, Führer des hessischen Landesmuseums, II, Darmstadt, 1955.

134. DEGERING (H. D.) and BOECKLER (Albert), *Die Quedlinburger Itala-Fragmente*, Berlin, 1932.

135. DEGRASSI (Nevio), *La 'sella plicatilis' di Pavia*, in *Arte del primo millennio. Atti del IIº convegno per lo studio dell'arte dell'alto medioevo*, *Pavia*, Turin, Viglongo, 1952.

136. DELEHAYE (Hippolyte), *Les Origines du culte des martyrs*, 2nd ed. Brussels, Société des Bollandistes, 1933. (1st ed. in 1912.)

137. DELORT (Émile), *Le Cimetière franc d'Ennery*, in *Gallia*, V, Paris, 1948, pp. 351-403.

138. DELVOYE (Charles), *Recherches récentes sur les origines de la basilique paléochrétienne*, in *Annuaire de l'Institut de philosophie et d'histoire orientales et slaves*, XIV, 1954-1957, pp. 205-228.

139. DEMOUGEOT (Émilienne), *Art des grandes invasions*, in *Histoire de l'art*, II, *L'Europe médiévale*, Paris, Gallimard, 1966. (Encyclopédie de la Pléiade.)

140. DESCHAMPS (Paul), *Étude sur la paléographie des inscriptions lapidaires de la fin de l'époque mérovingienne aux dernières années du XIIᵉ siècle*, in *Bulletin monumental*, 1929, pp. 5-88.

141. DHONDT (J.), *L'Essor urbain entre la Meuse et la mer du Nord à l'époque mérovingienne*, in *Studi in onore di A. Sapori*, Rome, 1957, pp. 55-78.

142. DOBERER (E.), *Zur Herkunft der Sigvaldplatte*, in *Österreichische Zeitschrift für Kunst und Denkmäler*, Folge, XVII, 1963, p. 168 sq.

143. DOPPELFELD (O.), *Das fränkische Frauengrab unter dem Chor des Kölner Domes*, in *Kölner Domblatt*, XX, 1961-1962, p. 103 sq.

144. DOPPELFELD (O.), *Das fränkische Knabengrab unter dem Chor des Kölner Domes*, in *Germania*, XLII, 1964, p. 156 sq.

145. DOPPELFELD (O.) and PIRLING (R.), *Fränkische Fürsten im Rheinland*, Düsseldorf, 1966.

146. DUCHESNE (Louis), *Fastes épiscopaux de l'ancienne Gaule*, 2nd ed. Paris, Fontemoing, 1907-1915, 3 vols. (1st ed. in 1893.)

147. DUCHESNE (Louis), *Origines du culte chrétien. Étude sur la liturgie latine avant Charlemagne*, 5th ed. Paris, E. de Boccard, 1925. (1st ed. in 1889.)

148. DUPONT (André), *Les Cités de la Narbonnaise première depuis les invasions germaniques jusqu'à l'apparition du Consulat*, Nîmes, Imprimerie de Chastenin frères et Alméras, 1942. (Thesis.)

149. DURAND-LEFEBVRE (M.), *Sarcophages mérovingiens de Paris*, in *Cahiers archéologiques*, VI, Paris, 1952, pp. 168-175.

150. DURLIAT (Marcel), *Un groupe de sculptures wisigothiques à Narbonne*, in *Études mérovingiennes. Actes des journées de Poitiers (1952)*, Paris, 1953, pp. 93-101.

151. DURLIAT (Marcel), *Les Autels de Septimanie du Vᵉ au VIIIᵉ siècle*, in *Actes du Vᵉ Congrès international d'archéologie chrétienne (1954)*, Vatican City, Paris, 1957, pp. 539-550.

152. DURLIAT (Marcel), *Quelques Sarcophages inédits [en Aquitaine]*, in *Cahiers archéologiques*, IX, Paris, 1957, pp. 23-32.

153. DURLIAT (Marcel), *L'Architecture espagnole*, Paris, Didier, 1966.

154. DUVAL (Noël), *Les Origines de la basilique chrétienne. État de la question*, in *Information d'histoire de l'art*, VII, Paris, 1962, pp. 1-19.

155. DYGGVE (Ejnar), *Il tempietto di Cividale*, in *Atti del IIº congresso internazionale di studi sull'alto medioevo*, Spoleto, 1953.

156. *Early Christian and Byzantine Art*, An Exhibition held at the Baltimore Museum of Art, Baltimore, 1947.

157. EBERSOLT (Jean), *Orient et Occident*, Paris, 1928.

158. EBERSOLT (J. G.), *Les Cimetières burgondes du Doubs et du Jura à l'époque barbare*, Besançon, 1950.

159. EGGERS (Hans Jürgen), WILL (Ernest), JOFFROY (René) and HOLMQVIST (Wilhelm), *Kelten und Germanen in Heidnischer Zeit*, Baden-Baden, Holle Verlag, 1964. French edition: *Les Celtes et les Germains à l'époque païenne*, Paris, A. Michel, 1965. (L'Art dans le monde, civilisations européennes.)

160. EISNER (J.), *Zwei Spangernhelme vom Baldenheimer Typus*, in *I.P.E.K.*, XIII-XIV, Berlin, 1939-1940, p. 145 sq.

161. ELBERN (V. H.), *Zu dem Relieffragment mit zwei Gekreuzigten in der Mellebaudis Memoria in Poitiers*, in *Jahrbuch Berliner Museen*, Neue Folge, III, Berlin, 1961, p. 149 sq.

162. ELBERN (V. H.), *Der fränkische Reliquienkasten und Tragaltar von Werden*, in *Das erste Jahrtausend*, I, Düsseldorf, 1962, pp. 436-470.

163. ELBERN (V. H.), *Das erste Jahrtausend*, I, II, Düsseldorf, 1962-1963. (Plates.)

164. ELLMERS (D.), *Zum Trinkgeschirr der Wikingerzeit*, in *Offa*, XXI-XXII, 1964-1965.

165. ESSEN (C. C. Van), *Reliefs décoratifs d'époque carolingienne à Rome*, in *Mededeelingen van het Nederlands Historisch Instituute Rome*, IX, The Hague, 1957, pp. 84-113.

166. *Études mérovingiennes. Actes des journées de Poitiers (1952)*, Paris, 1953.

167. *Evangeliorum quattuor Codex Cenannensis... prolegomenio auxerunt*, p. p. H. Alton and P. Meyer, Berne, Urs Graf Verlag, 1950, 2 vols.

168. *Evangeliorum quattuor Codex Durmachensis. The Book of Durrow*, p. p. Arthur Aston Luce, Otto Simes, P. Meyer and C. Bieler, Olten-Lausanne, Urs Graf Verlag, 1960. 2 folio vols.

169. *Evangeliorum quattuor Codex Lindisfarnensis*, p. p. T. D. Kendrick, T.J. Brown, R. L. S. Bruce-Mitford, H. Roosen-Runge, A. J. C. Ross, E. G. Stanley and A. G. A. Werner, Olten-Lausanne, Urs Graf Verlag, 1956-1960, 2 vols.

170. EWIG (E.), *Trier im Merovingenreich. Civitas, Stadt, Bistum*, Trier, 1954.

171. EWIG (E.), *Résidence et capitale pendant le haut Moyen Age*, in *Revue historique*, CCXXX, 1963, pp. 25-72.

172. *Exposition d'art byzantin*, Musée des Arts décoratifs, palais du Louvre, Paris, 1931.

173. EYGUN (F.), *Le baptistère Saint-Jean de Poitiers*, in *Gallia*, XXII, Paris 1964, pp. 137-161.

174. FAIDER-FEYTMANS (G.), *Les Fibules à rayons du cimetière mérovingien de Trivières (Hainaut)*, in *Annales de la Fédération archéologique et historique de Belgique, Congrès de Namur*, Brussels, 1938, pp. 3-8.

175. FAIDER-FEYTMANS (G.), *La Belgique à l'époque mérovingienne*, Brussels, 1964.

176. FEIST (P. H.), *Byzanz und die figurale Kunst der Merovingerzeit*, Byzantin. Beiträge, herg. von J. Jrmscher, Berlin, 1964, p. 399.

177. FELLETTI MAJ (Bianca Maria), *Ricostruzione di uno scudo longobardo da Castel Trosino*, in *Rendiconti della Pontificia Accademia romana di Archeologia*, XXXIV, Rome, 1961-1962, pp. 191-205.

178. FELLETTI MAJ (Bianca Maria), *Intorno a una fibula aurea dalla necropoli longobarda di Nocera Umbra*, *Commentari*, XII, 1961, p. 3.

179. FELLETTI MAJ (Bianca Maria), *Echi di tradizione antica nella civiltà artistica in età longobarda in Umbria*, in *Ricerche sull'Umbria tardo-antica e pre-romanica, II Convegno di studi umbri, Gubbio, 1964*, Perugia, 1965, p. 317 sq.

180. FETTICH (N.), *Der zweite Schatz von Szilágysomlyó*, in *Archaeologia Hungarica*, VIII, Budapest, 1932.

181. FÉVRIER (Paul-Albert), *Sculpture paléochrétienne de Saint-Julien d'Oule*, in *Cahiers archéologiques*, XII, 1962, pp. 89-98.

182. FÉVRIER (Paul-Albert), *Le Développement urbain en Provence, de l'époque romaine à la fin du XIVe siècle. Archéologie et histoire urbaine*, Paris, E. de Boccard, 1964. (Thesis.)

183. FILLITZ (Hermann), *Die Spätphase des 'langobardischen' Stiles. Jahrbuch der kunsthistorischen Sammlungen in Wien*, LIV, Vienna, 1958, p. 7 sq.

184. FINGERLIN (G.), *Grab einer adligen Frau aus Güttingen*, in *Badische Fundberichte*, Heft 4. Freiburg-im-Breisgau, 1964.

185. FLAVIGNY (R.) and CHIROL (E.), *Deux plaques mérovingiennes inédites de Saint-Ouen de Rouen*, in *Études mérovingiennes. Actes des journées de Poitiers (1952)*, Paris, 1953, p. 111 sq.

186. FLEURY (Michel) and FRANCE-LANORD (Albert), *Les Bijoux mérovingiens d'Arnegonde*, in *Art de France*, I, Paris, 1961, pp. 7-17.

187. FONTAINE (J.), *Isidore de Séville et la culture classique dans l'Espagne wisigothique*, Paris, Études augustiniennes, 1959, 2 vols. (Thesis.)

188. *Forma Orbis Romani. Carte archéologique de la Gaule romaine [et chrétienne]*, Paris, Union académique internationale et C.N.R.S. (In course of publication since 1931.)

189. FORMIGÉ (Jules), *Remarques diverses sur les baptistères de Provence*, in *Mélanges Fr. Martroye*, Paris, 1940, pp. 167-190.

190. FORSYTH (Gordon), *The Church of St Martin at Angers*, Princeton University Press, 1953. (Text and Atlas.)

191. FOSSARD (Denise), *Les Chapiteaux de marbre du VIIe siècle en Gaule. Style et évolution*, in *Cahiers archéologiques*, II, Paris, 1947, pp. 69-85.

192. FOSSARD (Denise), *Répartition des sarcophages mérovingiens à décor en France*, in *Études mérovingiennes. Actes des journées de Poitiers (1952)*, Paris, 1953, pp. 117-125.

193. FOSSARD (Denise), *La Chronologie des sarcophages d'Aquitaine*, in *Actes du Ve Congrès international d'archéologie chrétienne (1954)*, Vatican City-Paris, 1957, pp. 321-335.

194. FOSSARD (Denise), *Le Décor des sarcophages mérovingiens en plâtre moulé et l'influence de l'orfèvrerie*, in *Bulletin de la Société nationale des Antiquaires de France*, Paris, 1961, pp. 62-67.

195. FOSSARD (Denise), *Décors mérovingiens des bijoux et des sarcophages de plâtre*, in *Arts de France*, III, 1963, pp. 30-39.

196. FOURNIER (Gabriel), *Le Peuplement rural en basse Auvergne durant le haut Moyen Age*, Paris, Presses Universitaires de France, 1962. (Thesis.)

197. FOURNIER (Gabriel), *Les Mérovingiens*, Paris, Presses Universitaires de France, 1966. (Que sais-je?)

198. FRANCE-LANORD (Albert) and FLEURY (Michel), *Das Grab der Arnegundis in Saint-Denis*, in *Germania*, XL, 1962, p. 341 sq.

199. FRANCOVICH (G. de), *Arte carolingia ed ottoniana in Lombardia*, in *Römisches Jahrbuch für Kunstgeschichte*, VI, 1942-1944, pp. 113-255.

200. FRANCOVICH (G. de), *L'arte siriaca e il suo influsso sulla pittura medioevale nell'Oriente e nell'Occidente*, in *Commentari*, anno II, fascicolo I e II, Florence, Le Monnier, 1951: I, pp. 3-16, and II, pp. 75-83.

201. FRANCOVICH (G. de), *Il problema delle origini della scultura cosiddetta 'longobarda'*, in *Atti del I^o congresso internazionale di studi longobardi*, Spoleto, 1951, pp. 256-273.

202. FRANCOVICH (G. de), *Il ciclo pittorico della chiesa di S. Giovanni a Münster (Müstair) nei Grigioni*, in *Arte lombarda*, II, 1956, p. 28 sq.

203. FRANCOVICH (G. de), *Osservazioni sull'altare di Ratchis a Cividale e sui rapporti tra occidente e oriente nei secoli VII° e VIII° D. C.*, in *Scritti di storia dell'arte in onore di Mario Salmi*, Rome, 1961, p. 173 sq.

204. FREMERSDORF (Fritz), *Zur Geschichte des fränkischen Rüsselbechers*, in *Wallraf-Richartz Jahrbuch*, II-III, Cologne, 1934, p. 23 sq.

205. FREMERSDORF (Fritz), *Zwei wichtige Frankengräber aus Köln*, in *I.P.E.K.*, XV-XVI, Berlin, 1941-1942, p. 124 sq.

206. FREMERSDORF (Fritz), *Das fränkische Reihengräberfeld von Köln-Müngersdorf*, I, II, in *Germanische Denkmäler der Völkerwanderungszeit*, vol. XV, Berlin, 1944.

207. FREMERSDORF (Fritz), *Cologne gallo-romaine et chrétienne*, in *Mémorial d'un voyage d'études de la Société nationale des Antiquaires de France en Rhénanie (1951)*, Paris, 1953, pp. 91-140.

208. FREMERSDORF (Fritz), *Zu dem blauen Glasbecher aus dem Reihengräberfeld von Pfalheim (Kr. Ellmangen), Germanisches Nationalmuseum Nürnberg*, in *Kölner Jahrbuch*, I, 1955, p. 33 sq.

209. *Frühmittelalterliche Kunst. Neue Beiträge zur Kunstgeschichte des 1. Jahrtausends*, Baden-Baden, Verlag für Kunst und Wissenschaft, 1954.

210. FUCHS (S.), *Geschlossene Grabfunde der Reihengräberfelder von San Giovanni in Cividale*, Udine, 1943.

211. FUCHS (S.), *Kunst der Ostgotenzeit*, Berlin, 1944.

212. FUCHS (S.) and WERNER (J.), *Die langobardischen Fibeln aus Italien*, Berlin, 1950.

213. GABRIELLI (N.), *Le miniature delle omelie di S. Gregorio*, in *Arte del primo millennio, Atti del IIº Convegno per lo studio dell'arte dell'alto medio evo tenuto presso l'Università di Pavia (1950)*, Turin, Viglongo, 1952, pp. 301-311.

214. GAILLARD (G.), *La Représentation des évangélistes à l'Hypogée des Dunes*, in *Études mérovingiennes. Actes des journées de Poitiers (1952)*, Paris, 1953, p. 135 sq.

215. GALASSI (Giuseppe), *Roma o Bisanzio*, I, *I mosaici di Ravenna e le origini dell'arte italiana* (nova edizione); II, *Il congedo classico e l'arte nell'alto medioevo*, Rome, Istituto poligrafico di Stato, 1953; xv, p. 301, and VII, p. 683.

216. GANSHOF (F. L.), *Étude sur le développement des villes entre Loire et Rhin au Moyen Age*, Brussels, 1943.

217. GANTNER (Joseph), *Histoire de l'art en Suisse, des origines à la fin de l'époque romane*, Neuchâtel, v, Attinger, 1941.

218. GARSCHA (Frederich), *Das völkerwanderungszeitliche Fürstengrab von Altlussheim*, in *Germania*, 20, 1936, pp. 191-198.

219. GARSCHA (Frederich), *Zum Grabfund von Altlussheim*, in *Jahrbuch des Römisch-Germanischen Zentralmuseums in Mainz*, VII, Mainz, 1960, p. 315 sq.

220. GAUTHIER (Marie-Madeleine), *Première Campagne de fouilles dans le sépulcre de Saint-Martial de Limoges*, in *Cahiers archéologiques*, XII, 1962, pp. 205-248.

221. GINHART (K.), *Der fünfundzwanzigste karolingische Flechtwerkstein in Kärnten*, in *Carinthia*, I, 1957, p. 218 sq.

222. GIRARD (R.), *Fouilles à Saint-Laurent de Grenoble. Campagne de 1960 à 1964*, in *Bulletin du Comité des travaux historiques*, 1964, pp. 347-369.

223. GISCHIA (Léon), MAZENOD (Lucien) and VERRIER (Jean), *Les Arts primitifs français. Art mérovingien, art carolingien, art roman*, Paris, Arts et métiers graphiques, 1941.

224. GLAZEMA (P.), *Kunst en Schoonheid uit de vroege Middeleeuwen. De merowisgsche Grafvelden van Alphen, Rhenen en Maastricht*, Amersfoort, 1955.

225. GLAZEMA (P.) and YPEY (J.), *Merovingische Andachtskunst*, Baarn, 1965.

226. GOLDSCHMIDT (Adolph), *Die deutsche Buchmalerei*, I, *Die karolingische Buchmalerei*, Florence-Munich, Pantheon, 1928, 2 vols.

227. GÓMEZ MORENO (M.), *Iglesias mozárabes*, Madrid, 1919, 2 vols.

228. GOSSE (H.-A.), *Notice sur d'anciens cimetières trouvés soit en Suisse, soit dans le canton de Genève et principalement dans celui de la Balme*, in *Mémoire de la Société d'histoire et d'archéologie de Genève*, IX, 1853 and 1855.

229. GRABAR (André), *Plotin et les origines de l'esthétique médiévale*, in *Cahiers archéologiques*, I, Paris, 1945, pp. 7-14.

230. GRABAR (André), *Martyrium. Recherches sur le culte des reliques et l'art chrétien antique*, Paris, A. Maisonneuve, 1946-1947, 2 vols. of text and 1 vol. of plates. (Collège de France, Fondation Schlumberger pour les études byzantines.)

231. GRABAR (André), *Les Ampoules de Terre sainte* [at Monza and Bobbio], Photographs by Denise Fourmont. Paris, Klincksieck, 1958.

232. GRABAR (André), *Le Premier Art chrétien*, Paris, Gallimard, 1966. ('L'Univers des Formes'). English translation: *The Beginnings of Christian Art*, Thames & Hudson, London, and Odyssey Press, New York, 1967.

233. GRABAR (André), *L'Age d'or de Justinien*, Paris, Gallimard, 1966. ('L'Univers des Formes'). English translation: *Byzantium, From the Death of Theodosius to the Rise of Islam*, Thames & Hudson, London, 1967, and *The Golden Age of Justinian*, Odyssey Press, New York, 1967.

234. GRABAR (André) and NORDENFALK (Carl), *Le haut Moyen Age. De la fin de l'époque romaine au XIᵉ siècle*, Geneva, Skira, 1957. ('Les grands siècles de la peinture'). English translation: *Early Medieval Painting, From the 4th to the 11th Century*, Geneva, Skira, 1957.

235. GRELLE (A.), *I rilievi del duomo di Aversa*, in *Napoli Nobilissima*, IV, 1965, p. 157.

236. GRENIER (Albert), *Manuel d'archéologie gallo-romaine*, Paris, A. et J. Picard, 1931-1960, 4 tomes in 7 vols.

237. GRIFFE (Élie), *Les Premiers Lieux de culte chrétien en Gaule*, in *Bulletin de littérature ecclésiastique*, LVIII, 1957, pp. 129-150.

238. GRÖBBELS (J. W.), *Der Reihengräberfund von Gammertingen*, Munich, 1905.

239. GRÜNEISEN (W. de), *Sainte-Marie-Antique*, Rome, Bretschneider, 1911, 2 vols. (1 of text, 1 of plates.)

240. GUYAN (W. U.), *Das alamannische Gräberfeld von Beggingen-Löbern*, Basel, 1958.

241. HAMANN-MACLEAN (R. H.), *Frühe Kunst im westfränkischen Reich*, Leipzig, 1939.

242. HAMANN-MACLEAN (R. H.), *Merovingisch oder Frühromanisch?* in *Jahrbuch des Römisch-Germanischen Zentralmuseums in Mainz*, IV, Mainz, 1957, p. 161 sq.

243. HAMPEL (Joseph), *Die Altertümer des frühen Mittelalters in Ungarn*, I-III, Brunswick, 1905.

244. HARBAUER (J. M.), *Zu den Schretzheimer Funden*, in *Jahrbuch des historischen Vereins Dillingen*, IX, 1896, p. 219 sq.

245. HASELOFF (Arthur), *Die vorromanische Plastik in Italien*, Berlin, 1936.

246. HASELOFF (Günther), *Der Abtsstab des heiligen Germanus in Delsberg*, in *Germania*, XXXIII, 1955, p. 210.

247. HASELOFF (Günther), *Die langobardischen Goldblattkreuze. Ein Beitrag zur Frage nach dem Ursprung von Stil II*, in *Jahrbuch des Römisch-Germanischen Zentralmuseums in Mainz*, III, Mainz, 1956, p. 143 sq.

248. HASELOFF (Günther), *Principi mediterranei dell'arte barbarica*, in *Settimane di studio del Centro italiano di studi sull'alto medioevo*, IX, Spoleto, 1962, p. 477 sq.

249. HAUCK (Karl), *Germanische Bilddenkmäler des frühen Mittelalters*, in *Deutsche Vierteljahrsschrift für Literatur und Geistesgeschichte*, 1957, p. 349.

250. HÉBRARD (Jean), *Anciens Autels du diocèse de Montpellier*, Montpellier, 1942. (Mimeographed.)

251. HENRY (Françoise), *La Sculpture irlandaise pendant les douze premiers siècles de l'ère chrétienne*, Paris, Leroux, 1933.

252. HENRY (Françoise), *Irish Art in the Early Christian Period*, 2nd ed., London, Methuen, 1947.

253. HENRY (Françoise), *Early Monasteries, Beehive Huts, and Dry-Stone Houses in the Neighbourhood of Caerviceen and Waterville (Co. Kerry)*, in *Proceedings of the Royal Irish Academy*, section C, LVIII, 1956-1957, pp. 45-166.

254. HENRY (Françoise), *L'Art irlandais*, La Pierre-qui-Vire, Zodiaque, 1963-1964, 3 vols. ('La Nuit des temps'.)

255. HEMPEL (Heinz Ludwig), *Zum Problem der Anfänge der AT-Illustration*, in *Zeitschrift für die alttestamentliche Wissenschaft*, LXIX, Berlin, 1957, pp. 103-131.

256. HERBERT (J. A.), *Illuminated Manuscripts*, London, 1911.

257. HESSEN (Otto), *I nastri decorativi aurei della ricca tomba femminile longobarda di Torino-Lingotto*, in *Bollettino della Società piemontese di archeologia e di belle arti*, n. s., XVI-XVII, 1962-1963, p. 31 sq.

258. HIGOUNET (Charles), *La Gaule mérovingienne*, in *L'Information historique*, XVI, 1954, pp. 63-66 and 107-110.

259. HIGOUNET (Charles), GARDELLES (J.) and LAFAURIE (J.), *Bordeaux pendant le haut Moyen Age*, Bordeaux, Fédération historique du Sud-Ouest, 1963. *(Histoire de Bordeaux*, vol. II.)

260. HOLMQVIST (Wilhelm), *Zur Herkunft einiger germanischer Figurendarstellungen*, in *I.P.E.K.*, XII, Berlin, 1938, p. 78 sq.

261. HOLMQVIST (Wilhelm), *Kunstproblem der Merovingerzeit*, Kunglig Vitterhets Historie och Antikvitet Akademien, handlingar, Stockholm, 1939.

262. HOLMQVIST (Wilhelm), *Germanic Art during the First Millennium A. D.*, Stockholm, 1955.

263. HOLMQVIST (Wilhelm), *Barbarian Europe*, in *Encyclopedia of World Art*, V, McGraw Hill, New York and London, 1961.

264. HOLTER (K.), *Das alte und neue Testament in der Buchmalerei nördlich der Alpen*, in *Settimane di studio del Centro italiano di studi sull'alto medioevo*, X, Spoleto, 1963, pp. 413-471.

265. HOMBURGER (Otto), *Ein vernichtetes Denkmal merovingischer Baukunst aus frühkarolingischer Zeit, der 'Rachio-Codex' der Bongarsiana*, in *Festschrift Hans R. Hahnloser*, Stuttgart, 1961, pp. 185-206.

266. HOMBURGER (Otto), *Die illustrierten Handschriften der Bürgerbibliothek Bern. Die vorkarolingischen und karolingischen Handschriften*, Berne, Bürgerbibliothek, 1962.

267. HUBERT (Jean), *La Châsse dite « de Mummole » à Saint-Benoît-sur-Loire*, in *Bulletin de la Société nationale des Antiquaires de France*, 1930, pp. 115-117.

268. HUBERT (Jean), *Les Monuments funéraires de l'église de Saint-Dizier en Alsace*, in *Bulletin monumental*, Paris, 1935, pp. 215-235.

269. HUBERT (Jean), *Le Trône de Dagobert*, in *Demarteion*, I, 1935, pp. 17-29.

270. HUBERT (Jean), *L'Art pré-roman*, Paris, Van Oest, 1938.

271. HUBERT (Jean), *Ce que nous pouvons savoir de l'architecture religieuse en Gaule au Ve siècle*, in *Saint-Germain d'Auxerre et son temps*, Auxerre, 1950, pp. 15-25.

272. HUBERT (Jean), *Les Cathédrales doubles et l'histoire de la liturgie*, in *Atti del primo convegno internazionale di studi longobardi*, Spoleto, 1951, pp. 167-176.

273. HUBERT (Jean), *Les Grandes Voies de circulation à l'intérieur de la Gaule mérovingienne d'après l'archéologie*, in *Actes du VIe Congrès international d'études byzantines*, II, Paris, 1951, pp. 183-199.

274. HUBERT (Jean), *Les Cryptes de Jouarre*, Melun, Imprimerie de la préfecture de Seine-et-Marne, 1952.

275. HUBERT (Jean), *L'Architecture religieuse du haut Moyen Age en France. Plans, notices et bibliographie*, Paris, Imprimerie nationale, 1952. (Bibliothèque de l'École pratique des Hautes Études. Section des sciences religieuses. Collection chrétienne et byzantine.)

276. HUBERT (Jean), *L'Époque mérovingienne*, in René Huyghe, *L'Art et l'Homme*, II, Paris, Larousse, 1958, pp. 237-240.

277. HUBERT (Jean), *Évolution de la topographie et de l'aspect des villes de Gaule du Ve au Xe siècle*, in *Settimane di studio del Centro italiano di studi sull'alto medioevo*, VI, 1958 (1959), pp. 529-602.

278. HUBERT (Jean), *Les Relations artistiques entre les diverses parties de l'ancien empire romain pendant le haut Moyen Age*, in *Settimane di studio del Centro italiano di studi sull'alto medioevo*, XI, 1963, pp. 453-649.

279. HUBERT (Jean), *Les Cathédrales doubles de la Gaule*, in *Genava (Mélanges Louis Blondel)*, n. s., XI, 1963, pp. 105-125.

280. HUBERT (Jean), *L'Érémitisme et l'archéologie*, in *L'eremitismo in Occidente*, Milan, 1964, pp. 469-490. (Publication of the Catholic University of Milan, 3rd series.)

281. HUBERT (Jean), *Le décor du palais de Naranco et l'art de l'Europe barbare*, in *Symposium sobre cultura asturiana de la alta edad media*, Oviedo, 1967, pp. 151-160.

282. HUEBENER (Wolfgang), *Zur chronologischen Gliederung des Gräberfeldes von San Pedro de Alcántara, Vega del Mar*, in *Madrider Mitteilungen*, VI, 1965, pp. 195-214.

283. HUGLO (Michel), *Un tonaire du graduel de la fin du VIIIe siècle (Paris, B.N., Lat. 13159). Revue grégorienne*, 1952, pp. 176 sq., 224 sq.

284. HUNGER (Herbert), *Antikes und mittelalterliches Buch- und Schriftwesen*, in *Geschichte der Textüberlieferung der antiken und mittelalterlichen Literatur*, I, Zurich, Atlantis Verlag, 1961, pp. 108-147.

285. JALABERT (Denise), *La Flore sculptée des monuments du Moyen Age en France. Recherches sur les origines de l'art français*, Paris, A. et J. Picard, 1965.

286. JENNY (W. A.), *Die Kunst der Germanen im frühen Mittelalter*, Berlin, 1943.

287. JENNY (W. A.) and VOLBACH (W. F.), *Germanischer Schmuck des frühen Mittelalters*, Berlin, 1933.

288. JULLIAN (Camille), *Histoire de la Gaule*, Paris, Hachette, 1908 [1907]-1920, 6 vols.

289. JURASCHEK (Franz von), *Die Apokalypse von Valenciennes*, in *Veröffentlichungen der Gesellschaft für österreichische Frühmittelalterforschung* Heft 1, Linz, n. d.

290. JURASCHEK (Franz von) and JENNY (Wilhelm von), *Die Martinskirche in Linz. Ein vorkarolingischer Bau in seiner Umgestaltung zur Nischenkirche*, Linz, 1949.

291. KAUTZSCH (R.), *Die langobardische Schmuckkunst in Oberitalien*, in *Römisches Jahrbuch für Kunstgeschichte*, v, 1941, p. 1 sq.

292. KEMPF (T. K.), *Ausgrabungen au den Gelände des Trierer Domes*, in *Germania*, XXIX, 1951, pp. 47-58.

293. KEMPF (T. K.), *Les Premiers Résultats des fouilles de la cathédrale de Trèves*, in *Mémorial d'un voyage d'études de la Société nationale des Antiquaires de France en Rhénanie (1951)*, Paris, 1953, pp. 153-162.

294. KEMPF (T. K.), *Die Entwicklung des Stadtgrundrisses von Trier*, in *Trierer Jahrbuch*, 1953, pp. 5-22.

295. KENDRICK (Thomas Downing), *Polychrome Jewellery in Kent*, in *Antiquity*, VII, 1933, p. 429 sq.

296. KENDRICK (Thomas Downing), *Anglo-Saxon Art to A. D. 900*, London, Methuen, 1938.

297. KENDRICK (Thomas Downing), *The Sutton Hoo Ship Burial*, London, 1947.

298. KHATCHATRIAN (Armen), *Les Baptistères paléo-chrétiens. Plans, notices et bibliographie*, Paris, Klincksieck, 1962, 402 plans. (École pratique des Hautes Études. Section des sciences religieuses. Collection chrétienne et byzantine.)

299. KIRCHNER (Joachim), *Die Heimat des Eginocodex*, in *Archiv für Urkundenforschung*, X, 1928, pp. 111-127.

300. KIRSCH (Johann Peter), *Le Cimetière burgonde de Fétigny*, in *Archives de la Société d'histoire du canton de Fribourg*, IV, 1899, p. 479 sq.

301. KITZINGER (E.), *Römische Malerei vom Beginn des 7. bis zur Mitte des 8. Jahrhunderts*, Munich, 1936.

302. KITZINGER (E.), *The Coffin Reliquary*, in *The Relics of St. Cuthbert*, Studies by various authors, collected and edited by C. F. Battiscombe, Oxford-London, Oxford University Press, 1956, pp. 202-304.

303. KITZINGER (E.), *Hellenistic Heritage in Byzantine Art*, in *Dumbarton Oaks Papers*, 17, 1963.

304. KLAUSER (Theodor), *Reallexikon für Antike und Christentum, Sachwörterbuch zur Auseinandersetzung des Christentums mit der antiken Welt*, Stuttgart, Hiersemann, 1950 sq.

305. KLAUSER (Theodor), *Studien zur Entstehungsgeschichte der christlichen Kunst III*, in *Jahrbuch für Antike und Christentum*, III, 1960, pp. 112-133.

306. KOEHLER (W.), *The Fragments of an Eighth-Century Gospelbook in the Morgan Library (M. 564)*, in *Studies in Art and Literature for Belle da Costa Greene*, Princeton University Press, 1954, pp. 238-265.

307. KRAUTHEIMER (Richard), *Il transetto nella basilica paleocristiana*, in *Actes du Ve Congrès international d'archéologie chrétienne (1954)*, Vatican City-Paris, 1957, pp. 283-290.

308. KRAUTHEIMER (Richard), *Corpus basilicarum christianarum Romae*, Vatican City, in course of publication since 1958.

309. KRAUTHEIMER (Richard), *Mensa - Coemeterium - martyria*, in *Cahiers archéologiques*, XI, Paris, 1960, pp. 15-40.

310. KÜHN (Herbert), *Das Kunstgewerbe der Völkerwanderungszeit*, in *Geschichte des Kunstgewerbes*, edited by H. T. Bossert, I, Berlin, 1928.

311. KÜHN (Herbert), *Die germanischen Greifenschnallen der Völkerwanderungszeit*, in *I.P.E.K.*, Berlin, 1934, p. 77 sq.

312. KÜHN (Herbert), *Die vorgeschichtliche Kunst des Deutschlands*, Berlin, 1935.

313. KÜHN (Herbert), *Die Zikadenfibeln der Völkerwanderungszeit*, in *I.P.E.K.*, Berlin, 1936, pp. 85-106.

314. KÜHN (Herbert), *Die Reiterscheiben der Völkerwanderungszeit*, in *I.P.E.K.*, XII, Berlin, 1938, pp. 95-115.

315. KÜHN (Herbert), *Eine Goldstatuette der Völkerwanderungszeit*, in *I.P.E.K.*, Berlin, XII, 1938, p. 177.

316. KÜHN (Herbert), *Die grossen Adlerfibeln der Völkerwanderungszeit*, in *I.P.E.K.*, XIII-XIV, Berlin, 1939-1940, pp. 126-144.

317. KÜHN (Herbert), *Die germanischen Bügelfibeln der Völkerwanderungszeit in der Rheinprovinz*, Bonn, 1940, 2 vols.

318. KÜHN (Herbert), *Szenische Darstellungen der germanischen Völkerwanderungszeit*, in *I.P.E.K.*, XV-XVI, Berlin, 1941-1942, pp. 280-282.

319. KÜHN (Herbert), *Die Danielschnallen der Völkerwanderungszeit*, in *I.P.E.K.*, XV-XVI, Berlin, 1941-1942, pp. 140-170.

320. KÜHN (Herbert), *Die Lebensbaum- und Beterschnallen der Völkerwanderungszeit*, in *I.P.E.K.*, XVII, Berlin, 1943-1948, pp. 35-58.

321. KÜHN (Herbert), *Die germanischen Bügelfibeln der Völkerwanderungszeit in der Rheinprovinz*, II, *Bügelfibeln der Völkerwanderungszeit in Süddeutschland*, Graz, 2nd ed. 1965.

322. *Kunst des frühen Mittelalters*, Berner Kunstmuseum, Berne, 1949.

323. *Kunstschätze der Lombardei, 500 vor Christus bis 1800 nach Christus*, Kunsthaus, Zurich, 1949.

324. LA BAUME (P.), *Das fränkische Gräberfeld Junkersdorf bei Köln*, in *Das erste Jahrtausend*, II, Düsseldorf, 1964, p. 679 sq.

325. LA CROIX (Le Père Camille de), *Hypogée martyrium de Poitiers*, Paris, Didot et Cie, 1883.

326. LA CROIX (Le Père Camille de), *Cimetières et sarcophages mérovingiens du Poitou*, in *Bulletin archéologique du Comité des travaux historiques*, 1886, pp. 275-298.

327. LADENBAUER-OREL (H.), *Linz-Zizbau, Das bayerische Gräberfeld an der Traunmündung*, Vienna, 1960.

328. LAFAURIE (Jean), *Le Trésor de Gourdon (Saône-et-Loire)*, in *Bulletin de la Société nationale des Antiquaires de France*, 1958, p. 61-76.

329. LAMOTTE (Dom Odon), *Description des mosaïques de la Daurade à Toulouse (1633)*, in *Cahiers archéologiques*, XIII, Paris, 1962, pp. 261-266.

330. LANTIER (Raymond), *Le Cimetière wisigothique d'Estagel*, in *Gallia*, I, 1942, pp. 176-205.

331. LANTIER (Raymond), *Plaque funéraire de terre cuite mérovingienne*, in *Jahrbuch des Römisch-Germanischen Zentralmuseums in Mainz*, I, Mainz, 1954, p. 237 sq.

332. LANTIER (Raymond) and HUBERT (Jean), *Les Origines de l'art français*, Paris, Le Prat, 1947.

333. LARRIEU (Mary), *Chapiteaux en marbre antérieurs à l'époque romane dans le Gers*, in *Cahiers archéologiques*, XIV, 1964, pp. 109-158.

334. LASSUS (Jean), *Sanctuaires chrétiens de Syrie*, Paris, 1947.

335. LASTEYRIE (Ferdinand de), *Description du trésor de Guarrazar*, Paris, 1860.

336. LATOUCHE (Robert), *Les Grandes Invasions et la crise de l'Occident au Vᵉ siècle*, Paris, Éditions Montaigne, n. d. [1946].

337. LATOUCHE (Robert), *Les Origines de l'économie occidentale (IVᵉ-XIᵉ siècle)*, Paris, Albin Michel, 1956. (L'évolution de l'humanité, 23.)

338. LATOUCHE (Robert), *Gaulois et Francs. De Vercingétorix à Charlemagne*, Paris-Grenoble, Arthaud, 1965.

339. LAUGARDIÈRE (Maurice de), *L'Église de Bourges avant Charlemagne*, Paris-Bourges, Tardy, 1951.

340. LAUR-BELART (R.), *Eine alemannische Goldgriffspata aus Kleinhüningen bei Basel*, in *I.P.E.K.*, XII, Berlin, 1938, pp. 126-138.

341. LAWRENCE (Marion), *Maria Regina*, in *The Art Bulletin*, VII, 1925, p. 150 sq.

342. LE BLANT (Edmond), *Inscriptions chrétiennes de la Gaule antérieures au VIIIᵉ siècle*, Paris, Didot frères, 1856-1865, 2 vols.

343. LE BLANT (Edmond), *Étude sur les sarcophages chrétiens antiques de la ville d'Arles*, Paris, Hachette, 1878. *Unpublished documents on the history of France.*

344. LE BLANT (Edmond), *Les Sarcophages chrétiens de la Gaule*, Paris, 1886.

345. LE BLANT (Edmond), *Nouveau Recueil des inscriptions chrétiennes de la Gaule antérieures au VIIIᵉ siècle*, Paris, Hachette 1892. *Unpublished documents on the history of France.*

346. LECLERCQ (Dom H.), *Manuel d'archéologie chrétienne depuis les origines jusqu'au VIIIᵉ siècle*, Paris, Letouzey et Ané, 1907, 2 vols.

347. LE GENTILHOMME (P.), *Mélanges de numismatique mérovingienne*, Paris, Les Belles-Lettres, 1940.

348. LE GENTILHOMME (P.), *Le Monnayage et la circulation monétaire dans les royaumes barbares en Occident (Vᵉ-VIIIᵉ siècle)*, in *Revue numismatique*, 5th series, VII, 1943, pp. 45-112.

349. LEHMANN (Edgar), *Der frühe deutsche Kirchenbau. Die Entwicklung seiner Raumanordnung bis 1080*, Berlin, 1938; 2nd ed. Berlin, 1949, 1 vol. of text and 1 vol. of plates.

350. LEHMANN (Edgar), *Von der Kirchenfamilie zur Kathedrale*, in *Kunsthistorische Studien. Festschrift Friedrich Gerke*, Baden-Baden, 1962, pp. 21-37.

351. LELONG (Charles), *La Vie quotidienne en Gaule à l'époque mérovingienne*, Paris, Hachette, 1963.

352. LEROQUAIS (Victor), *Les Sacramentaires et les missels manuscrits des bibliothèques publiques de France*, Paris-Mâcon, Protat, 1924, 3 vols and 1 vol. of plates.

353. LEROQUAIS (Victor), *Les Psautiers manuscrits latins des bibliothèques publiques de France*, Paris-Mâcon, Protat, 1940, 2 vols.

354. LESNE (Émile), *Histoire de la propriété ecclésiastique en France*, Lille, Facultés catholiques, 1910-1943, 6 vols. (Mémoires et travaux des Facultés catholiques de Lille.)

355. LESTOCQUOY (Jean), *Le Paysage urbain en Gaule du Vᵉ au IXᵉ siècle*, in *Annales*, VIII, 1953, pp. 159-172.

356. LIÉNARD (Félix), *Archéologie de la Meuse*, Verdun, 1881-1885, 3 vols. and 3 atlases.

357. LINAS (Charles de), *Les Origines de l'orfèvrerie cloisonnée...* Paris, 1877-1878, 2 vols.

358. LINAS (Charles de), *Le Reliquaire de Pépin à Conques*, in *Gazette archéologique*, XII, 1887, p. 37 sq.

359. LINDENSCHMIT (Ludwig), *Die Altertümer unserer heidnischen Vorzeit*, I-V, Mainz, 1858-1911.

360. LINDENSCHMIT (Ludwig), *Handbuch der deutschen Altertumskunde*, I, *Merovingische Zeit*, Brunswick, 1880.

361. LIPINSKY (Angelo), *Der Theodolindenschatz im Dom zu Monza*, in *Das Münster*, XIII, 1960, pp. 146-173.

362. LOMBARD (Maurice), *L'Évolution urbaine pendant le haut Moyen Age*, in *Annales*, XII, 1957, pp. 7-28.

363. LONGNON (Auguste), *Géographie de la Gaule au VIᵉ siècle*, Paris, Hachette, 1878.

364. L'ORANGE (Hans Peter), *L'originaria decorazione del tempietto cividalese*, in *Atti del IIᵒ congresso internazionale di studi sull'alto medioevo*, Spoleto, 1953, p. 98 sq.

365. LOT (Ferdinand), *La Fin du monde antique et le début du Moyen Age*, Paris, La Renaissance du livre, 1927. (L'évolution de l'humanité, 31.)

366. LOT (Ferdinand), *Les Invasions germaniques. La pénétration mutuelle du monde barbare et du monde romain*, Paris, Payot, 1935.

367. LOT (Ferdinand), *Les Invasions barbares et le peuplement de l'Europe*, Paris, Payot, 1937.

368. LOT (Ferdinand), *Recherches sur la population et la superficie des cités remontant à la période gallo-romaine*, I, Paris, 1945; II, Paris, 1950; III, Paris, 1953. Champion. (Bibliothèque de l'École pratique des Hautes Études, Nos. 287, 296.)

369. LOT (Ferdinand), PFISTER (Christian) and GANSHOF (François-Louis), *Les Destinées de l'Empire en Occident de 395 à 888*, 2nd ed. Paris, P.U.F., 1940. (1st ed. in 1935.)

370. LOUIS (René), *Les Églises d'Auxerre des origines au XIᵉ siècle*, Paris, Clavreuil, 1952.

371. LOWE (Elias Avery), *Codices latini antiquiores*, Part VI, *France*, Oxford, Clarendon Press, 1953. xxx-47 p.

372. LOWE (Elias Avery), *The 'Script of Luxeuil', a Title vindicated*, in *Revue bénédictine*, 1953, pp. 132-142.

373. McGURK (P.), *The Irish Pocket Gospel Book*, in *Sacris erudici*, VIII, Bruges, 1956, p. 260 sq. (Bretons-Landévennec.)

374. McGURK (P.), *Latin Gospel Books from A. D. 400 to A. D. 800*, Paris-Brussels-Antwerp-Amsterdam, Érasme, 1961. (Publications of *Scriptorium*, V.)

375. MAILLÉ (Marquise A. de), *Vincent d'Agen et saint Vincent de Saragosse*, Melun-Paris, D'Argences, 1949.

376. MAILLÉ (Marquise A. de), *Recherches sur les origines chrétiennes de Bordeaux*, Paris, A. et J. Picard, 1959.

377. MALE (Émile), *La Fin du paganisme en Gaule et les plus anciennes basiliques chrétiennes*, Paris, Flammarion, 1950.

378. *Les Manuscrits à peintures en France du VIIᵉ au XIIᵉ siècle*, Paris, Bibliothèque nationale, 1954. (Exhibition catalogue.)

379. MARIONI (G.) and MUTINELLI (C.), *Guida storico-artistico di Cividale*, Udine, 1958.

380. MARTEL (Pierre) and BARRUOL (Guy), *Sites et monuments de Haute-Provence. Les monuments du haut Moyen Age. Inventaire*, Apt, 1964. (Les Alpes de lumière, 34.)

381. MARTÍNEZ SANTA-OLALLA (J.), *Chronologie der Gliederung des westgotischen Kunstgewerbes in Spanien*, in *I.P.E.K.* [1934], Berlin, 1935, p. 44 sq.

382. MARTÍNEZ SANTA-OLALLA (J.), *Nuevas Fibulas aquiliformes hispano-visigodas*, in *Archivo español de arqueologia*, XIV, 1940-1941, p. 33 sq.

383. MASAI (François), *Essai sur les origines de la miniature dite irlandaise*, Brussels, Érasme, 1947, 146 p. (Publications of *Scriptorium*.)

384. MASAI (François), *Observations sur le Psautier dit de Charlemagne*, Paris, *B.N., Lat. 13159*, in *Scriptorium*, VI, 1952, pp. 299-303.

385. *Mémorial d'un voyage d'études de la Société nationale des Antiquaires de France en Rhénanie (1951)*, Paris, Klincksieck, 1953.

386. MENGARELLI (R.), *La necropoli barbarica di Castel Trosino*, in *Monumenti antichi*, XII, Rome, 1902.

387. MERTENS (J.), *Recherches archéologiques dans l'abbaye mérovingienne de Nivelles*, in *Archeologia belgica*, 1961, pp. 89-113.

388. MICHELI (Geneviève-Louise), *L'Enluminure du haut Moyen Age et les influences irlandaises. Histoire d'une influence*, Brussels, Éditions de la Connaissance, 1939, XIII, p. 232. (Thesis.)

389. MICHON (Étienne), *Les Sarcophages de saint Drausin, de Soissons, de la Valbonne et de Castelnau-de-Guers au musée du Louvre et les sarcophages chrétiens dits de l'école d'Aquitaine ou du sud-ouest de la France*, in *Mélanges Schlumberger*, II, Paris, 1924, pp. 376-387.

390. MINARD (Dom Pierre), *L'Évangéliaire oncial de l'abbaye Sainte-Croix de Poitiers. Ses pièces inédites et ses particularités*, in *Revue Mabillon*, Abbaye Saint-Martin de Ligugé, 1943, pp. 1-22.

391. MOLINIER (Émile), *Histoire générale des arts appliqués à l'industrie du Vᵉ à la fin du XVIIIᵉ siècle*, IV, *L'Orfèvrerie religieuse et civile*, Paris, 1902.

392. MONACO (Giorgio), *Oreficerie longobarde a Parma*, Parma, 1955.

393. MONNERET DE VILLARD (Ugo), *Le transenne di S. Aspreno e le stoffe alessandrine*, in *Aegyptus*, IV, 1923, p. 64 sq.

394. MOOSBRUGGER (R.) and LEU (R.), *Die Schweiz im Frühmittelalter*, in *Repertorium der Ur- und Frühgeschichte der Schweiz*, V, 1959, p. 15 sq.

395. MORACCHINI (Geneviève), *Note sur la basilique paléochrétienne Santa Laurina d'Aleria (Corse)*, in *Études corses*, 1960, pp. 51-63.

396. MORACCHINI (Geneviève), *L'Architecture médiévale et paléochrétienne de la Corse*, in *Revue archéologique*, Paris, Presses universitaires de France, 1960, II, pp. 51-62.

397. MORACCHINI (Geneviève), *Le Pavement en mosaïque de la basilique paléochrétienne et du baptistère de Mariana (Corse)*, in *Cahiers archéologiques*, XIII, 1962, pp. 137-160.

398. MOREAU (Frédéric), *Album des principaux objets recueillis dans les sépultures de Caranda (Aisne)*, Saint-Quentin, 1877-1898, 4 vols. and general table by J. Pilloy, Paris, 1908.

399. MOREY (Charles Rufus), *The Landévennec Gospels, a Breton Illuminated Manuscript of the Ninth Century*, New York, The New York Public Library, 1929.

400. MOREY (Charles Rufus), *The Gospel Book of Landévennec*, in *Art Studies*, 1931, p. 263 sq.

401. MOREY (Charles Rufus), *Early Christian Art, an Outline of the Evolution of Style and Iconography in Sculpture and Painting from Antiquity to the 8th Century*, Princeton University Press, 1953, 3rd ed.

402. MÜLLER (Iso), *Disentiser Klostergeschichte (700-1512)*, Einsiedeln and Cologne, Benzinger, 1942.

403. MUSSET (Lucien), *L'Église d'Evrecy (Calvados) et ses sculptures préromanes*, in *Bulletin de la Société des Antiquaires de Normandie*, LIII, 1955-1956, pp. 116-163.

404. MUSSET (Lucien), *Deux-Jumeaux. Résultats des fouilles*, in *Bulletin de la Société des Antiquaires de Normandie*, LVI, 1961-1962, pp. 469-525. *Arch-stones and stone reliefs with pre-Romanesque decorations.*

405. MUSSET (Lucien), *Aux origines du christianisme normand. De l'art païen à l'art chrétien*, in *Art de Basse-Normandie*, 1964, No. 34, pp. 13-18.

406. MUSSET (Lucien), *Les Invasions. Les vagues germaniques*, Paris, 1965.

407. MUTINELLI (C.), *La necropoli longobarda di S. Stefano in Pertica in Cividale*, in *Quaderni della Face*, XIX, 1960, p. 1 sq.

408. NEES (Mechtildis), *Rheinische Schnallen der Völkerwanderungszeit*, Bonn, 1935.

409. NEUMÜLLER (Dom Willibrord) and HOLTER (Kurt), *Der Codex Millenarius*, Graz-Cologne, H. Böhlaus, n. d. [1959], 195 p. (Forschungen zur Geschichte Oberösterreichs, 6.)

410. NEUSS (Wilhelm), *Die Apocalypse des heiligen Johannes in der altspanischen und altchristlichen Bibelillustration*, Münster, 1931, 2 vols., 296 p.

411. NORDENFALK (Carl), *On the Age of the earliest Echternach Manuscripts*, in *Acta archaeologica*, III, Copenhagen, Levin & Munksgaard, 1932, pp. 57-62.

412. NORDENFALK (Carl), *Vier Kanontafeln eines spätantiken Evangelien-Buches*, Göteborg, Elanders Bok, 1937. (Göteborgs Kungl. Vettenkapsoch Vitterhets samlingar, Handling, 5.)

413. NORDENFALK (Carl), *Die spätantiken Kanontafeln, kunstgeschichtliche Studien über die eusebianische Evangelien-Konkordanz in den vier ersten Jahrhunderten ihrer Geschichte...* Göteborg, O. Isacsons, 1938, 2 vols. including 1 of plates.

414. NORDENFALK (Carl), *Before the Book of Durrow*, in *Acta archaeologica*, XVIII, Copenhagen, 1947, pp. 141-174.

415. NORDENFALK (Carl), *The Beginning of Book Decoration*, in *Essays in honor of Georg Swarzenski*, Berlin-Chicago, 1951, pp. 9-20.

340

416. NORDENFALK (Carl), *The Apostolic Canon Tables*, in *Essais en l'honneur de Jean Porcher*. *Gazette des Beaux-Arts*, 1963, VIe période, LXII, Paris-New York, 1963, pp. 17-34.

417. NORDHAGEN (P. J.), *The Earliest Decorations in Santa Maria Antiqua and their date*. *Acta ad archaeologiam et artium historiam pertinentia*, I, Rome, 1962, p. 53.

418. NOWOTHNIG (W.), *Das merovingische Gräberfeld von Rosdorf bei Göttingen*, in *Göttinger Jahrbuch*, 1958, pp. 31-35.

419. OAKESHOTT (Walter), *Classical Inspiration in Medieval Art*, London, Chapman & Hall, 1959.

420. ODOBESCO (A.), *Le Trésor de Pétrossa*, Paris, 1900.

421. OMONT (Henry), *Un nouveau manuscrit illustré de l'Apocalypse au IXe siècle. Notice du ms. latin, Nouv. Acq., 1132 de la Bibliothèque nationale*, in *Bibliothèque de l'École des chartes*, LXXXIII, 1922, p. 273 sq.

422. *Ori e argenti dell'Italia antica*, Turin, 1961.

423. OTTO (W.), *Die karolingische Bilderwelt*, LXXVIII, s, Munich, 1957. (Selbstverlag des kunsthistorischen Seminars der Universität München.)

424. PAESELER (Wilhelm), *Das Ingelheimer Relief mit den Flügelpferden*, in *Mainz und der Mittelrhein. Festschrift W. F. Volbach*, Mainz, 1966, pp. 45-140.

425. PALOL SALELLAS (P. de), *Bronces hispanovisigodos de origen mediterraneo*, Barcelona, 1950.

426. PALOL SALELLAS (P. de), *Arqueologia paleocristiana y visigoda*, Madrid, 1954.

427. PALOL SALELLAS (P. de), *Westgotische liturgische Bronzen in Spanien*, in *Neue Beiträge zur Kunstgeschichte des I. Jahrtausends*, II, Baden-Baden, 1954.

428. PALOL SALELLAS (P. de), *Esencia del arte hispánico de la época visigoda : romanismo y germanismo*, in *Settimane di studio del Centro italiano di studi sull'alto medioevo*, III, Spoleto, 1956, pp. 65-126, 38 pl.

429. PALOL SALELLAS (P. de), *Spanien. Kunst des frühen Mittelalters*, Munich, Hirmer, 1965. English edition: *Early Medieval Art in Spain*, New York and London, 1966.

430. PANAZZA (G.), *Lapide e sculture paleocristiane e preromaniche di Pavia*, in *Arte del primo millennio. Atti del IIo convegno per lo studio dell'arte dell'alto medioevo, Pavia*, Turin, 1950, p. 211 sq.

431. PANAZZA (G.), *Gli scavi, l'architettura e gli affreschi della chiesa di S. Salvatore in Brescia*, in *Atti dell'ottavo congresso di studi sull'alto medioevo*, II, Milan, 1962, p. 5 sq.

432. PANAZZA (G.), *Note sul materiale barbarico trovato nel Bresciano*, in *Problemi della civiltà. Scritti in onore di G. P. Bognetti*, Milan, 1964, p. 146 sq.

433. PANOFSKY (Erwin) and SAXL (Fritz), *Classical Mythology in Mediaeval Art*, in *Metropolitan Museum Studies*, IV, 2nd part, 1933, pp. 228-280.

434. PARROT (André), *Glyptique de Mari et mythologie orientale. Les origines du symbolisme évangélique*, in *Studia Mariana*, edited by A. Parrot, Leyden, E. J. Brill, 1950.

435. PASQUI (U.) and PARIBENI (Roberto), *Nocera Umbra*, in *Monumenti antichi*, XXV, Rome, 1918, col. 244 sq.

436. PERONI (A.), *La decorazione a stucco in S. Salvatore a Brescia*, in *Arte lombarda*, V, 1961, p. 187 sq.

437. PERRAT (Charles), *Saint-Irénée de Lyon*, in *Bulletin de la Société nationale des Antiquaires de France*, 1945-1947, pp. 172-173.

438. PESCH (Christian) and STAVENHAGEN (Georg von), *Die Basilica St. Gereon zu Köln*, Cologne, Greven, 1952.

439. PIJOAN (José), *Summa Artis*, VIII, *Arte barbaro y prerománico desde el siglo IV hasta el año 1000*, Madrid, Espasa-Calpe, 1942.

440. PILLOY (J.), *Études sur d'anciens lieux de sépulture dans l'Aisne*, Paris, 1885-1906, 3 vols.

441. PIRENNE (H.), *Die Geburt des Abendlandes* (German translation of *Mahomet et Charlemagne*), Berlin, 1939.

442. PIRLING (R.), *Ein fränkisches Fürstengrab aus Krefeld*, in *Germania*, XLII, 1964, pp. 186-216.

443. PLAT (Gabriel), *L'Art de bâtir en France, des Romains à l'an 1100, d'après les monuments anciens de la Touraine, de l'Anjou et du Vendômois*, Paris, Van Oest, 1939.

444. PORCHER (Jean), *Aux origines de la lettre ornée médiévale*, in *Mélanges Tisserant*, V, 2. Vatican City, 1964, pp. 273-276.

445. POST (P.), *Der kupferne Spangenhelm*, in *Bericht der römisch-germanischen Kommission*, XXXIV, Frankfurt am Main, Römisch-germanische Kommission (1951-1953), 1954, p. 115 sq.

446. PROU (Maurice), *Catalogue des monnaies mérovingiennes de la Bibliothèque nationale*, Paris, Rollin & Fucardent, 1892.

447. PROU (Maurice), *La Gaule mérovingienne*, Paris, May, n. d. [1897].

448. PUIG I CADAFALCH (José), *L'Art wisigothique et ses survivances*, Paris, F. de Nobele, 1961. (Posthumous publication of a study finished in 1944.)

449. RADEMACHER (Franz), *Der trierer Egbertschrein*, in *Trierer Zeitschrift*, XI, 1936, p. 144 sq.

450. RADEMACHER (Franz), *Die fränkische Goldscheiben-Fibeln aus dem Rheinischen Landesmuseum in Bonn*, Munich, 1940.

451. RENNER (Dorothee), *Die durchbrochenen Zierscheiben der Merovingerzeit*, in *Kataloge vor- und frühgeschichtlicher Altertümer*, Band 18, Römisch-Germanisches Zentralmuseum in Mainz, Mainz, 1967.

452. REYMOND (Maxime), *Le Cimetière barbare de Saint-Sulpice*, in *Revue Charlemagne*, I, 2, 1911, p. 4 sq.

453. RHE (Gy) and FETTICH (N.), *Jutas und Öskü*, in *Skutika*, IV, Prague, 1931.

454. RICCI (Seymour de), *Catalogue of a Collection of Germanic Antiquities belonging to J. P. Morgan*, New York, 1910-1911.

455. RICE (David Talbot), *The Beginnings of Christian Art*, London, 1957.

456. RICHÉ (Pierre), *Les Invasions barbares*, Paris, Presses universitaires de France, 1953. (Que sais-je?).

457. RICHÉ (Pierre), *Éducation et culture dans l'Occident barbare, VIe-VIIIe siècle*, Paris, Éditions du Seuil, 1962.

458. RICKERT (Margaret), *La Miniature anglaise des origines jusqu'à la fin du XIIe siècle*, Milan, 1959.

459. RIEGL (Alois), *Die spätrömische Kunstindustrie nach den Funden in Österreich und Ungarn*, I, 1901, II 1923, Vienna, 1923.

460. RIEGL (Alois), *Die spätrömische Kunstgewerbe*, II, *Kunstgewerbe des frühen Mittelalters*, bearbeitet von E. A. Zimmermann, Vienna, 1923.

461. ROBLIN (Michel), *Cités ou citadelles? Les enceintes romaines du Bas-Empire d'après l'exemple de Paris*, in *Revue des Études anciennes*, LIII, 1951, pp. 301-311.

462. ROEREN (R.), *Das alamannische Reihengräberfeld von Schretzheim*, Tübingen, 1952. (Dissertation.)

463. ROOSENS (Heli), *Quelques mobiliers funéraires de la fin de l'époque romaine dans le nord de la France. Dissertationes Archaeol. Gandenses*, VII, Bruges, 1962.

464. ROSS (M. C.), *Arts of the Migration Period*, in *The Walters Art Gallery*, with an Introduction and Historical Survey by P. Verdier, Baltimore, 1961.

465. ROSS (M. C.), *Catalogue of the Byzantine and Early Mediaeval Antiquities in the Dumbarton Oaks Collection*, II, Washington (D. C.), 1962-1965.

466. ROUSTAN (François), *La Major et le premier baptistère de Marseille*, Marseille, Flammarion & Vaillant, 1905.

467. RUPP (Herta), *Die Herkunft der Zelleneinlage und die Almandinscheibenfibeln im Rheinland*, in *Rheinische Forschungen zur Vorgeschichte*, II, 1937.

468. RUPP (Herta), *Eine merovingische Goldschmiedewerkstatt im Neuwieder Becken*, in *I.P.E.K.*, XII, Berlin, 1938, p. 116 sq.

469. SABBE (E.), *L'Importation des tissus orientaux en Europe occidentale au Moyen Age*, in *Revue belge de philologie et d'histoire*, XXXIII, Brussels, 1955, p. 68 sq.

470. SALIN (Bernhard), *Die altgermanische Tierornamentik*, Stockholm, new edition, 1935.

471. SALIN (Édouard), *Le Cimetière barbare de Lezéville*, Nancy, 1922.

472. SALIN (Édouard), *Rhin et Orient. Le Haut Moyen Age en Lorraine d'après le mobilier funéraire*, Paris, 1939.

473. SALIN (Édouard), *La Civilisation mérovingienne d'après les sépultures, les textes et le laboratoire*, Paris, A. et J. Picard, 1949-1959, 4 vols.

474. SALIN (Édouard), *Sur les influences orientales dans la France de l'Est à l'époque mérovingienne*, in *Revue archéologique de l'Est et du Centre-Est*, I, 1950, pp. 129-153.

475. SALIN (Édouard), *Sépultures gallo-romaines et mérovingiennes dans la basilique de Saint-Denis*, in *Monuments et Mémoires Piot*, XLIX, Paris, 1957, pp. 93-128.

476. SALIN Édouard) and FRANCE-LANORD (Albert), *Le Fer à l'époque mérovingienne*, Paris, Geuthner, 1943.

477. SALIN (Édouard) and FRANCE-LANORD (Albert), *Le Trésor d'Airan*, in *Monuments et Mémoires Piot*, XLIII, Paris, 1949, pp. 119-135.

478. SALMI (Mario), *La basilica di S. Salvatore di Spoleto*, Florence, 1951.

479. SALMI (Mario), *Stucchi e littostrati nell'alto medioevo italiano*, in *Atti dell'ottavo congresso di studi sull'alto medioevo*, I, Milan, 1962, pp. 21-51.

480. SALMI (Mario), *S. Salvatore di Spoleto, il tardo antico e l'alto medioevo*, in *Settimane di studio del Centro italiano di studi sull'alto medioevo*, IX, Spoleto, 1962, p. 497. sq.

481. SALMI (Mario), *Tardo antico e alto medioevo in Umbria*, in *Atti del IIe convegno di studi umbri, Gubbio, 1964*, Perugia, 1965, pp. 99-118.

482. SALMON (Dom Pierre), *Le Lectionnaire de Luxeuil*, Rome, Abbey of St Jerome, 1944-1953.

483. SANTANGELO (A.), *Cividale. Catalogo delle cose d'arte*, Rome, 1936.

484. SAUER (C.), *Tombes mérovingiennes à Dangolsheim*, in *C.A.H.A.*, CXXXII, 1952, p. 49 sq.

485. SCAPULA (Jean), *Le Cimetière mérovingien de « Villers-Derrière » à Gyé-sur-Seine (Aube)*, in *Revue archéologique de l'Est et du Centre-Est*, II, 1951, p. 148 sq.

486. SCHAFFRAN (E.), *Die Kunst der Langobarden in Italien*, Jena, 1941.

487. SCHÄHLE (W.), *Das Fürstengrab von Pouan*, Munich, 1956. (Dissertation.)

488. SCHLUNK (Helmut), *Arte visigodo*, in *Ars Hispaniae*, II, Madrid, 1947.

489. SCHLUNK (Helmut), *The Crosses of Oviedo*, in *The Art Bulletin*, XXXII, 1950, p. 107 sq.

490. SCHLUNK (Helmut), *Die Auseinandersetzung der christlichen und der islamischen Kunst... bis zum Jahre 1000*, in *Settimane di studio del Centro italiano di studi sull'alto medioevo*, Spoleto, 1965, pp. 903-973.

491. SCHMIDT (B.), *Die späte Völkerwanderungszeit in Mitteldeutschland*, Veröffentlichung des Landesmuseums für Vorgeschichte in Halle an der Saale, Heft 18, Halle, 1961.

492. SCHOPPA (H.), *Der fränkische Friedhof bei Eltville im Rheingau-Kreis*, in *Nassauische Annalen*, LXI, 1950, p. 1 sq.

493. SCHWARTS (J.), *A propos d'ustensiles « coptes » trouvés en Europe occidentale*, in *Bulletin de la Société d'archéologie copte*, XIV, 1958, p. 51 sq.

494. SESTON (William) and PERRAT (Charles), *Une basilique funéraire à Lyon*, in *Revue des études anciennes*, XLIX, Paris, 1947, pp. 139-150.

495. *Settimane di studio del Centro italiano di studi sull'alto medioevo*. Since 1951.

496. STEIN (E.), *Geschichte des spätrömischen Reiches* : I, Vienna, 1928; II, *Histoire du Bas-Empire*, Paris - Brussels, 1949.

497. STEINGRÄBER (E.), *Ein merovingisches Taschenreliquiar*, in *Münchner Jahrbuch*, VII, 1956, p. 27.

498. STERN (Henri), *Quelques ivoires d'origine supposée gauloise*, in *Cahiers archéologiques*, VII, Paris, 1954, p. 109 sq.

499. STERN (Henri), *Recueil général des mosaïques de la Gaule*, Paris, Centre national de la Recherche scientifique, 1958-1963, in course of publication since 1957, 3 vols. issued. (Supplements to *Gallia*, X.)

500. STERN (Henri), *Mosaïques de pavement préromanes et romanes en France*, in *Cahiers de civilisation médiévale*, V, 1962, pp. 13-33.

501. STIEREN (A.), *Ein neuer Friedhof fränkischer Zeit in Soest*, in *Germania*, XIV, 1930, p. 166. sq.

502. STOLL (H.), *Die Alamannengräber von Hailfinger in Württemberg*, in *Germanische Denkmäler der Völkerwanderungszeit*, IV, Berlin-Leipzig, 1939.

503. STOLL (Robert), *L'Art roman en Grande-Bretagne*, Paris, Braun, 1966. *Photographs and notices of early medieval carvings.*

504. STONE (Lawrence), *Sculpture in Britain: The Middle Ages*, Pelican History of Art, London and Baltimore, 1955.

505. *Storia di Milano*, II, Milan-Rome, Fondazione Treccani degli Alfieri per la storia di Milano, 1954.

506. STROHEKER (K. F.), *Der senatorische Adel im spätantiken Gallien*, Tübingen, 1943; and also: *Madrider Mitteilungen* IV, 1963, p. 107 sq.

507. SULZBERGER (S.), *Un exemple d'influence copte sur un manuscrit précarolingien (B. N., Lat. 12168)*, in *Scriptorium*, IX, Brussels, 1955, pp. 263-267.

508. SWARZENSKI (Hans), *Miniaturen des frühen Mittelalters*, Berne, Laupen, Iris Verlag, 1951, 23 p.

509. SWOBODA (K. M.), *In den Jahren 1950 bis 1957 erschienene Werke zur Kunst des frühen Mittelalters*, in *Kunstgeschichtliche Anzeigen*, Neue Folge, III, 1959, p. 138 sq.

510. SWOBODA (K. M.), in *Kunstgeschichtliche Anzeigen*, Neue Folge, VI, 1963-1964, p. 38 sq. (Bibliography.)

511. TACKENBERG (K.), *Über einige wenig bekannte Reiterscheiben*, in *Germania*, XXVIII, 1944-1950, p. 250.

512. TAGLIAFERRI (A.), *Arte longobarda. La scultura figurativa su marmo*, Cividale, 1961.

513. TARALON (Jean), *Le Trésor de Conques*, in *Bulletin de la Société nationale des Antiquaires de France*, 1954-1955, pp. 47-54.

514. TARALON (Jean), *Les Trésors des églises de France*, Paris, Hachette, 1966.

515. TEA (Eva), *La basilica di Santa Maria Antiqua*, Milan, Vita e Pensiero, 1937, XIV, 418 p.

516. TERRASSE (Henri), *L'Espagne du Moyen Age*, Paris, Fayard, 1966. (Civilisation et Arts.)

517. TESSIER (Georges), *Le Baptême de Clovis*, Paris, Gallimard, 1964.

518. TESTINI (P.), *Archeologia cristiana. Nozioni generali delle origini alla fine del secolo VI. Propedeutica. Topografia cimiteriale. Epigrafia. Edificio di culto*, Rome-Paris, Desclée, 1959.

519. THIEROT (Amaury) and LANTIER (Raymond), *Le Cimetière mérovingien du Maltrat à Vouciennes*, in *Revue archéologique*, 6th series, XV, 1940, p. 210 sq.

520. THIRY (G.), *Die Vogelfibeln der germanischen Völkerwanderungszeit*, Bonn, 1939.

521. TIKKANEN (Johan Jakob), *Die Psaltenillustration im Mittelalter*, Helsinki-Leipzig, 1895-1903, 320 pages.

522. TORP (Hjalmar), *Il problema della decorazione originaria del tempietto longobardo di Cividale del Friuli*, in *Quaderni della Face*, Udine, 1959, p. 5.

523. TRAVERSI (Gino), *Architettura paleocristiana Milanese*, Milan, Ceschina, 1964.

524. *Les Trésors des églises de France*. Musée des Arts décoratifs, Paris, 1965.

525. *Trésors du Moyen Age en Italie*, Petit Palais, Paris, 1952.

526. TSCHUMI (Otto), *Burgunder, Alemannen und Langobarden in der Schweiz*, Berne, 1945.

527. TSELOS (D.), *A Greco-Italian School of Illuminators and Fresco Painters. Its Relations to the principal Reims Manuscripts and to the Greek Frescoes in Rome and Castelseprio*, in *The Art Bulletin*, XXXVIII, 1956, pp. 1-30.

528. VACANDARD (Elphège), *L'Idolâtrie en Gaule au VI*e *et au VII*e *siècle*, in *Revue des questions historiques*, XLV, 1899, I, pp. 414-454.

529. VAN BERCHEM (Max) and CLOUZOT (Étienne), *Mosaïques chrétiennes du IV*e *au X*e *siècle*, Geneva, Imprimerie du *Journal de Genève*, 1924.

530. VAN DER MEER (Frederic), *Altchristliche Kunst*, Cologne, 1960.

531. VAN DER MEER (Frederic) and MOHRMANN (Christine), *Atlas de l'Antiquité chrétienne*, Paris-Brussels, Éditions Sequoia, 1960.

532. VAN MOE (Émile A.), *La Lettre ornée dans les manuscrits du VIII*e *au XII*e *siècle*, Paris, Éditions du Chêne, 1943.

533. VEECK (Walter), *Die Alamannen in Württemberg*, in *Germanische Denkmäler der Völkerwanderungszeit*, I, Berlin-Leipzig, 1931.

534. VEECK (Walter), *Ein reiches alemannisches Frauengrab aus Täbingen*, in *Germania*, XVI, Berlin, 1932, pp. 58-61.

535. VENTURI (Adolfo), *Storia dell'arte italiana*, II and III, Milan, 1902-1903.

536. VERCAUTEREN (F.), *Étude sur les « civitates » de la Belgique Seconde*, Brussels, Académie royale de Belgique, 1934.

537. VERZONE (Paolo), *L'architettura religiosa dell'alto medio evo nell'Italia settentrionale*, Milan, Esperia, 1942, 2nd ed., 1961.

538. VERZONE (Paolo), *L'arte preromanica in Liguria ed i rilievi decorativi dei 'secoli barbari'*, Turin, Viglongo, 1945.

539. VERZONE (Paolo), *Le chiese cimiteriali cristiane a struttura multiplice nell'Italia settentrionale*, in *Arte del primo millennio*, Turin, 1952, pp. 28-41.

540. VIEILLARD (May), *Les Canons d'Évangéliaires de la basse Antiquité*, C. R., in *Cahiers archéologiques*, I, Paris, 1945, pp. 113-123. (Cf. C. Nordenfalk, *Die spätantiken Kanontafeln.)*

541. VIEILLARD - TROIEKOUROFF (May), *La Cathédrale de Clermont du V*e *au XIII*e *siècle*, in *Cahiers archéologiques*, XI, Paris, 1960, pp. 199-247.

542. VIEILLARD - TROIEKOUROFF (May), *Les Sculptures et objets précieux retrouvés dans les fouilles de 1860 à 1886 à Saint-Martin de Tours*, in *Cahiers archéologiques*, XIII, Paris, 1962, pp. 85-118.

543. VIEILLARD - TROIEKOUROFF (May), FOSSARD (D.), CHATEL (E.) and LAMY-LASSALLE (C.), *Les Anciennes Églises suburbaines de Paris (IV*e*-X*e *siècle)*, in *Mémoires de la Société de l'histoire de Paris et de l'Ile-de-France*, XI, 1950, pp. 18-282.

544. VIEILLARD (René), *Recherches sur les origines de la Rome chrétienne. Les églises romaines et leur rôle dans l'histoire et la topographie de la ville depuis la fin du monde antique jusqu'à la formation de l'État pontifical. Essai d'urbanisme chrétien*, 2nd ed., Rome, Edizioni di Storia e letteratura, 1959.

545. VILLARD (André), *L'Art de Provence*, Paris-Grenoble, Arthaud, 1957. (Art et paysages.)

546. *Villes épiscopales de Provence (Aix, Arles, Fréjus, Marseille, Riez) de l'époque gallo-romaine au Moyen Age*, by F. Benoit, P.-A. Février, J. Formigé, H. Rolland. Introduction by J. Hubert, Paris, Klincksieck, 1954.

547. VINSKI (Z.), *Die archäologischen Denkmäler der grossen Völkerwanderungszeit in Syrmien*, in *Situla*, II, Ljubliana, 1957, p. 3 sq.

548. VIOLANTE (C.) and FONSECA (Cosimo Damiano), *Ubicazione e dedicazione delle cattedrali dalle origini al periodo romanico nelle città dell'Italia centrosettentrionale*, in *Il romanico pistoiese. Atti del I° convegno internazionale di studi medioevali di storia dell'arte, Pistoia, 1964*, Pistoia, 1966, pp. 303-352.

549. VIVES (J.), *Inscripciones cristianas de la España romana y visigoda*, Barcelona, 1942.

550. VOGT (E.), *Das alamannische Gräberfeld am alten Gotterbarmweg in Basel*, in *Indicateur d'antiquités suisses*, XXXII, 1930, p. 145 sq.

551. VOGT (E.), *Interpretation und museale Auswertung alamannischer Grabfunde*, in *Zeitschrift für schweizerische Archäologie und Kunstgeschichte*, XX, 1960, p. 70 sq.

552. VOLBACH (W. F.), *Metallarbeiten des christlichen Kultes*, Katalog 9 des Römisch-Germanischen Zentralmuseums in Mainz, Mainz, 1921.

553. VOLBACH (W. F.), *Zur Bronzepfanne von Güttingen*, in *Germania*, VII, 1933, p. 42 sq.

554. VOLBACH (W. F.), *Oriental Influences in Animal Sculpture of Campania*, in *The Art Bulletin*, XXIV, 1942, p. 172 sq.

555. VOLBACH (W. F.), *Elfenbeinarbeiten der Spätantike und des frühen Mittelalters*, Katalog 7 des Römisch-Germanischen Zentralmuseums in Mainz, Mainz, 1952.

556. VOLBACH (W. F.), *Frühmittelalterliche Elfenbeinarbeiten aus Gallien*, in *Festschrift des Römisch-Germanischen, Zentralmuseums in Mainz*, I, 1952 Mainz, p. 44 sq.

557. VOLBACH (W. F.), *Il tesoro di Conoscio*, in *Atti del secondo convegno di studi umbri, Gubbio*, Perugia, Università degli studi, 1964, pp. 303-316.

558. VOLBACH (W. F.) and HIRMER (M.), *Frühchristliche Kunst*, Munich, 1958. English translation: *Early Christian Art*, Thames & Hudson, London, and Abrams, New York, 1962.

559. *Vom Altertum zum Mittelalter*, bearbeitet von R. Noll. Führer durch das Kunsthistorisches Museum, Nr. 8. Vienna, 1958.

560. *Vorläufer und Anfänge christlicher Architektur, Früher deutscher Kirchenbau*. Colloquy held at Munich in April 1953, in *Kunst-Chronik*, VI, 1953, pp. 229-266.

561. WAGNER (E.), *Fundstätten und Funde aus vorgeschichtlicher, römischer und alemannisch-fränkischer Zeit im Grossherzogtum Baden*, I, II, Tübingen, 1908-1911.

562. WALD (E. T. de), *The Stuttgart Psalter. Biblia Folio 25. Württembergische Landesbibliothek, Stuttgart*, Princeton University Press, 1930, 132 p.

563. WALKER (Robert M.), *Illustrations to the Priscillian Prologues in the Gospel Manuscripts of the Carolingian Ada School*, in *The Art Bulletin*, XXX, 1948, pp. 1-10.

564. WARD-PERKINS (John Bryan), *The Sculpture of Visigothic France*, in *Archaeologia or Miscellaneous Tracts relating to Antiquity*, published by the Society of Antiquaries of London, LXXXVII, Oxford, 1938, pp. 79-128.

565. WARD-PERKINS (John Bryan), *A Carved Marble Fragment at Riom (Puy-de-Dôme) and the Chronology of the Aquitanian Sarcophagi*, in *The Antiquaries Journal*, XL, Oxford University Press, 1950, pp. 25-34.

566. WEISE (G.), *Zwei fränkische Königspfalzen*, Tübingen, 1923. *Excavations at Quierzy-sur-Oise and Samoussy*.

567. WEITZMANN (Kurt), *Illustrations in Roll and Codex. A Study of the Origin and Method of Text Illustration*, Princeton University Press, 1947.

568. WEITZMANN (Kurt), *The Fresco Cycle of S. Maria di Castelseprio*, Princeton University Press, 1951, VIII, p. 103. (Cf. M. Schapiro, *Art Bulletin*, XXXIV, 1952, p. 147.)

569. WEITZMANN (Kurt), *Narration in Early Christendom*, in *American Journal of Archaeology*, LXI, 1957, pp. 83-91.

570. WEITZMANN (Kurt), *Ancient Book Illumination*, Cambridge (Mass.), Harvard University Press, 1959.

571. WEITZMANN (Kurt), *The Survival of Mythological Representations in Early Christian and Byzantine Art and their Impact on Christian Iconography*, in *Dumbarton Oaks Papers*, XIV, 1960, pp. 44-68.

572. WEITZMANN (Kurt), *Geistige Grundlagen und Wesen der makedonischen Renaissance. (Arbeitsgemeinschaft in Forschungen des Landes Nordrhein-Westfalen*, CVII, 1963.)

573. WERCKMEISTER (O. K.), *Three Problems of Tradition in Pre-Carolingian Figure-Style*, in *Proceedings of the Royal Irish Academy*, LXIII, Section C, No. 5, 1963, pp. 167-189.

574. WERCKMEISTER (O. K.), *Die Bilder der drei Propheten in der Biblia Hispalense*. Madrider Mitteilungen, IV, 1963, p. 141.

575. *Werdendes Abendland an Rhein und Ruhr*, Exhibition at the Villa Hügel, Essen, 1956.

576. WERNER (Joachim), *Münzdatierte austrasische Grabfunde*, Berlin-Leipzig, 1935.

577. WERNER (Joachim), *Die byzantinische Scheibenfibel aus Capua und ihre germanischen Verwandten*, in *Acta archaeologica*, VII, Copenhagen, 1936, p. 57 sq.

578. WERNER (Joachim), *Italisches und koptisches Bronzegeschirr des 6. und 7. Jahrhunderts nordwärts der Alpen*, in *Mnemosynon Th. Wiegand*. Munich, 1938, p. 74 sq.

579. WERNER (Joachim), *Der Fund von Ittenheim*... Strasbourg, 1943.

580. WERNER (Joachim), *Zur Herkunft der frühmittelalterlichen Spangenhelme*, in *Prähistorische Zeitschrift*, XXXIV-XXXV, 1949-1950, p. 178.

581. WERNER (Joachim), *Die Schwerter von Imola, Herbrechtingen, und Endrebacke*, in *Acta archaeologica*, XXI, Copenhagen, 1950, p. 45 sq.

582. WERNER (Joachim), *Das alemannische Fürstengrab aus Wittislingen*, Munich, 1950.

583. WERNER (Joachim), *Zur ornamentgeschichtlichen Einordnung des Reliquiars von Beromünster*, in *Frühmittelalterliche Kunst in den Alpenländern, Actes du IIIe Congrès international pour l'étude du haut Moyen Age*, Olten-Lausanne, 1951, p. 107 sq.

584. WERNER (Joachim), *Ein langobardischer Schild von Ischl an der Alz*, in *Bayerische Vorgeschichteblätter*, Heft XVIII-XIX, Munich, 1951-1952, p. 45 sq.

585. WERNER (Joachim), *Das alemannische Gräberfeld von Bülach*, in *Monographien zur Ur- und Frühgeschichte der Schweiz*, IX, Basel, 1953.

586. WERNER (Joachim), *Das alemannische Gräberfeld von Mindelheim*, in *Materialhefte zur Bayerischen Vorgeschichte*, VI, Kollmünz, 1955.

587. WERNER (Joachim), *Die Byzantinischen Gürtelschnallen des 6. und 7. Jahrhunderts aus der Sammlung Diergardt*, in *Jahrbuch für Vor- und Frühgeschichte*, I, Cologne, 1955, pp. 36-48.

588. WERNER (Joachim), *Beiträge zur Archäologie des Attila Reiches*, in *Bayerische Akademie der Wissenschaften. Philosophisch-historische Klasse*, Abhandlung, Neue Folge 38 A, Munich, 1956.

589. WERNER (Joachim), *Byzantinische Gürtelschnalle aus Riva S. Vitale*, in *Sibrium*, III, 1957, p. 79 sq.

590. WERNER (Joachim), *Katalog der Sammlung Diergardt, Köln*, I-II, Munich, 1961-1962.

591. WERNER (Joachim), *Die Langobarden in Pannonien. Beiträge zur Kenntnis der langobardischen Bodenfunde vor 568*, Munich, 1962.

592. WILL (Ernest), *Recherches dans l'abbatiale de Saint-Quentin*, in *Cahiers archéologiques*, IX, Paris, 1957, pp. 165-186.

593. WILL (Ernest), *Le Relief cultuel gréco-romain*, Paris, E. de Boccard, 1956, 494 p. (Thesis.)

594. WILL (Robert) and HIMLY (F.-J.), *Les Édifices religieux en Alsace à l'époque préromane, V^e-Xe siècles*, in *Revue d'Alsace*, XCIII, 1954, pp. 36-76.

595. WILPERT (Joseph), *Die römischen Mosaiken und Malereien der kirchlichen Bauten vom 4. bis 13. Jahrhundert*, Freiburg-im-Breisgau, 1924.

596. WILSON (D. M.), *A Ring of Queen Arnegonde*, in *Germania*, XLII, 1964, p. 265 sq.

597. WIT (J. de), *Die Miniaturen des Virgilius Vaticanus*, Amsterdam, Swets & Zeitlinger, 1959.

598. WORMALD (F.), *The Miniatures in the Gospels of St. Augustine (Corpus Christi College ms. 286)*, Cambridge University Press, 1954, IX, p. 17.

599. WRIGHT (D. H.), *The Codex Millenarius and its Model*, in *Münchner Jahrbuch der bildenden Kunst*, III, Folge, XV, 1964, p. 37 sq.

600. WUILLEUMIER (Pierre), AUDIN (Amable) and LEROI-GOURHAN (André), *L'Église et la nécropole Saint-Laurent dans le quartier lyonnais de Choulans*, Lyon, Audin, 1949. (Institut des Études rhodaniennes de l'Université de Lyon, 4.)

601. ZEISS (Hans), *Die Grabfunde aus dem spanischen Westgotenreich*, Berlin-Leipzig, 1934.

602. ZEISS (Hans), *Das Goldblattkreuz von Stabio (Kanton Tessin) und verwandte Denkmäler*, in *Festschrift für E. Tatarinoff*, Solothurn, 1938, pp. 61-69.

603. ZEISS (Hans), *Die Bedeutung Burgunds für die Plattier- und Tauschierkunst der Merovingerzeit*, in *Forschungen und Fortschritte*, XXIX-XXX, 1939, p. 369 sq.

604. ZEISS (Hans), *Die frühbyzantinische Fibel aus Mengen*, in *Germania*, XXIII, 1939, pp. 269-273.

605. ZEISS (Hans), *Das Heilsbild in der germanischen Kunst des frühen Mittelalters*, in *Sitzungsberichte der Bayerischen Akademie der Wissenschaften. Philologisch-historische Klasse*, Munich, 1941, p. 38 sq.

606. ZEISS (Hans), *Die germanischen Grabfunde des frühen Mittelalters zwischen mittlerer Seine und Loiremündung*, XXXI, Berlin, 1942, in *Berichte der Römisch-Germanischen Kommission*.

607. ZIMMERMANN (E. H.), *Vorkarolingische Miniaturen*, Berlin, 1916-1918. 4 vols. of plates, 1 vol. of text (XII, 330 p.).

608. ZOVATTO (Paolo Lino), *Il tempietto di Cividale e i minori studi*, in *Felix Ravenna*, III, XIII, 1954, pp. 49-64.

609. ZOVATTO (Paolo Lino), *Il ciborio di S. Giorgio in Valpolicella ed altre sculture longobarde e ravennati*, III, XXXVIII, 1964, pp. 96-115.

610. ZÜRN (Hans), *Ein neues alemannisches Gräberfeld in Sontheim an der Brenz*, in *Fundberichte aus Schwaben*, Neue Folge, XVI, 1962, pp. 183-186.

BIBLIOGRAPHICAL INDEX

GENERAL

1, 2, 3, 4, 5, 6, 7, 12, 13, 14, 16, 17, 18, 19, 21, 35, 37, 39, 51, 52, 53, 73, 75, 87, 90, 98, 102, 104, 111, 117, 118, 119, 122, 123, 125, 128, 131, 133, 134, 136, 139, 140, 141, 145, 146, 147, 148, 156, 157, 159, 163, 166, 170, 171, 172, 175, 176, 179, 182, 183, 187, 188, 196, 197, 199, 209, 211, 215 II, 216, 217, 223, 224, 225, 227, 229, 230, 232, 233, 236, 237, 241, 242, 243, 245, 248, 252, 254, 258, 259, 261, 262, 263, 270, 273, 276, 277, 278, 280, 286, 288, 296, 303, 304, 305, 312, 322, 323, 324, 332, 334, 336, 337, 338, 346, 351, 354, 355, 356, 359, 360, 362, 363, 365, 366, 367, 368, 369, 375, 376, 377, 385, 394, 401, 405, 406, 419, 426, 428, 429, 433, 434, 439, 441, 447, 448, 453, 455, 456, 457, 461, 464, 465, 472, 473, 474, 476, 481, 486, 488, 490, 491, 495, 496, 503, 505, 506, 509, 510, 514, 516, 517, 518, 524, 525, 526, 528, 530, 531, 533, 535, 536, 538, 544, 545, 546, 549, 558, 559. 572, 575, 580, 588, 591, 593, 605.

PART ONE

ARCHITECTURE

General Works: 15, 35, 49, 55, 59, 65, 100, 108, 109, 112, 116, 120, 121, 127, 128, 130, 138, 151, 153, 154, 161, 162, 188, 189, 190, 230, 244, 250, 271, 272, 275, 279, 290, 298, 307, 308, 309, 325, 334, 349, 350, 377, 396, 430, 431, 443, 518, 523, 537, 544, 548, 560, 561, 594, 595, 600.

Specialized Works: 41, 44, 45, 46, 47, 48, 50, 60, 61, 62, 63, 64, 66, 67, 68, 76, 79, 81, 84, 96, 99, 101, 107, 112, 115, 129, 155, 173, 189, 190, 202, 203, 207 210, 220, 222, 235, 239, 253, 259, 268, 274, 281, 282 290, 292, 293, 294, 297, 325, 327, 339, 356, 364, 370, 379, 380, 387, 393, 395, 397, 402, 420, 431, 432, 435, 436, 437, 438, 449, 466, 478, 480, 481, 483, 494, 515, 541, 543, 550, 561, 579, 581, 584, 589, 592, 600, 608 609.

SCULPTURE

General Works: 14, 21, 26, 30, 31, 44, 67, 94, 115, 135, 140, 142, 150, 151, 165, 176, 181, 185, 191, 201, 203, 221, 235, 250, 251, 281, 285, 331, 333, 342, 345, 393, 401, 403, 404, 430, 489, 504, 512, 518, 538, 542, 549, 554, 565, 593, 609.

Cemeteries and Burials: 8, 23, 24, 27, 40, 43, 54, 80, 86, 87, 88, 89, 92, 105, 106, 114, 137, 143, 144, 158, 174, 178, 184, 198, 205, 206, 218, 219, 224, 228, 238, 240, 244, 257, 297, 300, 326, 330, 386, 398, 407, 418, 440, 442, 452, 463, 471, 475, 484, 485, 487, 492, 501, 502, 518, 519, 534, 539, 551, 566, 576, 582, 585, 586, 601, 606, 610.

Sarcophagi: 44, 85, 91, 93, 149, 152, 192, 193, 194, 195, 343, 344, 389, 565.

PART TWO

PAINTING

General Works: 14, 21, 22, 29, 33, 69, 70, 71, 72, 74, 76, 112, 155, 200, 202, 213, 214, 215, 234, 249, 255, 260, 301, 329, 341, 364, 401, 417, 431, 436, 479, 515, 522, 547, 568, 571, 595, 607, 608.
Book Painting: 56, 57, 69, 71, 82, 95, 97, 167, 168, 169, 226, 234, 255, 256, 264, 265, 266, 283, 284, 289, 299, 306, 352, 353, 371, 372, 373, 374, 378, 383, 384, 388, 390, 399, 400, 409, 410, 411, 412, 413, 414, 415, 416, 421, 423, 444, 458, 482, 507, 508, 521, 527, 532, 540, 562, 563, 567, 569, 570, 573, 574, 597, 598, 599.
Mosaics: 20, 215 I, 329, 397, 499, 500, 529, 595.

PART THREE

APPLIED ARTS
General Works: 6, 25, 27, 35, 87, 164, 204, 245, 247, 287, 291, 310, 311, 323, 357, 381, 391, 434, 454, 459, 460, 470, 493, 552, 590.
Bronzes: 425, 427, 553, 578.
Ivories: 498, 555, 556.
Coins: 58, 328, 347, 348, 446.
Jewellery: 8, 9, 10, 11, 23, 32, 34, 36, 38, 42, 77, 78, 83, 105, 110, 113, 115, 124, 126, 132, 160, 162, 174, 177, 178, 180, 186, 195, 204, 208, 212, 231, 246, 247, 257, 267, 269, 287, 291, 295, 302, 313, 314, 315, 316, 317, 318, 319, 320, 321, 323, 335, 340, 357, 358, 361, 381, 382, 391, 392, 408, 420, 422, 424, 445, 449, 450, 451, 462, 467, 468, 477, 497, 511, 513, 520, 542, 547, 557, 577, 583, 584, 587, 589, 596, 602, 603, 604.
Textiles: 103, 393, 469.

List of Illustrations

Unless otherwise specified, the reference numbers in parentheses refer to other entries in the List of Illustrations and to the corresponding plates.

Frontispiece. Merovingian (Lombard) Art. *Lion Plaque for a Shield (detail).* 7th century. Historisches Museum, Berne. Gilt bronze. (Arts of Mankind Photo.)

Found in 1833 near Stabio in the grave of a Lombard warrior, with many similar objects. (Cf. 302.)

1. **ECHTERNACH.** *Echternach Gospels: Lion, Symbol of St Mark. (Cf. 168.)* Mid-8th century. Folio 75 verso, MS Lat. 9389, Bibliothèque Nationale, Paris. Miniature painting on vellum, 13¼ × 10 in. (B.N. Photo.)

2. Art of the Late Empire. **FRÉJUS, Baptistery.** *The Dome and Its Drum Pierced with Windows.* 5th century. In situ. (Arts of Mankind Photo.)

The dome of this baptistery enables us to form some idea of the lantern-towers which were built over the choir of the early basilicas and which are mentioned or described in several texts of the Merovingian period.

3. Art of the Late Empire. **FRÉJUS, Baptistery.** *View of the Interior.* 5th century. In situ. (Arts of Mankind Photo.)

Around the baptismal font, polygonal in shape, can be seen vestiges of the columns which supported a ciborium. (Cf. 322 A & B.)

4. Art of the Late Empire. **FRÉJUS, Baptistery.** *External View.* 5th century. In situ. (Arts of Mankind Photo.)

The building has been over-restored in our time, but its original proportions have been strictly preserved. Much of the square base on which it stands is now underground; this base was originally surrounded by a portico.

5. Early Christian Art. **ALBENGA, Baptistery.** *View of the Interior.* 5th-6th century. In situ. (Arts of Mankind Photo.)

Decagonal outside and octagonal inside, with radiating apses and niches, the baptistery measures 46 ft at its widest point. Large fragments of the original wall mosaics and openwork closure slabs of the windows have been preserved. (Cf. 6.)

6. Early Christian Art. **ALBENGA, Baptistery.** *Mosaic decorating one of the Vaults. (Cf. 5.)* 5th-6th century. In situ. (Arts of Mankind Photo.)

7. Early Christian Art. **MILAN, San Lorenzo.** *West Colonnade of the Atrium.* 4th-5th century. In situ. (Arts of Mankind Photo.)

The columns are nearly 10 ft high.

8. Early Christian Art. **MILAN, San Lorenzo.** *External View from the South-east.* 4th-5th century. In situ. (Arts of Mankind Photo.)

Built on a square plan, with exedrae and corner towers, the church is 157 ft wide and 115 ft high. For its plan, see A. GRABAR, The Golden Age of Justinian, Odyssey Press, New York, or Byzantium, The Age of Justinian, Thames and Hudson, London, The Arts of Mankind, 1966, Fig. 397. The Early Christian structure of the upper parts of the church was until recently concealed by architectural and decorative elements added in the 16th century.

9. **MILAN, San Lorenzo.** *View of the Interior from the South-east.* 4th-5th century. In situ. (Arts of Mankind Photo.)

10. **MILAN, San Lorenzo.** *View of the Interior from the South-east.* 4th-5th century. In situ. (Arts of Mankind Photo.)

11. **MARSEILLES, Church of Saint-Victor.** *Crypts of Notre-Dame-de-Confession, originally an Early Christian mausoleum.* 5th century. In situ. (Arts of Mankind Photo.)

View from the south (the building is oriented towards the north). In the centre is the nave, with arcades opening on what were originally the side aisles. In the foreground, the columns of the atrium. In the early 19th century the original marble columns with capitals were replaced by stone columns. (Cf. 13, 334.)

12. **MARSEILLES, Church of Saint-Victor, Crypts of Notre-Dame-de-Confession.** *Mosaic decorating the intrados of an arch on the west side of the atrium.* 5th century. In situ. (Arts of Mankind Photo.)

13. **MARSEILLES, Church of Saint-Victor, Crypts of Notre-Dame-de-Confession.** *Vine pattern decorating the intrados of an arch at the entrance of the east aisle. (Cf. 11.)* 5th century. In situ. Stucco. (Arts of Mankind Photo.)

14. **MARSEILLES, Abbey of Saint-Victor.** *Altar.* 5th century. Musée d'Archéologie, Château Borély, Marseilles. Carrara marble, 70 × 44 in. (Arts of Mankind Photo.)

The four pilasters supporting the altar are modern. (Cf. 15.)

15. **MARSEILLES, Abbey of Saint-Victor.** *Altar: detail of the decorated edges of the altar slab (front, back and one side).* 5th century. Musée d'Archéologie, Château Borély, Marseilles. (Arts of Mankind Photo.)

Note the Greek inscription engraved on the front edge below the monogram of Christ and the doves on either side of it. (Cf. 14.)

16. **ARLES, Cemetery of Les Aliscamps.** *Sarcophagus of Concordius, Bishop of Arles (died c. 390).* 4th century. Musée Lapidaire Chrétien, Arles. Proconnesus marble, lid 86½ × 9½ × 31 in.; coffin 86 × 23½ × 31½ in. (Arts of Mankind Photo.)

The epitaph is engraved on the tablet in the centre.

17. *Reliquary Shrine probably representing the Martyrium of the Holy Sepulchre at Jerusalem.* About 5th century. Musée Lapidaire, Narbonne. White marble of the Pyrenees, 49 × 35½ in. (Arts of Mankind Photo.)

The front was closed by a metal screen whose sealing sockets are still visible. Discovered at Narbonne in the substructure of a defensive turret on the city walls, not far from the first cathedral.

18. *Decorative Pilaster from a Church (detail).* 5th century. Musée Lapidaire Chrétien, Arles. Marble, 34 × 65 in. (Arts of Mankind Photo.)

19. **SAINT - MAXIMIN - LA - SAINTE - BAUME (Var), Basilica of Sainte-Madeleine, Crypt** (originally an Early Christian mausoleum). *Engraved slab: The Virgin as a Child and Servant of the Temple.* About 5th century. In situ. Marble, height 65 in. (Arts of Mankind Photo.)

This theme, certified by the inscription engraved above the figure, is taken from the apocryphal Gospels.

20. **SAINT - MAXIMIN - LA - SAINTE - BAUME (Var), Basilica of Sainte-Madeleine, Crypt.** *Engraved slab: Abraham's Sacrifice.* About 5th century. In situ. Marble, height 62 in. (Arts of Mankind Photo.)

21. **SAINT - MAXIMIN - LA - SAINTE - BAUME (Var), Basilica of Sainte-Madeleine, Crypt.** *Engraved slab: Daniel in the Lions' Den.* About 5th century. In situ. Marble, height 64 in. (Arts of Mankind Photo.)

22. **AUXERRE, Church of Saint-Germain** (originally in the basilica erected by Queen Clotilda, 493-545). *Slab with the Monogram of Christ.* 493-545. In situ. Stone with cavities for inlays of glass paste. Diameter of monogram 23 in. (Arts of Mankind Photo.)

Queen Clotilda, at some undetermined time between her arrival in Gaul (493) and her death (545), had a basilica erected in place of the oratory containing the body of St Germanus, Bishop of Auxerre (died 448). The only remaining vestige of the basilica is this slab with the monogram of Christ; preserved during the Middle Ages in the masonry of the main altar of the upper church, it was removed in the 17th century and embedded in one of the niches of the crypt.

23. Merovingian Art. **POITIERS, Convent of Sainte-Croix.** *Reading Desk attributed to St Radegunda who, about 555, founded the Convent of the Holy Cross at Poitiers and died there in 587.* 6th century. Abbey of Sainte-Croix, Route de Gençay at Saint-Benoît. Wood, length at the base 10¼ in., width 7½ in., height 6 in. (Arts of Mankind Photo.)

The traditional attribution is confirmed by the iconography of the woodcarvings (see the perspective view showing the back of the desk, No. 120.)

24. Merovingian Art. **CHARENTON-DU-CHER, Abbey founded about 620.** *Sarcophagus with engraved designs. (Cf. 25 showing the other side.)* 7th century. Musée du Berry, Bourges. Marble. (Arts of Mankind Photo.)

25. Merovingian Art. **CHARENTON-DU-CHER, Abbey.** *Sarcophagus with engraved decoration, detail. (Cf. 24 showing the other side.)* 7th century. Musée du Berry, Bourges. (Arts of Mankind Photo.)

26. Merovingian Art. **GÉMIGNY (Loiret).** *Fragment of a disk forming part of a mould for making patens.* About 6th century. Musée Historique de l'Orléanais, Orléans. Fine-grained limestone, 4⅛ × 4 in.; the original disk had a diameter of 6½ in. (Museum Photo - Martin.)

The inscriptions help to identify the figure of the Saviour ([SALV]ATOR) and those of three angels (VRIEL, RAGVEL, [RA]FAEL).

27. Merovingian Art. **TOULOUSE, Church of Saint-Sernin.** *Sarcophagus, reliefs in the central part.* 6th-7th century. Musée des Augustins, Toulouse. Marble of the Pyrenees, height 21 in. (Arts of Mankind Photo.)

The sculptor has imitated the hunting scenes on pagan sarcophagi carved in Italy and exported to Gaul in the 2nd or 3rd century.

28. Merovingian Art. **TOULOUSE, Church of Notre-Dame de la Daurade.** *Capital.* 5th-6th century. Musée des Augustins, Toulouse. Marble of the Pyrenees, height 11 in. (Arts of Mankind Photo.)

29. Merovingian Art. **TOULOUSE, Notre-Dame de la Daurade.** *Column, detail of the carving.* 5th-6th century. Louvre, Paris. Marble of the Pyrenees. (Arts of Mankind Photo.)

30. Merovingian Art. **VIENNE (Isère), Church of Saint-Pierre** (formerly the Basilica of the Apostles, now the Archaeological Museum). *View of the Interior from the west.* 5th-11th century. In situ. (Photo Musées de Vienne.)

The arcading with marble columns and capitals lining the side walls recalls the superimposed orders of the architecture of the Late Empire. (Cf. 328.)

31. Merovingian Art. **VIENNE (Isère), Church of Saint-Pierre.** *Sarcophagus with engraved designs.* 6th-7th century. In situ. White marble. (Photo Denise Fourmont, Paris.)

In the 10th century (as attested by an inscription of that period engraved on the lid), the remains of St Leonian were placed in this sarcophagus; he had been abbot of Saint-André of Vienne in the early 6th century.

32. Merovingian Art. **LANGEAIS (Indre-et-Loire).** *Stele with engraved designs.* 6th-7th century. Musée Archéologique de Touraine, Tours. Stone, 8 ¼ × 13½ × 1½ in. (Photo Jean Hubert, Paris.)

The dead man's epitaph is accompanied by an engraved hunting scene which, like the bas-relief on the Toulouse sarcophagus (cf. 27), imitates the pagan reliefs on antique tombs.

33. Merovingian Art. **SELLES-SUR-CHER, Basilica** (founded by King Childebert I between 542 and 558). *Columns and capitals re-used on the façade of the 12th-century church.* 6th and 12th century. In situ. Marble, height of the capitals 11½ in. (Arts of Mankind Photo.)

The Romanesque arcading recalls the superimposed orders of the early basilicas. (Cf. 30 and 34-37.)

34. Merovingian Art. **SELLES-SUR-CHER, Basilica.** *Capital.* 6th century. In situ. Marble, height 11½ in. (Arts of Mankind Photo.)

The column is antique; the abacus of the capital dates from the Romanesque period. (Cf. 33.)

35. Merovingian Art. **SELLES-SUR-CHER, Basilica.** *Capital. (Cf. 33.)* 6th century. In situ. Marble, height 11½ in. (Arts of Mankind Photo.)

36-37. Merovingian Art. **SELLES-SUR-CHER, Basilica.** *Reconstruction of*

the pattern, based on the equilateral triangle, used to work out the proportions of a capital. 6th century. In situ. Marble, height 11½ in. (Arts of Mankind Photo and drawing by Claude Abeille.)

The use of elementary geometry can also be observed in the ground plan of early medieval churches. (Cf. 33.)

38. **School of Reims.** *Utrecht Psalter, detail: Church with a lantern-tower.* 9th century. University Library, Utrecht. Vellum. (Photo Utrecht University Library.)

The lantern-tower, resting on a drum pierced with windows, existed already in the religious architecture of the Late Empire. It seems to have been a characteristic feature of the churches built in Gaul in the Merovingian period. It survived in France until the Romanesque period.

39. Merovingian Art. **SOISSONS and PARIS.** *Coffin of St Drausius, Bishop of Soissons (died after 667) with lid from another tomb at Saint-Germain-des-Prés, Paris. (Cf. 40.)* Louvre, Paris. Marble, length 7 ft. (Arts of Mankind Photo.)

40. Merovingian Art. **SOISSONS.** *Central part of the coffin of St Drausius, Bishop of Soissons (died after 667). (Cf. 39.)* 7th century. Louvre, Paris. Marble. (Arts of Mankind Photo.)

41. Merovingian Art. **NANTES, Cathedral** (consecrated by Bishop St Felix about 558). *Capital decorated with a cross and acanthus leaves.* Mid-6th century. Musée Dobrée, Nantes. Marble, 26¾ × 25 × 15¾ in. (Arts of Mankind Photo.)

Work on the cathedral began before 548 under Bishop Eumerius.

42. Merovingian Art. **NANTES, Cathedral.** *Capital.* Mid-6th century. Musée Dobrée, Nantes. Marble, 10½ × 12½ × 29½ in. (Arts of Mankind Photo.)

43. Merovingian Art. **VERTOU (Loire-Atlantique), Abbey** (founded by St Martin, died c. 601). *Capital.* 6th-7th century. Musée Dobrée, Nantes. White limestone, 7 × 11 × 10½ in. (Arts of Mankind Photo.)

Capital discovered in 1850 when a Romanesque wall of the church of Vertou was demolished.

44. Merovingian Art. **VERTOU (Loire-Atlantique), Abbey.** *Capital.* 6th-7th century. Musée Dobrée, Nantes. White limestone, 8¼ × 11¾ × 9 in. (Arts of Mankind Photo.)

Discovered as above (cf. 43).

45. Merovingian Art. **POITIERS.** *Baptistery of Saint-Jean, seen from the south-east. (Cf. 324.)* About 7th century. In situ. (Arts of Mankind Photo.)

46. Merovingian Art. **POITIERS.** *Baptistery of Saint-Jean, seen from the north-east. (Cf. 324.)* About 7th century. In situ. (Arts of Mankind Photo.)

47. Merovingian Art. **POITIERS.** *Baptistery of Saint-Jean, north front.* About 7th century. In situ. (Arts of Mankind Photo.)

48. Merovingian Art. **POITIERS.** *Baptistery of Saint-Jean, south front (detail).* About 7th century. In situ. (Arts of Mankind Photo.)

49. Merovingian Art. **POITIERS, Baptistery of Saint-Jean.** *Ancient Capital re-used inside the baptistery.* About 7th century. In situ. Marble. (Arts of Mankind Photo.)

The stone abacus above the capital dates from the Romanesque period.

50. Merovingian Art. **POITIERS, Baptistery of Saint-Jean.** *Ancient Capitals re-used inside the baptistery in the Romanesque period.* About 7th century. In situ. Marble. (Arts of Mankind Photo.)

51 A. Merovingian Art. **ANTIGNY (Vienne).** *Sarcophagus.* 7th century. Baptistery of Saint-Jean, Poitiers. Stone. (Arts of Mankind Photo.)

51 B. Merovingian Art. **POITIERS, Cemetery of Saint-Lazare.** *Sarcophagus.* 7th century. Baptistery of Saint-Jean, Poitiers. Stone. (Arts of Mankind Photo.)

51 C. Merovingian Art. **POITIERS, Cemetery of Sainte-Catherine.** *Sarcophagus.* 7th century. Baptistery of Saint-Jean, Poitiers. Stone, length 70 in., width at the head 28¾ in., width at the foot 13¾ in. (Arts of Mankind Photo.)

Rounded lid found in 1831.

51 D. Merovingian Art. **POITIERS, Cemetery of Saint-Lazare.** *Sarcophagus.* 7th century. Baptistery of Saint-Jean, Poitiers. Stone. (Arts of Mankind Photo.)

52. Merovingian Art. **POITIERS, Baptistery of Saint-Jean.** *Pilasters decorating the outer walls (casts).* About 7th century. In situ. The originals are of stone. (Arts of Mankind Photo.)

53. Merovingian Art. **POITIERS, Baptistery of Saint-Jean.** *Sculptured Slab decorating the outer wall (cast).* About 7th century. In situ. The original is of stone. (Arts of Mankind Photo.)

54. Merovingian Art. **MAZEROLLES (Vienne), Church.** *Sculptured Slab embedded in a wall (cast).* 7th century. Cast preserved in the Baptistery of Saint-Jean, Poitiers. The original is of stone. (Arts of Mankind Photo.)

The monastery of Mazerolles was rebuilt by Ansoaldus, Bishop of Poitiers, in the late 7th century (c. 678-697). The same design, also enclosed in a circle, appears on a piece of stamped terracotta (Musée Dobrée, Nantes) from the monastery of Vertou founded by St Martin (died c. 601).

55. African Art. **MASCLIANAE (Hajeb El Aiun), Tunisia.** *Panel representing Adam and Eve standing, with haloes, separated by the tree with the serpent coiling round it.* 6th century. Musée National du Bardo, Tunis. Stamped terracotta, length 10 to 10½ in., thickness ½ to ¾ of an inch. (Photo Direction des Musées Nationaux - Musée du Bardo, Tunis.)

Such terracottas are now assigned to the early period of the Byzantine occupation of North Africa.

56. Merovingian Art. **VERTOU (Loire-Atlantique), Monastery** (founded by St Martin, died c. 601). *Panel representing Adam and Eve tempted by the serpent.* 6th-7th century. Musée Dobrée, Nantes. Stamped terracotta, 8¼ × 7¾ × 3¼ in. (Arts of Mankind Photo.)

This panel bears a striking resemblance to No. 55. The elements of both derive from a common origin: the Christian art of the Late Empire.

57. African Art. **HENSHIR KAMOR, Tunisia.** *Panel representing Christ (?).* 6th century. Musée National du Bardo, Tunis. Stamped terracotta, length 10 to 10½ in., thickness ½ to ¾ of an inch. (Photo Direction des Musées Nationaux - Musée du Bardo, Tunis.)

The director of the Bardo Museum has kindly provided the following information: 'The face and the circle are heightened with white; this circle is enclosed between two others, one painted grey, the other red. The panel is thought to represent Christ.'

58. Merovingian Art. **PARIS, Cemetery of Saint-Marcel.** *Panel representing a head with gaping mouth, the brow surmounted by a cross.* 7th century.

Musée Carnavalet, Paris. Terracotta, about 37½ × 32 × 12½ in. (Photo Denise Fossard, Paris.)

The resemblance to No. 57 is evident: both derive from the Christian art of the Late Empire.

59. Merovingian Art. **NANTES, former church of Saint-Similien.** *Figured Panel imitating the antique.* 7th century. Musée Dobrée, Nantes. Red terracotta, 8 × 5 × 1¾ in. (Arts of Mankind Photo.)

A considerable number of figured terracottas have been brought together in the Nantes museum. Most of them appear to come from interior friezes and from cornices supporting a ceiling. In this respect, as in so many others, early medieval builders followed the practices of the Late Empire.

60. Merovingian Art. **VERTOU (Loire-Atlantique).** *Fragment of an Incised Pediment originally representing two confronted doves on either side of a vase.* 6th-7th century. Musée Dobrée, Nantes. White limestone, 7½ × 8¼ in. (Arts of Mankind Photo.)

Found in 1875 in the rubble of the Romanesque church of Vertou.

61. Merovingian Art. **VERTOU (Loire-Atlantique).** *Fragment of a Pediment.* 6th-7th century. Musée Dobrée, Nantes. White limestone, 9 × 8 × 4 in. (Arts of Mankind Photo.)

62. Merovingian Art. **NANTES, former church of Saint-Similien.** *Fragment of a Cornice.* 7th century. Musée Dobrée, Nantes. White marble, 8 × 6 × 4¼ in. (Arts of Mankind Photo.)

In the present state of our knowledge, this fragment cannot be dated with any certainty.

63. Merovingian Art. **NANTES, former church of Saint-Similien.** *Panel with the Sacred Monogram.* 7th century. Musée Dobrée, Nantes. Red stamped terracotta, 8 × 8¼ × 3 in. (Arts of Mankind Photo.)

Compare with the terracotta panel from Vertou (No. 56) representing Adam and Eve. Dimensions and style are the same. These terracottas, cast in moulds in specialized workshops, went to make up friezes and revetments. The stone friezes of the early Romanesque churches are the last expression of a decorative art handed down by the Late Empire.

64. Merovingian Art. **VERTOU (Loire-Atlantique), Abbey** (founded by St Martin, died c. 601). *Fragment of a Pediment (or a panel) decorated with*

a six-rayed star. 6th-7th century. Musée Dobrée, Nantes. White limestone, 34 × 8¼ × 4 in. (Arts of Mankind Photo.)

This motif is very similar in both size and design to those decorating the pediments of the baptistery of Saint-Jean, Poitiers (No. 48).

65. Merovingian Art. **NANTES, former church of Saint-Similien.** *Arch-stone with a Figure holding in its right hand a ball-topped rod and raising its left forearm.* 7th century. Musée Dobrée, Nantes. Red stamped terracotta, 13 × 5½ × 3½ in. (Arts of Mankind Photo.)

Several arch-stones of this type have been found, and others representing a monogrammed cross with Alpha and Omega. Judging by their shape and size, these stones came from arches or round-headed windows with an inner diameter of about two feet. These carvings, the handiwork of the Merovingian stone-carvers of the lower Loire, appear to have been used as models by the sculptors who made the historiated arch-stones which decorate 12th-century churches in the west of France.

66. Merovingian Art. **SAINT-DENIS, Basilica.** *Part of a Closure Slab.* Merovingian period. Dépôt lapidaire, Basilica of Saint-Denis. A cast of the whole slab has been made on the basis of a large extant fragment in white limestone, 28½ × 24½ in. (Arts of Mankind Photo.)

The fragment was found by Jules Formigé during excavations carried out in the nave of the basilica.

67. Merovingian Art. **SAINT-DENIS, Basilica.** *Closure Pilaster.* Merovingian period. Dépôt lapidaire, Basilica of Saint-Denis. White limestone. (Arts of Mankind Photo.)

Found in the excavation of the nave. This counter-curve motif occurs in exactly the same form in gold filigree-work of the 6th and 7th centuries.

68. Merovingian Art. **POITIERS, Cimetière des Dunes.** *Hypogeum ('Hypogée des Dunes'), Overall View from the west.* 7th century. In situ. Stone. (Arts of Mankind Photo.)

This burial vault formed part of a cemetery situated on one of the limestone plateaux (called locally 'dunes') to the east of Poitiers, near the Roman road from Bourges to Poitiers by way of Argenton. It was discovered on December 24, 1878, by le Père de la Croix during a systematic excavation of the cemetery. (Cf. 70, 76, 332 A & B.)

69. Merovingian Art. **POITIERS, Cimetière des Dunes.** *Drawing by le Père de la Croix. Reconstruction of the longitudinal section of the Hypogeum.* 7th century. Inside dimensions: length 18 ft, width 10 ft. The stairway is 3½ ft wide and just under 15 ft in length. (After C. de la Croix, *Hypogée-Martyrium de Poitiers*, Paris 1883, Pl. XX.)

Le Père de la Croix gave the ancient name 'hypogeum' to this burial vault, which originally lay only partially underground. It was designed to house a tomb, an altar and stone reliquary shrines. There were many burial vaults of this type in Merovingian Gaul. It was called a memoria *or* crypta, *the word* crypta *being used, then as in Roman times, to designate any vaulted structure. An inscription engraved on the door-head records that this* memoria *contained the tomb of Abbot Mellebaude, 'debitor of Christ.'*

70. Merovingian Art. **POITIERS, Cimetière des Dunes.** *Hypogeum ('Hypogée des Dunes'): Three Steps of the Stairway.* 7th century. In situ. A. 39 × 8¼ in.; B. 37½ × 10 in.; C. 39 × 8½ in. (Arts of Mankind Photo.)

Each step has a different decoration (fishes, ivy scroll, twined snakes), to which was no doubt attributed a magical or prophylactic power such, it was hoped, as would protect the vault from tomb-robbers. (Cf. 68, 332 A & B.)

71. Merovingian Art. **POITIERS, Cimetière des Dunes.** *Hypogeum ('Hypogée des Dunes'): Magical Inscription engraved on the threshold of the entrance.* 7th century. In situ. Engraved stone, 27½ × 9½ in. (Arts of Mankind Photo.)

It reads: GRAMA GRVMO ANA - AY CAX PI/IX. *The meaning of this esoteric anagram remains a riddle.*

72. Merovingian Art. **POITIERS, Cimetière des Dunes.** *Drawing by le Père de la Croix. Cross-section of the Hypogeum, from the west.* 7th century. (After C. de la Croix, *Hypogée-Martyrium de Poitiers*, Paris 1883, Pl. XXI.)

This reconstruction shows the architecture and paintings as they were found when the hypogeum was discovered. Note the painted, cube-shaped altar and the decorative painting on the east wall. (Cf. 73.)

73. Merovingian Art. **POITIERS, Cimetière des Dunes.** *Hypogeum ('Hypogée des Dunes'): Lower Part of the Altar.* 7th century. In situ. Stone, 22 × 33½ in. (Arts of Mankind Photo.)

The front of the altar was adorned with a painted cross; the cavities contained inlays of glass paste. Its original aspect is shown in No. 72. In the foreground, a step decorated with rosettes and bearing an engraved inscription (now incomplete) exhorting men not to liken themselves to God and not to seek any glorification beyond the confession of their sins and the doing of good works. (Cf. 72.)

74. Merovingian Art. **POITIERS, Cimetière des Dunes.** *Hypogeum ('Hypogée des Dunes'): View of the North Side of the Sanctuary.* 7th century. In situ. Stone. (Arts of Mankind Photo.)

In the left foreground, the base and fragment of a column which may have been part of a stone lectern. On the far right, the base of a monumental cross. Under the arcosolium, the remains of a stone reliquary shrine in the form of a tomb, whose front was decorated with a row of figures in flowing robes. (Cf. 332 A & B.)

75. Merovingian Art. **POITIERS, Cimetière des Dunes.** *Copy by le Père de la Croix. Hypogeum ('Hypogée des Dunes'): Copy of a Painted Inscription formerly in the North Arcosolium.* 7th century. (After C. de la Croix, *Hypogée-Martyrium de Poitiers*, Paris 1883, Pl. X, No. 2.)

Inscription commemorating the translation of relics on the 3rd and 9th of December. In accordance with the custom of the time, the year is not indicated. The lettering of the painted and engraved inscriptions in the hypogeum enables it to be safely attributed to the 7th century.

76. Merovingian Art. **POITIERS, Cimetière des Dunes.** *Hypogeum ('Hypogée des Dunes'): Base of a Monumental Cross.* In situ. Stone, 29½ × 24¾ in. (Arts of Mankind Photo.)

As Victor Elbern has shown, this fragment of sculpture representing the good and the bad thief formed the base of a monumental cross. This cross would, however, have been too big for the memoria of Abbot Mellebaude. It may have stood in the sanctuary of a large funerary basilica located in this same cemetery; such basilicas were often built at this period in the suburbs of cathedral towns. Mellebaude may have been abbot of this basilica. Another possibility is that the cross stood in the cemetery itself, like the sculptured crosses of Great Britain and Ireland. (Cf. 68.)

77. Merovingian Art. **JOUARRE, Abbey.** *The North Crypt seen from the south-west.* 7th century. In situ. Stone and marble. (Arts of Mankind Photo.)

On the right, the tomb of the first abbess, St Theodechilde. On the left, the tomb of Bishop Agilbert. The 12th-century vaulting rests on columns surmounted by marble capitals dating to the 7th century. (Cf. 340 A & B.)

78. Merovingian Art. **JOUARRE, Abbey.** *North Crypt with, at the back, the south crypt known as the crypt of St Ebregesilus, bishop of Meaux in the 7th century. (Cf. 340 A & B.)* 7th century. In situ. (Arts of Mankind Photo.)

79. Merovingian Art. **JOUARRE, Abbey, north crypt.** *West Wall.* 7th century. In situ. Stone. (Arts of Mankind Photo.)

Decorative stonework imitating the masonry of Roman architecture. The same succession of squares, lozenges and polygons appears on the façades of the triumphal gate of the Abbey of Lorsch dating to the late 8th century (see The Carolingian Empire, The Arts of Mankind, 196?).

80. Merovingian Art. **JOUARRE, Abbey, north crypt.** *Capital.* 7th century. In situ. Marble of the Pyrenees. (Arts of Mankind Photo.)

The column itself is antique, re-used here. The abacus is Romanesque. All the capitals in the Jouarre crypts are carved in Pyrenean marble; they appear to have been made to order, for they are much more stylized than those of Notre-Dame de la Daurade, Toulouse (cf. 28), and those at Selles-sur-Cher of the 6th century (cf. 33-36).

81. Merovingian Art. **JOUARRE, Abbey, north crypt.** *Capital.* 7th century. In situ. Marble of the Pyrenees. (Arts of Mankind Photo.)

This capital is the only one whose foliage carving reveals the influence of the spiny acanthus leaves on Byzantine capitals of the mid-6th century.

82. Merovingian Art. **JOUARRE, Abbey, north crypt.** *Cenotaph under the Sarcophagus of the first abbess, St Theodechilde.* Late 7th-early 8th century. In situ. Local stone. (Arts of Mankind Photo.)

The marble capital is genuine, but the column is a 19th-century copy. (Cf. 83.)

83. Merovingian Art. **JOUARRE, Abbey, north crypt.** *Cenotaph of the first abbess, St Theodechilde, detail. (Cf. 82.)* Late 7th-early 8th century. (Arts of Mankind Photo.)

84. Merovingian Art. **JOUARRE, Abbey, north crypt.** *Tomb of Bishop Agilbert (died c. 680), with the Last Judgment.* 7th century. In situ. Local limestone. (Arts of Mankind Photo.)

(Cf. 85, 86, 87 and 89, short side of the sarcophagus.)

85. Merovingian Art. **JOUARRE, Abbey, north crypt.** *Tomb of Bishop Agilbert, detail of the Last Judgment on the front.* 7th century. In situ. (Arts of Mankind Photo.)

The faithful are represented with upraised arms; those with a sash round their loins are no doubt the elect—an iconographic peculiarity of which this sarcophagus provides the only known example. (Cf. 84, 86, 87.)

86. Merovingian Art. **JOUARRE, Abbey, north crypt.** *Tomb of Bishop Agilbert, detail of the Last Judgment on the front. (Cf. 84, 85, 87.)* 7th century. In situ. (Arts of Mankind Photo.)

87. Merovingian Art. **JOUARRE, Abbey, north crypt.** *Tomb of Bishop Agilbert, detail of the Last Judgment on the front. (Cf. 84-86.)* 7th century. In situ. (Arts of Mankind Photo.)

88. Merovingian Art. **JOUARRE, Abbey, north crypt.** *Tomb of Bishop Agilbert, detail of the short side at the head: Winged Man of the Vision of the Apocalypse (cast). (Cf. 89.)* 7th century. In situ. Original made of stone. (Arts of Mankind Photo.)

89. Merovingian Art. **JOUARRE, Abbey, north crypt.** *Tomb of Bishop Agilbert, detail of the short side at the head: Christ enthroned between the four Evangelist Symbols (cast).* 7th century. In situ. (Arts of Mankind Photo.)

The animals and winged man look away from Christ, in accordance with an iconographic practice peculiar to Asia Minor, Egypt and Cappadocia. (Cf. 84, front of the sarcophagus, and 88.)

90. Merovingian Art. **JOUARRE, Abbey, north crypt.** *Tomb of Abbess Agilberta.* 7th century. In situ. (Arts of Mankind Photo.)

This sarcophagus stands against the south wall of the crypt. The genuine fragments of the early medieval carvings were completed with copies in the 19th century.

91. Merovingian Art. **JOUARRE, Abbey, north crypt.** *Stele: censing angel and another figure.* 7th century. In situ. Soft local limestone. (Arts of Mankind Photo.)

This figure group, like the sarcophagus of Bishop Agilbert, is carved in soft limestone. Though not by the same sculptor, the two works have so much in common, particularly in the treatment of faces, that they must be pretty nearly contemporary.

92. Insular Art. **MONASTERBOICE, County Louth.** *Muiredach Cross.* Early 10th century. In situ. Stone, 10½ ft × 6½ ft × 19½ in. (Irish Tourist Board Photo, Paris.)

According to the inscription engraved on the lower part, this cross was made for Abbot Muiredach (died 924). Though no earlier, then, than the beginning of the 10th century, it represents a tradition of figure carving which had been successfully practised in the British Isles since the early Middle Ages.

93. Insular Art. **RUTHWELL (Dumfrieshire), Church.** *Shaft of a Cross, detail: Healing of the Blind Man.* Last quarter of the 7th century. In situ. Stone, height 17 ft 3 in. (After T.D. Kendrick, *Anglo-Saxon Art, To A.D. 900*, Methuen, London 1938, Pl. XLVIII, 1.)

Scene of the life of Christ.

94. Insular Art. **BEWCASTLE (Cumberland).** *Shaft of a Cross, detail: Christ.* Late 7th century. In situ. Stone. (After T.D. Kendrick, *Anglo-Saxon Art, To A.D. 900*, Methuen, London 1938, Pl. XLVIII, 2.)

95. Insular Art. **JEDBURGH (Roxburghshire).** *Fragment of the Shaft of a Cross.* Late 7th century (?). Jedburgh Museum. Stone. (Photo Ministry of Public Building and Works, Edinburgh.)

96. Insular Art. **EASBY (Yorkshire).** *Shaft of a Cross: Christ and the Apostles.* Early 9th century. Victoria and Albert Museum, London. Stone. (Museum Photo.)

97. Insular Art. **EASBY (Yorkshire).** *Shaft of a Cross.* Early 9th century. Victoria and Albert Museum, London. Stone. (Museum Photo.)

98. Spanish Art. **SAN PEDRO DE LA NAVE (Zamora).** *View of the Church from the south-west.* Second half of the 7th century. In situ. Length 69 ft, width of the transept 55 ft. (Photo Enric Gras, Barcelona.)

Monastic church on a cruciform plan. The Spanish churches of this period are, like this one, quite small, but they are remarkable for the very fine masonry work of their walls and vaults, also for the beauty of their sculptured capitals.

99. Spanish Art. **SAN PEDRO DE LA NAVE (Zamora).** *View of the Interior.* Second half of the 7th century. In situ. Inner width of the choir 10 ft, inner width of the sanctuary 8½ ft. (Photo Enric Gras, Barcelona.)

The columns are not embedded in the walls but set flush against them as in ancient Roman architecture. The capitals are adorned with both figures and decorative motifs.

100. Spanish Art. **SAN PEDRO DE LA NAVE (Zamora).** *Capital with Figure Carvings: Daniel in the Lions' Den.* Second half of the 7th century. In situ. (Photo Enric Gras, Barcelona.)

While in the 7th century marble capitals continued to be widely used in Gaul owing to the presence on its soil of marble quarries and the Aquitanian workshops, Spanish sculptors were already practising the art of ingeniously carved stone capitals.

101. Spanish Art. **SAN PEDRO DE LA NAVE (Zamora).** *Capital with Figure Carvings: Abraham's Sacrifice. (Cf. 100.)* Second half of the 7th century. In situ. (Photo Enric Gras, Barcelona.)

102. Spanish Art. **QUINTANILLA DE LAS VIÑAS (Burgos), Church of Santa Maria.** *Christ between Two Angels.* 7th century (?). In situ. Stone. (Fotoarchiv Deutsches Archäologisches Institut, Madrid.)

This monastic church was probably built in the course of the 7th century. Only the transept (32 ft in width) and the sanctuary (square in plan) now remain; they contain some fine decorative carvings forming a frieze, and some figure reliefs carved by a less skilful hand.

103. Spanish Art. **OVIEDO, Church of Santullano (San Julian de los Prados).** Drawing by Don Magin Berenguer Alonso. *Copy (in part a reconstruction) of the Wall Paintings in the Transept.* 812-842. In situ. Drawings deposited at the Instituto de Estudios Asturianos, Oviedo. Length of the church 65 ft, width 39 ft. Two oratories (square in plan, each side measuring about 13 ft) form the arms of a kind of transept. (Photo Magin Berenguer Alonso, Oviedo.)

The church now stands in a suburb of Oviedo. It was built between 812 and 842 as an oratory of the country villa of King Alfonso. The fine paintings are now almost entirely effaced.

104. Spanish Art. **OVIEDO, Church of Santullano (San Julian de los Prados).** Drawing by Don Magin Berenguer Alonso. *Copy (in part a reconstruction) of the Wall Paintings situated above* the Entrance of the Sanctuary and the two Oratories. 812-842. In situ. Drawings deposited at the Instituto de Estudios Asturianos, Oviedo. (Photo Magin Berenguer Alonso, Oviedo.)

105. Spanish Art. **OVIEDO, Church of Santullano (San Julian de los Prados).** Drawing by Don Magin Berenguer Alonso. *Copy of the Paintings on the West Wall, in the Nave and South Aisle, and in the Transept.* Cross-section. 812-842. Drawings deposited at the Instituto de Estudios Asturianos, Oviedo. Length of nave and transept 49 ft. (Photo Enric Gras, Barcelona.)

106. Spanish Art. **SANTA MARIA DE NARANCO (near Oviedo).** *View of the Palace.* (Palace built during the reign of King Ramiro I, 842-850.) In situ. (Photo Enric Gras, Barcelona.)

This two-storeyed palace, built for a king, shows an even greater perfection in its proportions, masonry and decorative carvings than the buildings of the previous century (see Nos. 98, 99). This palace was converted in the 12th century into a church dedicated to the Virgin.

107. Spanish Art. **SANTA MARIA DE NARANCO (near Oviedo).** *Interior View of the Main Hall on the upper floor of the Palace built for King Ramiro I (842-850).* In situ. This upper hall, measuring 39 by 13 feet, is reached by a flight of twelve steps; at each end of it is an arcaded gallery or loggia, 10 ft long. (Photo Enric Gras, Barcelona.)

The internal construction of the upper hall is remarkable. Blind arcades, supported by coupled stone columns with spiral patterns, cover nearly the whole of the side walls. The semicircular vaulting is reinforced every six feet by cross-arches of bonded stonework.

108. Spanish Art. **SANTA MARIA DE NARANCO (near Oviedo).** *Gallery at the end of the upper hall of the Palace, architectural detail.* 842-850. In situ. (Photo Enric Gras, Barcelona.)

The stone disk between the arches is a notable survival of Roman architecture, and not, as some scholars have supposed, an imitation of barbarian metal shields.

109. Spanish Art. **SANTA MARIA DE NARANCO (near Oviedo).** *External Arcading of the Palace, detail.* 842-850. In situ. (Photo Enric Gras, Barcelona.)

This architecture, though contemporary with the reign of Charles the Bald, is absolutely foreign to the Carolingian renascence. *It owes its peculiarities and its high quality to the religious architecture which was practised in Spain in the 7th and 8th centuries and which undoubtedly benefited from influences stemming from the Byzantine East.*

110. Italian Art. **CASTELSEPRIO (Varese), Santa Maria Foris Portas.** *Overall View from the south-west.* 7th century. In situ. (Arts of Mankind Photo.)

The church of the ancient town of Castelseprio, summer residence of the archbishops of Milan, is one of the few in Italy that can safely be assigned to the 7th century. The church is timber-roofed throughout. It consists of a rectangular sanctuary measuring 32 by 16 ft, surrounded by a porch and three apses. The windows are keyhole-shaped.

111. Italian Art. **CASTELSEPRIO (Varese), Santa Maria Foris Portas.** *East Apse: The Flight into Egypt.* 8th century. In situ. Fresco, 43 × 55 in. (Arts of Mankind Photo.)

These remarkable paintings, of which only about ten panels remain intact, were discovered in 1944. Illustrating the childhood of Christ, they were disposed on the wall of the apse in three superimposed registers. The technique is Byzantine, but the choice of subjects and their arrangement conform to the practice of the Roman West.

112. Merovingian Art. **GRENOBLE, Saint-Laurent, crypt.** *East Apse.* 8th century. In situ. Diameter of the apse 9½ ft. (Arts of Mankind Photo.)

The triumphal arch, with voussoirs of alternating stone and brick, rests on twin colonnettes supported by a column —an arrangement which recalls the superimposed orders of the architecture of the Late Empire, and which was to be imitated a few years later at Germigny-des-Prés (see The Carolingian Empire, The Arts of Mankind, 1969). The three-cusped vault rests on wall arches which originally sprang from stucco colonnettes. Of the large cross and stucco scrollwork decorating the vault, only vestiges remain. The window is not ancient. (Cf. 113, 335 A & B.)

113. Merovingian Art. **GRENOBLE, Saint-Laurent, crypt.** *View of the Interior.* 8th century. In situ. (Arts of Mankind Photo.)

A typical example of columns set against the wall and of superimposed orders constituting a composite architectural pattern which dates from the Late Empire and which presumably existed in many buildings in Gaul from the 5th century to the end of the early Middle Ages. (Cf. 112, 335 A & B.)

114. Merovingian Art. **GRENOBLE, Saint-Laurent.** *Crypt, detail.* Marble capitals, stone abaci. (Arts of Mankind Photo.)

The columns come from ancient Roman monuments. The capitals too come from an earlier building, perhaps from a 6th century mausoleum, as R. Girard has conjectured. The thick abaci above the capitals date from the 8th century.

115. Merovingian Art. **GRENOBLE, Saint-Laurent, crypt.** *Capital.* 8th century. In situ. Marble capital, stone abacus. (Arts of Mankind Photo.)

The capital comes from an earlier building; the abacus, of the 8th century, has carvings similar to those made in upper Italy at the same period.

116. Merovingian Art. **GRENOBLE, Saint-Laurent, crypt.** *Capital with Carved Abacus of the same period.* 8th century. In situ. Capital and abacus both of stone. (Arts of Mankind Photo.)

The iconographic peculiarities of the stone abaci carved at the same time as a certain number of the capitals show that the present structure dates from the middle or second half of the 8th century.

117. Merovingian Art. **GRENOBLE, Saint-Laurent, crypt.** *Capital and Abacus.* 8th century. In situ. Stone capital. (Arts of Mankind Photo.)

This capital was to be imitated a few years later at Germigny-des-Prés (see The Carolingian Empire, Arts of Mankind, 1969*). The carving on the abacus recalls that of North Italian closure slabs and of friezes of the second half of the 8th century.*

118. Merovingian Art. **NARBONNE, Pilgrims' Church.** *Slab representing the Exaltation of the Cross.* 8th century. Musée Lapidaire, Narbonne. Marble, 39 × 21½ in. (Arts of Mankind Photo.)

The cross is held aloft by two figures. Above, two doves confronted on either side of a vase. Lower right, an animal identified by Marcel Durliat as the basilisk, symbol of evil. The vase shows the same distortions as the one on the abacus of a capital at Saint-Laurent, Grenoble (No. 117). Marcel Durliat has pointed out that an altar support in the church of Oupia is decorated with the same jewelled cross and the same group of doves as the Narbonne panel.

119 A & B. Lombard Art. **PAVIA, Monastery of Santa Maria della Pusterola** (now the diocesan seminary). *The Two Sides of the Tomb of Abbess Theodota.* About 735. Museo Civico Malaspina, Pavia. Cipolin from Val di Susa, 26 × 69 × 1½ in. (Arts of Mankind Photo.)

Flat-plane carving, a technique similar to that of the bas-reliefs made at the same period at Cividale. The Pavia carvings, however, rise to the level of a stricter, more finished art.

120. Merovingian Art. **POITIERS, Convent of Sainte-Croix.** *Reading Desk attributed to St Radegunda, seen from behind.* 6th century. Abbey of Sainte-Croix, Route de Gençay at Saint-Benoît. Wood, length at the base 10¼ in. (Arts of Mankind Photo.)

See No. 23 for the beautiful carvings on the top of the desk. Here one can judge of the beauty and harmony of the very simple supporting elements. These give us moreover some idea of what the wooden furniture of the Merovingian period must have been like; of that furniture excavations have revealed nothing. This illustration has been placed deliberately at the end of the chapter devoted to architecture. From furniture to timber architecture the distance is not so great. Of the latter, unfortunately, we know practically nothing in the Merovingian period, but the importance it assumed in the Carolingian period and throughout the Middle Ages makes it fitting that we should evoke it here, if only fleetingly.

121. **North Italy (Nonantula).** *Homilies of St Gregory: St Gregory blessing.* About 800. Folio 9 verso, MS CXLVIII, Biblioteca Capitolare, Vercelli. Miniature painting on vellum, 11 × 8½ in. (Arts of Mankind Photo.)

On the basis of the handwriting, Bernhard Bischoff has assigned this manuscript to the scriptorium of Nonantula.

122. **ROME, Church of Santa Maria Antiqua, presbyterium, detail.** *Maria Regina and an Angel.* 6th century. In situ. Fresco. (Photo De Antonis, Rome.)

In our plate only the figures of the Virgin and Child and the angel are reproduced in colour, so as to set them apart from the background figures, which represent the remains of frescoes of different periods. (Cf. 129.)

123. **ROME, Church of Santa Maria Maggiore, springing of the triumphal arch, detail.** *Superimposed registers: Scenes of the Life of the Virgin and*

the Childhood of Christ. (Cf. 124.) 5th century (432-440). In situ. Mosaic. (Photo De Antonis, Rome.)

124. **ROME, Church of Santa Maria Maggiore, triumphal arch, superimposed registers.** *Scenes of the Life of the Virgin and the Childhood of Christ. (Cf. 123, 125.)* 5th century (432-440). In situ. Mosaic. (Photo Anderson-Giraudon, Paris.)

125. **ROME, Church of Santa Maria Maggiore, right springing of the triumphal arch.** *Scenes of the Life of the Virgin and the Childhood of Christ. (Cf. 124.)* 5th century (432-440). In situ. Mosaic. (Photo De Antonis, Rome.)

126. **ITALY.** *Virgil's Aeneid, Codex Vaticanus. Aeneas and Achates watch the Construction of a City.* 5th century. Folio 13 recto, Vat. MS lat. 3225, Biblioteca Apostolica, Vatican City. Miniature painting on vellum, 6½ × 6¼ in. (Vatican Library Photo.)

127. **ITALY.** *Virgil's Aeneid, Codex Romanus. Dido, Aeneas and a Guest.* 5th century. Folio 100 verso, Vat. MS lat. 3867, Biblioteca Apostolica, Vatican City. Miniature painting on vellum. (Vatican Library Photo.)

128. **ROME.** *Virgin and Child with two Angels ('Virgin of Clemency').* Early 8th century. Left-hand side chapel, apse of Santa Maria in Trastevere, Rome. Canvas and wood, encaustic painting. Overall size, 64½ × 45½ in. Size of the painted surface, 60 × 41¼ in. (Photo De Antonis, Rome.)

129. **ROME, Church of Santa Maria Antiqua, west wall of the tribune.** *Fragment of an Annunciation: the Archangel Gabriel. (Cf. 122.)* 6th-7th century. In situ. Fresco. (Photo De Antonis, Rome.)

130. **ROME, Church of Santa Costanza, nave vault, detail.** *Bacchic Scenes: Grape Harvest.* 4th century. In situ. Mosaic. (Photo De Antonis, Rome.)

131. **ROME, Church of Santa Maria Antiqua, arch of the presbyterium.** *Reconstruction of the Paintings,* after W. de Grüneisen (1904). *(Cf. 132.)* In situ. (Photo De Antonis, Rome.)

132. **ROME, Church of Santa Maria Antiqua, arch of the presbyterium.** *Present State of the Paintings. (Cf. 131.)* 8th century. In situ. Fresco. (Photo De Antonis, Rome.)

133. **ROME, Church of Santa Maria Antiqua, left pillar of the nave.** *Angel of an Annunciation.* Early 8th century. In situ. Fresco. (Photo De Antonis, Rome.)

134. **CASTELSEPRIO (Varese), Church of Santa Maria Foris Portas.** *Nativity and Annunciation to the Shepherds.* 9th-10th century (?). In situ. Fresco. (Arts of Mankind Photo.)

135. **CASTELSEPRIO (Varese), Church of Santa Maria Foris Portas.** *Presentation in the Temple.* 9th-10th century (?). In situ. Fresco. (Arts of Mankind Photo.)

136. **BRESCIA, Church of San Salvatore, upper south wall of the nave.** *Head of a Saint.* Before 774. In situ. Fresco. (Arts of Mankind Photo.)

137. **ROME, Church of Santa Maria Antiqua, left side of the nave.** *The Story of Joseph (upper register) and Christ with the Fathers of the Church (lower register).* 8th century (757-767). In situ. Fresco. (Photo De Antonis, Rome.)

138. **CIVIDALE (Friuli), Church of Santa Maria in Valle, called the Tempietto.** *A Martyr.* Before 774. In situ. Fresco. (Photo A. Perissinotto, Padua.)

139. **CIVIDALE (Friuli), Church of Santa Maria in Valle, called the Tempietto.** *A Martyr.* Before 774. In situ. Fresco. (Photo A. Perissinotto, Padua.)

140. **ROME, Church of Santa Maria Antiqua, outer wall of the prothesis.** *Four Martyrs, 'those whose names God knows'.* About 741-752. In situ. Fresco. (Photo De Antonis, Rome.)

141. **North Africa or North-east Italy.** *Tours or Ashburnham Pentateuch: The Story of Joseph.* 7th century. Folio 44 recto, Nouv. acq. lat. 2334, Bibliothèque Nationale, Paris. Miniature painting on vellum, 14¾ × 13 in. (B.N. Photo.)

142. **MILAN, Church of Sant'Ambrogio, chapel of San Vittore in Ciel d'Oro.** *St Ambrose.* 5th century (c. 470). In situ. Mosaic. (Arts of Mankind Photo.)

143. **MILAN, Church of Sant'Ambrogio, chapel of San Vittore in Ciel d'Oro.** *St Maternus.* 5th century (c. 470). In situ. Mosaic. (Arts of Mankind Photo.)

144. **MILAN, Church of Sant'Ambrogio, chapel of San Vittore in Ciel d'Oro.** *St Protasius, detail.* 5th century (c. 470). In situ. Mosaic. (Arts of Mankind Photo.)

145. **North Italy.** *St Hilary, 'De Trinitate': Man's Head.* Late 6th century. Folio 355 verso, MS lat. 2630, Biblio-thèque Nationale, Paris. Drawing on vellum, size of the detail 2 × 1½ in. (B.N. Photo.)

146. **North Italy.** *Gospel Book of St Augustine: St Luke enthroned in an Arcade, with scenes of the Life of Christ between the columns. (Cf. 147.)* Late 6th century. Folio 129 verso, MS 286, Corpus Christi College Library, Cambridge. Miniature painting on vellum, 8 × 6 in. (Photo Stearn and Sons, Cambridge, by courtesy of the Master and Fellows of Corpus Christi College.)

147. **North Italy.** *Gospel Book of St Augustine: Scenes of the Life of Christ. (Cf. 146.)* Late 6th century. Folio 130 recto, MS 286, Corpus Christi College Library, Cambridge. Miniature painting on vellum, 8 × 6 in. (Photo Stearn and Sons, Cambridge, by courtesy of the Master and Fellows of Corpus Christi College.)

148. **ROME.** *Diptych of Boetius, inner leaves: left, Raising of Lazarus; right, St Jerome, St Augustine and St Gregory. (Cf. 149.)* 7th century. Museo Civico Cristiano, Brescia. Painted ivory, each leaf 14 × 5 in. (Arts of Mankind Photo.)

149. **ROME.** *Diptych of Boetius, outer leaves: the Consul Boetius represented twice, standing and seated on the curule chair. (Cf. 148.)* 487. Museo Civico Cristiano, Brescia. (Arts of Mankind Photo.)

150. **North-East Italy.** *Gospel Book called Codex Valerianus: Explicit.* About 675. Folio 202 verso, MS Clm 6224, Bayerische Staatsbibliothek, Munich. Miniature painting on vellum, 10 × 8¼ in. (Staatsbibliothek Photo.)

151. **North-East Italy.** *Gospel Book called Codex Valerianus: Incipit Page.* Folio 81 verso, MS Clm 6224, Bayerische Staatsbibliothek, Munich. Miniature painting on vellum, 10 × 8¼ in. (Staatsbibliothek Photo.)

152. **AUGSBURG.** *Gospel Book: Adoration of the Magi.* Early 9th century. Folio 24 recto, MS Clm 23631, Bayerische Staatsbibliothek, Munich. Miniature painting on vellum, 12 × 8¼ in. (Staatsbibliothek Photo.)

153. **AUGSBURG.** *Gospel Book: Massacre of the Innocents.* Early 9th century. Folio 24 verso, MS Clm 23631, Bayerische Staatsbibliothek, Munich. Miniature painting on vellum, 12 × 8¼ in. (Staatsbibliothek Photo.)

154. **VERONA.** *Homiliary of Egino (Codex Egino): St Augustine dictating to a Scribe.* Late 7th century. Folio 18 verso, MS Phill. 1676, Deutsche Staatsbibliothek, Berlin. Miniature painting on vellum, 15¼ × 12¼ in. (Deutsche Fotothek, Dresden-Döring.)

The medallion above the figures has been cut out.

155. **VERONA.** *Homiliary of Egino (Codex Egino): St Gregory.* Late 7th century. Folio 25 verso, MS Phill. 1676, Deutsche Staatsbibliothek, Berlin. Miniature painting on vellum, 15¼ × 12¼ in. (Deutsche Fotothek, Dresden-Döring.)

156. **North Italy.** *Compendium of Canon Law: Finding of the True Cross by St Helena.* First half of the 9th century. MS CLXV, Biblioteca Capitolare, Vercelli. Drawing on vellum. (Arts of Mankind Photo.)

157. **North Italy.** *Compendium of Canon Law: the Emperor Constantine burning the Arian Books.* First half of the 9th century. MS CLXV, Biblioteca Capitolare, Vercelli. Drawing on vellum. (Arts of Mankind Photo.)

158. **North Italy.** *Compendium of Canon Law: the Emperor Theodosius.* First half of the 9th century. MS CLXV, Biblioteca Capitolare, Vercelli. Drawing on vellum. (Arts of Mankind Photo.)

159. **North Italy.** *Compendium of Canon Law: the Apostles Peter and Paul. (Cf. 160, 161.)* First half of the 9th century. MS CLXV, Biblioteca Capitolare, Vercelli. Drawing on vellum. (Arts of Mankind Photo.)

160. **North Italy.** *Compendium of Canon Law: the Apostle Paul, detail. (Cf. 159.)* First half of the 9th century. MS CLXV, Biblioteca Capitolare, Vercelli. Drawing on vellum. (Arts of Mankind Photo.)

161. **North Italy.** *Compendium of Canon Law: the Apostle Peter, detail. (Cf. 159.)* First half of the 9th century. MS CLXV, Biblioteca Capitolare, Vercelli. Drawing on vellum. (Arts of Mankind Photo.)

162. **North Italy (Nonantula).** *Homiliary of St Gregory: Deacon Davidpertus, accompanied by St Peter, presenting his Book to Christ.* About 800. Folio 7 verso, MS CXLVIII, Biblioteca Capitolare, Vercelli. Miniature painting on vellum, 11¼ × 8½ in. (Arts of Mankind Photo.)

163. **North Italy (Nonantula)**. *Homiliary of St Gregory: Christ blessing.* About 800. Folio 8 recto, MS CXLVIII, Biblioteca Capitolare, Vercelli. Miniature painting on vellum, 11¼ × 8½ in. (Arts of Mankind Photo.)

164. **MUSTAIR (Grisons, Switzerland), Johanneskirche, nave.** *The Flight into Egypt, the Departure for Bethlehem.* 9th century. In situ. Fresco, about 67 × 59 in. (Arts of Mankind Photo.)

165. **MUSTAIR (Grisons, Switzerland), Johanneskirche, nave.** *Healing of the Deaf and Dumb Man, detail.* 9th century. In situ. Fresco. (Arts of Mankind Photo.)

166 A & B. **MUSTAIR (Grisons, Switzerland), Johanneskirche, nave.** *Scenes of the Life of Christ: A. Christ and the Children. - B. The Descent into Limbo.* 9th century. In situ. Fresco. (Arts of Mankind Photo.)

167 A & B. **MALLES VENOSTA (Italian Tyrol), Church of San Benedetto, left side wall.** *Figure Groups: A. Scenes of the Saints' Lives. — B. Scene of Martyrdom.* 9th century. In situ. Fresco. (Arts of Mankind Photo.)

168. **ECHTERNACH or NORTHUMBRIA (?).** *Echternach Gospels: the Lion, Symbol of St Mark. (Cf. 1.)* 8th century. Folio 75 verso, MS lat. 9389, Bibliothèque Nationale, Paris. Miniature painting on vellum, 13 × 10 in. (B.N. Photo.)

169. **IRELAND or NORTHUMBRIA.** *The Book of Kells: St John.* Late 8th century. Folio 291 verso, MS 58 (A I, 6), Trinity College Library, Dublin. Miniature painting on vellum, 12½ × 9¾ in. (Photo The Green Studio, Dublin.)

170. **IRELAND.** *The Book of Durrow: the Man, Symbol of St Matthew.* Late 7th century. Folio 21 verso, MS 57 (A IV, 5), Trinity College Library, Dublin. Miniature painting on vellum, 9½ × 6½ in. (Photo The Green Studio, Dublin.)

171. **LINDISFARNE (?).** *The Book of Lindisfarne: Decorated Initials XPI and Beginning of the Gospel according to St Matthew.* 8th century. Folio 29 recto, Cotton MS Nero D IV, British Museum, London. Miniature painting on vellum, 9½ × 8½ in. (Urs Graf Verlag Photo.)

172. **IRELAND, ROSCREA.** *The Book of Dimma: St Mark.* Mid-8th century. Folio 30 recto, MS 59, Trinity College Library, Dublin. Miniature painting on vellum, 7 × 5½ in. (Photo Belzeaux-Zodiaque, La Pierre-qui-Vire.)

173. **LINDISFARNE (?).** *The Book of Lindisfarne: St Luke and his Symbol.* 8th century. Folio 137 verso, Cotton MS Nero D IV, British Museum, London. Miniature painting on vellum, 11¾ × 9½ in. (Urs Graf Verlag Photo.)

174. **ECHTERNACH or NORTHUMBRIA (?).** *Echternach Gospels: the Man, Symbol of St Matthew.* 8th century. Folio 18 verso, MS lat. 9389, Bibliothèque Nationale, Paris. Miniature painting on vellum, 13 × 10 in. (B.N. Photo.)

175. **Northern France.** *Sacramentarium Gelasianum: Frontispiece (arch enclosing a cross, with Alpha and Omega dangling from its arms).* About 750. Folio 3 verso, Vat. Reg. lat. 316, Biblioteca Apostolica, Vatican City. (Vatican Library Photo.)

In the manuscript this leaf faces folio 4 recto. (Cf. 189.)

176. **CORBIE.** *St Ambrose, 'Hexaemeron': Incipit Page, with title in zoomorphic capitals.* Second half of the 8th century. Folio 1 verso, MS lat. 12135, Bibliothèque Nationale, Paris. Miniature painting on vellum, 13 × 8 in. (B.N. Photo.)

177 A. **FRANCE.** *Homiliary: Zoomorphic Initial Q(uod).* Mid-8th century. Folio 13 recto, Nouv. acq. lat. 1598, Bibliothèque Nationale, Paris. Miniature painting on vellum, size of the page 12¾ × 9½ in., size of the detail 2¾ × 6 in. (B.N. Photo.)

177 B. **FRANCE.** *Works of St Ambrose: Zoomorphic Initial D.* Mid-8th century. Folio 101 verso, MS lat. 1732, Bibliothèque Nationale, Paris. Miniature painting on vellum, size of the page 12¾ × 9½ in., size of the detail 1¾ × 2 in. (B.N. Photo.)

177 C. **FRANCE.** *Homiliary: Zoomorphic Initial P(ost).* Mid-8th century. Folio 15 recto, Nouv. acq. lat. 1598, Bibliothèque Nationale, Paris. Miniature painting on vellum, size of the page 12¾ × 9½ in., size of the detail 6¼ × 2¼ in. (B.N. Photo.)

177 D. **Provenance unknown.** *St Gregory, 'Job Commentaries': Zoomorphic Initial B(eatus).* Late 7th century. Folio 32 recto, Nouv. acq. lat. 2061, Bibliothèque Nationale, Paris. Miniature painting on vellum, size of the detail, 3½ × 2¼ in. (B.N. Photo.)

178. **LUXEUIL.** *St Gregory, 'Ezekiel Commentary': Carpet-pattern Page.* Second quarter of the 7th century. Folio 2 recto, MS lat. Q.v.I N 14, Saltykov-Shchedrin State Library, Leningrad. Miniature painting on vellum, 10¼ × 7³⁄₈ in. (Leningrad Library Photo.)

179. **LUXEUIL.** *Works of the Church Fathers, Codex Ragyntrudis: Carpet-pattern Page.* About 750. Folio 98 verso, Cod. Bonif. 2, Cathedral Museum, Fulda. Miniature painting on vellum, 7⁵⁄₈ × 11¼ in. (Photo Rolf Kreuder, Fulda.)

180. **CORBIE.** *Rule of St Basil: Arcades and Rosettes.* About 700. Folio 1 verso, MS lat. F.v.I N 2, Saltykov-Shchedrin State Library, Leningrad. Miniature painting on vellum, 12¼ × 8¾ in. (Leningrad Library Photo.)

181. **LUXEUIL.** *Sacramentary (Missale Gothicum): Arcades and Rosettes.* About 700. Folio 169 verso, Vat. Reg. lat. 317, Biblioteca Apostolica, Vatican City. Miniature painting on vellum, 6¾ × 10¼ in. (Vatican Library Photo.)

182. **North Italy (?).** *Eucherius of Lyons, 'Formulae Spirituales': Title in Capitals beneath an Arch, detail.* Late 7th century. Folio 23 verso, MS lat. 2769, Bibliothèque Nationale, Paris. Miniature painting on vellum, size of the page 9½ × 7 in., size of the detail 5½ × 6 in. (B.N. Photo.)

This detail covers about half the page.

183. **ITALY, BOBBIO (?).** *Gospel Book called Codex Usserianus Primus: Prophylactic Cross (colophon to St Luke, incipit to St Mark).* Late 6th-early 7th century. Folio 149 verso, MS 55 (A IV, 15), Trinity College Library, Dublin. Miniature painting on vellum, 7 × 4¾ in. (Trinity College Library Photo - The Green Studio, Dublin.)

Cross, or Chi Rho, painted in red and black. The handwriting of this manuscript resembles that of MS D 23 Sup. in the Ambrosiana, Milan, and of MS Clm 6224 in Munich (Françoise Henry).

184. **North-east France (?).** *Isidore of Seville, 'Contra Judaeos': Isidore presenting his Book to his Sister Florentina. (Cf. 186, 187.)* About 800. Folio 1 verso, MS lat. 13396, Bibliothèque Nationale, Paris. Drawing on vellum, 10½ × 7¼ in. (B.N. Photo.)

185. **Besançon Region (?).** *Lex Romana Visigothorum: A Lawgiver.* About 793. Folio 234 recto, MS 731, Stiftsbiblio-

thek, St Gall. Drawing on vellum, 8¼ × 5¼ in. (Arts of Mankind Photo.)

186. **North-east France (?).** *Isidore of Seville, 'Contra Judaeos': Isidore presenting his Book to his Sister Florentina, detail. (Cf. 184.)* About 800. Folio 1 verso, MS lat. 13396, Bibliothèque Nationale, Paris. (B.N. Photo.)

187. **North-east France (?).** *Isidore of Seville, 'Contra Judaeos': Isidore presenting his Book to his Sister Florentina, detail. (Cf. 184.)* About 800. Folio 1 verso, MS lat. 13396. (B.N. Photo.)

188. **Northern France, LAON (?).** *St Augustine, 'Quaestiones in Heptateuchon': Frontispiece.* Mid-8th century. Frontispiece, MS lat. 12168, Bibliothèque Nationale, Paris. Miniature painting on vellum, 11¾ × 8 in. (B.N. Photo.)

189. **Northern France.** *Sacramentarium Gelasianum: Cross, Initial and Decorative Letters.* About 750. Folio 4 recto, Vat. Reg. lat. 316, Biblioteca Apostolica, Vatican City. Miniature painting on vellum, 10¼ × 6¾ in. (Vatican Library Photo.)

In the manuscript this leaf faces the one reproduced here as No. 175.

190. **Northern France, LAON (?).** *St Augustine, 'Quaestiones in Heptateuchon': Decorative Letter and Incipit.* Mid-8th century. Folio 1 recto, MS lat. 12168, Bibliothèque Nationale, Paris. Miniature painting on vellum, 11¾ × 8 in. (B.N. Photo.)

191. **FLAVIGNY.** *Flavigny Gospels: Canon Tables.* Second half of the 8th century. Folio 15 recto, MS 4, Bibliothèque Municipale, Autun. Drawing on vellum, 13 × 8½ in. (Arts of Mankind Photo.)

192. **FLAVIGNY.** *Flavigny Gospels: Canon Tables. (Cf. 193, 194.)* Second half of the 8th century. Folio 8 recto, MS 4, Bibliothèque Municipale, Autun. Drawing on vellum, 12¾ × 8½ in. (Arts of Mankind Photo.)

193. **FLAVIGNY.** *Flavigny Gospels: Canon Tables, Symbol of St Matthew, detail. (Cf. 192.)* Second half of the 8th century. Folio 8 recto, MS 4, Bibliothèque Municipale, Autun. (Arts of Mankind Photo.)

194. **FLAVIGNY.** *Flavigny Gospels: Canon Tables, Symbol of St Mark, detail. (Cf. 192.)* Second half of the 8th century. Folio 8 recto, MS 4, Bibliothèque Municipale, Autun. (Arts of Mankind Photo.)

195. **Eastern France.** *Chronicle of Fredegarius: Two Men holding a Bow, with a Bird beneath it.* About 750. Folio 23 verso, MS lat. 10910, Bibliothèque Nationale, Paris. Drawing on vellum, 9½ × 6½ in. (B.N. Photo.)

196. **Eastern France.** *Chronicle of Fredegarius: Figure, detail.* About 750. Folio A, MS lat. 10910, Bibliothèque Nationale, Paris. Drawing on vellum, size of the page 9½ × 6½ in., size of the detail 2⅜ in. high. (B.N. Photo.)

197. **Eastern France.** *Chronicle of Fredegarius: Seated Female Saint.* About 750. Folio 75 verso, MS lat. 10910, Bibliothèque Nationale, Paris. Drawing on vellum, 9½ × 6½ in. (B.N. Photo.)

198. **Diocese of Meaux.** *Gellone Sacramentary: Historiated Initial, the Virgin Mary, and Decorated Letters.* About 790-795. Folio 1 recto, MS lat. 12048, Bibliothèque Nationale, Paris. Miniature painting on vellum, 11¾ × 7 in. (B.N. Photo.)

199. **Diocese of Meaux.** *Gellone Sacramentary: Decorated Initials, Evangelist Symbols. L (bull of St Luke, for Lucas), I (eagle of St John, for Johannes).* About 790-795. Folio 42 verso, MS lat. 12048, Bibliothèque Nationale, Paris. Miniature painting on vellum, size of the page 11¾ × 7 in., height of the bull 2 in., height of the eagle 4⅛ in. (B.N. Photo.)

200. **Diocese of Meaux.** *Gellone Sacramentary: Decorated Initial 0.* About 790-795. Folio 82 recto, MS lat. 12048, Bibliothèque Nationale, Paris. Miniature painting on vellum, size of the page 11¾ × 7 in., height of the letter 1⅝ in. (B.N. Photo.)

201. **Diocese of Meaux.** *Gellone Sacramentary: Historiated Initial and the Finding of the True Cross.* About 790-795. Folio 76 verso, MS lat. 12048, Bibliothèque Nationale, Paris. Miniature painting on vellum, height 2 in. (B.N. Photo.)

202. **Diocese of Meaux.** *Gellone Sacramentary: Decorated Initial I(ntercessio). (Cf. 177 A.)* About 790-795. Folio 106 recto, MS lat. 12048, Bibliothèque Nationale, Paris. Miniature painting on vellum, size of the page 11¾ × 7 in., height of the letter 2¾ in. (B.N. Photo.)

203. **Diocese of Meaux.** *Gellone Sacramentary: Te igitur, with Crucifixion.* About 790-795. Folio 143 verso, MS lat. 12048, Bibliothèque Nationale, Paris. Miniature painting on vellum, size of the page 11¾ × 7 in. (B.N. Photo.)

204. **CORBIE.** *Corbie Psalter: Historiated Initial B(eatus).* First quarter of the 9th century. Folio 1 verso, MS 18, Bibliothèque Municipale, Amiens. Tinted drawing on vellum, size of the page 11 × 6¾ in., size of the detail 9 × 5¼ in. (Arts of Mankind Photo.)

205. **CORBIE.** *Corbie Psalter: Historiated Initial Q(uid).* First quarter of the 9th century. Folio 46 recto, MS 18, Bibliothèque Municipale, Amiens. Tinted drawing on vellum, size of the page 11 × 6¾ in., height of the letter 6¼ in. (Arts of Mankind Photo.)

206. **CORBIE.** *Corbie Psalter: Historiated Initial with David and Goliath.* First quarter of the 9th century. Folio 123 verso, MS 18, Bibliothèque Municipale, Amiens. Tinted drawing on vellum, size of the page 11 × 6¾ in. (Arts of Mankind Photo.)

207. **CORBIE.** *Corbie Psalter: Historiated Initial, Song of Habakkuk.* First quarter of the 9th century. Folio 133 recto, MS 18, Bibliothèque Municipale, Amiens. Tinted drawing on vellum, size of the page 11 × 6¾ in., size of the detail 7 × 3 in. (Arts of Mankind Photo.)

208. **CORBIE.** *Corbie Psalter: Zoomorphic Initial A.* First quarter of the 9th century. Folio 68 verso, MS 18, Bibliothèque Municipale, Amiens. Tinted drawing on vellum, size of the page 11 × 6¾ in., height of the letter 2⅜ in. (Arts of Mankind Photo.)

209. **CORBIE.** *Corbie Psalter: Decorated Initial M.* First quarter of the 9th century. Folio 136 verso, MS 18, Bibliothèque Municipale, Amiens. Tinted drawing on vellum, size of the page 11 × 6¾ in., height of the letter 2⅜ in. (Arts of Mankind Photo.)

210. **CORBIE.** *Corbie Psalter: Decorated Initial, Presentation in the Temple.* First quarter of the 9th century. Folio 137 recto, MS 18, Bibliothèque Municipale, Amiens. Tinted drawing on vellum, size of the page 11 × 6¾ in., height of the letter 2⅜ in. (Arts of Mankind Photo.)

211. **AMIENS.** *Gospel Book of Sainte-Croix of Poitiers: Christ in Majesty.* Late 8th century. Folio 31 recto, MS 17, Bibliothèque Municipale, Poitiers. Miniature painting on vellum, 12 × 9 in. (Arts of Mankind Photo.)

212. **Northern France, CORBIE (?).** *Stuttgart Psalter, Psalm XVIII, 6-8: Christ succoured by the Hand of God, and a Soldier driven away by the Angel of God.* First quarter of the 9th century. Folio 23 recto, Württembergische Lan-

desbibliothek, Stuttgart. Miniature painting on vellum, size of the page 10½ × 7 in. (B.N. Photo.)

Facsimile reproduction after Ernest T. Dewald, The Stuttgart Psalter, Princeton University Press, 1930.

213. **Northern France, CORBIE (?).** *Stuttgart Psalter, Psalm CXLIII, 10: David and Goliath.* First quarter of the 9 th century. Folio 158 verso, Württembergische Landesbibliothek, Stuttgart. Miniature painting on vellum, size of the page 10½ × 7 in. (B.N. Photo.)

Facsimile reproduction after Ernest T. Dewald, The Stuttgart Psalter, Princeton University Press, 1930.

214. **SAINT-RIQUIER.** *Gallican Psalter ('Psalter of Charlemagne'): Christ between Two Angels, illustrating Psalm CIX, 'Tu es sacerdos in aeternum.'* 800. Folio 118 verso, MS lat. 13159, Bibliothèque Nationale, Paris. Miniature painting on vellum, 11 × 6¼ in. (B.N. Photo.)

215. Late Antique Art. *Head of an Empress.* 5th-6th century. Museo Archeologico, Castello Sforzesco, Milan. Marble, height 10½ in. (Arts of Mankind Photo.)

It has been suggested by R. Delbrück that this head may represent the Empress Theodora.

216. Merovingian Art. **GAUL.** *Leaf of a Diptych: St Peter, with a frieze of lambs in the arch.* 5th century. The Metropolitan Museum of Art, New York, Gift of J. Pierpont Morgan. Ivory, 11½ × 4¾ in. (Metropolitan Museum Photo.)

See No. 217 for the other leaf of this diptych, which came originally from Kranenburg.

217. Merovingian Art. **GAUL.** *Leaf of a Diptych: St Paul.* 5th century. The Metropolitan Museum of Art, New York, Gift of J. Pierpont Morgan. Ivory, 11½ × 4¾ in. (Metropolitan Museum Photo.)

See No. 216 for the other leaf of this diptych.

218. Merovingian (Byzantine) Art. **ITALY.** *Phalera (horse's harness ornament) with the figure of a helmeted warrior.* About 600. Musée Archéologique, Strasbourg. Embossed silver gilt, diameter 3½ in. (Arts of Mankind Photo.)

Found at Ittenheim in 1930 in the grave of a barbarian noble.

219. Merovingian (Byzantine) Art. **Byzantine East (?), RAVENNA (?).** *Pan decorated with a Hunting Scene (vena-*

tio) *and a circular Greek Inscription.* About 600. Hegaumuseum, Singen. Bronze, diameter 8¾ in. (Photo Staatliches Amt für Ur- und Frühgeschichte.)

Found in the Merovingian cemetery at Güttingen, grave No. 38.

220. Gaulish Art. **ARLES.** *Buckle of St Caesarius: Soldiers asleep beside the Tomb of Christ.* 6th century. Notre-Dame-la-Major, Arles. Ivory, 4 × 2 in. (Arts of Mankind Photo.)

A unique piece found in the tomb of St Caesarius (470-542) in the church of Saint-Trophime. It is an imitation of Burgundian bronze buckles.

221. Merovingian Art. *Liturgical Comb of St Lupus: Confronted Lions and the Tree of Life, with the Inscription PECTEN S. LUPI.* 7th-8th century. Cathedral Treasure, Sens. Ivory, with gold filigree, silver gilt and cabochons, 8¾ × 4¼ in. (Photo Giraudon, Paris.)

Comb attributed to St Lupus, archbishop of Sens (died 623).

222. Merovingian Art. *Decorated Tablets.* 6th-7th century. Chapel, Institution Saint-Martin, Angers. Wood formerly covered with wax. (Arts of Mankind Photo.)

Probably of Italiar (Lombard?) origin.

223. Merovingian (Germanic) Art. *Pair o Looped Fibulae.* Early 5th century. Kunsthistorisches Museum, Vienna. Silver gilt, green enamel, cabochons, glass paste and filigree work, 6¼ × 6¼ in. (Photo Meyer, Vienna.)

Found in a grave at Untersiebenbrunn, these fibulae are characteristic of Germanic art in the period of the migration of peoples.

224. Pontic Art (Art of the Goths). *Large Eagle-headed Fibula.* About 380. Academia Institutul de Archeologie, Bucharest. Gold inlaid with rock crystal and almandines (the latter lost), 10½ × 6 in. (without the pendants). (Academia Photo.)

This fibula was part of the treasure found at Petrossa.

225. Art of the East. **PONTUS.** *Sword.* Mid-5th century. Badisches Landesmuseum, Karlsruhe. Gold, iron and almandines, 12½ × 1⅞ in. (Museum Photo.)

Found at Altlussheim.

226. Sassanian Art. *Pendant.* About 400. Sammlung Nassauischer Altertümer, Wiesbaden Museum. Gold and almandines. (Photo Studio Boersch, Wiesbaden.)

Found at Wolfsheim in 1870 in a tomb treasure, with a coin of the emperor Valens (364-378). On the back, engraved in Pahlavi, is the name of its owner: Ardeshir I (?).

227. Merovingian (Frankish) Art. *Hilt and Ornaments from Two Different Swords.* Late 5th century. Cabinet des Médailles, Bibliothèque Nationale, Paris. Gold, iron and almandines. (Arts of Mankind Photo.)

Found at Tournai in 1653 in the tomb of King Childeric. The plate shows a proposed reconstruction.

228. Merovingian (Frankish) Art. *Ring with the Seal of King Childeric (galvanoplasty).* About 480. Copy in the Cabinet des Médailles, Bibliothèque Nationale, Paris. (B.N. Photo.)

The original ring (with other objects from the treasure of King Childeric) was stolen from the Bibliothèque Royale in 1831.

229. Merovingian (Frankish) Art. *Pair of Grasshopper Fibulae.* Late 5th century. Cabinet des Médailles, Bibliothèque Nationale, Paris. Gold and almandines. (B.N. Photo.)

Found at Tournai in 1653 in the tomb of King Childeric.

230. Merovingian (Frankish) Art showing Pontic influence. *Grasshopper Fibula.* Late 5th century. Musée des Beaux-Arts, Palais Saint-Pierre, Lyons. Silver gilt and almandines, width about 2 in. (Photo J. Camponogara, Lyons.)

Found at Beaurepaire (Isère) in 1841.

231. Merovingian (Frankish) Art showing Pontic influence. *Long Sword.* 6th century. Musée des Antiquités Nationales, Saint-Germain-en-Laye. Gold, iron and almandines. (Arts of Mankind Photo.)

Found at Lavoye in grave No. 319.

232. Merovingian (Frankish) Art showing Pontic influence. *Belt Buckle.* 5th-6th century. Musée de Cluny, Paris. Bronze gilt and almandines, 1¼ × 2½ in. (Arts of Mankind Photo.)

Found in 1868 in the cemetery of Tressan.

233. Merovingian (Burgundian) Art. *Chalice.* About 500. Cabinet des Médailles, Bibliothèque Nationale, Paris. Gold, filigree work, turquoises, glass paste, height 3 in. (Arts of Mankind Photo.)

Found in 1845 near Gourdon.

234. Merovingian (Burgundian) Art. *Paten (from above and from the side).* About 500. Cabinet des Médailles, Biblio-

thèque Nationale, Paris. Gold, filigree work, green and red cloisonné enamels, 8¼ × 5 in. (Arts of Mankind Photo.)

Paten and chalice (No. 233) found in 1845 near Gourdon with coins of Justinian I (527-565); they may have belonged to King Sigismund of Burgundy (died 524). (Cf. 235.)

235. Merovingian (Alamannic?) Art showing Ostrogothic influence. *Pair of Fish Fibulae.* 6th century. Schweizerisches Landesmuseum, Zurich. Gold, almandines and green cloisonné enamels, length 3½ in. (Photo De Bellet, Geneva.)

Found at Bülach in grave No. 14 of the Alamannic cemetery.

236. Merovingian (Frankish) Art. *Looped Fibula.* 6th century. Musée des Antiquités Nationales, Saint-Germain-en-Laye. Silver gilt, filigree work, almandines and stones, length 4 in. (Arts of Mankind Photo.)

Found in a cemetery at Jouy-le-Comte.

237. Italian Art. *Diptych, detail of the central part: Lamb enclosed in a Wreath.* Second half of the 5th century. Cathedral Treasure, Milan. Ivory ground, lamb of silver gilt, red and green stones, cloisonné technique. Overall size 14¾ × 11 in. (Arts of Mankind Photo.)

Diptych in five parts, probably used as a book cover. Decorated with Biblical scenes and the evangelist symbols.

238. Merovingian Art (Art of the Goths). *Fragment of a Horse's Harness consisting of two applied ornaments, formerly known as the 'Cuirass of Theodoric.'* About 500. Formerly Museo Nazionale, Ravenna (stolen about thirty years ago). Gold and almandines, cloisonné technique, height 6¾ in. (Photo Alinari, Florence.)

Found in 1854.

239. Merovingian (Frankish) Art. *Fragment of a Horse's Harness consisting of two applied ornaments.* Early 6th century. Landschaftsmuseum des Niederrheins, Schloss Linn, Krefeld. Gold, almandines and green glass, 9 × 8½ in. (Photo Römisch-Germanische Kommission, Frankfort.)

Discovered in 1962 in the grave of a Frankish chief and dated by a solidus of Anastasius I (491-518).

240. Merovingian Art (Art of the Goths). *Spread Eagle Fibula.* About 500. Germanisches Nationalmuseum, Nuremberg. Gold and almandines, cloisonné technique, height 4¾ in. (Museum Photo.)

Found at Domagnano. The companion piece to this fibula is in the collection of the Marquis de Ganay, Paris (the former collection of the Comtesse de Béhague). The eagle symbol appeared in the art of the Goths under the influence of the Scythians and the Alans.

241. Italian Art. ROME (?). *Covers of the Gospel Book of Queen Theodelinda.* About 600. Cathedral Treasure, Monza. Gold, precious stones, pearls and glass beads, antique cameos, cloisonné enamels. Size of the two covers together, 13½ × 10½ in. (Arts of Mankind Photo.)

Gift of Pope Gregory the Great, in 603, to Queen Theodelinda at Monza.

242. Merovingian (Visigothic) Art. *Pair of Eagle Fibulae.* 6th century. The Walters Art Gallery, Baltimore. Bronze gilt, rock crystal, and white, blue, red and green stones. Height 5¾ in. (Museum Photo.)

Found at Tierra de Barros, Estremadura.

243. Merovingian (Ostrogothic) Art. *Looped Fibula with Four Eagle Heads.* About 500. Museo Civico d'Arte Antica, Turin. Gold, almandines, emeralds. (Museum Photo.)

Found at Desana in 1938 in the grave of a woman.

244. Merovingian Art (Art of the Goths). ITALY (?). *Quadrangular Belt Buckle.* 6th century. Badisches Landesmuseum, Karlsruhe. Silver gilt, inlaid stones, length 4¾ in. (Museum Photo.)

245. Merovingian (Ostrogothic) Art. *Belt Buckle.* About 500. Museo Civico, Pavia. Silver gilt, stones, 2⅝ × 1⅞ in. (Arts of Mankind Photo.)

Found at Torre del Mangano, near Pavia.

246. Italian Art. ROME (?). *Jewelled Cross.* 6th century. Formerly in the Treasure of the Sancta Sanctorum, Museo Sacro, Vatican City, now lost. Gold, almandines and stones, 10 × 9½ in. (Vatican Library Photo.)

The arms were thickly incrusted with balsam.

247. Merovingian (Visigothic) Art. *Belt Buckle.* 6th century. Museo Arqueológico Nacional, Madrid. Bronze gilt, stones. (Museum Photo - David Manso.)

Found at Carpio de Tajo, near Toledo.

248. Merovingian (Visigothic) Art. *Jewelled Votive Crown of King Recceswinth, with the Inscription RECCESVINTHUS REX OFFERET.* About 653-672. Museo Arqueológico Nacional, Madrid, formerly Musée de Cluny, Paris. Gold and precious stones, diameter 7⅞ in. (Museum Photo - David Manso.)

Found at Fuente de Guarrazar in 1858 with a hoard of a dozen votive crowns, buried about 670.

249. Merovingian (Frankish) Art. *Jewellery of Queen Arnegonde: Round Fibulae, Large Pin, Belt Ornaments.* Second half of the 6th century. Direction des Antiquités historiques de la Région parisienne. Fibulae, gold and garnets. Pin, gold, silver and garnets. Belt ornaments, gold, silver, garnets, glass beads. Length of the pin 10⅜ in. (Arts of Mankind Photo.)

Jewellery discovered during excavations of the basilica of Saint-Denis, together with a seal ring bearing the name of Arnegonde, who was probably the wife of Clotaire I, son of Clovis.

250. Merovingian (Lombard) Art. *Round Fibula.* 7th century. Museo dell'Alto Medioevo, Rome. Gold, filigree work, diameter 3 in. (Photo De Antonis, Rome.)

Found at Castel Trosino in a grave, together with a unique and remarkable hoard of round fibulae.

251. Merovingian (Lombard) Art. *Round Fibula.* 7th century. Museo dell'Alto Medioevo, Rome. Gold, filigree work, with cloisonné inlays of glass paste. Diameter 3¾ in. (Photo De Antonis, Rome.)

Found at Castel Trosino in a grave, with a unique and remarkable hoard of round fibulae.

252. Merovingian (Frankish) Art. *Pair of Looped Fibulae.* First half of the 6th century. Römisch-Germanisches Museum, Cologne (property of the Cathedral Museum, Cologne). Gold and almandines, cloisonné technique. Length 3 in. (Museum Photo.)

Found in 1959 in a grave under Cologne Cathedral, and dated by coins, these fibulae show the influence of Italian art. The grave was that of a Merovingian princess.

253. Merovingian (Alamannic) Art. *S-shaped Fibula figuring a Two-headed Monster.* Second half of the 6th century. Württembergisches Landesmuseum, Stuttgart. Gold and almandines, length 1½ in. (Photo Karl Natter, Stuttgart.)

Found at Deisslingen (Württemberg) in 1930 in a woman's grave.

360

254. Merovingian (Anglo-Saxon) Art. *Round Fibula.* 7th century. City of Liverpool Museums. Gold, inlays, almandines and stones, cloisonné technique. Diameter 3¼ in. (Museum Photo.)

Found at Kingston.

255. Merovingian (Lombard) Art. *Round Fibula.* 7th century. Museo Nazionale di Antichità, Parma. Gold, almandines and blue stones, cloisonné technique. Diameter 2¾ in. (Photo Tosi, Parma.)

Found in 1950 in a grave at Parma.

256. Merovingian (Lombard) Art. *Round Fibula.* 6th-7th century. Museo Archeologico, Turin. Gold and almandines, cloisonné technique with setting of gold wire. Diameter 2⅛ in. (Gabinetto fotografico della Soprintendenza alle Antichità per il Piemonte, Turin.)

Found in a grave at Lingotto.

257. Merovingian Art. *Round Fibula.* Römisch-Germanisches Museum, Cologne (property of the Cathedral Museum, Cologne). Gold, filigree work, inlays of almandines and enamel, cloisonné technique. Diameter 1⅝ in. (Rheinisches Bildarchiv. Kölnisches Stadtmuseum.)

Found in 1959 in the grave of a Frankish princess under Cologne Cathedral.

258. Merovingian (Frankish) Art showing Burgundian influence. *Round Fibula.* 6th-7th century. Musée des Antiquités Nationales, Saint-Germain-en-Laye. Gold, with filigree work, diameter 2 in. (Arts of Mankind Photo.)

Found in a cemetery at Charnay-lès-Mâcon.

259. Merovingian (Frankish) Art. *Round Fibula.* About 600. Landesmuseum, Münster. Gold and almandines, cloisonné technique. (Museum Photo.)

Found at Soest in grave No. 106, and dated by coins of Justinian (527-565).

260. Merovingian (Alamannic) Art. *Round Fibula forming a Swastika-shaped Swirl of Animals.* Early 7th century. Museum, Dillingen an der Donau. Gold and almandines, cloisonné technique. (Photo Fink, Dillingen.)

Found at Schretzheim in grave No. 23.

261. Merovingian (Alamannic) Art. *Looped Fibula.* 7th century. Prähistorische Staatssammlung, Munich. Silver gilt with niello work, filigree and stones. Length 6¼ in. (Photo Elisabeth Römmelt, Munich.)

A unique piece, found at Wittislingen in 1881 in the grave of an Alamannic princess. On the back, inscribed in Latin, are the names Uffila and Wigerig.

262. Merovingian (Alamannic) Art. **West Germany (?).** *Round Fibula with Four Pairs of Twined Serpents forming a Cross.* 7th century. Prähistorische Staatssammlung, Munich. Gold, almandines, filigree and cloisonné technique. Diameter 3⅛ in. (Photo Elisabeth Römmelt, Munich.)

Found at Wittislingen in the grave of the same Alamannic princess as No. 261.

263. Merovingian (Frankish) Art. *Portable Altar of St Andrew, executed for Archbishop Egbert (977-993), front: in the centre, a Fibula with, in the centre of it, a solidus of the emperor Justinian (527-565).* 6th century, restored in the 10th (between 977 and 993). Cathedral Treasure, Trier. Gold and almandines, enamels, ivory and intaglios. (Photo Atelier Niko Haas, Trier.)

264. Merovingian (Frankish) Art. *Chalice of St Eligius.* About 600. Drawing of 1653. Original destroyed during the French Revolution. Gold and almandines, with blue, white and green stones. Height 10½ in., diameter at the rim 5¾ in., diameter of the stem 6¼ in. (After F. Cabrol and H. Leclercq, *Dictionnaire d'archéologie chrétienne et de liturgie*, II, Paris 1924, fig. 1902.)

Made for the Abbey of Chelles.

265. Merovingian (Alamannic) Art. **Provincial workshop of the Alamanno-Burgundian lands (?).** *Crook of St Germanus, detail.* Second half of the 7th century. Treasure of the Church of Saint-Marcel, Delémont (canton of Berne, Switzerland). Gold, silver, filigree and red stones on wood. Height 47 in., diameter 1 in. (Photo De Bellet, Geneva.)

Comes from Moutier-Grandval. Attributed to St Germanus of Trier (610-677), first abbot of the monastery of Grandval.

266. Merovingian (Frankish) Art. *Fragment of the Cross of St Eligius.* About 600. Cabinet des Médailles, Bibliothèque Nationale, Paris. The rest of the cross was destroyed in 1794. Gold; the almandines are lost. Size 4 × 4 in. (Arts of Mankind Photo.)

Made for the Abbey of Saint-Denis.

267. Flemish Art. **SAINT-DENIS, Abbey.** *Panel painting by the Master of Saint-Gilles, The Mass of St Giles, detail showing the high altar of Saint-Denis*

with the 'Carolingian cross of St Eligius' (?). 15th-century painting. The National Gallery, London. (Museum Photo, reproduced by courtesy of the Trustees.)

The altar table pictured here, mentioned in the 12th century by Abbot Suger (Migne, Patrologia latina, 186, col. 1233) and at that time still an antependium, was later used as a retable.

268. Merovingian (Alamannic) Art. **Workshops of the Abbey of Saint-Maurice-d'Agaune, made by UNDIHO and ELLO.** *Reliquary Casket of Teuderigus.* Late 7th century. Abbey Treasure, Saint-Maurice (canton of Valais, Switzerland). Gold, stones and cameo on a wooden support, cloisonné technique. Height 5 in. (Photo De Bellet, Geneva.)

On the back of the casket is the following inscription, each letter being enclosed in a lozenge: TEUDERIGUS PRESBITER IN HONORE SCI MAURICII FIERI IUSSIT AMEN. NORDOLAUS ET RIHLINDIS ORDENARUNT FABRICARE. VNDIHO ET ELLO FICERUNT.

269. Byzantine Art. *Emperors hunting, confronted on either side of a symbolic tree.* Late 8th century. Musée Historique des Tissus, Lyons. Silk, 28¾ × 28 in. (Photo Giraudon, Paris.)

Textile formerly belonging to the Abbey of Mozac (Puy-de-Dôme.)

270. Italian or Islamic (?) Art. *Hen with her Seven Chicks.* 7th century (?) Cathedral Treasure, Monza. Silver gilt, garnets and sapphires. Diameter 18 in., height to the hen's tail 10½ in. (Arts of Mankind Photo.)

Said by tradition to be a gift of Queen Theodelinda to the basilica of Monza. However, several present-day scholars (Toesca, Grabar, Monneret de Villard) consider it to be a later work, perhaps Muslim, of the 11th or 12th century.

271. Merovingian (Lombard) Art. *Frontal Plaque of a Helmet: King Agilulf (591-616) enthroned, with an inscription:* VICTORIA D(OMINO) N(OSTRO) AGILUL(FO) REGI. About 600. Museo Nazionale, Palazzo del Bargello, Florence. Bronze gilt. (Photo Alinari, Florence.)

Found at Val di Nievole. (Cf. 272.)

272. Merovingian (Lombard) Art. *Frontal Plaque of a Helmet, detail: King Agilulf enthroned. (Cf. 271.)* About 600. Museo Nazionale, Palazzo del Bargello, Florence. (Photo Alinari, Florence.)

273. Merovingian (Lombard) Art. **CIVI-DALE, Santa Maria in Valle, Tempietto.** *Six Holy Women and Decoration of the Entrance Wall.* Late 8th century. In situ. Stucco. Figures life-size. (Photo Osvaldo Böhm, Venice.)

The dating has been questioned: see E. Dyggve, Atti del Congresso internazionale di Studi sull'alto medioevo, 1952, Spoleto, p. 75, and G. de Francovich, Römisches Jahrbuch, IV, 1942-1944, p. 135. (Cf. 274-276.)

274. Merovingian (Lombard) Art. **CIVI-DALE, Santa Maria in Valle, Tempietto, entrance wall, detail.** *Three Holy Women. (Cf. 273.)* Late 8th century. In situ. (Gabinetto fotografico nazionale, Rome.)

275. Merovingian (Lombard) Art. **CIVI-DALE, Santa Maria in Valle, Tempietto.** *Decoration of the Entrance Wall, detail. (Cf. 273.)* Late 8th century. In situ. Stucco. (Photo Osvaldo Böhm, Venice.)

276. Merovingian (Lombard) Art. **CIVI-DALE, Santa Maria in Valle, Tempietto, entrance wall.** *Portal Lunette with Palmettes and Vine Patterns, detail. (Cf. 273.)* Late 8th century. In situ. Stucco. (Gabinetto fotografico nazionale, Rome.)

277. Merovingian (Lombard) Art. **CIVI-DALE, San Giovanni Evangelista.** *Altar of Duke Ratchis: Christ in Majesty with Two Angels.* About 740. Chapter Room, San Martino, Cividale. Stone. (Photo Scala, Florence.)

Inscribed dedication by Duke Pemmo (died 737) and by Ratchis (744-749), Duke, then King, of the Lombards. (Cf. 279 and 281 for the other sides of the altar.)

278. Merovingian (Lombard) Art. *Closure Slab of Magister Ursus, in honour of Duke Ilderic Dagileopa of Spoleto.* 8th century. San Pietro in Valle, Ferentillo. Marble, 43 × 80½ in. (Photo Soprintendenza ai Monumenti dell'Umbria.)

The two Orants are presumably Ilderic and Ursus. Inscription: URSUS MAGISTER FECIT. Lombard style highly simplified and geometric.

279. Merovingian (Lombard) Art. **CIVI-DALE, San Giovanni Evangelista.** *Altar of Duke Ratchis, side: Adoration of the Magi. (Cf. 277, 280, 281.)* About 740. Chapter Room, San Martino, Cividale. (Photo Scala, Florence.)

280. Merovingian (Lombard) Art. **CIVI-DALE, San Giovanni Evangelista.** *Altar of Duke Ratchis, side: Adoration of the Magi, detail. (Cf. 279.)* About 740. Chapter Room, San Martino, Cividale. (Photo Scala, Florence.)

281. Merovingian (Lombard) Art. **CIVI-DALE, San Giovanni Evangelista.** *Altar of Duke Ratchis, side: The Visitation.* About 740. Chapter Room, San Martino, Cividale. (Photo Scala, Florence.)

Cf. 277 and 279 for the other sides of the altar.

282. Merovingian Art. **AVERSA, Cathedral.** *Knight fighting a Dragon.* 11th century (?), showing Merovingian survivals. In situ. Marble, 66 × 21½ in. (Photo Bulloz, Paris.)

283. Merovingian Art. *Helmet of a Prince, adorned with Birds pecking Grapes.* Early 6th century. Mittelrhein Landesmuseum, Mainz. Copper and iron. (Museum Photo.)

Found at Planig in 1939 in a richly furnished tomb.

284. Merovingian Art. *Belt Buckle representing a Wolf.* Museo Arqueologico, Barcelona. (Photo Enric Gras, Barcelona.)

The authenticity of this piece has been in part contested by Martin Almagro.

285. Merovingian (Visigothic) Art. *Belt Buckle.* 6th-7th century. Musée de Cluny, Paris. Bronze gilt, 4¾ × 2¾ in. (Arts of Mankind Photo.)

Found at Castel, now Castelsagrat (Tarn-et-Garonne), in a cemetery.

286. Merovingian (Frankish) Art. *Clasp of a Bag.* Early 6th century. Musée des Antiquités Nationales, Saint-Germain-en-Laye. Gold and almandines, length 4¾ in. (Arts of Mankind Photo.)

Found at Lavoye in grave No. 319.

287. Merovingian (Frankish) Art, showing Mediterranean influence. *Tankard with Christological Scenes.* About 500. Musée des Antiquités Nationales, Saint-Germain-en-Laye. Stamped bronze relief on wood, height 7 in. (Arts of Mankind Photo.)

Found at Lavoye in grave No. 319. This work, like those from Vermand, illustrates the development from Early Christian reliefs of the 4th and 5th centuries.

288. Merovingian (Gaulish) Art. *Leaf of a Diptych used as a Book Cover, detail: Virgin and Child with Two Angels.* Early 7th century. Treasure, Church of Saint-Andoche, Saulieu. Ivory, 9½ × 6½ in. (Photo Studio R. Rémy, Dijon.)

289. Merovingian (Gaulish) Art. *Leaf o, the Saint-Lupicin Diptych used as the cover of a Gospel Book, central detail: Virgin and Child.* 6th century. MS lat. 9384, Bibliothèque Nationale, Paris. Ivory, overall size 14¼ × 11¾ in. (B.N. Photo.)

290. Merovingian (Gaulish) Art. *Leaf of a Diptych: St Peter.* 6th-7th century. The Metropolitan Museum of Art, New York, Gift of George Blumenthal, 1941. Ivory, 9 × 4¼ in. (Metropolitan Museum Photo.)

Came from the Abbey of Mettlach.

291. Merovingian (Germanic) Art, showing Mediterranean influence. **METZ, Church of Saint-Pierre-aux-Nonnains.** *Central Part of a Closure Slab: Christ beneath an Arch.* About 613-620. Musée Central, Metz. Jura limestone, 38 × 21½ in. (Arts of Mankind Photo.)

292. Merovingian (Burgundian) Art. *Belt Buckle with an Orant.* 7th century. Musée d'Art et d'Histoire, Geneva. Bronze, length 5 in., patterned with scorings and interlaces. (Photo De Bellet, Geneva.)

Found at La Balme in a Burgundian cemetery. The standing Orant, with uplifted arms, has a rudimentary Medusa's head engraved on its chest. This piece belongs to the group of Burgundian 'Orant buckles' executed under Mediterranean influence but still in a highly barbarian style.

293. Merovingian (Frankish) Art. *Round Openwork Fibula, with bearded head of Christ in the centre and sacred monogram.* 6th-7th century. Cabinet des Médailles, Bibliothèque Nationale, Paris. Gold and stones, diameter 2½ in. (B.N. Photo.)

Found at Limons in 1885.

294. Merovingian (Frankish) Art. *Reliquary Casket of St Liudger: Christ between Two Angels represented as Orants.* 8th century. Church of St Liudger, Essen-Werden. Plaques of bone on a wooden core, 8¾ × 15¾ in. (Photo Paul Wirtz, Essen-Werden.)

The original arrangement has been modified. Formerly at the Abbey of Werden.

295. Merovingian (Frankish) Art. **NIE-DERDOLLENDORF, Christian Cemetery.** *Tomb Stele: front, Dead Man armed with a sword, combing his hair,*

with a snake overhead; back, *Haloed Christ holding a spear.* Late 7th century. Rheinisches Landesmuseum, Bonn. Limestone, height 17 in. (Museum Photo.)

This tombstone is important for the light it throws on the Christianized Franks' conception of the Other World.

296. Merovingian (Frankish) Art. **GON-DORF.** *Tomb Stele: Saint or Christ between Two Doves; in the corners, birds' heads (griffins symbolizing the Other World).* 7th-8th century. Rheinisches Landesmuseum, Bonn. Limestone, 33 × 26¼ in. (Museum Photo.)

297. Merovingian (Alamannic) Art. **Workshop of South-west Germany.** *Reliquary Casket: in the centre, a Holy Knight slaying a Dragon in a large medallion, with smaller medallions around it; on the lid, Daniel between Lions which are turning away from him.* 7th century. Church of Ennabeuren (Württemberg). Copper plate on a wooden core, height 3½ in. (Photo Dr Hellmut Hell, Reutlingen.)

A typical example of the syncretism of early medieval Christian art.

298. Merovingian (Frankish) Art. *Round Fibula: Adoration of the Magi.* 7th century. Rheinisches Landesmuseum, Trier. Bronze, diameter 2¼ in. (Museum Photo.)

Found in a grave at Minden. One of the most telling pieces of evidence for the Mediterranean influence on Germanic art north of the Alps.

299. Merovingian (Lombard) Art. *Disk: in the centre, Mounted Knight with a Lance; around him, interlaces of animals.* About 600. Museo Archeologico Nazionale, Cividale. Gold, diameter 1⁷⁄₈ in. (Photo Scala, Florence.)

Found near Udine in a cemetery.

300. Merovingian (Lombard) Art. *Cross decorated with eight Heads alternating with eight Stones.* 7th century. Museo Archeologico Nazionale, Cividale. Laminated gold, garnet and lapis lazuli, height 4¼ in. (Photo Scala, Florence.)

Found at Cividale in 1874 in the so-called tomb of Gisulf (died 611) in Piazza Paolo Diacono. This is the most precious of the 'gold-leaf Lombard crosses,' which were generally sewn on the shroud and interred with the dead man.

301. Merovingian (Lombard) Art. *Ornamental Plaque from a Shield, representing a knight with lowered lance.*

7th century. Historisches Museum, Berne. Cast bronze gilt, length 4 in. (Arts of Mankind Photo.)

Found in 1833 in a cemetery at San Pietro, near Stabio. Also in the Berne museum are similar ornaments representing a lion (see No. 302) and a stylized tree; in the Locarno museum is another lion. Further shield ornaments can be seen at Lucca, Paris (Musée de Cluny) and Munich (Prähistorische Staatssammlung; below, No. 303).

302. Merovingian (Lombard) Art. *Ornamental Plaque from a Shield, representing a Lion. (Cf. Frontispiece and 301.)* 7th century. Historisches Museum, Berne. (Arts of Mankind Photo.)

303. Merovingian (Lombard) Art. *Ornamental Plaque from a Shield, representing a Griffin.* 7th century. Prähistorische Staatssammlung, Munich. Chased bronze, length 3¼ in. (Photo Elisabeth Römmelt, Munich.)

Found in 1905 in a grave at Ischl an der Alz (Upper Bavaria).

304. Merovingian (Alamannic) Art. *Openwork Disk representing a Horseman with lowered lance.* 7th century. Stadtmuseum, Esslingen. Bronze, diameter 3¼ in. (Photo Aeckerle, Esslingen.)

Found in 1908 at Oberesslingen (Württemberg). Disks of the same type can be seen at Karlsruhe (from Bräunlingen), Stuttgart (from Oberesslingen) and Zurich (from Heftenbach).

305. Merovingian Art. *Belt Buckle: Daniel in the Lions' Den.* Musée Cantonal d'Archéologie et d'Histoire, Lausanne. Tin-plated bronze, overall length 4 in., width 2¼ in. (Photo De Bellet, Geneva.)

Found at Ecublens (Vaud) in 1903.

306. Merovingian (Alamannic) Art. *Openwork Disk: Hercules (?), with animals' heads on the rim.* First half of the 7th century. Fürstlich Hohenzollernsches Museum, Sigmaringen. Bronze, diameter 3¼ in. (Photo Dr Hellmut Hell, Reutlingen.)

Found in 1904 in a grave at Gammertingen with coins of the emperor Maurice copied by the Lombards (c. 610).

307. Merovingian (Frankish) Art. *Belt Buckle: Demon with arms ending in birds' heads with interlaces.* 7th century. Musée des Antiquités, Rouen. Bronze, height 4½ in. (Photo Ellebé, Rouen.)

Found at Criel-sur-Mer.

308. Merovingian (Bavarian) Art. *Openwork Disk: Three Winged Horses on the run.* 7th century. Prähistorische Staatssammlung, Munich. Silver-damascened iron, diameter 3⁷⁄₈ in. (Photo Elisabeth Römmelt, Munich.)

Found in 1920 at Mühltal an der Isar in grave No. 28. Evidence of the imitation of Mediterranean Christian motifs by the recently converted Bavarians.

309. Merovingian (Aquitanian) Art. *Belt Buckle: Fabulous Animals in medallions, with their heads slewed round.* 7th century. Musée des Beaux-Arts, Troyes. Bronze. (Arts of Mankind Photo.)

Found in 1890 at Troyes in the Clamart or the Madeleine cemetery. Belongs to the group of 'Aquitanian buckles,' a type of belt buckle peculiar to southern Gaul which probably took form under Late Roman influence.

310. Merovingian (North German) Art. *Scabbard: Warrior with a Wolf Mask.* 7th century. Formerly Staatliche Museen, Berlin, now lost. Cast in Römisch-Germanisches Zentralmuseum, Mainz. Silver and iron, length 13¾ in. (Photo Römisch-Germanisches Centralmuseum, Mainz.)

Found in a grave at Gutenstein.

311. Merovingian (Frankish) Art. *Reliquary Casket of Mumma or St Mommola: lower part, Rosette and Star Ornaments; upper part, the Twelve Apostles (?).* 8th century. Abbey Church, Saint-Benoît - sur - Loire. Copper - plated wood, embossed, length 5 in., height 4¼ in., width 2 in. (Arts of Mankind Photo.)

Discovered in 1642 in the altar foundations of Notre-Dame. On the back, Latin inscription: MUMMA FIERI IUSSIT IN AMORE SCE MARIE †ET SCI PETRI.

312. Merovingian Art. *Reliquary Casket. Virgin and Child between St Peter and St Paul.* 8th century. Musée de Cluny, Paris. Embossed bronze gilt on a wooden core, 3½ × 3¾ in. (Arts of Mankind Photo.)

313. Merovingian Art. *Reliquary Casket: Christ blessing, between the Archangels Gabriel and Michael.* 8th century. Treasure, Church of Saint-Evroult, Mortain. Embossed copper gilt on a beechwood core, 5½ × 4⅛ × 2 in. (Photo Archives des Monuments historiques.)

The casket bears a Runic inscription: 'May God assist Eada who made this chrismal.'

314. Pre-Romanesque Art. *Reliquary Casket of Pippin II of Aquitaine (817-838)*. About 1000, made of Merovingian and Carolingian fragments. Treasure, Church of Sainte-Foy, Conques. Embossed gold leaf, with filigree work, hard stones, pearls, mother-of-pearl, glass paste, glass and translucid enamels, on a wooden core, 7¼ × 7¼ × 3½ in. (Photo Tournier, Rodez.)

The Crucifixion appears to have been made for another object. Beneath the arms of the cross, confronted birds above fantastic animals. Inscribed in scrolls are the names of Longinus and the sponge-bearer Stephaton.

315. Merovingian Art. *Reliquary Casket of Bishop Altheus: on the front, the Virgin and St John*. Late 8th century; the embossed flower on the top is of the 17th century. Cathedral Treasure, Sion (canton of Valais, Switzerland). Silver gilt on a wooden core, with cloisonné enamels, length 7 in. (Photo De Bellet, Geneva.)

Bears a dedicatory inscription of Bishop Altheus of Sion (780-799) to the Virgin.

316. Carolingian Art. *Reliquary Casket: on the front, Stones set in the form of a Cross*. About 780. Staatliche Museen, Berlin, Stiftung Preussischer Kulturbesitz. Gold and embossed silver gilt on an oak core, with cloisonné enamels, pearls, gems and stones. Size 6¼ × 5¾ in. (Photo Elsa Postel, Berlin.)

Comes from the collegiate church of Enger. According to legend, this casket was a gift of Charlemagne for the baptism of Duke Widukind (785), whose remains were deposited in it.

317. Merovingian Art. **VIENNE (Isère).** *Plan of the pre-Carolingian Cathedral Complex*. 5th-early 6th century. (After Jean Vallery-Radot, *L'Ancienne Cathédrale Saint-Maurice de Vienne*, in *Bulletin Monumental*, CX, 1952, p. 299.)

The present cathedral stands on the site of the church of Saint-Sauveur, founded in the early 11th century. It is located on the north side of the ancient cathedral complex, which was built in the 5th or early 6th century, and was in part rebuilt in the 13th century. It was demolished during the Revolution but the position of the buildings is recorded on an old plan. The arrangement of the three churches and the irregularity of their orientation suggest that they were erected on the site of pagan temples.

318. **GENEVA.** *Plan of the Ancient Cathedral and Baptistery*. (After Louis Blondel, *Les Premiers Edifices chré-*tiens de Genève, de la fin de l'époque romaine à l'époque romane*, in *Genava*, new series, V, 1957, Fig. 1, pp. 97-128.)

The remains of the cathedral church of Notre-Dame were found in 1956 under the Temple de l'Auditoire, on the north side of the present cathedral. The foundations of the latter were excavated several times in the 19th and the early 20th century. The difficult task of studying and analysing the ancient vestiges was carried out by Louis Blondel, who considered the earliest of them to date from the 5th century.

319. **PARIS.** *Plan of the Ancient Cathedral Complex*. (After Jean Hubert, *Les Origines de Notre-Dame de Paris*, in *Revue d'Histoire de l'Église de France*, L, 1964, Fig. 2, p. 9.)

The position and vestiges of the churches that no longer exist were revealed by excavations made in 1711, 1847, 1858 and 1967, and the information thus obtained is supplemented by plans dating from the 18th century.

320. Merovingian Art. **CIMIEZ, now part of Nice.** *Plan of the Ancient Cathedral and its Baptistery*. (After Fernand Benoît, in *Gallia*, XIV, 2, 1956, p. 236.)

These early Christian constructions were built up from the Roman baths and the dependencies of a ruined villa situated on the outskirts of the Roman town. They were discovered by chance in 1955. No place-name had preserved the memory of them.

321. Merovingian Art. **MARSEILLES.** *Plan of the Ancient Cathedral Complex and Baptistery*. (After François Roustan, *La Major et le premier baptistère de Marseille*, Marseilles 1905, Pl. XXVIII.)

The excavations of 1850-1854 brought to light the mosaic pavements, the marble columns and extensive remains of the baptistery which, with the Lateran baptistery in Rome, was one of the largest of early Christian Europe. Of all this material, nothing has been preserved.

322 A & B. **FRÉJUS.** *Section and Plan of the Baptistery*. 5th-early 6th century. (After Paul-Albert Février, *Forum Iulii* [i.e. Fréjus], in *Itinéraires ligures*, 13, 1963, Fig. 59, p. 75, and Fig. 66, p. 83.)

This building, dating to the 5th century or the early years of the 6th, was originally surrounded by a portico. (Cf. 3.)

323. **ANGERS.** *Ancient Cathedral Complex*. (After Victor Godard-Faultrier, *Fouilles de la place du Ralliement à Angers*, in *Mémoires de la Société* d'Agriculture, Sciences et Arts d'Angers, XXI, 1879, p. 148 and Pl. VIII.)

Plan of the church of Notre-Dame et Saint-Maurille, of the baptistery west of its façade, and of a small hypocaust chamber which may have served as the liturgical bath for the celebration of baptism. These buildings, situated in a suburb of the ancient Roman town, may have constituted the earliest cathedral complex.

324. Merovingian Art. **POITIERS.** *Plan of the Baptistery of Saint-Jean. (Cf. 45, 46.)* About 7th century. (After Jean Hubert, *Le Baptistère de Poitiers et l'emplacement du premier groupe épiscopal*, in *Cahiers Archéologiques*, VI, 1952, p. 139.)

325. **RIEZ.** *Plan of the Baptistery*. (After Maxime Belmont, *Baptistère de Riez*, in *Actes du Ve Congrès international d'archéologie chrétienne à Aix-en-Provence, 1955*, Vatican City & Paris, 1957, p. 108.)

The excavations of 1926 showed that the baptistery was surrounded by porticoes on at least three sides. The plan remains that of the original building. The upper parts were considerably modified in the Romanesque period.

326. Merovingian Art. **TOULOUSE.** *Interior Elevation and Plan of the Basilica of Notre-Dame de la Daurade (early print)*. Possibly late 5th, more probably early 6th century. (Photo Bibliothèque Nationale, Paris. After Dom Jacques Martin, *La Religion des Gaulois*, Paris, 1727, Vol. I, Pl. IV, p. 146.)

This brick church, pulled down in 1761, was decorated with gold-ground mosaics (hence the name 'Daurade'), disposed on several registers in the arcading. All that now remains of the church are a few columns and marble capitals.

327 A & B. Merovingian Art. **COLOGNE.** *Section and Plan of the Church of St Gereon*. (After T.K. Kempf, *Frühchristliche Funde und Forschungen in Deutschland*, in *Actes du Ve Congrès d'archéologie chrétienne à Aix-en-Provence, 1954*, Vatican City & Paris, 1957, Fig. 2, p. 65.)

This is the 'basilica of the golden saints' mentioned in the writings of Gregory of Tours and dating from the late 4th century. During the restorations necessitated by the damage it suffered during the last war, all the essential elements of the original building were found under the interior structure added in the Gothic period.

328. Merovingian Art. **VIENNE (Isère)**. *Plan of the Church of Saint-Pierre.* Second half of the 5th century. (After Jean Hubert, *L'Architecture religieuse du haut Moyen-Age en France*, Paris 1952, Pl. XVI, Fig. 48.)

Basilica erected extra muros and originally dedicated to the Holy Apostles; in it, many of the bishops of Vienne were interred. (Cf. 30.)

329. Merovingian Art. **TARRAGONA**. *Plan of the Basilica of San Fructuoso del Francoli.* 5th or 6th century. (After *Xº Congreso internacional de Arte de la Alta Edad Media*, Madrid 1962, p. 32.)

330. Merovingian Art. **VICENZA**. *Plan of the Ancient Basilica dedicated to Sts Felix and Fortunatus.* 5th and 6th centuries. (After Paolo Verzone, *L'Architettura religiosa dell'alto medio evo nell'Italia settentrionale*, Milan 1942, Fig. 15, p. 40.)

331. Merovingian Art. **SAINT-BER-TRAND-DE-COMMINGES (Haute-Garonne)**. *Plan of the Funerary Basilica.* (After A.W. Clapham, *English Romanesque Architecture before the Conquest*, Oxford, Clarendon Press, 1930, Fig. 4, p. 11.)

This church used to be attributed to the 4th century, but there are no grounds for such an early dating. Its foundation was undoubtedly subsequent to the Vandal invasions which devastated south-western Gaul in 408.

332 A & B. Merovingian Art. **POITIERS**. *Section and Plan of the Hypogeum ('Hypogée des Dunes') discovered in 1878 by le Père Camille de la Croix.* (After le Père Camille de la Croix, *Monographie de l'hypogée-martyrium de Poitiers*, Paris 1883, and L. Levillain, *La 'Memoria' de l'abbé Mellebaude*, in *Bulletin de la Société des Antiquaires de l'Ouest*.)

Characteristic features of its engraved and painted inscriptions date this structure to the 7th century. (Cf. 68, 70, 74.)

333 A & B. Merovingian Art. **MUJELEIA, Syria**. *Section and Plan of a Burial Vault.* (After M. de Vogüé, *Syrie centrale. Architecture civile et religieuse du Iᵉʳ au VIIᵉ siècle*, Vol. II, Paris 1865-1877, Pl. 88.)

A little earlier than the Poitiers hypogeum but quite similar to it, this small Syrian monument shows that the same customs and practices obtained throughout Christendom in the period of the Late Empire.

334. Merovingian Art. **MARSEILLES**. *Plan of the Mausoleum erected beside the quarry where the martyr St Victor had been buried, and dating to the Late Empire.* 5th century. (After Fernand Benoît, *Le Martyrium rupestre de l'abbaye Saint-Victor*, in *Comptes rendus de l'Académie des Inscriptions et Belles-Lettres*, 1966, p. 121.)

This mausoleum, converted into an oratory, was known in the Middle Ages as Notre-Dame-de-Confession; from this name it was assumed, wrongly, that the building had been, in the 5th century, the first church of the monastery. During the recent excavations carried out by Fernand Benoît, bones were brought to light inside the building. It has never had either a door or an apse. It is a sort of triumphal arch preceded by an atrium without any portico. (Cf. 11.)

335 A & B. Merovingian Art. **GRENO-BLE**. *Section and Plan of the 'Crypt' of Saint-Laurent.* (After R. Girard, *Fouilles à Saint-Laurent de Grenoble, Campagnes de 1960 à 1964*, in *Actes du LXXXIXᵉ Congrès national des Sociétés savantes, Lyon, 1964*, Paris, 1965, Fig. 9, p. 353.)

This funerary oratory of the 8th century only became a crypt when the choir of a priory church founded in the 11th century was built on top of it. Recent excavations have shown that even the original oratory was preceded on this spot by antique structures of the very early Middle Ages; from these perhaps came some of the marble capitals re-used inside the 8th-century oratory. (Cf. 112, 113.)

336. **KILDRENAGH, Ireland**. *Plan of the Monastery.* (After Françoise Henry, *Early Monasteries, Beehive Huts and Dry-Stone Houses in the Neighbourhood of Caherciveen and Waterville* [Co. Kerry], in *Proceedings of the Royal Irish Academy*, LVIII, Section C, No. 3, February 1957, Dublin, Fig. 13, p. 89.)

This plan and the next show clearly how rough and simple were the structures in which the monks of the British Isles (and also of north Brittany) voluntarily chose to live in the 6th and 7th centuries.

337. **WEST FEAGHMAAN, Ireland**. *Plan of the Monastery. (Cf. 336.)* (After Françoise Henry, *Early Monasteries, Beehive Huts and Dry-Stone Houses in the Neighbourhood of Caherciveen and Waterville* [Co. Kerry], in *Proceedings of the Royal Irish Academy*, LVIII, Section C, No. 3, February 1957, Dublin, Fig. 14, p. 91.)

338. Merovingian Art. **SAINT-MAURICE (Valais), Switzerland**. *Plan of the Successive Basilicas erected in honour of St Maurice and his companions at the monastery of Saint-Maurice-d'Agaune founded in Late Antiquity under the crag where they suffered martyrdom.* Late 4th century/5th-6th century (516-520)/late 6th century (after 574)/late 8th century. (After Louis Blondel, *Aperçu sur les édifices chrétiens dans la Suisse occidentale avant l'an mille*, in *Art du Haut Moyen-Age dans la région alpine. Actes du IIIᵉ Congrès international pour l'étude du Haut Moyen-Age*, September 9-14, 1951, Urs Graf Verlag, Olten-Lausanne, 1954, Fig. 116, p. 284, Fig. 117-118, p. 285, Fig. 119, p. 286, Fig. 120, p. 287.)

The orientation of the 6th-century baptistery is very different from that of the church, and much more correct. This fact seems to indicate that a total reconstruction of the monastery had been planned at that time.

339. **ROMAINMOTIER (Vaud), Switzerland**. *Plan of the Successive Churches of the Benedictine Monastery.* Founded about 636. 8th-11th century. (After Albert Naef, *Les Phases constructives de l'église de Romainmôtier*, in *Indicateur d'Antiquités suisses*, new series VII, Zurich 1905-1906, Pl. XXI.)

The substructures of the successive churches were brought to light in 1904 under the present church, formerly a Cluniac priory. The smallest church dates from the foundation of the monastery, about 636. The second was perhaps dedicated to Sts Peter and Paul by Pope Stephen II during his visit to Romainmôtier in December 753. The present church dates from the 11th and 12th centuries.

340 A & B. Merovingian Art. **JOUARRE (Seine-et-Marne)**. A. *Plan of the Excavations of the Cemeterial Church carried out in 1843 and 1869. - B. Position of the Ancient Churches of the Abbey, after a plan of 1780 and the excavations of 1843 and 1869.* Abbey founded in the 7th century, shortly after 630. (After Jean Hubert, *L'Art pré-roman*, Paris 1938, Pl. I b, and Jean Hubert, *Les Cryptes de Jouarre*, Melun 1952, p. 9.)

A. *Plan by Abbé Thiercelin. (Cf. 77, 78.)*

341. Merovingian Art. **NIVELLES, Belgium**. *The Ancient Churches of the Abbey, after the excavations of Jacques Mertens: Saint-Pierre, Notre-Dame, Saint-Paul.* 7th century. (After Jacques Mertens, *Recherches archéologiques dans l'abbaye mérovingienne de Nivelles*, in *Archaeologia Belgica*, 1961, p. 110, Fig. 14.)

A characteristic example of the unplanned layout of the buildings of a 7th-century monastery.

342. **MANGLIEU (Puy-de-Dôme).** *Plan o, the Abbey in the Middle Ages.* The east end of the north church and the substructure of the south church probably date to the 8th century. (After Jean Hubert, *Les Églises et les anciens bâtiments monastiques de l'abbaye de Manglieu au début du VIII*e *siècle,* in *Bulletin de la Société nationale des Antiquaires de France,* 1958, p. 62.)

343. **CASA HERRERA (Badajoz), Spain.** *Plan of the Early Christian Basilica.* (After Marcel Durliat, *L'Architecture espagnole,* Toulouse-Paris 1966, Fig. 9, p. 42.)

344. **SILCHESTER (Hampshire).** *Plan of the Church brought to light in 1892 near the forum of the ancient Roman town.* (After F. Cabrol and H. Leclercq, *Dictionnaire d'archéologie chrétienne et de liturgie,* s.v. *Bretagne (Grande-),* Paris 1903, Vol. II, col. 1175, Fig. 1631.)

This church, oriented to the west like the great Constantinian churches of Rome, contained a fine mosaic pavement.

345. **COMO (Lombardy).** *Plan of the Ancient Church of Santi Apostoli, later renamed Sant'Abbondio.* (After Paolo Verzone, *L'Architettura religiosa dell'alto medio evo nell'Italia settentrionale,* Milan 1942, p. 19, Fig. 7.)

Excavations of 1863. A very early tradition attributes the foundation of this church to the bishop St Amanzio (died c. 450). This bishop and several of his successors were buried in the church.

346. **SAINT-ROMAIN-D'ALBON (Drôme).** *Plan of an Ancient Church, after the excavations of 1875.* (After J. Duc, *Essais historiques sur la commune d'Albon,* Valence 1900, p. 34.)

The earliest tombs found in this church are dated by their epitaphs from 467 to 516.

347. Merovingian Art. **SAINT-BLAISE (Bouches-du-Rhône).** *Plan of the Basilica.* 5th or 6th century. (After Henri Rolland, *Fouilles de Saint-Blaise,* supplements to *Gallia,* III, Paris 1951, p. 164, and Henri Rolland, *Saint-Blaise,* in *Villes épiscopales de Provence,* Paris 1954, appendix, p. 45.)

This church, mentioned in 829 as being dedicated to St Peter, stood inside the ancient oppidum of Ugium. Its foundations and mosaic pavement were cleared in excavations conducted by Henri Rolland.

348. Merovingian Art. **ANGERS.** *Plan o, the Church of Saint-Martin, in its first state, after the excavations of George H. Forsyth.* (After George H. Forsyth, *L'Église Saint-Martin d'Angers,* in *Bulletin monumental,* CX, 1952, p. 209.)

349. **CANTERBURY.** *Plan of the Ancient Church of Sts Peter and Paul (excavations of 1924.)* (After A.W. Clapham, *English Romanesque Architecture before the Conquest,* Oxford, Clarendon Press, 1930, Fig. 6, p. 18.)

We know from Bede that this was the main church of the monastery founded east of the town by St Augustine in 597. It was erected to house the tombs of Augustine and later bishops, also the tombs of the kings. Augustine died in 604 and the church was not consecrated until 613; his tomb stood in the north porch, the south porch being reserved for royal tombs. In the 8th century an altar was placed in the north porch dedicated to the pope St Gregory the Great (died 604).

350. **RECULVER (Kent).** *Plan of the Ancient Church of St Mary.* (After A.W. Clapham, *English Romanesque Architecture before the Conquest,* Oxford, Clarendon Press, 1930, Fig. 8, No. 1, p. 23.)

This church, founded in 669 by Egbert, king of Kent, was pulled down in 1805. Its foundations were cleared in excavations made in 1926 and 1927.

351. **LYONS.** *Plan of the Ancient Church of Saint-Laurent discovered in 1947 in the suburb of Choulans, in the southeastern part of Lyons.* (After P. Wuilleumier, A. Audin and A. Le Roi-Gourhan, *L'Église et la nécropole Saint-Laurent dans le quartier lyonnais de Choulans. Études archéologiques* et anthropologiques, Lyons 1949, Fig. 2, p. 10.)

This basilica dates to the 6th century. Tomb inscriptions in its cemetery indicate that the latter was in use around 550 and above all around 650-656.

352. **SAINT-AMBROIX (Cher).** *Plan o, the Excavations of 1909 and 1910, showing the substructures of the monastery founded at Ernodorum by Ambrose, bishop of Cahors, and abandoned in the time of the Norman invasions.* 8th century. (After Colonel Thil and P. de Goy, *Les Découvertes des Champs-Saint-Hilaire à Saint-Ambroix,* in *Mémoires de la Société des Antiquaires du Centre,* XXXIV, 1911, p. 24.)

353. Merovingian (Frankish) Art. *Fibula.* 8th century. Hessisches Landesmuseum, Darmstadt. Gold leaf on bronze, with cameo and stones, diameter 3¼ in. (Museum Photo.)

Found at Molsheim.

354. *Map of the Heritage of Antiquity at the end of the 4th century.* After Jean Hubert.

355. *Map of the Migrations from the 3rd to the 5th century.* After W.F. Volbach.

356. *Map of Gaul and Neighbouring Lands in the time of King Dagobert (629-639).* After Jean Hubert.

357. *Map of the Monasteries founded in Gaul in the 7th century.* After Jean Hubert.

358. *Map of Art Forms.* After Jean Hubert, Jean Porcher and W.F. Volbach.

359. *Map of the Citadel Towns of the late 3rd century which became the seat of a Bishop.* After Jean Hubert.

360. *Distribution Map of Marble Carvings (Sarcophagi and Capitals) from the Toulouse Region (7th century).* After Jean Hubert.

361. *Distribution Map of Objects of Adornment from Aquitaine (7th century).* After Jean Hubert.

The plans were drawn by Claude ABEILLE, the maps by Jacques PERSON.

Glossary-Index

AACHEN (AIX-LA-CHAPELLE). City in western Germany where Charlemagne built his palace, *p.* 299; *map* 358.

ABACUS. Uppermost part of a stone capital, *p.* 86, 99, 100; *fig.* 115-117.

ABRAHAM'S SACRIFICE. The patriarch Abraham was bidden by God to sacrifice his son Isaac on Mount Moriyya (*Genesis*, XXII). This scene is represented on a capital in the church of San Pedro de la Nave and on an engraved slab at Saint-Maximin, *p.* 86; *fig.* 20, 101.

ACANTHUS. Prickly plant of the Mediterranean region, whose serrated leaves have served as a pattern of ornamentation ever since Antiquity (e.g. Corinthian capitals), *p.* 212, 311; *fig.* 81.

ACHATES. The faithful companion of Aeneas in Virgil's *Aeneid*, *fig.* 126.

ACTAEON. A huntsman in Greek mythology who, having surprised Artemis (Diana) bathing, was changed by the goddess into a stag and torn to pieces by his own hounds, *p.* 199.

ADALARD or ADALHARD (St) [c. 751-826]. Cousin german of Charlemagne and Abbot of Corbie. He was the counsellor of Pepin, King of Italy (812-814). After Charlemagne's death, he was banished to Noirmoutier but was reconciled with the king in 822, *p.* 202.

ADRIANOPLE. City in Thrace (present-day Edirne, Turkey), on the Marica. A stoutly fortified outpost of Constantinople. The emperor Valens was killed there in 378 fighting against the Visigoths, *p.* XII; *map* 354.

ADRIATIC SEA, *p.* 128.

AFRICA, *p.* XII, 48, 257.

AFRICA (NORTH). Roughly corresponds to the present-day Maghreb. Occupied by the Vandals from 429 on, then reconquered in part by Justinian in 534, *p.* 288.

AGILBERT (St) [died c. 680-690]. Born in Paris, studied in Ireland, bishop of Wessex, then bishop of Paris (c. 667-c. 675), died at Jouarre, where the tomb thought to be his stands in the north crypt, *p.* 72, 73; *fig.* 77, 84-89, 91.

AGILBERTA (St). Sister of the bishop of Meaux, St Ebregesilus, she was the second abbess of Jouarre, where she died about 684, *p.* 78; *fig.* 90.

AGILOFINGS. First dynasty of the Dukes of Bavaria, founded by Agilulf, a Frankish warrior who is supposed to have invaded Bavaria in 533, *p.* 131.

AGILULF. King of the Lombards (591-616), converted to Catholicism. Plaque of Agilulf at Florence (Bargello), *p.* 165, 247; *fig.* 271, 272.

AGNELLUS (486-569). Archbishop of Ravenna (556-569), *p.* 247.

AIRAN. Small town in France (Calvados), on the Muance, 20 km. east of Caen. A woman's grave was discovered there containing objects apparently of Pontic-Danubian workmanship, *p.* 215.

ALAMANNI or ALEMANNI. A group of Germanic tribes established between the upper Danube and the middle Rhine. Often at war with the Romans in the 3rd-4th centuries in their attempts to cross the Rhine. In 406 they settled in Alsace and the Palatinate, founding a kingdom in the 5th century, *p.* XII, 218, 313.

ALANS. Nomadic tribe who invaded South Russia about the time of the birth of Christ and were enslaved by the Huns. Part of the tribe aided the Huns in their invasion of Europe, *map* 355.

ALARIC I (c. 370-410). King of the Visigoths (396-410), he devastated Thrace and Greece as far as the Peloponnesus, then invaded Italy (402) but was repulsed. Returning in 408, he captured Rome (August 24, 410), devastated South Italy and was preparing to invade Sicily when he died on the banks of the Busento, *p.* XII; *map* 355.

ALBENGA. Town on the Italian Riviera, about 60 km. from the French frontier. Its baptistery is one of the oldest in Europe, *p.* 3, 5; *fig.* 5, 6; *maps* 354, 358.

ALBON. Village in France (Drôme), 28 km. south of Vienne. Ancient church in the hamlet of Saint-Romaind'Albon, built between 467 and 516 (dated by funerary inscriptions), *p.* 33; *fig.* 346; *map* 358.

ALEXANDRIA. City in Lower Egypt on the Mediterranean, founded by Alexander the Great in 332 B.C. Capital of the Ptolemies, then a Roman province from 30 B.C. on. A leading centre of intellectual and religious life in ancient times, *p.* 229, 288.

ALFONSO II of the Asturias (759-842). Son of Fruela I. King of Oviedo in 783 and then from 791 to 835, *p.* 89; *fig.* 105.

ALPS, *p.* XI, 97, 128, 138, 209, 231, 311, 312, 313.

ALTHEUS. Bishop of Sion (Switzerland) from 772 to 814. In his time Charlemagne presented to the abbey of Saint-Maurice, of which Altheus was abbot from 804, a number of precious objects including an altar frontal of solid gold, *p.* 285; *fig.* 315.

ALTLUSSHEIM. Village in West Germany (Baden-Württemberg), on the Rhine, 5 km. south-east of Speyer. The tomb of a barbarian warrior-chief was found there in 1932, *p.* 215.

AMBO. A large pulpit and reading desk in the early churches, *p.* 247.

AMBROSE (St). Father and Doctor of the Church (c. 340-397), archbishop of Milan (374-397). Friend of St Augustine, whom he baptized, *p.* 128, 137; *fig.* 142, 176, 177B.

AMIENS. City in northern France (Somme), on the river Somme. Ancient capital of the Ambiani; fell to Clotaire after the death of Clovis, *p.* 202; *fig.* 211; *maps* 358, 359.

ANASTASIUS I (c. 430-518). Emperor of the East (491-518). A Monophysite, he broke with Rome and persecuted the orthodox Christians. He built the city walls of Constantinople which bear his name, cf. *fig.* 239.

ANDELFINGEN. Town in Switzerland (canton of Zurich), 18 km. south-east of Schaffhausen, *p.* 312.

ANDENNE. Town in Belgium (Namur), on the Meuse, 16 km. east of Namur, founded in the 7th century by St Begga, mother of Pepin of Heristal, *p.* 281.

ANDERNACH. Town in West Germany (Rhine Palatinate), 17 km. west of Koblenz. The ancient Antunnacum of the Romans, *p.* 265, 268.

ANDREW (St). One of the twelve Apostles, brother of Peter, *p.* 238; *fig.* 263.

ANGERS. City in western France (Maine-et-Loire), conquered by Childeric in 471. The church of Saint-Martin stands on the site of an earlier church dating to the 7th century, *p.* 33, 212; *fig.* 323, 348; *maps* 358, 359.

ANGILBERT (St) [c. 745-814]. Pupil of Alcuin, minister and ambassador of Pepin. He had a child by Bertha, Charlemagne's daughter. In 790 he was made abbot of Saint-Riquier, *p.* 83.

ANGLES. A Germanic people established for the most part on the east coast of Schleswig-Holstein. After many sea raids from the 2nd to the 4th century, they colonized England, together with the Saxons and Frisians, in the 5th and above all in the 6th century. From their name come the words 'England' and 'English', *p.* XIII; *maps* 355, 356.

ANIMAL STYLE. Germanic ornamentation developed in North Germany in the 6th century under Roman influences. At first it combined vine tendrils and meander patterns with highly simplified animal forms (Animal Style I). During the 7th century it absorbed elements of Mediterranean ornamentation (braided ribbons). The result was Animal Style II, a typically Germanic mode of expression which survived in Scandinavia until the 9th and 10th centuries, *p.* 277, 312, 313.

ANSOALD. Bishop of Poitiers (c. 678-c. 697), a relative of St Leger, *p.* 40; *fig.* 54.

ANTEPENDIUM. An altar frontal of repoussé metal (gold or silver), *fig.* 267.

ANTICHRIST. Antagonist of Christ. A personage born of pre-Christian apocalyptic superstitions, symbolizing wickedness and impiety, whom Christ was to conquer forever at his second coming, *p.* 195.

ANTIGNY. Village in France (Vienne), 3 km. from Saint-Savin and 45 km. east of Poitiers, *fig.* 51A; *map* 358.

ANTIOCH. Capital of the ancient Seleucid Empire, present-day Antakya (Turkey), *p.* 288.

APAHIDA. Village in Rumania, on the Somes Mic, 15 km. north-east of Cluj, *p.* 218.

AQUEDUCT. Artificial channel for conveying water from one place to another, either subterranean or above-ground, *p.* 34.

AQUILEIA. Town in north-east Italy, on the Adriatic. Capital of the Roman xth region of Venetia et Histria. Devastated by Attila in 452, it was abandoned for a time during the Lombard invasions of 568, *p.* 3; *map* 354.

AQUITAINE (AQUITANIA). Under Caesar, one of the three great regions of Gaul. Taken by the Visigoths in 413, it was conquered by Clovis in 507, *p.* XII, 30, 34, 35, 47, 62, 64, 279, 312; *maps* 356, 361.

ARABS. A Semitic people given political and religious unity by Mohammed. In the 7th and 8th centuries they conquered Egypt, Syria, Asia Minor, Persia, North Africa and Spain. They were defeated at Poitiers (732) in their attempt to conquer Gaul, *p.* XIII, 62, 77, 84, 128, 215, 257, 313.

ARCH. See TRIUMPHAL ARCH.

ARDASHIR I. First Persian king of the Sassanid dynasty (A.D. 224-241), *p.* 215; *fig.* 226.

ARIANISM. 4th-century heresy propagated by Arius and his disciples. They maintained that the Trinity comprises three separate, heterogeneous substances. The Father alone is eternal, he alone is God. Christ, the Son of God, is a created being, and so not God in the fullest sense. Condemned by the Council of Nicaea (325), which declared Christ consubstantial with the Father, this heresy was ended by the Council of Antioch (379) and the Council of Constantinople (381), *p.* XIV, 114.

ARISTOTLE (384-322 B.C.). Greek philosopher whose writings had an immense influence on medieval thinkers, *p.* XIV.

ARIUS (c. 280-336). Heresiarch, priest at Alexandria in 315, began to propagate Arianism in 318. Excommunicated by the Council of Nicaea (325), he took refuge in Illyria, *p.* XIV, 114.

ARLES. City in south-eastern France (Bouches-du-Rhône), on the Rhone. A Roman colony from the time of Julius Caesar, chief city of Viennensis Secunda, conquered by the Visigoths in 477. The Early Christian cemetery preserved on the south-east side of the Roman defensive wall gives a good idea of the cemeteries *extra muros* which were a common feature of cathedral towns down to the end of the Middle Ages, *p.* 15, 211; *fig.* 16, 18; *maps* 354, 356, 358.

ARMENIA. Region in Asia Minor between Anatolia and the Iranian plateau, now divided between Turkey, Iran and the U.S.S.R., *p.* 1, 33.

ARNEGONDE (c. 525-570). Frankish queen, wife of Clotaire I, mother of Chilperic I. A stone sarcophagus thought to be hers (it was identified by a royal seal ring found in it) was brought to light in 1954 in excavations of the basilica of Saint-Denis, *fig.* 249.

ARRAS. City in northern France (Pas-de-Calais). Famous in antiquity under the name of Atrebatum. Destroyed

during the barbarian invasions, it was rebuilt around 500 by St Vaast, *p.* 238.

ASHBURNHAM PENTATEUCH. Another name for the Tours Pentateuch, a famous illuminated manuscript stolen from the Tours Library in the 19th century by Count Libri, who sold it to the English bibliophile the Earl of Ashburnham (1797-1878). After a campaign led by the French scholar Léopold Delisle, it was returned to the Bibliothèque Nationale in Paris, *fig.* 141.

ASIA MINOR, *p.* 1, 288; *fig.* 89.

ATHAULF. King of the Visigoths (410-415). Brother-in-law of Alaric, whom he succeeded after the latter's death in 410, he led the Visigoths into Gaul in 412. In 414 he married Galla Placidia, sister of the Roman Emperor Honorius, and set up a government in Aquitaine. Murdered at Barcelona in 415, *p.* XII.

ATTILA. King of the Huns established in Pannonia in 434, he invaded Gaul, advanced as far as Orléans and was defeated on the Catalaunian Plains (battle of Châlons, 451). In 452 he invaded Italy, devastated the north and spared Rome at the request of Pope St Leo. He returned to Pannonia where he died in 453, *p.* 22, 215; *map* 355.

AUGSBURG. City in West Germany (Bavaria), chief city of Swabia, at the confluence of the Lech and the Wertach. Founded by Augustus, *fig.* 152, 153; *map* 358.

AUGUSTINE (St). Father of the Latin Church (354-430). Son of St Monica, he was converted at Milan and baptized by St Ambrose. He settled at Hippo (Bône), where he became a priest (391), then bishop of Hippo (396), *p.* 128, 178; *fig.* 147, 154, 188, 190.

AUGUSTINE (St). Apostle of England from 596 and first bishop of Canterbury (596), where he died in 605, *p.* 33, 132, 157.

AUSTRIA, *p.* 100, 215.

AUTUN. City in central France (Saône-et-Loire), east of the Morvan. One of the three cities of Lugdunensis Prima under Augustus. Taken by the Burgundians (427) and ravaged by the Huns (451). Church of Saint-Martin founded and built between 589 and 600 by Queen Brunhilda, who was buried there after her execution in 613. The old church was pulled down in 1781, *p.* XII, 27, 32; *maps* 354, 359.

AUVERGNE, *p.* 22, 32, 289.

AUXERRE. City of north-central France (Yonne), on the river Yonne. In the 4th century, chief city of Lugdunensis Quarta, ravaged by Attila in 451. Basilica erected just outside the town by Queen Clotilde between 493 and 545 over the tomb of bishop St Germanus (died 448), *p.* 13, 21, 27; *fig.* 22; *maps* 356, 358, 359.

AVARS. A nomadic people of Eastern origin, related to the Huns. In 565-570 they settled in Lower Austria and made incursions as far as Constantinople, *p.* 271.

AVERSA. City in South Italy (Campania), 16 km. north of Naples. Founded in 1030, about 3 miles from the ancient town of Atella which had been destroyed, *p.* 257; *fig.* 282.

BALME (LA). Hamlet in eastern France (Haute-Savoie), commune of Magland. Site of a Burgundian cemetery, where two belt buckles of the 7th century, representing Daniel, were found, *p.* 278; *fig.* 292.

BAPTISTERY. Edifice located beside the cathedral church where the sacrament of baptism was administered, *p.* 3, 13, 32, 33, 40, 48, 57, 247, 248; *fig.* 2-6, 45-50, 52, 53.

BARBARIANS. Term applied by the Romans to all peoples foreign to them. Today it is used to designate the Germanic peoples (Ostrogoths, Visigoths, Vandals, Alamanni, Lombards, Alans, Suevi, Franks, Angles, Saxons) who invaded the Roman Empire from the 4th to the 6th century, *p.* XI, XII, XV, 1, 12, 16, 25, 128, 131, 155, 287.

BASEL. City of north-west Switzerland (canton of Basel-Stadt), on the Rhine, at the meeting-point of the Swiss, French and German frontiers, *map* 354.

BASIL (St). Doctor of the Church (c. 330-379). Pupil of the rhetorician Libanios at Constantinople. Lived at first as a hermit, then became a priest (362) and bishop of Caesarea (370). Resolutely opposed the Arians, *fig.* 180.

BAWIT. Site in Middle Egypt, in the desert 5 miles west of Deirut esh-Sherif. Monastery founded by St Pacomius and transformed by St Apollo (c. 380), *p.* 159.

BEDE (St). Anglo-Saxon monk at the monastery of Jarrow (673-735). A famous historian, he wrote a *Historia ecclesiastica gentis Anglorum* (721) and *De ratione temporum, p.* 78, 81, 155.

BELISARIUS (c. 494-565). General in the service of the Byzantine Emperor Justinian I. Destroyed the kingdom of the Vandals in Africa (533-534), fought against the Ostrogoths in Italy (536-548) and saved Constantinople from the Huns (559), *p.* XIII.

BENEDICT BISCOP (St). English Benedictine (c. 628-690), founder and abbot of the abbeys of Wearmouth and Jarrow. He collected illuminated manuscripts and owned part of the library of Cassiodorus, *p.* 157, 159.

BENEVENTO. City in South Italy (Campania), in the valley of the Calore. This region owed allegiance to the Emperor of the East until 545. In 571 it became the Lombard Duchy of Benevento, *p.* XIII; *maps* 354, 356, 358.

BENOIT (Fernand). French archaeologist (born 1892), member of the Académie des Inscriptions et Belles-Lettres, *p.* 15.

BERLIN, *p.* 225, 243, 278, 285, 312.

BEROMÜNSTER. Town in Switzerland (canton of Lucerne), south of the Hallwilersee, *p.* 311.

BEWCASTLE. Village and parish in north Cumberland, 15 miles northeast of Carlisle, *fig.* 94: *map* 358.

BLACK SEA. See PONTUS EUXINUS.

BLONDEL (Louis). Swiss archaeologist and architect (1885-1966), *p.* 22.

BOBBIO. Town in central Italy (Emilia). Monastery founded in 612 by St Columban, a famous intellectual centre in the Middle Ages, *p.* 157, 159, 165; *fig.* 183; *map* 358.

BOETIUS (Anicius Manlius Flavius). Member of the famous gens Anicia (c. 450-500), praetorian prefect of Italy, twice prefect of Rome, then consul under Odoacer (487). Father of the philosopher, *p.* 136; *fig.* 148, 149.

BOETIUS (Anicius Manlius Severinus). Roman philosopher, poet and statesman (c. 470-524), author of the *Consolation of Philosophy*. His Latin translations of Greek authors helped to diffuse the doctrines of the Neo-Platonists and Aristotle. Held office under Theodoric but died in prison, *p.* 136.

BONN. City in West Germany, on the Rhine, some 50 km. south of Cologne, *p.* 265, 312.

BOURRASSÉ (Abbé Jean-Jacques). French historian and archaeologist (1813-1870), *p.* 47.

BOURBON-L'ARCHAMBAULT. Small town in central France (Allier), 23 km. from Moulins. Stone quarries, *p.* 69.

BRACTEATE (Latin *bractea* = thin sheet of metal). Coins and coin effigies of the time of the great invasions and the Merovingian period. Barbarian imitations of Roman coins and medals, and generally dated according to this reference. Some are chased on both sides, some on one side only; the latter are very thin sheets and the image appears in sunk carving on the obverse, *p.* 199, 268, 273.

BRÄUNLINGEN. Town in West Germany (Baden), in the Black Forest, 16 km. south of Villingen, *p.* 275.

BRÉHIER (Louis). French archaeologist (1866-1951), *p.* 245.

BRESCIA. City in North Italy (Lombardy), at the foot of the Alps. Seat of a Lombard duchy for a few years in the 8th century. Basilica of San Salvatore, ancient church of a monastery founded in 753 by Aistolf, king of the Lombards. Museum of medieval Christian art (in the former church of Santa Giulia), *p.* 121, 136, 312; *fig.* 136; *map* 358.

BRIE. Ancient district in France, around Meaux, *p.* 78, 81.

BRIOUDE. Town in France (Haute-Loire), made famous by St Julian and St Avitus. Church of Saint-Julien built about 476 and mentioned by Gregory of Tours, *p.* 32; *map* 356.

BRITISH ISLES, *p.* 47, 71, 78, 81, 83, 113, 131, 155, 157, 162, 178, 202.

BRITTANY. Ancient province of France. From the mid-5th to the 7th century, it was invaded and occupied by Celts from the British Isles fleeing the Angles, *p.* x.

BRUNHILDA (c. 534-613). Daughter of Athanagild, she became the wife of Sigebert, king of Austrasia from 565 to 575, then of Merovaeus. Tortured and executed by order of Clotaire II, she was buried in the church of Saint-Martin at Autun, *p.* 24, 27, 32.

BUCHAREST. Capital of Rumania, in the Wallachian plain, about 30 miles from the Danube, *p.* 218.

BUCKLES. Large numbers of ornamented belt buckles have been found in early medieval graves, *p.* 59, 215, 229, 243, 246, 257, 265, 268, 277-279, 311-313; *fig.* 220, 232, 244, 245, 249-253, 284, 285, 292, 307, 309; *map* 361.

BÜLACH. Small town in Switzerland (canton of Zurich), 19 km. north of Zurich. Site of an Alamannic cemetery, *p.* 221; *fig.* 235; *map* 358.

BURGOS, *p.* 84.

BURGUNDIANS. Germanic tribe which appears in the first century A.D. in the Baltic area, then on the middle Vistula; probably of Scandinavian origin. During the 3rd century they moved westwards, crossing the Rhine near Mainz (406) and founding a kingdom near Worms. Attacked by the Huns (436), they fled southwards and in 443 were allowed by Aetius to settle as *foederati* in Sapaudia (i.e. French Switzerland and the southern foothills of the French Jura around Geneva), *p.* 16, 22, 265, 277-279, 312, 313; *map* 355.

BURGUNDY, *p.* 178; *map* 356.

BYZANTIUM. See CONSTANTINOPLE.

CABALISTIC FORMULA. In the Hypogeum of Poitiers, *p.* 59, 60; *fig.* 71.

CAHORS. City of south-western France (Lot), enclosed by the river Lot. Occupied by the Visigoths (c. 471), it was ravaged by the Franks in 513. Building activity of the bishop St Desiderius (Didier), *p.* 34, 92; *map* 359.

CALLISTUS. Bishop of Cividale (726-?). He built the baptistery of Cividale (c. 730), *p.* 247, 248.

CAMEO. Gem carved in relief, *p.* 231, 313.

CAMPANIA. Region of South Italy extending from the Garigliano to the Gulf of Policastro, *p.* 257.

CANON TABLES. Tables of concordances in the Gospels, first drawn up by Eusebius of Caesarea (died 339) and represented at the beginning of Gospel Books, *p.* 159, 178, 188; *fig.* 191-194.

CANTERBURY. City in south-east England (Kent), about 50 miles from London. In the 5th century it was occupied by the Saxons and became the capital of the kingdom of Kent in 560. St Augustine settled there in 597, founding a monastery and becoming the first bishop of England, *p.* 33; *fig.* 349; *maps* 356, 358.

CAPITAL. Head or uppermost member of a column (in marble or stone) supporting the architrave or the springing of an arch. Near the Pyrenean marble quarries, capitals were carved and from there transported over long distances, *p.* 29-31, 35, 48, 67, 68, 99, 245, 312; *fig.* 28, 30, 33-37, 41-44, 49, 50, 77, 80-82, 99-101, 114-117; *map* 360.

CAPPADOCIA. Central region of Asia Minor in antiquity. Capital, Caesarea of Cappadocia, *p.* 77.

CAPUA. City in South Italy (Campania), in a bend of the Volturno, 33 km. north of Naples, *p.* 257.

CAROLINGIAN MINUSCULE. A minuscule book hand, very clear and distinct, developed in France during the reign of Charlemagne and based on the Roman cursive, *p.* 202.

CAROLINGIAN RENASCENCE. Art current of the Carolingian period: a deliberate reversion to the art of antiquity sponsored by Charlemagne, *p.* XII, XVI, 93, 94, 99, 102, 212, 288.

CAROLINGIANS. Second line of the kings of France (751-987), *p.* XIV, 20, 105, 107, 131, 183, 202, 206.

CARPET PATTERN. Rectangular ornament, usually on a gold ground, consisting of vine tendrils and various motifs decorating the frontispiece or initial page of an illuminated manuscript, *fig.* 178, 179.

CASA HERRERA. Locality in Spain, near Merida (province of Badajoz), *fig.* 343; *map* 358.

CASSIODORUS (c. 480-c. 575). Roman statesman and author who enjoyed the favour of Odoacer and Theodoric. Founded the monastery of Vivarium (Calabria) where he died, *p.* 195.

CASTELSEPRIO. Village in North Italy (Lombardy), on the right bank of the Olona, some 27 km. north of Milan and 14 km. from Varese. In the church of Santa Maria Foris Portas a large sequence of wall paintings was discovered in 1944, *p.* 93-95, 121, 128, 250; *fig.* 110, 111, 134, 135; *map* 358.

CASTEL TROSINO. Small town in central Italy (Marche), 6 km. from Ascoli Piceno. Site of a Lombard cemetery rich in grave goods of the 6th and 7th centuries, *p.* 231, 234, 311; *map* 358.

CATTANEO (Raffaele). Italian architect and archaeologist (1861-1889), *p.* 245, 250.

CELTS. An Indo-Germanic people who, first settling in Central Europe, were gradually driven back towards the Atlantic Ocean. At the time of the Roman conquest of Gaul, the Celts occupied an area bounded on the east by the Alps and the Rhine, on the south-east by the Durance and the Rhone, on the south by the Mediterranean and the Pyrenees, on the south-west by the Garonne, on the west by the Atlantic, on the north by the Seine and the Marne, *p.* 81.

CESARIUS OF ARLES (St) [470-542]. Became a monk at Lérins (Hyères) at the age of twenty, then a priest at Arles and finally bishop of Arles (503-542). One of the great churchmen and preachers of his day, *p.* 211; *fig.* 220.

CHALICE, *p.* 221, 241, 243; *fig.* 233, 264.

CHALON-SUR-SAONE. City in France (Saône-et-Loire), on the right bank of the Saône. At the end of the 6th century it was the capital of Gontran, king of Burgundy, *p.* 260, 277; *map* 359.

CHAMPAGNE. Ancient province of France (capital, Troyes), *p.* 69.

CHAMPAGNE (SOUTHERN). Natural region forming part of the French province of Champagne. Wooden church of the late Middle Ages, *p.* 290.

CHARENTON-DU-CHER. Town in France (Cher), 11 km. east of Saint-Amand-Mont-Rond. Remains of an abbey founded in 620 by St Cholan, *fig.* 24, 25; *map* 358.

CHARLEMAGNE (742-814). Eldest son of Pepin the Short, king of the Franks in 768 with his brother Carloman, then alone from 771. Crowned emperor in 800 at Rome by Pope Leo III, *p.* XIII, 102, 123, 150, 195, 199, 202, 250, 288, 289; *fig.* 214, 316.

CHARNAY-LÈS-MACON. Village in east-central France (Saône-et-Loire), 4 km. from Mâcon. Site of a Merovingian cemetery of the 6th and 7th centuries, *p.* 221, 234; *fig.* 258.

CHELLES. Small town in France (Seine-et-Marne), on the Marne. Residence of the Merovingian kings. Abbey founded about 660 by St Bathilda, *p.* 241; *map* 358.

CHER. Tributary of the Loire (220 miles), *p.* 69.

CHEVALIER (Mgr Casimir). French archaeologist (1825-1893), *p.* 47.

CHILDEBERT I. Son of Clovis and Clotilda, king of the Franks (511-558), *p.* 27, 29.

CHILDERIC I (c. 436-481). King of the Franks (457-481). Member of the house of Merovaeus and father of

Clovis I. He reigned over the Salic Franks. He fixed his residence at Tournai, where his tomb was discovered in 1653, *p. 218; fig. 227-229.*

CHILPERIC I (539-584). Son of Clotaire I, king of the Franks (561-584). Husband of Fredegund, *p. 24.*

CHOSROES II (590-628). King of the Sassanid dynasty. Preserved at the Bibliothèque Nationale, Paris, is an inlaid gold cup traditionally known as the 'Cup of Chosroes' or the 'Cup of Solomon.' It belonged to the treasure of Saint-Denis and is said to have been a gift to Charlemagne from Harun al-Rashid, *p. 218.*

CHRODEGANG (St) [712?-766]. Bishop of Metz (742-766) and reformer of the cathedral clergy, he was also a minister of Pepin the Short, king of Austrasia, *p. 289.*

CHUR. Town in eastern Switzerland, capital of the canton of the Grisons (Graubünden), on the Plessur. Of Roman origin, *p. 272, 281.*

CIBORIUM. A canopy standing on columns and covering the high altar in early medieval churches, *p. 32, 245, 247, 250, 312; fig. 3.*

CIMIEZ. Ancient town in France (Alpes-Maritimes), on the Riviera, now part of Nice. Under the name of Cemenelium, it was the capital of the Vediantii. In the 4th century it was one of the eight cities of the Maritime Alps; wrecked in the 6th. Ancient cathedral and baptistery, ancient abbey church of Saint-Pons, *fig. 320; map 358.*

CIMITILE. Town in South Italy (Campania), 35 km. from Naples. Ancient cemetery of Nola, *p. 257.*

CIVATE. Small town in Lombardy (Como), 6 km. from Lecco and 56 km. north-east of Milan. The church of San Pietro al Monte, 5 km. from Civate, is famous, *p. 250.*

CIVIDALE DEL FRIULI. Town in north-east Italy (Venezia Giulia), 17 km. from Udine. The ancient Forum Julii, it gave its name to Friuli of which it was the capital. Alboin made it the capital of the first Lombard duchy in Italy in 568. It later became a Frankish duchy, *p. 121-123, 128, 200, 247, 248, 250, 271, 272, 311; map 358.*
Church of Santa Maria in Valle (Tempietto), *fig. 138, 139, 273-276.*
Church of San Martino, altar of Duke Ratchis or Pemmo, *fig. 277, 279-281.*
Cross of Gisulf, *fig. 300.*
Gold Disk, *fig. 299.*

CIVITA CASTELLANA. Town in central Italy (Latium), 57 km. from Rome. In the cathedral, a marble relief with a hunting scene (8th century), *p. 257.*

CLERMONT. City in central France (Puy-de-Dôme), today called Clermont-Ferrand. Conquered in the 5th century by the Visigoths, then taken by Clovis (507). 5th-century church of Saint-Antolien mentioned by Gregory of Tours, *p. 32; map 356.*

CLOISONNÉ. Art of inlaying coloured stones or enamels between partitions *(cloisons)* made of wire fillets, usually of gold. This technique was revived in Northern Europe from the 3rd to the 5th century under Oriental (Hunnish) influences, *p. 178, 218, 221, 225, 231, 234, 238, 243, 313.*

CLOSURE SLABS. Ornamental stone slabs used to close off a tomb or the sanctuary of a church, *p. 55, 100, 101, 265, 312; fig. 19-22, 66, 118, 119, 291.*

CLOTILDA (St). Daughter of Chilperic and wife of Clovis (c. 475-545), *p. 21, 24, 27.*

CLOVIS I (466-511). Son of Childeric I and king of the Franks (481-511), of the Merovingian line. He conquered northern Gaul in 486 and made Paris his residence. In 507 he subdued the areas occupied by the Visigoths as far as the Garonne. Converted to Catholicism about 496, *p. 24, 27.*

CLUNY, *p. 275.*

CODEX. A manuscript book of vellum leaves, written on both recto and verso and assembled in signatures, in contrast to the scroll or *volumen.* Examples: *fig. 126, 127, 150, 154, 155, 179, 183.*

COINS. Many coins have been found in Germanic graves and in buried treasures. Placed in the graves as an obol for Charon, they provide valuable evidence for the dating of burials. They indicate the reign of an emperor or king roughly corresponding to the lifetime of the dead man, and so constitute a *terminus post quem* for his burial, *p. 268, 288.*

COLOGNE (KÖLN). City in West Germany (Rhineland-Westphalia). Capital of the Roman province of Lower Germany, then of the Ripuarian Franks. Church of Sankt Gereon mentioned by Gregory of Tours: extensive remains of the original building were brought to light as a result of the damage caused by air raids in the last war, *p. 1, 5, 231, 245, 260; fig. 252, 257, 327A & B; maps 354, 356, 358-359.*

COLUMBAN (St). Irish monk (c. 540-615), missionary and reformer, and founder of the abbeys of Luxeuil and Bobbio, *p. 64, 165.*

COMO. City in North Italy (Lombardy) at the south-west end of the Lake of Como. The ancient Roman colony of Novum Comum, it became a bishopric about 379, *p. 250.*

CONCORDIUS. Bishop of Arles (c. 374-c. 400), *fig. 16.*

CONDAT. Former name of the abbey of Saint-Claude (Jura), *p. 289.*

CONQUES. Town in south-western France (Aveyron), 32 km. north-west of Rodez. Abbey of Sainte-Foy, famous from Carolingian times as a pilgrimage centre, *p. 285; fig. 314; map 358.*

CONSTANS I (320-350). Third son of Constantine the Great and Emperor of the West (337-350), *p. XII.*

CONSTANTINA or CONSTANTIA (c. 318-354). Daughter of Constantine the Great, she married her cousin Annibalianus, then Gallus, appointed Caesar by Constantius II. She died in Bithynia and was buried in Rome on the Via Nomentana (Mausoleum of Santa Costanza), *p. 115.*

CONSTANTINE THE GREAT (c. 285-337). Roman Emperor (306-337). In 330 he transferred the seat of government to Constantinople, *p. XII, XIV, 13, 115, 143, 209; fig. 157.*

CONSTANTINE II (316-340). Eldest son of Constantine the Great and Emperor of the West (337-340), *p. X.*

CONSTANTINE IV (654-685). Eldest son of Constans II and Emperor of the East (668-685), he resisted the Arabs and by re-establishing religious unity with Rome strengthened the Empire, *p. 113.*

CONSTANTINOPLE. Capital of the Empire of the East, built from 324 to 330 by Constantine the Great on the site of the ancient Byzantium. Present-day Istanbul, *p. XII, XIII, XIV, 3, 112, 113, 121, 229, 287; maps 354, 355.*

CONSTANTINOPLE (Councils of). The second church council, convoked in 381 by Theodosius, confirmed the condemnation of Arianism by the Council of Nicaea. The sixth church council (680-681) condemned monothelitism, *p. 113.*

CONSTANTIUS II (317-361). Second son of Constantine the Great and Emperor of the East (337-361), *p. XII.*

COPELANZ (LA). Village in Switzerland (canton of Vaud), near Oron, 16 km. south-east of Lausanne. Here was found a gold fibula representing a haloed horseman trampling on serpents (6th-7th century), *p.* 271.

COPTIC ART. The art of Christian Egypt. It appears to have influenced the carvings on the sarcophagus of Bishop Agilbert at Jouarre, *p.* 72, 74, 77, 188.

COPTS. Name of the Christian Egyptians separated from the Catholic Church after the 5th century. In the first centuries of Christianity, the Copts exerted a considerable influence owing to the development of monasticism in Egypt, to such famous places of pilgrimage as the tomb of St Menas (died 296) at Abu Mina, and finally to the exodus of Coptic monks and artists following the Arab invasion in the 7th century, *p.* 74, 77, 178, 188, 260, 277, 312.

CORBIE. Small town in northern France (Somme), 25 km. east of Amiens. Abbey founded between 657 and 661 by Queen Bathilda, regent for her son Clovis III. It adopted the Benedictine rule about 700 and was reformed by Abbot Adalard about 820. The *Corbie Psalter* is now in the Amiens Library, *p.* 123, 165, 178, 188, 195, 200, 202, 206; *fig.* 176, 180, 204, 210, 212, 213; *map* 358.

COULANDON. Village in central France (Allier), 6 km. from Moulins. Stone quarries, *p.* 69.

CRIEL-SUR-MER. Small town in northern France (Seine-Maritime), in the valley of the Yères, 22 km. north-east of Dieppe and 2 km. from the English Channel, *p.* 278.

'CROSS OF THE ARDENNES.' Processional cross of gold leaf and copper on a wooden core, dating from about 850, *p.* 313.

CRYPT. In antiquity, in the writings of Gregory of Tours, and until the end of the early Middle Ages, the word *crypta* denoted a vaulted structure, a funerary hypogeum or a church annex, which could be either subterranean or aboveground, *p.* 64, 66; *fig.* 11, 12, 19-21, 77-91, 112-117.

CYRUS (St). According to the legend, St Julitta fled from Tarsus (Cilicia) early in the 4th century with her three-year-old son Cyrus to escape Diocletian's persecution of the Christians. But she was recognized as a Christian and martyred with her son, *p.* 124, 139.

DAGILEOPA (Ilderic). Duke of Spoleto (8th century), successor of Transamondo. For him the altar of the abbey of San Pietro in Valle at Ferentillo was made, *p.* 250; *fig.* 278.

DAGOBERT I. Son of Clotaire II. King of the Franks (629-639), *p.* 238; *map* 356.

DAILLENS. Village in Switzerland (canton of Vaud) on the west slope of the Jorat, 2.5 km. north-east of Cossonay. Site of a Burgundian cemetery where two buckles were found representing Daniel in the lions' den (7th century), *p.* 277.

DANIEL. Hebrew prophet, principal personage of the Book of Daniel. Captive at Babylon where he underwent many trials because of his faith. Daniel in the lions' den was one of the most popular symbolic themes of early medieval art, *p.* 86, 265, 277, 278; *fig.* 21, 100, 297, 305.

DANUBE. River of Central Europe (1725 miles long), flowing from the Black Forest to the Black Sea, *p.* XII, 215, 312.

DARMSTADT. City in West Germany (Hesse), 28 km. south of Frankfurt, *p.* 313.

DAUPHINÉ. Ancient province of south-eastern France (capital, Grenoble), *p.* 27.

DAVID. Second king of Israel (c. 1010-970 B.C.). Slew the Philistine giant Goliath. He transformed the twelve tribes into a homogeneous nation, conquered Jerusalem and made it the centre of Jewish religious life, *p.* 195; *fig.* 206, 213.

DELÉMONT. Town in north-western Switzerland (canton of Berne), 45 km. south-west of Basel, *p.* 243; *fig.* 265; *map* 358.

DESANA. Village in North Italy (Piedmont), near Vercelli, where in 1938 a woman's grave of the 6th century was discovered, *p.* 225; *map* 358.

DESCHAMPS (Paul). French archaeologist and art historian (born 1888), *p.* 245.

DESIDERIUS (?-after 774). King of the Lombards, crowned in 757 by Pope Stephen II. Taken prisoner by Charlemagne in 774, he died at Corbie or Liège, *p.* 123, 200, 202.

DESIDERIUS or DIDIER (St) [595-655]. Bishop of Cahors (630-655), *p.* 34, 92.

DIANA. Ancient Italian goddess of the moon, later assimilated to Artemis, *p.* 199.

DIJON. City in eastern France (Côte-d'Or), former capital of the Duchy of Burgundy. Formed part of the ancient kingdom of the Burgundians, *p.* 69.

DIMMA (8th century). Bishop of Condeire or Connon (Ireland). Cousin of St Brecan, he was educated at the monastery of Lynally. He is said to have copied sacred texts for St Cronan of Roscrea, *fig.* 172.

DIOSCORIDES (Pedanius). Greek physician of the first century A.D., author of *De Materia Medica*, *p.* 202.

DIPTYCH. Hinged tablet of ivory, wood or sheet metal. The inner sides, coated with wax, could be written on with a stylus. In the period of the Late Empire, the outer sides were often richly carved (consular diptychs), *p.* 209, 212, 221, 263, 265; *fig.* 216, 217, 237.

DOEG. An Edomite, chief of Saul's herdsmen, who told him of David's flight. At Saul's command he slew 85 of the priests of Nob and devastated the city. Symbol of Antichrist, *p.* 195.

DOMAGNANO. Small town in the Republic of San Marino (central Italy), *p.* 222.

DONATISM. Schism which throughout the 4th century divided the African churches on the issue of the 'traditors,' i.e. bishops or priests who during the Roman persecutions gave up to the pagan authorities the Scriptures and sacred vessels. The schism began in 311 as a protest against the election of Caecilian as bishop of Carthage; the Donatists had a rival bishop elected by a synod, first Majorinus, then, after his death, Donatus. Condemned by three councils (Rome 313, Arles 314, Milan 316), Donatism died out in 411, *p.* XIV.

DOTZHEIM. Residential suburb of Wiesbaden, 3.2 km. west of the city centre, *p.* 268.

DRAUSIUS (St). A native of Soissons, he became archdeacon, then bishop of Soissons (c. 658-c. 674), *fig.* 39, 40.

DURHAM. Borough of northern England, in the county of the same name, some 70 miles north of York, *map* 358.

DURROW. Irish village (Co. Offaly), 3 miles north-west of Tullamore (formerly Daimhaig). Monastery founded about 504 by St Columban. *Book of*

Durrow, illuminated manuscript of the 7th century, *p.* 159, 160; *fig.* 170; *map* 358.

DYGGVE (Ejnar). Danish archaeologist and architect (1887-1961), *p.* 250; *fig.* 273.

EADFRID or EADFRITH. Bishop of Lindisfarne (698-721), who probably wrote out the *Book of Lindisfarne*, *p.* 159.

EASBY. Abbey about a mile east of Richmond (Yorkshire), in the valley of the Swale, *fig.* 96, 97; *map* 358.

EBERSOLT (Jean). French archaeologist, *p.* 245.

EBREGESILUS (St). Bishop of Meaux (late 7th century), *p.* 67; *fig.* 78.

ECCLESIUS (St) [died 534]. Archbishop of Ravenna (521-532), *p.* 247.

ECHMIADZIN. Town in U.S.S.R. (Republic of Armenia), west of Erivan, seat of the primate of the Armenian Church, *p.* 265.

ECHTERNACH. Ancient abbey on the German frontier of the Duchy of Luxembourg. Founded in 698 by St Willibrord. Secularized in 1793. *Echternach Gospels*, illuminated manuscript, *p.* 31, 157, 160; *fig.* 1, 168, 174; *map* 358.

EDESSA. City in northern Mesopotamia (present-day Urfa, Turkey). The church of St Sophia was famous in early times, *p.* 32.

EGINO OF VERONA (died 802). Bishop of Verona in the late 8th century (he is recorded there in 797). One of the artisans of the Carolingian renascence, for he brought many manuscripts from Italy to Reichenau and composed a Homiliary at the request of Charlemagne, *p.* 139; *fig.* 154, 155.

EGYPT, *p.* 77, 113, 188, 257, 259, 277.

ELBERN (Victor). Contemporary German archaeologist, *p.* 62.

ELIGIUS or ELOI (St). Born near Limoges (c. 588-660). He became a goldsmith in Paris, then master of the mint under Clotaire II and Dagobert, and was appointed bishop of Noyon (641), *p.* 62, 240, 241, 243; *fig.* 264, 266, 267.

ELLO. Goldsmith (8th century), apparently a Swabian. One of the two makers of the casket of Teuderigus at Saint-Maurice, *p.* 243.

EMPIRE. See ROMAN EMPIRE.

ENGER. Town in West Germany, 8 km. north-east of Herford (Westphalia). Abbey church with the tomb of Widukind, *p.* 243, 285; *map* 358.

ENGERS. Town in West Germany (Rhine Palatinate), 20 km. north of Koblenz, *p.* 312.

ENGLAND, *p.* 33, 72, 132, 312.

ENNABEUREN. Town in West Germany (Württemberg), 12 km. from Urach, *p.* 268, 281; *fig.* 297.

ENTRINGEN. Small town in West Germany (Baden-Württemberg), some 20 km. south of Stuttgart, *p.* 218.

EPHESUS. City in Asia Minor (present-day Selçuk, Turkey), where two councils were held, including the 3rd church council convoked by Theodosius II in 431. It recognized the dual nature of Christ in a single person and proclaimed Mary the Mother of God, *p.* XIV, 107; *map* 354.

ERERUK. City in Armenia, *p.* 33.

EROS. Greek god of love, son of Aphrodite and Ares, lover and husband of Psyche, identified with Cupid by the Romans and often represented as a child, *p.* 115.

EUCHERIUS (St). Bishop of Lyons about 432, died about 449. Prolific author admired by Erasmus, *fig.* 182.

EUGENDE or OYEND (St). Assistant of St Lupicinus and later abbot of the monastery of Condat (present-day Saint-Claude in the Jura). Died in 510, *p.* 289.

EUSICIUS (St). Hermit at Pressigny, on the river Cher, where he died in 542. Childebert I erected a basilica over his tomb; this was the original church of Selles-sur-Cher, *p.* 29.

EUTYCHIUS or EUTYCHES (c. 375-c. 454). Greek heresiarch who affirmed the single, divine nature of Christ, condemned by the Council of Chalcedon (451) and exiled into Egypt, *p.* XIV.

EVANGELIST SYMBOLS. Representation of the four Evangelists by their symbols: an angel (Matthew), a winged lion (Mark), a winged bull (Luke), an eagle (John), *p.* 160, 178, 182, 248; *fig.* 1, 89, 168, 170, 173, 174, 193, 194, 199.

EWER. Pitcher or jug with a handle, *p.* 260; *fig.* 287.

EXPLICIT. Latin term (an abbreviation of *explicitus*, 'unfolded') placed at the end of medieval manuscripts to indicate the conclusion, *p.* 137; *fig.* 150.

EZEKIEL. Hebrew prophet who gave his name to the Book of Ezekiel in the Bible. Born into a family of priests and a captive at Babylon, he prepared the way for the restoration of Israel and of the new Temple of Jerusalem, *fig.* 178.

FANO. City in central Italy (Marche) on the Adriatic, 12 km. south-east of Pesaro, *p.* 225.

FARNESINA or Villa Farnese in Rome. In its gardens stands a Roman edifice of the first century A.D., whose stucco decorations, discovered in 1879, are now in the Museo Nazionale Romano, *p.* 113.

FATHERS OF THE CHURCH, *p.* 117, 124; *fig.* 137, 179.

FEAGHMAAN WEST. Site in southwest Ireland (Co. Kerry), on the north side of Valentia Island (Dingle Bay), *fig.* 337; *map* 358.

FERENTILLO. Town in central Italy (Umbria), 20 km. from Terni. Nearby is the abbey of San Pietro in Valle, founded in the 8th century, *p.* 250; *fig.* 278.

FÉTIGNY. Village in Switzerland (canton of Fribourg), on the left bank of the Broye, 28 km. west of Fribourg, *p.* 313.

FIBULA. The ornamental clasps or brooches of Antiquity and the early Middle Ages, *p.* 178, 215, 221, 222, 225, 234, 238, 241, 243, 246, 257, 265, 268, 271, 273, 281, 312, 313; *fig.* 223, 224, 235, 236, 240, 242, 243, 249-262, 293, 298. See also GRASSHOPPER FIBULAE.

FIESOLE. Town in Tuscany near Florence, *p.* 250.

FILIGREE. Ornamental work, consisting in the application of grains, beads or fine wire, usually of gold or silver, to objects of gold or silver. Much used in the Merovingian period to decorate gold fibulae and buckles, under the influence of Byzantine art, *p.* 221, 234, 238, 243, 279, 285.

FLAVIGNY. Benedictine abbey of Saint-Pierre de Flavigny founded in 720, destroyed by the Normans and rebuilt in the 10th century. Near it sprang up the small town of Flavigny-sur-Ozerain, 9 km. south-east of Les Laumes (Côte-d'Or, Burgundy), *p.* 178; *fig.* 191-194; *map* 358.

FLEURY-SUR-LOIRE. Former name of the abbey of Saint-Benoît-sur-Loire, *p.* 64, 281.

FLONHEIM. Town in West Germany (Rhineland), some 20 km. north of Worms, where the 5th-century grave of a barbarian chieftain was discovered, *p.* 218.

FLORENCE, *p.* 275; *map* 354.

FLORO, *p.* 312.

FORMIGÉ (Jules). French architect and archaeologist (1879-1960), *p.* 55; *fig.* 66, 67.

FORNOVO DI SAN GIOVANNI. Commune in North Italy (Bergamo), on the right bank of the Serio, *p.* 312.

FORTIFIED TOWNS. Roman towns of Gaul converted into strongholds in order to withstand the incursions of the barbarians, *p.* 12, 13; *map* 359.

FORTUNATUS (St). Born in Venetia, near Treviso (c. 530-609). Bishop of Poitiers in 599. Writer and poet, *p.* 22, 24, 32.

FRANCOVITCH (Geza de). Contemporary Hungarian archaeologist and art historian, *p.* 250; *fig.* 273.

FRANKS. Confederated Germanic tribes established in the 3rd century on the Lower Rhine. The leading tribes among them were the Salian and Ripuarian Franks at the mouths of the Rhine and Meuse and along the Scheldt and the Somme (4th century): these founded a kingdom under Clovis, *p.* XII, XIII, 16, 20, 105, 121, 257, 265; *maps* 355, 356.

FREDEGARIUS (Pseudo-). Anonymous author, probably a Burgundian, of the sequel to Gregory of Tours' *Historia Francorum*. His chronicle ends in 642, *p.* 188; *fig.* 195-197.

FREISING. City in West Germany (Bavaria), 32 km. north-east of Munich, *p.* 137; *map* 358.

FRÉJUS. Town on the French Riviera (Var), ancient capital of the Oxibiani. Its 5th-century baptistery is unique in France, *p.* 3, 32, 33; *fig.* 2-4, 322A & B; *maps* 354, 356, 358.

FRESCO. Technique of painting, colours being applied, with water as a vehicle, on a coat of fresh plaster. The lime of the ground is penetrated by the pigments and, converted by exposure into carbonate, acts as a binding material, *p.* 94, 150; *fig.* 110, 122, 129, 131-141, 164-167.

FRIBOURG. City in west-central Switzerland, in a bend of the river Sarine, capital of the canton of the same name, *p.* 313.

FRISIANS. A Germanic people in the region comprised between the mouths of the Rhine and the Ems. With the Angles and Jutes, they carried out sea raids against England and attempted to colonize it, *p.* XIII.

FRIULI. Region in north-east Italy (capital, Udine), now part of Venezia Giulia, *p.* 122, 202, 247, 271, 312.

GABRIEL. Archangel, *fig.* 129, 313.

GALLA PLACIDIA (c. 389-450). Daughter of Theodosius I and Galla, she first married the Visigoth Athaulf, brother-in-law of Alaric, in 414; then, in 417, Constantius, a general serving under Honorius, by whom she had two children, Honoria and Valentinian III. As a widow, she acted as regent (425) of the Empire of the West during the minority of Valentinian. Famous for her mausoleum at Ravenna, beside the church of San Vitale, *p.* 39.

GAMMERTINGEN. Town in West Germany (Württemberg), 24 km. from Sigmaringen. A woman's grave was found here in 1904 in an Alamannic cemetery, *p.* 278.

GANAY (Marquis de). Collection, *p.* 222.

GARNET. Stone much appreciated in the period of the barbarian invasions, especially the almandine. Generally imported from India, garnets were worked with gold, cut and inset on goffered sheets of metal. Much used on weapons, jewellery and various precious objects, *p.* 215, 218, 222, 231, 238, 241, 265.

GARONNE. River in south-western France, flowing from the Pyrenees to the Gironde estuary, *p.* 12, 34.

GAUL. In Antiquity and the early Middle Ages, the region bounded by the Rhine, the Alps, the Mediterranean, the Pyrenees and the Atlantic, roughly corresponding to modern France, *p.* XII, XIII, 1, 3, 12, 15, 16, 20, 21, 25, 27, 30, 32-35, 40, 42, 47, 48, 64, 69, 74, 92, 101, 102, 105, 113, 123, 128, 155, 165, 178, 188, 202, 209, 212, 259, 265, 287-289; *map* 356.

GELASIANUM. See SACRAMENTARIUM GELASIANUM.

GÉLIMER. Last Vandal king of Africa (530-534), *map* 355.

GELLONE. Abbey founded in 804 by St William, duke of Aquitaine, at Saint - Guilhem - le - Désert (Hérault), near Montpellier, *p.* 188, 206; *fig.* 198-203; *map* 358.

GÉMIGNY. Village in central France (Loiret), 11 km. from Patay, *fig.* 26; *map* 358.

GENEVA. City in Switzerland, at the west end of the Lake of Geneva. In the 4th century it became the chief town of the Genevenses and the second city of the Viennensis. About 474, capital of the Sapaudia of the Burgundians, then conquered by the Franks in 534, *p.* 22, 277, 278; *fig.* 318; *maps* 354, 356, 358, 359.

GENEVIEVE (St). Born at Nantes c. 429, died in Paris in 512, and buried in the basilica of the Holy Apostles founded by King Clovis I, *p.* 27.

GENSERIC or GAISERIC. Vandal king of Africa (428-477). Landed in Africa in May 429 and in 435 obtained for his people the status of *foederati*. On October 19, 439, he captured Carthage and overran the North African coast as far as Tripolitania. By 442 he had occupied Proconsularis, Byzacena and part of Numidia and Tripolitania: this was the Vandal Empire. With his fleet Genseric made incursions in the Mediterranean, *p.* XII; *map* 355.

GEOMETRIC ART. Style of ornamentation composed of motifs regularly or geometrically disposed, *p.* 30, 31.

GEORGE (c. 769-799). Bishop of Ostia, then bishop of Amiens. Translator into Latin of a Universal Chronicle, *p.* 202.

GEPIDS. A Teutonic people akin to the Goths, *map* 355.

GERMANI, *p.* 20, 21, 312.

GERMANUS (St) [c. 389-448]. Born at Auxerre, he studied in Rome, became an advocate and was appointed *dux* of his native town. Bishop of Auxerre in 418. Sent to England in 429 by Pope Celestine to fight the Pelagians. Died at Ravenna July 31, 448, his body being brought back to Auxerre. Over his tomb Queen Clotilda erected a basilica which gave rise to the abbey of Saint-Germain, *p.* 27.

GERMANUS (St) [c. 494-576]. Born near Autun. Bishop of Paris before 558. Died May 28, 576. Buried under the side porch of the church of the Holy Cross and St Vincent (later known as Saint-Germain-des-Prés), founded by King Childebert I, *p.* 27.

GERMANUS OF TRIER (St) [610-677]. Founder and first abbot of the monastery of Moûtier-Grandval or Münster (canton of Berne, Switzerland), *p.* 243; *fig.* 265.

GERMANY, *p.* 12, 238, 313.

GERMIGNY-DES-PRÉS. Village in central France (Loiret), near the Loire, 30 km. east of Orléans and 6 km. north-west of Saint-Benoît-sur-Loire (the former abbey of Fleury). Villa and oratory erected here about 800 by Theodulf, bishop of Orléans and abbot of Fleury. This oratory became in the Middle Ages a priory of Saint-Benoît-sur-Loire, then a parish church. It was unfortunately rebuilt on mistaken lines by the architect Lisch in 1869, *p.* 27, 95.

GESTA DAGOBERTI. A chronicle compiled about 835 at the abbey of Saint-Denis, *p.* 243, 259.

GISULF I. Nephew of Alboin, king of the Lombards, and duke of Friuli (died 611), *p.* 271.

GOLGOTHA. Place of crucifixion at Jerusalem, *p.* 188.

GOLIATH. Philistine giant killed by David with a sling, *p.* 195.

GONDORF. Town in West Germany (Rhine Palatinate), on the left bank of the Moselle, 25 km. south-west of Koblenz, *p.* 265.

GONTRAN (St) [c. 545-592]. Son of Clotaire II and king of Burgundy (561-592), *p.* 259.

GOSPEL BOOK. Book containing the Gospel texts for all the masses of the year, *p.* 231. Examples: *fig.* 1, 241.

GOSPELS. Complete texts of the four Gospels of the New Testament, with or without the canon tables, *p.* 178; *fig.* 146, 147, 150-153, 168-174, 183, 191-194, 211.

GOTHS. A Germanic people originally dwelling in Scandinavia and on the lower Vistula—the only one who achieved a successful synthesis of Roman and Germanic elements. The prestige enjoyed by the Goths among the Germanic tribes comes out clearly in the Niebelungen. They were early divided into two groups: Ostrogoths and Visigoths (i.e. East Goths and West Goths), *p.* XII, 16, 155, 211, 222, 225, 229; *map* 355.

GOURDON. Village in west-central France (Saône-et-Loire), 7 km. east of Montceau-les-Mines, where in 1845 a treasure was found consisting of a chalice, a paten and 104 coins of the first half of the 6th century, *p.* 218, 221, 241; *map* 358.

GRADO. Small town in north-eastern Italy (Friuli, Venezia Giulia), on the lagoon. It was the port of Aquileia, and here the inhabitants of Aquileia, fleeing before Attila and later the Lombards, took refuge, *p.* 231.

GRASSHOPPER FIBULAE. Gold, silver or bronze fibulae in the form of grasshoppers, often inlaid with precious stones and generally found in pairs in graves. This motif, of Oriental origin, was transmitted to Merovingian art by way of South Russia and Hungary at the time of the Hunnish invasions. It may be a symbol of immortality. Among the oldest pieces known are the grasshopper fibulae from the tomb of the Frankish king Childeric at Tournai, also called bee fibulae. Cf. a fibula from Beaurepaire (Musée des Beaux-Arts, Lyons), *p.* 218; *fig.* 229, 230.

GREAT BRITAIN, *p.* XIII, 20, 33, 72, 78, 160.

GREECE, *p.* 202, 288.

GREGORY THE GREAT (St) [c. 540-604]. Prefect of Rome (572-574). As Pope (590-604), he defended the states of the Church against the Lombards and evangelized England. His writings made him one of the founders of medieval Christian spirituality, *p.* 115, 143, 202, 231; *fig.* 121, 148, 155, 162, 177D, 178, 241.

GREGORY OF TOURS (St). Churchman and historian (538 or 539-594), born at Clermont. Bishop of Tours in 573. Author of the *Historia Francorum*, *p.* 5, 13, 22, 24, 27, 32, 155.

GRENOBLE. City in south-eastern France (Isère). Taken by the Burgundians, then by the Franks, it held out against the Lombards in 673. Crypt of the church of Saint-Laurent, *p.* 27, 97-101, *fig.* 112-117, 335A & B; *maps* 358, 359.

GRISONS or GRAUBÜNDEN. Easternmost canton of Switzerland, between Austria and Italy, *p.* 150, 250.

GUARRAZAR (Fuente de). Locality in central Spain, near Guadamur (province of Toledo), where in 1858 a treasure of Visigothic crosses and crowns was discovered, *p.* 231, 241; *fig.* 248; *map* 358.

GÜLTLINGEN. Small town in West Germany (Baden-Württemberg), some 30 km. south-east of Pforzheim. In 1901 the tomb of an Alamannic chief was found here, *p.* 218.

GUMMERSMARK. Locality in Denmark (Sjaelland), between Ringsted and Köge, where some brooches decorated with animal forms were discovered, *p.* 312.

GUTENSTEIN. Town in West Germany (Konstanz), *p.* 280.

GÜTTINGEN. Town in northern Switzerland (canton of Thurgau), on the left bank of the Lake of Constance. Site of an Alamannic cemetery of the Merovingian period, *p.* 211, 271; *map* 358.

HABAKKUK. The eighth of the lesser prophets, *p.* 195; *fig.* 207.

HALLE. City in East Germany, on the Saale, some 50 km. north-west of Leipzig, *p.* 271.

HEIDINGSFELD. Town in West Germany (Baden), 10 km. south-west of Würzburg, *p.* 312.

HELENA (St). Mother of Constantine the Great (c. 250-330). She had churches erected at Bethlehem and Jerusalem, *p.* 143; *fig.* 156.

HELVETIA, *p.* 101.

HEPTATEUCH. The first seven books of the Old Testament: Pentateuch, Book of Joshua, and Judges, *p.* 178; *fig.* 188, 190.

HERACLIUS I (c. 575-641). Emperor of the East (610-641), *p.* 113.

HERCULES. Latin name for Heracles, *p.* 278; *fig.* 306.

HEROD THE GREAT (74-4 B.C.). King of the Jews (40-4 B.C.), *p.* 138.

HERULI. A German people dwelling in the Danish islands, who with the Goths migrated to the Pontic steppe in the 3rd century. Under pressure from the Huns, they were driven westwards again, beyond the Danube, *p.* XII; *map* 355.

HEXAEMERON. A treatise on the six days of the Creation: the best known are those of St Basil and St Ambrose, *fig.* 176.

HILARY or HILARIUS (St) [c. 315-c. 367]. Bishop of Poitiers (350-367), exiled in Phrygia (356-360) for his adherence to orthodox Christianity. Author of the *De Trinitate, fig.* 145.

HOMILY. A discourse or sermon read or pronounced to an audience, *fig.* 154, 155, 177A & C.

HONORIUS (Flavius) [384-423]. Son of Theodosius I and Emperor of the West (395-423), *p.* XII.

HORMISDAS (St). As Pope (514-523) he restored the unity of the Church and had the Canons of the Greek Church translated into Latin, *p.* 229.

HORNHAUSEN. Town in East Germany (Saxony), west of Magdeburg. Here in 1874 was found a tombstone representing Wotan on horseback with his spear and buckler (8th century), *p.* 271.

HORSEMAN. The most popular theme in Germanic art both before and after their conversion to Christianity, *p.* 272, 275; *fig.* 297, 299.

HUNGARY, *p.* 229.

HUNS. A nomadic Asiatic people of horsemen who invaded Europe in a series of devastating incursions during the 4th and 5th centuries. Under the leadership of Attila (died 453) they penetrated as far as Gaul, but their power was broken in 451 at the battle of Châlons, in Champagne (Catalaunian Plains), where they were turned back by the Roman legions under Aetius, reinforced by Germanic troops. The Huns then retreated into Italy and Pannonia, *p.* XII, 215; *map* 355.

ICONOCLASM. Image breaking: the doctrine of a strong party in the Byzantine Empire in the 8th and 9th centuries which opposed the use of images and regarded as idolatrous the representation of Christ, the Virgin and saints. Iconoclasm ended on March 11, 843, with the victory of orthodoxy, *p.* XIV, 62, 202, 250.

INDIA, *p.* 215, 259.

INGOMER. Son of Clovis I and Clotilda. Died in infancy, *p.* 24.

NITIAL (ORNAMENTAL). In illuminated manuscripts, a large initial at the beginning of a chapter or paragraph, often elaborately adorned with arabesques, figures, etc., and sometimes filling the entire page, *p.* 137, 157, 159, 160, 165, 178, 188, 195, 199, 206; *fig.* 171, 176, 177A, B, C, D, 189, 190, 198-210.

INTERLACE. A pattern of surface decoration consisting of straps or ribbons often elaborately interwoven, *p.* 100, 159, 212, 225, 265, 271, 281, 311, 312.

INTRADOS. The under surface of an arch or vault, *p.* 11, 117; *fig.* 12, 13.

IRELAND, *p.* XIII, 72, 81, 157, 277.

ISAAC (Sacrifice of). See ABRAHAM'S SACRIFICE.

ISIDORE OF SEVILLE (St). Doctor of the Church (c. 560-636). Succeeded his brother Leander, in 601, as archbishop of Seville. A prolific author, *fig.* 184, 186, 187.

ITALY, *p.* XIII, 13, 15, 20, 25, 32, 33, 47, 97, 99-102, 105, 107, 113, 121, 128, 132, 137, 150, 165, 188, 195, 202, 206, 211, 222, 229, 231, 234, 241, 245, 246, 250, 257, 268, 287, 288, 311-313.

ITTENHEIM. Village in north-east France (Bas-Rhin), 13 km. west of Strasbourg, where in 1930 the grave of a Merovingian noble was discovered, *p.* 211, 275; *map* 358.

IVORY, *p.* 105, 209, 211, 221, 245, 250, 288; *fig.* 216, 217, 288-290.

IVREA. City in north-west Italy (Piedmont), on the Dora Baltea, *map* 358.

JEDBURGH. Town in south-eastern Scotland (Roxburgh), in the region of the royal abbeys of the Scott country, between Selkirk and Kelso, *fig.* 95; *map* 358.

JEROME (St). Father and Doctor of the Church (c. 347-420), author of the Latin translation of the Bible known as the Vulgate, *p.* 202; *fig.* 148.

JERUSALEM, *p.* 278; *fig.* 17.

JESSE. Bishop of Amiens (from 799) but deposed in 831. Died in 836, *p.* 202.

JEWELLERY (BARBARIAN), *p.* 55, 231, 241, 243, 268, 287.

JOB (BOOK OF). A book of the Old Testament, *fig.* 177D.

JOHN THE BAPTIST (St). Son of Zacharias and Elizabeth. In 27 he baptized Christ on the banks of the Jordan. In 28 he was beheaded by order of Herod Antipas, *p.* 150.

JOHN THE EVANGELIST (St). Son of Salome and Zebedee, brother of James the Greater. Author of the fourth Gospel and the Book of Revelation. Died c. 100, *p.* 117, 182, 285; *fig.* 169, 199, 315.

JOHN VII. Pope (705-707), *p.* 116, 117, 119, 123.

JOSEPH. Son of Jacob and Rachel. His story is told in Genesis 37-50, *p.* 124; *fig.* 137, 141.

JOUARRE. Former Benedictine abbey in northern France (Seine-et-Marne), 3 km. south of Ferté-sous-Jouarre, founded about 630 by St Adon. Crypts, *p.* 31, 64-78, 81, 84, 289; *fig.* 77-91, 340A & B; *map* 358.

JOUY-LE-COMTE. Hamlet in northern France (Val-d'Oise), near Parmain, 38 km. north of Paris, *p.* 221; *fig.* 236.

JOVINIAN. Roman heresiarch (died c. 412), who maintained that baptism and grace suffice and that works are useless. Excommunicated in 380 by Pope Siricius, *p.* 202.

JULITTA. Mother of St Cyrus, *p.* 124, 139.

JUMIÈGES. Former Benedictine abbey in Normandy, 28 km. north-west of Rouen (Seine-Maritime), founded in 654 by St Philibert, *p.* 64.

JURA, *p.* 289.

JUSTINIAN I (482-565). Byzantine Emperor (527-565), builder of St Sophia of Constantinople and husband of Theodora, *p.* XIII, 107, 113, 238, 245, 288.

JUTES. A Germanic tribe apparently originating in southern Jutland. According to Bede, they settled in Kent, the Isle of Wight and part of Hampshire. But their role and movements have not yet been clarified, *p.* XIII.

KÄRLICH. Town in West Germany (Rhine Palatinate), in the suburbs of Koblenz, *p.* 313.

KARLSRUHE. City in West Germany (Baden-Württemberg), on the Rhine, near the French frontier, *p.* 225, 275.

KELLS or CEANANNUS MOR. Town in eastern Ireland (Co. Meath), on the Blackwater, 12 miles north-west of An Uaimh. Monastery founded in the 6th century by St Columkille, where the *Book of Kells* was written, *p.* 159, 160; *fig.* 169; *map* 358.

KENT. County in south-eastern England, bordering on the Strait of Dover and the lower Thames, *p.* 231.

KILDRENAGH. Site in Ireland (Co. Kerry), on Valentia Island, *fig.* 336; *map* 358.

KINGSTON. Town in England (Kent), near Dover, *p.* 231; *fig.* 254.

KLEINHÜNINGEN. Former locality in the canton of Basel (Switzerland), part of the city of Basel since 1893. Site of an Alamannic grave of the 5th-6th century, *p.* 218, 221.

KOBLENZ. City in West Germany (Rhine Palatinate), at the confluence of the Moselle and the Rhine. Occupied by the Romans from 9 B.C., taken by the Franks about 500. Fortified *villa* of Nicetius, bishop of Trier, near the city, *p.* 22.

KOCHEM or COCHEM. Small town in West Germany (Moselle), 56 km. south-west of Koblenz, *p.* 267.

KRANENBURG. Village in West Germany (North Rhineland - Westphalia), 8 km. west of Cleves, near the Dutch frontier, *p.* 209.

KREFELD-GELLEP. City in West Germany (Rhineland-Westphalia), 23 km. south-west of Duisburg. The tomb of a Frankish chief was found here in 1962, dated to the 5th-6th century by a *solidus* of Anastasius I, *p.* 222, 231, 241, 260; *fig.* 239; *map* 358.

KYMATION. A conventional design in antique art, resembling a series of waves (Greek *kyma* = wave), *p.* 212.

LA CROIX (Révérend Père Camille de). Belgian archaeologist and Jesuit (1831-1911), *fig.* 68, 69, 72, 75.

LAMB. Symbol originally given to Christ by John the Baptist (John I, 29). Appears in Christian art from the 4th century on, *p.* 115, 221, 311; *fig.* 216, 237.

LANGEAIS. Village in central France (Indre-et-Loire), on the right bank of the Loire, 24 km. west of Tours, *fig.* 32; *map* 358.

LANTERN-TOWER. A tower pierced with windows admitting light into the part of the church over which it stands, *p.* 1, 32; *fig.* 2, 38.

LAON. City in northern France (Aisne). Formed part of the kingdom of Soissons, then of Austrasia. Taken by Pepin in 742. Two abbeys: Saint-Jean founded in 641 by St Salaberga; and Saint-Vincent, *p.* 165, 178, 206; *fig.* 188, 190; *map* 358.

LATER EMPIRE. Term the designating Roman Empire from 235 to 476, *p.* 3, 13, 27, 32, 34, 39, 40, 42, 47, 48, 84, 100.

LAUNEBOLDE. Duke of Aquitaine who, with his wife Berethrude, erected a

basilica in honour of St Saturninus at Toulouse about 570, *p.* 24.

LAVIGNY. Village in French Switzerland (canton of Vaud), 7.5 km. west of Morges, near the Lake of Geneva. Burgundian and Alamannic cemeteries here have yielded weapons, ornaments and belt buckles (7th century), *p.* 277.

LAVOYE. Village in north-eastern France (Meuse), 30 km. north of Bar-le-Duc. Frankish graves of the Merovingian period, *p.* 218, 260; *fig.* 231, 286, 287; *map* 358.

LAWRENCE (St). Roman deacon of Pope Sixtus, martyred in 258, *p.* 7.

LAZARUS. Brother of Mary and Martha, raised from the dead by Jesus (John XI, 1-44), *p.* 136; *fig.* 148.

LENINGRAD. City in the U.S.S.R. on the Gulf of Finland, *fig.* 178, 180.

LEO III. Bishop of Cimitile (c. 680-690), *p.* 257.

LIBER PONTIFICALIS. A series of biographies of the popes from the 6th century on, *p.* 231.

LIMOGES. City in west-central France (Haute-Vienne), on the river Vienne, *p.* 241.

LIMONS. Village in central France (Puy-de-Dôme), 24 km. west of Thiers, on the left bank of the Allier, *p.* 265; *map* 358.

LINDISFARNE (HOLY ISLAND). Small island off the coast of Northumberland, in north-eastern England. Monastery founded in 635 by St Aidan. *Book of Lindisfarne*, *p.* 159; *fig.* 171, 173; *map* 358.

LINGOTTO. Suburb of Turin (Piedmont, Italy), *p.* 231, 241; *fig.* 256; *map* 358.

LIUDGER or LUDGER (St). Native of the Frisian islands (743-809). He evangelized central Germany and became the first bishop of Münster (804-809), *fig.* 294.

LIUTPRAND. Son of Ansprand and king of the Lombards (713-744), *p.* XIII.

LIVIA (House of). House of the first century A.D. on the Palatine, in Rome, famous for its wall paintings (in the Museo delle Terme, Rome), *p.* 113.

LOIRE. French river flowing from the Massif Central north and then west into the Bay of Biscay (625 miles long), *p.* 12, 20, 34, 42, 48, 55, 69, 312.

LOMBARDS. A Germanic people perhaps of Scandinavian origin, who settled along the Elbe and then in lower Austria. In the 5th century they moved into Pannonia, becoming *foederati*; then, in 568, under their king Alboin, they descended into Italy and there founded a kingdom which lasted until 774, *p.* XIII, 20, 94, 102, 105, 113, 128, 131, 200, 202, 231, 238, 247, 250, 257, 271, 273, 275, 311-313; *map* 356.

LOMBARDY. Region in North Italy bounded by Switzerland, the Po, Lake Maggiore and the river Ticino, Lake Garda and the Mincio, *p.* 71, 155, 178, 200, 234, 312; *map* 356.

LONDON, *p.* 243; *fig.* 267; *maps* 354, 356.

LOPICENUS. Bishop of Modena (died 750), *p.* 247.

LORSCH. Town in West Germany (Hesse). Former abbey founded near Mainz in 764 and rebuilt on a nearby site in 774, *p.* 40, 67, 289.

LUCCA. City in central Italy (Tuscany), *p.* 247; *map* 358.

LUKE (St). Physician of Antioch, companion of St Paul. Author of the third Gospel and the Acts of the Apostles, which are distinguished by their classical Greek, *p.* 132, 178; *fig.* 146, 173 199.

LUPICIN or LUPICINUS (St). Brother of St Romanus, he founded the monastery of Lauconne in the Jura (later called Saint-Lupicin) and succeeded his brother as abbot of Saint-Claude (Jura). Died about 480, *fig.* 289.

LUPUS or LOUP (St). Bishop of Sens (c. 610-623), *p.* 211; *fig.* 221.

LUXEUIL or LUXEUIL-LES-BAINS. Town in eastern France (Haute-Saône), where about 590 St Columban founded an abbey which became an outstanding spiritual centre, *p.* 165; *fig.* 178, 179, 181; *map* 358.

LYONS. City in east-central France (Rhône), at the confluence of the Rhône and the Saône. Part of the Burgundian, then of the Frankish kingdom, *p.* 238; *maps* 354, 356, 358. Church of Saint-Irénée. An inscription discovered in 1946 and soundings have revealed that the chevet of the 'crypt' mentioned by Gregory of Tours was the apse of a pagan funerary basilica of the 2nd or 3rd century, *p.* 32. Church of Saint-Laurent (6th century). Rediscovered during excavations in 1947, along with fifteen epitaphs of the

MONASTERBOICE. Village in Ireland (Co. Louth), 5 miles north-west of Drogheda, *fig.* 92; *map* 358.

MONCEAU-LE-NEUF-ET-FAUCOUZY. Village in northern France (Aisne), 22 km. north of Laon, *p.* 268.

MONKS and MONASTICISM, *p.* 288, 289.

MONOTHELITISM. Heresy of those who held that Christ had but one will. An edict (Ecthesis) published by the Emperor Heraclius in 638 asserted the doctrine of the single will and forbade further debate, *p.* XIV.

MONTE CASSINO. The most famous monastery in Italy (Latium), 140 km. south-east of Rome, founded about 529 by St Benedict, destroyed by the Lombards in 581, rebuilt by Abbot Petronax in 720, then wrecked again by the Saracens in 883, *p.* 202.

MONTESQUIOU-FEZENSAC (Comte Blaise de). Contemporary French archaeologist, *p.* 241.

MONZA. City in North Italy (Lombardy), 15 km. from Milan. It was the capital of the Lombard kingdom and Queen Theodelinde enriched it with churches and treasures, *p.* 222, 231, 245; *fig.* 241, 270; *maps* 356, 358.

MORKEN. Town in West Germany (Rhineland), near Bonn. Site of a rich tomb of a Frankish noble, discovered in 1955; in the dead man's mouth was found a *solidus* of Tiberius II (578-582), *p.* 260.

MORTAIN. Town in north-western France (Manche), 45 km. north of Fougères. Reliquary casket, *p.* 282; *fig.* 313.

MOSAICS, *p.* 5, 12, 27, 32, 77, 97, 105, 222, 260, 275, 312; *fig.* 6, 12, 123-125, 130, 142-144.

MOSELKERN. Town in West Germany (Moselle), on the left bank of the Moselle, 40 km. south-west of Koblenz, *p.* 267.

MOSELLE. Tributary of the Rhine (320 miles long), *p.* 24, 265.

MOUTIER-GRANDVAL (in German, MÜNSTER). Town in north-western Switzerland (canton of Berne), 52 km. south-west of Basel, on the Birs. Abbey founded about 640 by St Germanus of Trier, then a monk sent out from the abbey of Luxeuil. The main church was dedicated to Our Lady. Excavations made in 1872 brought to light the original foundations of the church of St Peter, which contained many graves, *p.* 64.

MÜHLTAL. Town in West Germany (Bavaria), 40 km. south of Munich. Site of a woman's grave discovered in 1920, containing a round plaque representing three winged quadrupeds, *p.* 279.

MUIREDACH. Abbot of Monasterboice (Ireland), died in 924, *fig.* 92.

MUJELEIA (Syria), *fig.* 333A & B.

MUMMA. Name of the donatrix of a reliquary casket to the abbey of Saint-Benoît-sur-Loire, *p.* 281; *fig.* 311.

MUNDOLSHEIM. Village in north-eastern France (Bas-Rhin), 7 km. north of Strasbourg, *p.* 215.

MUNICH. City in West Germany, capital of Bavaria, on the Isar, *p.* 137, 275, 279.

MÜNSTER. City in West Germany (Westphalia), on the Aa, *p.* 312.

MÜNSTER. See MOUTIER - GRAND-VAL.

MÜSTAIR. Village in eastern Switzerland (Grisons), near the Italian frontier. Three-apsed church of St John (Johanneskirche), with wall paintings: some, discovered in 1894, were detached and placed in the Landesmuseum, Zurich, in 1909; the rest, discovered in 1947, have been left *in situ*. Unfortunately these paintings have been over-restored, *p.* 95, 150, 250; *fig.* 164-166; *map* 358.

NAMUR. City in Belgium, on the left bank of the Meuse: the Namurcum Castrum of the Merovingians, *p.* 281, 312.

NANCY. City in north-eastern France (Meurthe-et-Moselle), *p.* 268.

NANTES. City in Brittany, on the lower Loire. Cathedral consecrated about 558; its marble capitals are in the Musée Dobrée, *p.* 32, 40; *fig.* 41, 42, 59, 62, 63, 65; *maps* 354, 356, 358, 359.

NAPLES, *p.* 257; *map* 354.

NARANCO. Palace of King Ramiro I (842-850), about a mile from Oviedo (north-western Spain). Converted into a church between 905 and 1065, called Santa Maria de Naranco, *p.* 91; *fig.* 106-109; *map* 358.

NARBONNE. City in southern France (Aude), one of the oldest cities of Gaul. Taken by the Visigoths in 414. Reliquary of the Holy Sepulchre: carved panel representing the exaltation of the Cross, *p.* 101, 165; *fig.* 17, 118; *maps* 354-356, 358, 359.

NARSES (c. 478-568). General under Justinian, who distinguished himself in putting down the Nika riots (532), then in reconquering Italy. He defeated Totila (552) and Teias (October 1, 552), drove the Franks and Alamanni out of Italy, and exterminated the Ostrogoths. He reorganized Italy as a province of the Byzantine Empire, *p.* XIII.

NESTORIUS (c. 380-451). Monk at Antioch, then patriarch of Constantinople in 428. He taught that the Virgin was not the mother of God but the mother of Christ, and that the two natures of Christ are not united substantially but accidentally. Condemned in 431 by the Council of Ephesus, he was deposed and exiled, *p.* XIV.

NICAEA. City in Bithynia (Asia Minor), on Lake Ascanius (present-day Iznik). The first church council was held here from May 20 to July 25, 325: it condemned Arianism and fixed the date of Easter, *p.* 143; *map* 354.

NICE. See CIMIEZ.

NICETUS (St). Bishop of Trier in 527, died in 566, *p.* 22, 24.

NIEDERDOLLENDORF. Village in West Germany (Rhine Palatinate), 43 km. south of Cologne, on the Rhine, *p.* 265, 267.

NIVELLES. Town in Belgium (Brabant), 31 km. south of Brussels. Excavations carried out in 1961 by Jacques Mertens revealed the complete ground-plans of the three monastery churches of the 7th century, dedicated to St Peter (later to St Gertrude), Our Lady and St Paul, *p.* 31, 64, 67, 289; *fig.* 341; *map* 358.

NOCERA UMBRA. Town in central Italy (Umbria), 20 km. north of Foligno, *p.* 231, 243, 312.

NORCIA. Small town in central Italy (Umbria, province of Perugia), 20 km. south of Spoleto. Birthplace of St Benedict, *p.* 225.

NORMANDY. Ancient province of north-western France (capital, Rouen), *p.* 69.

NORTHUMBRIA. Anglo-Saxon kingdom of northern England (capital, York), *p.* 81.

NOUAILLÉ. Village in west-central France (Vienne), 10 km. south-east of Poitiers. Former abbey founded in the second half of the 7th century. It had two churches, one dedicated to St Hilary (then to St Junian), the other to Our Lady. The first is now the parish church of the village; the second has been privately owned since the Revolution, together with some of the monastic buildings dating to the Middle Ages, *p.* 64.

NOYON. City in northern France (Oise), 25 km. north-east of Compiègne, *p.* 241; *maps* 356, 359.

NUREMBERG. City in West Germany (Bavaria), capital of Franconia, *p.* 222, 313.

ODOACER (c. 434-493). Head of the Roman army, of Germanic origin. Proclaimed king in 476, he deposed the last emperor Romulus Augustulus and became patrician of the Roman Empire. He was killed by Theodoric at Ravenna, *p.* XII.

OPUS INCLUSORIUM. Type of gem-setting used in cloisonné jewellery, *p.* 221.

OPUS RETICULATUM. Masonry whose lozenge-shaped joints form a network or web design, *p.* 67.

ORANT. Figure with upraised hands, in an attitude of prayer, *p.* 74, 265, 278; *fig.* 85, 292.

ORIENTALS (Colonies of), *p.* 250, 288.

ORLÉANS. City in central France (Loiret), *p.* 259; *maps* 355, 356, 359.

OSTIA. Town in central Italy, 23 km. from Rome, a suburbicarian diocese founded in 830 by Pope Gregory IV just east of the ancient Roman town, which had been the seaport of Rome, at the mouth of the Tiber, *p.* 202; *map* 354.

OSTROGOTHS. The East Goths, who founded an empire on the Black Sea in the 4th century. Driven westwards by the Huns, they settled in Italy in the 5th century and founded an empire (493) under Theodoric (capital, Ravenna). Largely wiped out in a series of wars, they were exterminated in 553 by the Byzantine general Narses, near Vesuvius, *p.* XII, XIII, 222, 225, 229, 231, 241, 260, 312; *map* 355.

OVIEDO. City in north-western Spain, capital of the province of the same name. In the present suburb of Santullano, church of San Julian de los Prados (c. 812), *p.* 89, 91; *fig.* 103-105; *maps* 355, 358.

PAINTING (WALL), *p.* 13, 32, 77, 89, 105, 107, 116-124, 250; *fig.* 103-105, 111.

PALATINE (Mount). One of the seven hills of ancient Rome, residence of the emperors, *p.* 105.

PALESTINE, *p.* xv, 312.

PANNONIA. Roman province on the lower Danube, roughly corresponding to present-day Hungary, *p.* 229.

PARENZO. Town in Yugoslavia (now called Porec), on the west side of the Istrian peninsula, at the head of the Adriatic, *p.* 231.

PARIS. Two Merovingian churches: Church of the Apostles, built by King Clovis I between 496 and 511. Church of the Holy Cross and St Vincent (later called Saint-Germain-le-Doré, then Saint-Germain-des-Prés), built by King Childebert I between 542 and 558, *p.* 13, 27, 64, 72, 218, 222, 241, 243, 263, 275, 282; *fig.* 58, 227-229, 232-234, 266, 319; *maps* 354, 356, 358, 359.

PARMA. City in north-central Italy (Emilia), where in 1950 a round fibula of the 7th century was found in a Lombard grave, *p.* 231; *fig.* 255.

PASPELS. Village in eastern Switzerland (Grisons), 3 km. south-east of Rothenbrunnen, *p.* 272.

PATEN. A small dish or plate of precious metal used in the Eucharistic service, *p.* 221, 241, 245, 313; *fig.* 26, 234.

PAUL (St). Apostle of the Gentiles, *p.* 143, 150, 282; *fig.* 159, 160, 217, 312.

PAUL (St). Egyptian recluse, the first hermit to withdraw into the Thebaid (died 342), *p.* 64.

PAUL I (c. 700-767). Pope (757-767), brother and successor of Stephen II. He made an alliance with the Franks against the Lombards and welcomed Greek monks exiled to the West as a result of Iconoclasm, *p.* 116, 124.

PAUL THE DEACON or PAUL WARNEFRIED. Lombard priest, historian and poet (720-799), he left Italy after the fall of the Lombard kingdom and settled at the court of Charlemagne at Aachen, *p.* 155, 202.

PELAGIUS II (520-590). Roman of Gothic origin, pope (579-590). He opposed the schism of Aquileia and rebuilt the church of San Lorenzo fuori le Mura, *p.* 115.

PEMMO. Duke of Friuli (died c. 737), *p.* 248, 250.

PENTATEUCH. First five books of the Old Testament (Genesis, Exodus, Leviticus, Numbers, Deuteronomy). Tours or Ashburnham Pentateuch, *p.* 128; *fig.* 141.

PEPIN OF AQUITAINE (803-838). Second son of Louis the Debonair and king of Aquitaine (817-838), *p.* 285; *fig.* 314.

PEPIN THE SHORT (c. 715-768). Younger son of Charles Martel, mayor of the palace (741-751) and king of the Franks (751-768). To Pope Stephen II he gave the Exarchate of Ravenna, *p.* XIII, 202.

PERSIANS. The name applies in this book to the Persians of the Sassanid dynasty (A.D. 226-651), *p.* XIII, 159, 195, 200, 215, 311.

PERUGIA. City in central Italy (Umbria), 165 km. south-east of Florence, *p.* 275.

PETER (St). The first of the Apostles (died 64), *p.* 143, 150, 282; *fig.* 159, 161, 216, 290, 312.

PFULLINGEN. Town in West Germany (Württemberg), 40 km. south of Stuttgart, where in 1840 a round gold fibula was found in an Alamannic cemetery, *p.* 238, 243.

PHALERA. A metal boss or disk worn on the head or breast of a horse, *p.* 211, 275; *fig.* 218.

PIETROASA. Locality in Rumania (province of Buzow), 100 km. north-east of Bucharest, where in 1837-1838 a barbarian treasure hoard was found, *p.* 218; *fig.* 224.

PIPPIN. See PEPIN.

PLANIG. Town in West Germany (Rhine Palatinate), some 25 km. west of Mainz. The 6th century grave of a rich barbarian noble was found here in 1939, *p.* 218, 260.

PLATO (8th century). Father of Pope John VII. Of Greek origin, he was curator of the Roman palace where the exarch's lieutenant resided, *p.* 116.

PLIEZHAUSEN. Town in West Germany (Württemberg), south of Stuttgart, where a 7th-century fibula representing a horseman with his lance was found in a grave, *p.* 272, 273, 280.

PLINY THE YOUNGER (Caius Plinius Caecilius Secundus). Latin author (A.D. 62-c. 114), nephew of Pliny the Elder, *p.* 165.

PLOTINUS. Neo-Platonic philosopher (A.D. c. 205-c. 269), who taught with success in Rome. He retained only the three hypostases (soul, intelligence and unity) of Plato and syncretized the mysticism of his period, *p.* XIV.

relics are in the church of Saint-Sernin, Toulouse, *p.* 24.

SAULIEU. Small town in eastern France (Côte-d'Or), 38 km. south-east of Avallon. 8th-century abbey, *p.* 265; *fig.* 288.

SAVOY (SAVOIE). Historical region of south-eastern France, inhabited by the Allobroges before the Roman conquest. Occupied by the Burgundians in 443, then by the Franks in 534. In 888 it became part of the kingdom of Burgundy, *p.* 22.

SAXONS. A Germanic people dwelling between the Elbe and the Sieg, active as sea raiders in the 3rd and 4th centuries. In the 5th, they conquered the eastern third of Great Britain. Charlemagne undertook to subdue and Christianize them (772-804), *p.* XIII; *maps* 355, 356.

SCHRETZHEIM. Town in West Germany (Bavaria), 50 km. east of Ulm. Site of a vast Merovingian cemetery, *p.* 234.

SCRAMASAX. Short sword used by the German tribes, with a single cutting edge and a fluted blade, *p.* 218.

SEDULIUS (Caius Caelius). Latin priest and poet (5th century), author of the *Carmen Paschale*, *p.* 182.

SEINE. River in northern France, flowing into the English Channel (480 miles long), *p.* 34, 35, 68, 69, 218, 312.

SELLES-SUR-CHER. Town in north-central France (Loir-et-Cher), on the river Cher, 40 km. west of Vierzon. Marble capitals and columns of the basilica founded before 558 by Childebert I, over the tomb of the hermit St Eusicius, *p.* 29, 35; *fig.* 33-37; *map* 358.

SENS. City in north-central France (Yonne), *p.* 211, 245; *fig.* 221; *maps* 356, 359.

SEPTIMANIA. Part of the province of Narbonnensis I held by the Visigoths after the battle of Vouillé (507). It owed its name to the seven bishoprics comprised in the diocese of Narbonne: Béziers, Maguelonne, Elne, Nîmes, Agde, Lodève, Carcassonne, *p.* 92.

SHRINES, *p.* 60, 282; *fig.* 74, 311-313.

SICILY, *p.* 257.

SIGISMUND (St). Son and successor of Gondebaud and king of the Burgundians (516-523). Defeated by the sons of Clovis, he was killed by Clodomir (524), *p.* 218.

SIGUALDUS. Patriarch of Aquileia (762-776), *p.* 248, 271.

SILCHESTER. Small town in southern England (Hampshire), about 6 miles from Basingstoke. The ancient Roman town of Calleva Atrebatum, *fig.* 344; *map* 358.

SIMOCATTA (Theophylactes). Byzantine author of the 7th century, born in Egypt. Prefect and imperial secretary at Constantinople. He wrote the *History of the Emperor Mauricius (582-602)*, an important source of information about the Persians and the Slavs, *p.* 231.

SIMURGH. In Persian mythology, a gigantic mythical bird which acted as a tutelary genius, *p.* 195.

SION (SITTEN). City in south-central Switzerland (canton of Valais), the Sedunum of the Romans. Seat of a bishop, *p.* 285; *fig.* 315; *map* 358.

SIXTUS III (St). Pope (432-440). He restored many churches in Rome, *p.* 107.

SOEST. City in West Germany (Westphalia). Site of a large Merovingian cemetery, *p.* 234, 312; *map* 358.

SOISSONS. City in northern France (Aisne), in Roman times part of Belgica II. In the 5th century, capital of a kingdom taken over by Clovis after the defeat of Syagrius (486), *p.* 311; *fig.* 39, 40; *maps* 356, 359.

SOLIDUS. Gold coin of the Late Empire, first issued in 325 by Constantine the Great, *p.* 238; *fig.* 239, 263.

SOLNHOFEN. Small town in West Germany (Bavaria), *p.* 250.

SOLOGNE. Region south of the Parisian basin, lying between the Cher and the Loire, *p.* 69.

SPAIN. Roman province in 27 B.C. From the 5th to the 7th century, kingdom of the Visigoths. From 711, under Moorish domination, except for the Asturias, Leon and the Pyrenees, *p.* XII, 13, 20, 27, 33, 47, 71, 84, 91, 92, 95, 113, 225, 287, 311.

SPATHA. Longsword of the Germans. The hilt and sheath were often richly adorned with gold and almandines or silver demascening, *p.* 218. Example: *fig.* 231.

SPOLETO. City in central Italy (Umbria). Capital of a semi-independent Lombard duchy, whose status was changed by Charlemagne when he conquered

the Lombard state. Basilica of San Salvatore (or San Crocifisso), attributed to the 5th century and remarkable for a beautifully designed façade, *p.* XIII, 39, 250; *maps* 354, 358.

STABIO. Town in Italian Switzerland (canton of Ticino). One mile north of Stabio is San Pietro, *p.* 273, 275, 311; *map* 358.

STEPHEN (St). One of the seven deacons and the first Christian martyr. Condemned by the Sanhedrin for blasphemy and stoned at the gates of Jerusalem (some time between A.D. 31 and 36), *p.* 150.

STEPHEN II. Pope (752-757) who crowned Pepin the Short in 754 at Saint-Denis, *p.* XIII, 202.

STILICHO (Flavius). Roman general of Vandal origin (c. 360-408). He served under Theodosius and Honorius, and defeated Alaric. Lost his commanding position and his life as a result of court intrigues, *p.* XII.

STRASBOURG. City in north-eastern France (Bas-Rhin), on the Rhine. Taken by the Alamanni, then recovered by the Romans. One of the four cities of Germania Superior, *p.* 271, 289; *map* 359.

STRONGHOLDS. See FORTIFIED TOWNS.

STRZYGOWSKI (Josef). Austrian archaeologist and art historian (1862-1941), *p.* 250.

STUCCO. A fine plaster made of lime or gypsum with sand and pounded marble, used for internal decoration. Ancient stuccoes are often as hard as stone. Stuccowork of Saint-Victor, Marseilles, and Saint-Laurent, Grenoble, *p.* 12, 100, 113, 200, 250; *fig.* 13, 112, 273-276.

STUTTGART. City in West Germany (Baden-Württemberg), *p.* 206, 272, 312; *fig.* 212, 213.

SUEVI. A Germanic people who crossed the Rhine in 406-407 and penetrated into Spain in 409. In 411 they occupied the southern part of Galicia, then the northern part, founding a state around Braga (now in north-western Portugal), *p.* XII; *map* 355.

SUTTON HOO. Locality near Woodbridge in eastern England (Suffolk), where in 1939 the tomb of a Saxon prince was found, including a ship fully equipped for the voyage to the Other World, but without the prince's body. The tomb contained a rich burial treasure, including a large silver plate bearing the stamp of Anastasius I (491-518) and Merovingian coins dated 650-670, *p.* 159, 234, 271, 272, 280; *map* 358.

SWITZERLAND, *p.* 34, 97, 99, 101, 250.

SWORDS, *p.* 215, 218, 265, 280. Examples: *fig.* 225, 227, 231, 310.

SYAGRIUS (St) [c. 520-600]. Bishop of Autun about 561, died in 600. Often mentioned in the writings of his contemporaries Gregory of Tours, Fortunatus and Gregory the Great, *p.* 27.

SYAGRIUS (c. 430-486). Gallo-Roman chieftain who ruled the territory left to the Romans in Gaul (464-486), *map* 355.

SYRIA, *p.* 3, 33, 250, 259, 260, 287, 312.

SYRO-EGYPTIAN ART, *p.* 3, 35.

TÄBINGEN. Small town in West Germany (Baden-Württemberg), about 105 km. south-west of Stuttgart. Alamannic cemetery, *p.* 238, 312.

TARRAGONA. City in north-eastern Spain (Catalonia), *map* 358.
Church of San Fructuoso del Francoli, *fig.* 329.

TERRACOTTA RELIEFS. Used as wall decorations, *p.* 48; *fig.* 55-60, 63, 65, 101.

TEUDERIGUS or TEUDERICUS. Priest at the abbey of Saint-Maurice (Valais, Switzerland), who in the 7th century had a gold reliquary casket made, *p.* 243; *fig.* 268.

TEXTILES, *p.* 3, 178, 188, 231, 257, 259, 260, 275, 288, 312; *fig.* 269.

THEODECHILDE or THELCHILDE (St). First abbess of Jouarre (7th century), *p.* 64, 71, 289; *fig.* 77, 82, 83.

THEODELINDA. Lombard queen (died 625), daughter of a Bavarian duke. Her second husband was Agilulf, king of the Lombards (591-616). Under Theodelinda's influence, the king and his people abjured Arianism and were converted to Roman Catholicism. In 603 Pope Gregory the Great sent her precious gifts (together with a letter, still extant) for the baptism of her son, out of gratitude for her successful efforts to reconcile the Lombards with the pope. This 'treasure of Theodelinda' is still in part preserved in Monza cathedral, *p.* 222, 231, 245; *fig.* 241, 270.

THEODORE. Archbishop of Ravenna (late 7th century), *p.* 247, 311.

THEODORE OF TARSUS or OF CANTERBURY (St). Missionary (602-690), born at Tarsus, who became archbishop of Canterbury in 668. He reformed the Anglo-Saxon clergy and founded many monasteries, *p.* 157.

THEODORIC I or THIERRY I. Eldest son of Clovis I and king of Austrasia (511-534), *p.* 22.

THEODORIC THE GREAT (c. 454-526). King of the Ostrogoths. In 488 he descended into Italy, sent by the Byzantine Emperor Zeno to drive out Odoacer, whom he had assassinated in 493. He then organized a state with Ravenna as its capital. His so-called 'cuirass' found in 1854 is probably part of a saddle or harness, *p.* XIII, 107, 136, 222; *fig.* 238; *map* 355.

THEODOSIUS I THE GREAT (c. 347-395). Roman Emperor from 379 with Gratian, then alone from 393. In 382 he gave the Goths the status of *foederati* or allies of the Romans, *p.* XII, XIV, 209, 247; *fig.* 158.

THEODOTA. A girl of noble family, wooed by the Lombard king Cunipertus. She withdrew to the convent of Santa Maria at Pavia, of which she became abbess (died 720) and which later took her name, *p.* 71; *fig.* 119A & B.

THEODULF (c. 750-821). Bishop of Orléans from about 781 and abbot of Saint-Benoît-sur-Loire. About 800-806 he built the *villa* and oratory of Germigny, now Germigny-des-Prés. Theologian, poet and hymn-writer, *p.* 92, 95.

THEOPHYLACTOS (c. 1050-c. 1107). Disciple of Michael Psellos and archbishop of Ochrida, then the capital of Bulgaria. A skilled exegete, he wrote the *Education of Rulers* for Constantine, son of Michael VII, who had been his pupil, *p.* 195.

TIBERIUS II. Byzantine Emperor (578-582), *p.* 24.

TICINO. Italian-speaking canton of Switzerland, on the south side of the Alps, *p.* 273, 311; *map* 355.

TIERRA DE BARROS. Locality in southwestern Spain, 40 km. south of Badajoz, *p.* 225.

TIMBER CONSTRUCTIONS. Something is known of the wooden buildings of the Late Empire and the early Middle Ages from writings of the period, from occasional representations of them, and from excavations which have revealed the forms of posts driven into the ground.

TOESCA (Pietro). Italian art historian (1877-1962), *p.* 245.

TOKOR (Armenia). Church, *p.* 33.

TOLEDO. City in central Spain, on the Tagus, 70 km. south of Madrid, *p.* 231, 257; *maps* 354, 356, 358.

TONGRES. City in Belgium (Limburg), *p.* 265.

TOREUTICS. The art of metalworking (embossing, chasing, etc.), *p.* 211, 245.

TORSLUNDA. Town in Sweden (Öland), on the Strait of Kalmar, where in a grave various objects were found representing masked warriors executing a ritual battle dance (7th century), *p.* 280.

TOTILA. King of the Ostrogoths of Italy (541-552). He resumed the offensive against the Byzantines, pushing as far as Naples (543). Occupied Rome in 546 and 549. Conquered all Italy, Corsica, Sardinia and Sicily (550). Defeated by Narses in 552 and died in flight, *p.* XIII.

TOULOUSE. City in south-western France (Haute-Garonne). In the 4th century, one of the six cities of Narbonnensis I. Capital of the kingdom of the Visigoths (419) until taken by Clovis (508). Church of Saint-Sernin (St Saturninus, apostle of Toulouse), *p.* 22, 24, 35, 48, 211, 225, 257; *fig.* 27-29, 326; *maps* 354-356, 358-360.

TOURNAI. City in south-west Belgium, on the Scheldt. Tomb of the Frankish king Childeric I (457-481), discovered in the cloister of Saint-Brice in 1653. The treasure found in it was presented to Louis XIV in 1665 and later deposited in the Bibliothèque Royale, Paris, whence it was stolen in 1831: only a few pieces were found in the Seine and recovered. This treasure was one of the most significant discoveries ever made bearing on the art and culture of the Merovingian Franks, *p.* 218; *maps* 354, 358.

TOURS. City in west-central France (Indre-et-Loire), on the Loire. In the 4th century, the leading town of Lugdunensis III. Taken by the Visigoths (473), then by Clovis (507). Its third bishop was St Martin, over whose tomb the basilica of Saint-Martin was built (consecrated in 472). Monastic scriptoria produced many illuminated manuscripts (School of Tours), *p.* 27 32, 128, 289; *maps* 354, 356, 359.

TRADITIO LEGIS. Scene representing St Peter receiving from Christ the scroll of the new Law, *p.* 115.

TRANSPORT. Long-distance transport of capitals, sarcophagi and closure slabs, *p.* 35, 68, 69, 288.

TREBUR. Village in West Germany (Hesse), 18 km. north-west of Darmstadt, *p.* 312.

TREE OF LIFE. Tree whose fruit conferred immortality. Ancient symbol taken over in Christian art (symbol of the might and Resurrection of Christ), *p.* 211, 279.

TRESSAN. Village in south-western France (Hérault), 30 km. west of Montpellier. Site of a cemetery, discovered in 1868, which yielded objects of the 6th century, *p.* 218; *fig.* 232; *map* 358.

TRIANGLE (Equilateral). Pattern used in working out the proportions of capitals, *p.* 31; *fig.* 36, 37.

TRIER (TREVES). City in West Germany (Rhine Palatinate). In the 3rd century, capital of the 'Gallo-Roman Empire' (258-273), *p.* 1, 3, 15, 22, 238, 260, 265, 268; *maps* 354, 355, 358.

TRIUMPHAL ARCH. In Latin basilicas, the great arch leading into the choir or sanctuary (chancel arch), *p.* 11, 99, 107, 116, 183, 311; *fig.* 13, 112, 123, 124, 125.

TROYES. City in north-eastern France (Aube), on the Seine. Its most famous bishop was St Lupus (Loup). Over his tomb the famous abbey of Saint-Loup was erected in the 5th century, *p.* 215, 279; *fig.* 309; *map* 359.

TUNISIA, *fig.* 55, 57.

TURIN. City in north-western Italy (Piedmont), on the upper Po, *p.* 231.

UNCIALS. A majuscule script derived from Roman capitals, *p.* 165, 188, 195, 199, 202.

UNDIHO. A 7th-century goldsmith, probably Swabian, one of the two makers of the reliquary casket of Teuderigus at Saint-Maurice, *p.* 243.

UNIVERSALS (Quarrel over). A controversy among the Schoolmen over the origin and nature of general ideas, *p.* XIV.

UNTERSIEBENBRUNN. Town in Austria, near Vienna, where in 1910 the grave of a Germanic princess was found, *p.* 215.

USSERIANUS (Codex). Manuscript belonging to James Usher (1580-1626), archbishop of Armagh. He left many exegetical writings, *fig.* 183.

UTRECHT. City in the central Netherlands, south of the Zuyderzee. Utrecht Psalter (c. 820), *fig.* 38.

VAL DI NIEVOLE. Valley in Tuscany (province of Pistoia), near Lucca, *p.* 247; *fig.* 271.

VALENS (Flavius). Roman Emperor of the East (364-378), *fig.* 226.

VALENTINIAN I. Roman Emperor of the West (364-375). Drove the Alamanni from Gaul, consolidated the Rhine frontier, and put an end to Saxon raids in Roman Britain, *p.* XII.

VALERIANUS. Copyist of the Bible in the 7th century, *p.* 137, 165; *fig.* 150, 151.

VALPOLICELLA. Village in North Italy (Verona), famous for its marble quarries, *p.* 312.

VANDALS. A Germanic people driven westwards by the Hunnish invasion, they overran Gaul and reached Spain in 409. In 429 they moved into North Africa, establishing an empire from Carthage to Constantine which was overthrown in 534 by Belisarius, *p.* XII; *map* 355.

VATICAN CITY, *p.* 222, 231, 275.

VENASQUE. Town in south-eastern France (Vaucluse), 13 km. from Carpentras, *p.* 39.

VERCELLI. City in North Italy (Piedmont): a Roman municipium, then a Lombard duchy, then a Frankish county. In the Chapter Library, several illuminated manuscripts, *p.* 139, 143, 188; *fig.* 156-163; *map* 358.

VERMAND. Small town in northern France (Aisne), 12 km. south of Saint-Quentin. Frankish cemetery discovered in the 19th century, *p.* 260.

VERONA. City in North Italy (Venetia), on the Adige. A Roman colony, an important city under the Empire, and a capital under Theodoric and under Charlemagne's successors, *p.* 128, 139, 143, 275; *fig.* 154, 155; *maps* 354, 358.

VERTOU. Village in western France (Loire-Atlantique), 9 km. south-east of Nantes. Abbey, *p.* 40; *fig.* 43, 44, 56, 60, 61, 64; *map* 358.

VEUREY-VOROIZE. Village in south-eastern France (Isère), 20 km. north-west of Grenoble. Ancient cemetery in the nearby hamlet of Saint-Ours, where excavations made in 1856 brought to light some 30 graves of the early Middle Ages, *p.* 33.

VEXILLUM. Flag or standard, *p.* 195.

VICENZA. City in North Italy, *map* 358. Basilica of Sts Felix and Fortunatus, *fig.* 330.

VICTOR (St). Martyred at Marseilles, *p.* 11.

VIENNA. Austria, *p.* 202; *fig.* 223; *map* 354.

VIENNE. City in south-eastern France (Isère), on the Rhone. In the 4th century, capital of the Viennensis. Taken in 463 by the Burgundians, who made it their second capital after Chalon. Church of Saints-Apôtres, founded in the 5th century (later called Saint-Pierre and now serving as the Archaeological Museum), *p.* 27, 32; *fig.* 30, 31, 317, 328; *maps* 354, 356, 358-359.

VILLA, *p.* 13, 22, 33.

VINCENT (St). Deacon and martyr (died 304). Born at Huesca, educated at Saragossa, he was taken to Valencia with his bishop Valerius and martyred. His relics were at one time in Saint-Germain-des-Prés, Paris, *p.* 27.

VINESHOOTS. Symbol of Christ the Saviour (after John xv, 1), *p.* 12, 247, 250, 311; *fig.* 276.

VIRGIL (Publius Vergilius Maro). Latin poet (c. 70-19 B.C.), *p.* 112, 113, 178; *fig.* 126, 127.

VISIGOTHS. A Germanic people from Scandinavia who migrated to the region of the Black Sea. Driven westwards by the invasion of the Huns (375), they sought refuge within the Roman Empire. Under Alaric they devastated Greece. In 401 Alaric led them into Italy. In 413 they overran the Narbonnensis and (temporarily)Aquitaine. They settled in Spain, where they founded a Visigothic kingdom which lasted till the Moorish invasion (711), *p.* XII, 20, 22, 24, 27, 225, 241, 257, 278, 279, 311; *fig.* 185; *maps* 355, 356.

VITRUVIUS (Marcus Vitruvius Pollio). Roman architect and engineer (first century B.C.), author of the *De Architectura* in ten books, *p.* 31.

WALL PAINTING. See PAINTING.

WALLS (CITY). The defensive walls of the Late Empire, curving or rectilinear, crenellated and flanked with towers, girded only those parts of the old open city which were best suited for defence, *p.* 12, 13.

WARNEBERTUS. Bishop of Soissons (674-676), whose reliquary casket is identified with the one at Beromünster (Switzerland), *p.* 311.

WENDEL. Small town in Sweden (Uppland), 120 km. north of Uppsala. Excavations made in the late 19th century brought to light the tombs of 14 Nordic chieftains in full dress, with their wives, horses, weapons and domestic animals, *p.* 271.

WERDEN. City in West Germany, part of Essen since 1929, *p.* 267; *map* 358.

WESTPHALIA. Province of West Germany which, with the North Rhineland, forms one of the Länder, *p.* 234, 285.

WIDUKIND. Saxon chief who rebelled against Charlemagne in 778. Subdued in 785, he was baptized at Attigny, *fig.* 316.

WIESBADEN. City in West Germany (Hesse), *p.* 268.

WIESOPPENHEIM. Town in West Germany (Rhine Palatinate), 24 km. from Worms, on the Rhine, *p.* 260.

WIGERIG. Rhenish goldsmith of the 7th century, *p.* 238.

WILLIBRORD (St) (658-739). Born in Northumberland, he studied in Ireland. Sent to Rome, then to Frisia as a missionary (690). He established his seat at Utrecht, then founded the abbey of Echternach (698) where he died, *p.* 160.

WITTISLINGEN. Small town in West Germany (Bavaria), some 50 km. east of Ulm. Tomb of an Alamannic princess, discovered in 1881, whose grave goods are the finest ever brought to light, *p.* 238; *map* 358.

WOLFSHEIM. Town in West Germany (Rhine Palatinate), 15 km. north-west of Worms, where the richly furnished tomb of a warrior was found in 1870, *p.* 215, 218; *map* 358.

WOODEN BUILDINGS. See TIMBER CONSTRUCTIONS.

WOODEN HUTS. Dwellings of the hermits and the early cenobites, as at Condat (later Saint-Claude) in the French Jura, *p.* 289.

WORMS. City in West Germany (Rhine Palatinate), on the Rhine, *p.* 260, 313.

WULFF (Oskar). German art historian (1864-1946), *p.* 245.

WÜRZBURG. City in West Germany (Bavaria), on the Main, *p.* 312.

YVERDON. Town in French Switzerland (canton of Vaud), on the Lake of Neuchâtel. In the museum, two bronze buckles (7th century) representing Daniel, in a very barbarian style, *p.* 278.

ZACHARIAS (St). Pope (741-752). Of Greek origin, he formed an alliance with Pepin the Short against the Lombards and sent out St Boniface to evangelize Germany, *p.* 122, 123.

After the death of Jean PORCHER, the documentation concerning his chapter was completed by Dominique BOZO.

Maps

MODERN NAMES	ANCIENT NAMES			MODERN NAMES	ANCIENT NAMES	
Actium	*Actium*	G 5		Nantes	*Namnetes*	B 3
Adrianople	*Hadrianopolis*	H 4		Naples	*Neapolis*	E 4
Agrigento	*Akragas* or *Agrigentum*	E 5		Narbonne	*Narbo Martius*	C 4
Aix	*Aquae Sextae*	D 4		Narona	*Narona*	F 4
Albenga	*Albingaunum*	D 4		Nicaea	*Nicaea*	H 4
Aleria	*Aleria*	D 4		Nicomedia or Izmit	*Nicomedia*	H 4
Ancona	*Ancona*	E 4		Nikopolis	*Nicopolis*	G 5
Aquileia	*Aquileia*	E 3		Nîmes	*Nemausus*	C 4
Arcar	*Ratiaria*	G 4		Numantia	*Numantia*	B 4
Argos	*Argos*	G 5		Orléansville	*Castellum Tingitanum*	C 5
Arles	*Arelate*	C 4		Ostia	*Ostium* or *Ostia*	E 4
Athens	*Athenae*	G 5		Palermo	*Panormus*	E 5
Autun	*Augustodunum*	C 3		Paris	*Parisii*	C 3
Barcelona	*Barcino*	C 4		Pergamum	*Pergamon*	H 5
Basel	*Basilea*	D 3		Périgueux	*Vesunna* or *Petrocorii*	C 3
Benevento	*Beneventum*	E 4		Pharsala	*Pharsalus*	G 5
Bergamo	*Bergomum*	D 3		Pisa	*Pisae*	E 4
Bordeaux	*Burdigala*	B 4		Poitiers	*Pictavi*	C 3
Bourges	*Bituriges*	C 3		Ravenna	*Ravenna*	E 4
Braga	*Bracara Augusta*	A 4		Reggio	*Rhegium*	E 4
Brindisi	*Brundisium*	F 4		Rome	*Roma*	E 4
Cadiz	*Gades*	A 5		Rouen	*Rotomagus*	C 3
Cagliari	*Calaris* or *Caralis*	D 5		Saintes	*Santones*	B 3
Carthage	*Carthago*	E 5		Salonica	*Thessalonica*	G 4
Carthagena	*Nova Carthago*	B 5		Sardis	*Sardes*	H 5
Cologne	*Colonia Agrippina*	D 2		Sétif	*Sitifis*	D 5
Constantine	*Cirta* or *Constantina*	D 5		Seville	*Hispalis*	A 5
Constantinople	*Constantinopolis* or *Nova Roma*	H 4		Solin	*Salona*	F 4
Constanza or Costanza	*Tomi*	H 4		Smyrna	*Smyrna*	H 5
Cordova	*Corduba*	B 5		Split	*Spalato*	F 4
Corinth	*Corinthus* or *Korinthia*	G 5		Spoleto	*Spoletium*	E 4
Crotona	*Croton*	F 5		Stobi	*Stobi*	G 4
Djemila or Jemila	*Cuicul*	D 5		Sremska Mitrovica	*Sirmium*	F 4
Dover	*Dubris*	C 2		Syracuse	*Syracusae*	F 5
Ephesus	*Ephesus*	H 5		Tabarka	*Thabraca*	D 5
Epidaurus	*Epidaurus*	G 5		Tangier	*Tingis*	A 5
Florence	*Florentia*	E 4		Tarento	*Tarentum*	F 4
Fréjus	*Forum Iulii*	D 4		Tarrasa	*Egara*	C 4
Geneva	*Genava*	D 3		Timgad	*Thamugadi*	D 5
Genoa	*Genua*	D 4		Tipasa	*Tipasa*	C 5
Hippo	*Hippo Regius*	D 5		Toledo	*Toletum*	B 5
Lauriacum	*Lauriacum*	E 3		Toulouse	*Tolosa*	C 4
London	*Londinium*	B 2		Tournai	*Turnacum*	C 2
Lyons	*Lugdunum*	C 3		Tours	*Turones*	C 3
Mainz	*Moguntiacum*	D 2		Tralles	*Tralli* or *Tralles*	H 5
Malaga	*Malaca*	B 5		Trier	*Treveri*	D 3
Mantua	*Mantua*	E 3		Valencia	*Valentia Edetanorum*	B 5
Marseilles	*Massilia*	D 4		Varna	*Odessos* or *Odessus*	H 4
Merida	*Emerita*	A 5		Verona	*Verona*	E 3
Messina	*Messana*	F 5		Vienne (Gaul)	*Vienna*	C 3
Metz	*Mettis*	D 3		Vienna (Illyria)	*Vindobona*	F 3
Milan	*Mediolanum*	D 3		Virunum	*Virunum*	E 3
Miletus	*Miletus*	H 5		York	*Eboracum*	B 2
				Zadar or Zara	*Jadera*	F 4

356 - GAUL AND NEIGHBOURING LANDS IN THE TIME OF DAGOBERT (629-639). AFTER J. HUBERT.

30°　　　　35°　　　　40°　　　　45°　　　　50°　　　　55°

Volkhov　　　*Volga*

0   100   200   300 kilometres
0   100   200   300 miles

Dniepr

50°

Beresina

Oural

Pripet

Desna   *Seim*   *Don*   *Volga*

HUNS (375)

ALANS (c. 400)

Bug   HUNS (375)   **A L A N S**   CASPIAN   45°

O S T R O G O T H S
(200-375)   *HUNS*   SEA

Prut   **HERULI**

Siret   (270-316)

OTHS

Danube

B L A C K   S E A   40°

(378)

Byzantium •

Simav

Tigris

Gediz   35°

Menderes

B Y Z A N T I N E   E M P I R E   *Euphrates*

45°

Rhodes   30°   35°   40°

CYPRUS

■ ARCHITECTURE □ MANUSCRIPTS ★ ORNAMENTS

Aachen	□ E 2		Guarrazar	★ C 5		Reculver	■ D 2
Albenga	■ E 4		Güttingen	★ E 3		Reichenau	□ E 3
Albon	■ D 3		Iona	□ B 1		Riez	■ E 4
Amiens	□ D 3		Ittenheim	★ E 3		Romainmôtier	■ E 3
Angers	■ C 3		Ivrea	□ E 3		Rome	□★ F 4
Antigny	■ D 3		Jarrow	□ C 2		Roscrea	□ B 2
Arles	■★ D 4		Jedburgh	■ C 1		Ruthwell	■ C 1
Augsburg	□ F 3		Jouarre	■ D 3		Saint-Ambroix	■ D 3
Auxerre	■ D 3		Kairouan	■ F 5		Saint-Benoît-sur-Loire	★ D 3
Benevento	□ F 4		Kells	□ B 2		Saint-Bertrand-de-Comminges	■ D 4
Besançon	□ E 3		Kildrenagh	■ A 2		Saint-Blaise	■ D 4
Bewcastle	■ C 1		Krefeld	★ E 2		Saint-Denis	■★ D 3
Bobbio	□ E 4		Langeais	■ D 3		Saint Gall	□ E 3
Brescia	□ F 3		Laon	□ D 3		Saint-Maurice	★ E 3
Bülach	★ E 3		Lavoye	★ D 3		Saint-Maximin	■ E 4
Canterbury	□ D 2		Limons	★ D 3		Saint-Riquier	□ D 2
Casa Herrera	■ B 5		Lindisfarne	□ C 1		S. Fructuoso del Francoli	■ D 4
Castelseprio	■□ E 3		Lingotto	★ E 3		S. Pedro de la Nave	■ B 4
Castel Trosino	★ F 4		Lucca	□ F 4		Sankt Paul im Lavanttal	□ F 3
Charenton-du-Cher	■ D 3		Luxeuil	□ E 3		S. Maria de Naranco	■ B 4
Chelles	★ D 3		Lyons	■ D 3		Selles-sur-Cher	■ D 3
Cimiez	■ E 4		Mainz	★ E 2		Silchester	■ C 2
Cividale	□ F 3		Malles (Mals)	□ F 3		Sion	★ E 3
Cologne	★ E 2		Manglieu	■ D 3		Soest	★ E 2
Como	■ E 3		Marseilles	■ E 4		Spoleto	□ F 4
Conques	★ D 4		Mazerolles	■ D 3		Stabio	★ E 3
Corbie	□ D 3		Meaux	□ D 3		Sutton Hoo	□★ D 2
Delémont	★ E 3		Metz	★ E 3		Toledo	★ C 5
Desana	★ E 3		Milan	■□ E 3		Toulouse	■★ D 4
Durham	□ C 2		Molsheim	★ E 3		Tournai	★ D 2
Durrow	□ B 2		Monasterboice	■ B 2		Tressan	★ D 4
Easby	■ C 2		Monza	★ E 3		Trier	★ E 3
Echternach	□ E 3		Müstair	□ F 3		Tunis	■ F 5
Enger	★ E 2		Nantes	■ C 3		Vercelli	□ E 3
Feaghmaan	■ A 2		Narbonne	■ D 4		Verona	□ F 3
Flavigny	□ D 3		Nivelles	■ D 2		Vertou	■ C 3
Freising	□ F 3		Nonantula	□ F 4		Vicenza	■ F 3
Fréjus	■ E 4		Oviedo	■ B 4		Vienne	■ D 3
Fulda	□ E 2		Paris	■ D 3		Werden	★ E 2
Gellone	□ D 4		Pavia	■★ E 3		Wittislingen	★ F 3
Gémigny	■ D 3		Poitiers	■ D 3		Wolfsheim	★ E 3
Geneva	■ E 3		Quintanilla de las Viñas	■ C 4		York	□ C 2
Gourdon	★ D 4		Ravenna	□ F 4			
Grenoble	■ E 3						

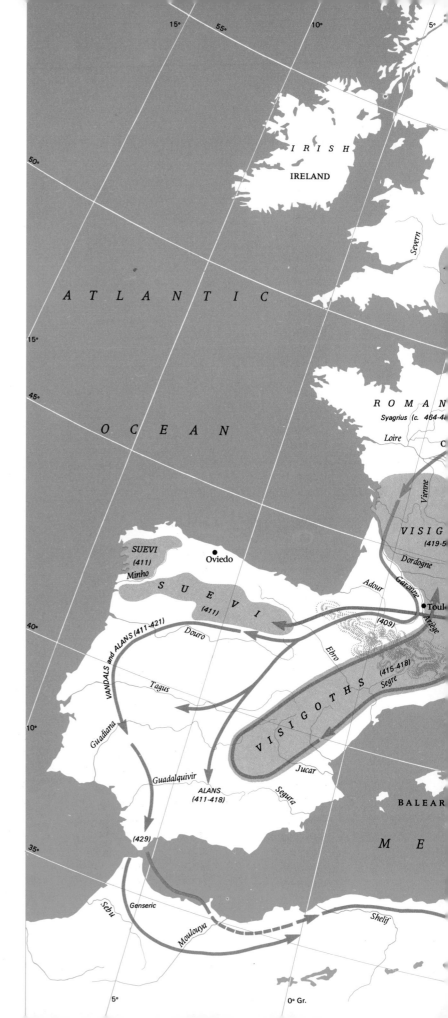

I R I S H

IRELAND

Severn

A T L A N T I C

O C E A N

R O M A N

Syagrius (c. 464-4...

Loire

Vienne

VISIG
(419-5...

Dordogne

Adour *Garonne*

● Toul...

Ariège

SUEVI
(411)
Minho

● Oviedo

S U E V I
(411)

(409)

Ebro

VANDALS and ALANS (411-421)

Douro

VISIGOTHS (415-418)

Segre

Tagus

V I S I G O T H S

Guadiana

Jucar

Guadalquivir

ALANS
(411-418)

Segura

BALEAR...

M E

(429)

Sebu *Genseric*

Shelif

Moulouya

Dark colours: start of migrations.
Light colours: temporary occupations.
Arrows and dates: paths of migrations.

GOTHS-GEPIDS
VISIGOTHS-OSTROGOTHS

HUNS

ALANS-VANDALS

BURGUNDIANS

SUEVI

ANGLES-SAXONS

355 - THE MIGRATIONS FROM THE THIRD TO THE
FIFTH CENTURY. AFTER W.F. VOLBACH. ▶

NORTH SEA

GOTHS

ANGLES HERULI

Œsel

Gotland

BALTIC

Öland

SEA

Bornholm

Dvina

Niemen

GOTHS
(150)

GEPIDS
(250)

Narev

Vistula

Bug

(550)

(450)

SAXONS

Elbe

Aller

Ems

BURGUNDIANS
(150-250)

Warta

Styr

ANGLO-SAXONS

Thames

(450)

Trent

SUEVI
(c. 170)

Oder

VANDALS
(c. 400)

Oder

Vistula

Dniestr

FRANKS

(408-409)

Scheldt

Rhine

Weser

Saale

Somme

Oise

Meuse

S
6)

Mainz
(407)

VANDALS

Main

Eger

Trier
(430)

Moselle

(451)

(436)

BURGUNDIANS
(260)

Neckar

Vltava

SUEVI
(200-403)

VANDALS

Tisza

Loir

léans

(451)

Seine

Meuse

Danube

(413-436)

(407)

Saône

Rhine

SUEVI

Lake of Constance

Inn

Raba

Drave

HUNS

Attila
(434-453)

GEPIDS

Mures

Olt

Indre

Cher

Allier

Doubs

BURGUNDIANS
(443)

Rhône

OTHS

07)

Lot

Loire

Isère

OSTROGOTHS
(403)

Adda

Po

Save

VISIG

Tarn

ouse

Rhône

Durance

Tanaro

(412-413)

Ticino

(454)

Adige

Piave

Arles

Narbonne
(414)

Arno

(408)

Ravenna
Theodoric
(473-526)

(401)

CORSICA

Tiber

Vardar

Strimma

Maritsa

Rome

Alaric (410)

SARDINIA

ICS

(410)

DITERRA

(455)

SICILY

Medjerda
(439)

Carthage

VANDALS
(435-534)
Gelimer (+ 534)

N E A N

S E A

CRETE

(395)

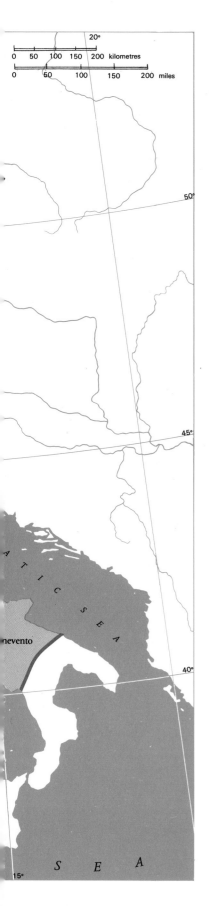

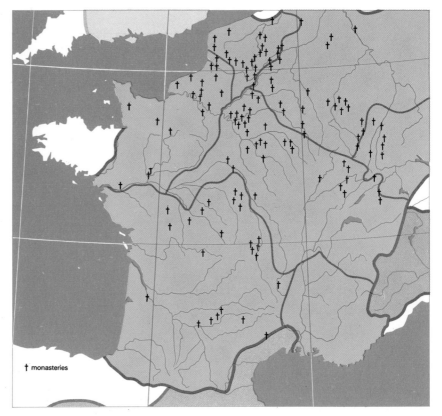

357 - MONASTERIES FOUNDED IN GAUL IN THE SEVENTH CENTURY.   AFTER J. HUBERT.

† monasteries

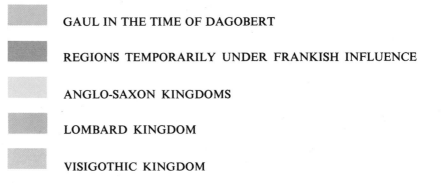

GAUL IN THE TIME OF DAGOBERT

REGIONS TEMPORARILY UNDER FRANKISH INFLUENCE

ANGLO-SAXON KINGDOMS

LOMBARD KINGDOM

VISIGOTHIC KINGDOM

DIOCESE

OF

GREAT BRITAIN

IRELAND

York

Trent

Severn

Thames

London

Dover

FRISIAN

Ems

Scheldt

Tournai

Meuse

Rhine

Cologne

Somme

Main

Rouen

Eure

Oise

Seine

Paris

Marne

Trier

Ne

Metz

Seine

Moselle

Meuse

ALAMANN

Mayenne

D   I   O   C   E   S   E

Nantes

Tours

Loir

Cher

Loire

Yonne

Rhine

Basel

Indre

Bourges

I

Poitiers

Autun

Saône

Doubs

Saintes

Vienne

O   F   G   A   U   L

Allier

Lyons

Geneva

Périgueux

Loire

Be

Bordeaux

Dordogne

Vienne

Isère

Milan

Lot

Rhône

Adda

Adour

Garonne

Durance

Pô

Ticino

Braga

Toulouse

Tarn

Nimes

Arles

Albenga

Tanaro

Genoa

Ariège

Aix

Reg

Narbonne

Marseilles

Fréjus

Pisa

Douro

Ebro

Minho

Numantia

Segre

Tarrasa

CORSICA

Barcelona

Aleria

D   I   O   C   E   S   E

Tagus

Toledo

Merida

Guadiana

Jucar

Valencia

O   F   S   P   A   I   N

Guadalquivir

Cordova

Segura

SARDINIA

Seville

BALEARICS

Cadiz

Malaga

Carthagena

Cagliari

Tangier

M   E   D   I   T   E   R   R

Sebu

Tipasa

Shelif

Moulouya

Orléansville

Hippo

DIOCESE OF SPAIN

Setif

Djemila

Tabarca

Cartha

Constantine

Medjerda

D   I   O   C   E   S   E   O   F   A   F   R   I   C   A

Timgad

A   T   L   A   N   T   I   C

O   C   E   A   N

Roman Empire at the
end of the 4th century

Limits of dioceses   Limits of provinces

ANCIENT NAMES	MODERN NAMES		ANCIENT NAMES	MODERN NAMES	
Actium	Actium	G 5	*Miletus*	Miletus	H 5
Agrigentum or *Akragas*	Agrigento	E 5	*Moguntiacum*	Mainz	D 2
Albingaunum	Albenga	D 4	*Namnetes*	Nantes	B 3
Aleria	Aleria	D 4	*Narbo Martius*	Narbonne	C 4
Ancona	Ancona	E 4	*Narona*	Narona	F 4
Aquae Sextae	Aix	D 4	*Neapolis*	Naples	E 4
Aquileia	Aquileia	E 3	*Nemausus*	Nîmes	C 4
Arelate	Arles	C 4	*Nicaea*	Nicaea	H 4
Argos	Argos	G 5	*Nicomedia*	Nicomedia	H 4
Athenae	Athens	G 5	*Nicopolis*	Nikopolis	G 5
Augustodunum	Autun	C 3	*Nova Carthago*	Carthagena	B 5
Barcino	Barcelona	C 4	*Numantia*	Numantia	B 4
Basilea	Basel	D 3	*Odessos* or *Odessus*	Varna	H 4
Beneventum	Benevento	E 4	*Ostia* or *Ostium*	Ostia	E 4
Bergomum	Bergamo	D 3	*Panormus*	Palermo	E 5
Bituriges	Bourges	C 3	*Parisii*	Paris	C 3
Bracara Augusta	Braga	A 4	*Pergamon*	Pergamum	H 5
Brundisium	Brindisi	F 4	*Petrocorii* or *Vesunna*	Périgueux	C 3
Burdigala	Bordeaux	B 4	*Pharsalus*	Pharsala	G 5
Calaris or *Caralis*	Cagliari	D 5	*Pictavi*	Poitiers	C 3
Carthago	Carthage	E 5	*Pisae*	Pisa	E 4
Castellum Tingitanum	Orléansville	C 5	*Ratiaria*	Arcar	G 4
Cirta or *Constantina*	Constantine	D 5	*Ravenna*	Ravenna	E 4
Colonia Agrippina	Cologne	D 2	*Rhegium*	Reggio	E 4
Constantinopolis			*Roma*	Rome	E 4
or *Nova Roma*	Constantinople	H 4	*Rotomagus*	Rouen	C 3
Corduba	Cordova	B 5	*Salona*	Solin	F 4
Corinthus or *Korinthia*	Corinth	G 5	*Santones*	Saintes	B 3
Croton	Crotona	F 5	*Sardes*	Sardis	H 5
Cuicul	Djemila	D 5	*Sirmium*	Sremska Mitrovica	F 4
Dubris	Dover	C 2	*Sitifis*	Sétif	D 5
Eboracum	York	B 2	*Smyrna*	Smyrna	H 5
Egara	Tarrasa	C 4	*Spalato*	Split	F 4
Emerita	Merida	A 5	*Spoletium*	Spoleto	E 4
Ephesus	Ephesus	H 5	*Stobi*	Stobi	G 4
Epidaurus	Epidaurus	G 5	*Syracusae*	Syracuse	F 5
Florentia	Florence	E 4	*Tarentum*	Tarento	F 4
Forum Iulii	Fréjus	D 4	*Thabraca*	Tabarka	D 5
Gades	Cadiz	A 5	*Thamugadi*	Timgad	D 5
Genava	Geneva	D 3	*Thessalonica*	Salonica	G 4
Genua	Genoa	D 4	*Tingis*	Tangier	A 5
Hadrianopolis	Adrianople	H 4	*Tipasa*	Tipasa	C 5
Hippo Regius	Hippo	D 5	*Toletum*	Toledo	B 5
Hispalis	Seville	A 5	*Tolosa*	Toulouse	C 4
Jadera	Zadar	F 4	*Tomi*	Constanza or Costanza	H 4
Lauriacum	Lauriacum	E 3	*Tralli* or *Tralles*	Tralles	H 5
Londinium	London	B 2	*Treveri*	Trier	D 3
Lugdunum	Lyons	C 3	*Turnacum*	Tournai	C 2
Malaca	Malaga	B 5	*Turones*	Tours	C 3
Mantua	Mantua	E 3	*Valentia Edetanorum*	Valencia	B 5
Massilia	Marseilles	D 4	*Verona*	Verona	E 3
Mediolanum	Milan	D 3	*Vienna*	Vienne (Gaul)	C 3
Messana	Messina	F 5	*Vindobona*	Vienna (Illyria)	F 3
Mettis	Metz	D 3	*Virunum*	Virunum	E 3
			Zara	Zadar	F 4

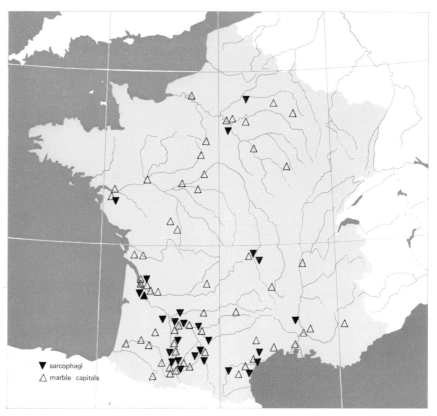

360 - MARBLE CARVINGS FROM THE TOULOUSE REGION (7TH CENTURY). AFTER J. HUBERT.

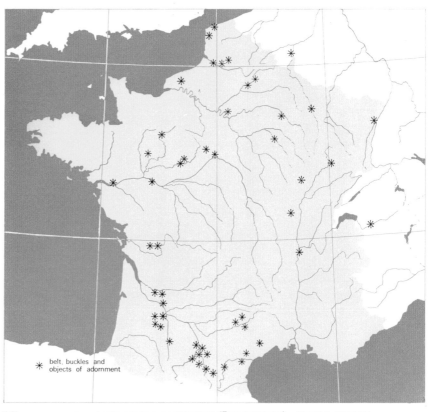

361 - OBJECTS OF ADORNMENT FROM AQUITAINE (7TH CENTURY). AFTER J. HUBERT.

A
B
C
0° Gr.
D

15°
10°
5°
5°

2

0   100   200   300   400   500 kilometres
0   100   200   300 miles

Iona

Jedburgh
Lindisfarne
Ruthwell
Bewcastle
Jarrow
Durham
Easby
York

I R E L A N D

N O R T H

S E A

Monasterboice
Durrow
Kells
Roscrea
Kildrenagh
Feaghmaan

50°

A T L A N T I C

Severn
Trent
Thames

Sutton Hoo
Silchester
Reculver
Canterbury

3

Rhine
Ems
Werden
Soest
Krefeld
Cologne
En
Tournai
Aachen
Saint-Riquier
Nivelles
Amiens
Corbie
Laon
Echternach
Mainz
Saint-Denis
Lavoye
Trier
Wolfish
Meaux
Jouarre
Molsheim
Paris
Chelles
Metz
Ittenheim
Neckar
Rhine
Wittisling

O C E A N

45°

Scheldt
Meuse
Seine
Eure
Marne
Moselle
Meuse

Nantes
Angers
Gémigny
Vertou
Langeais
St-Benoît-
sur-Loire
Auxerre
Luxeuil
Selles-sur-Cher
Cher
Flavigny
Güttingen
Re
Poitiers
Antigny
Saint-
Ambroix
Besançon
Delémont
Sa
Mazerolles
Bülach
Charenton-
du-Cher
Romainmôtier
Saint-Maurice
Müst

Mayenne
Loir
Loire
Yonne
Saône
Doubs

4

Vienne
Limons
Geneva
Sion
Stabio
Adda
Manglieu
Lyons
Castelseprio
Como
Gourdon
Vienne
Ivrea
Monza
Albon
Grenoble
Vercelli
Milan
Conques
Desana
Pavia
Toulouse
Gellone
Lingotto
Bobbio
Saint-Bertrand-
de-Comminges
Tressan
Arles
Riez
Albenga
Non
Narbonne
Saint-Blaise
Cimiez
Marseilles
Saint-Maximin
Fréjus

Allier
Vienne
Dordogne
Lot
Garonne
Tarn
Ariège
Rhône
Isère
Durance
Tanaro

Sta. María
de Naranco
Oviedo
Minho

S. Pedro
de la Nave
Quintanilla
de las Viñas
Duero

40°

Ebro
Segre

CORSICA

Casa Herrera
Guarrazar
Toledo
Tagus
Guadiana
Júcar

5

Guadalquivir
Segura

S. Fructuoso
del Francoli

SARDINIA

BALEARICS

T Y R

35°

M E D I T E R R

Sebu
Shelif
Medjerda
Tunis

6

B
5°
Moulouya
C
0° Gr.
D
5°
E
10°

Kairouan

Roman Empire at the
end of the 4th century

Limits of dioceses

Limits of provinces

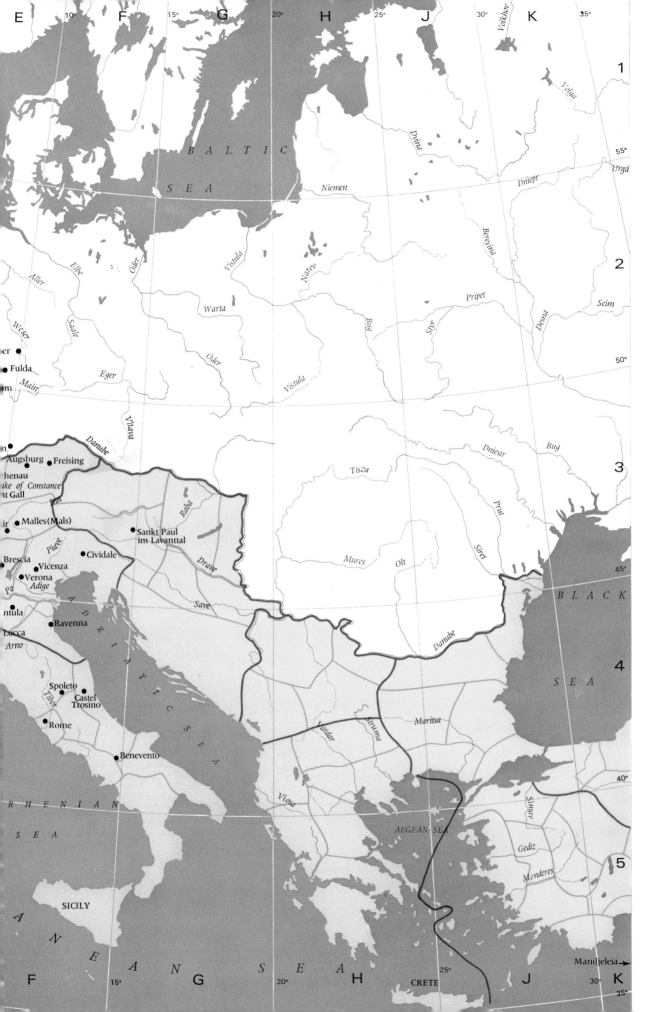

E 10° F 15° G 20° H 25° J 30° K 35°

1

BALTIC

SEA

Volkhov

Volga

Dvina

55°

Urga

Dniepr

Niemen

2

Elbe

Oder

Vistula

Narev

Beresina

Pripet

Seim

Aller

Saale

Bug

Styr

Desna

Weser

Warta

50°

Fulda

Oder

Eger

Vistula

Main

Vltava

Danube

Augsburg Freising

Dniestr

Bug

3

henau

ke of Constance

t Gall

Tisza

Prut

Inn

Raba

Malles (Mals)

Sankt Paul

im Lavanttal

45°

Piave

Drave

ir

Brescia Vicenza

Mures

Olt

Siret

Cividale

Verona

Adige

BLACK

Save

Danube

ntula

A

Ravenna

Lucca

D

Arno

R

4

I

SEA

Spoleto

A

Tiber

Castel

T

Trosino

I

Rome

C

Vardar

Struma

Maritsa

Benevento

S

40°

E

A

Viosa

Sipav

RHENIAN

AEGEAN SEA

Gediz

SEA

5

Menderes

SICILY

A

N

E

A

N

S

E

A

H

Mandjeleia →

F 15° A G 20° N H 25° S J 30° E K

CRETE

35°

359 - CITADEL TOWNS OF THE LATE THIRD CENTURY WHICH BECAME THE SEAT OF A BISHOP. AFTER J. HUBERT.

THIS, THE TWELFTH VOLUME OF 'THE ARTS OF MANKIND' SERIES, EDITED BY ANDRÉ MALRAUX AND ANDRÉ PARROT, HAS BEEN PRODUCED UNDER THE SUPERVISION OF ALBERT BEURET, EDITOR-IN-CHARGE OF THE SERIES, ASSISTED BY JACQUELINE BLANCHARD. THE BOOK WAS DESIGNED BY ROGER PARRY, ASSISTED BY JEAN-LUC HERMAN AND SERGE ROMAIN. THE TEXT AND THE PLATES IN BLACK AND WHITE WERE PRINTED BY L'IMPRIMERIE GEORGES LANG, PARIS ; PLATES IN COLOUR BY L'IMPRIMERIE DRAEGER FRÈRES, MONTROUGE. THE BINDING, DESIGNED BY MASSIN, WAS EXECUTED BY BABOUOT, GENTILLY.